Nelson's Guide to
Denominations

J. Gordon Melton

Published by
Thomas Nelson™
Since 1798

www.thomasnelson.com

Published in Nashville, Tennessee, by Thomas Nelson, Inc.

Thomas Nelson, Inc. titles may be purchased in bulk for educational, business, fundraising, or sales promotional use. For information, please email SpecialMarkets@ThomasNelson.com

Library of Congress Cataloging-in-Publication Data

Melton, J. Gordon.
Nelson's guide to denominations / J. Gordon Melton.
p. cm.
Includes index.
ISBN-13: 978-1-4185-0196-9
1. Christian sects—North America. 2. North America—Religion.
I. Title.
BR510.M45 2006
280—dc22
2006025462

ISBN-10: 1-41850-196-4
ISBN-13: 978-1-41850-196-9

Printed in the United States of America
1 2 3 4 5 6 7—11 10 09 08 07

CONTENTS

Preface

Any attempt to follow the trends in contemporary American religion soon forces a confrontation with several facts about church life. First and foremost, the religious community is incredibly diverse, and to comprehend the diversity one must deal with the fast-moving, ever-changing culture. Events have made us aware that America is now home not just to a Christian majority and Jewish minority, but to the whole spectrum of the world's religions—Buddhism, Hinduism, Islam—not to mention the smaller traditions such as Sikhism, Taoism, or Jainism. Along with the imported faiths, the longstanding dissenting faith in the West, the many diverse elements of which are now generally termed Western Esotericism, but more popularly known as the New Age, also has enjoyed a spectacular jump in popularity over the last century. And we would be remiss if we did not acknowledge the growth of organized unbelief as the champion of those who affirm their lack of interest in things religious.

In spite of the growth of the many different religious communities in America, however, the great majority of Americans still adhere to some form of Christianity—between 65 and 85 percent depending on how the count is made, what questions are asked, and where the boundaries are drawn. One of the great long-term trends in American religious life is the manner in which the country moved from a largely irreligious unchurched nation in the decades immediately after the American Revolution (in which only 10 to 15 percent of the citizenry were church members) to one in which more than two-thirds of Americans have chosen to adhere to a worshiping community. The price of churching the nation in the increasing climate of freedom that has pervaded modern culture, however, has been the splintering of the church into numerous separate communities—"denominations," for lack of a better term.

Through the twentieth century, Christians in the United States have divided into more than a thousand denominations, three times as many as had appeared by 1900. There is, of course, one simple explanation for the diversity—population. The country grew from 75 million residents to more than 280 million through the twentieth century. But that is too simplistic an answer. Looking back over the last century, we can see forces that unleashed bursts of religious creativity. The twentieth century began with the emergence of Pentecostalism, soon followed by the Fundamentalist-Modernist controversy. Within a decade, Pentecostalism divided into three major communities over theological differences. The Fundamentalist-Modernist controversy was not so much resolved through the 1920s as taken to a new stage as Fundamentalists divided into Neo-Evangelicals and separatist Fundamentalists, while Modernists left the popular Liberalism of the 1920s for Neo-Orthodoxy, ecumenical theologies, and various theological explorations based on new advances (changes) in science and philosophy. Conservatives countered with their own new theologies: dispensationalism, the Princeton theology, presuppositional apologetics, and dominion theology.

The major controversies that tended to split the American Christian community and produce new denominational bodies were countered by attempts to reconcile the differences or at least to minimize their disruptive effects. The larger denominations spawned an ecumenical movement, the major organizational expression being a set of church councils that operated at the national, state, and local level. Simultaneously, groups that shared a similar heritage and theological life have grouped themselves into familial communal structures. These ecumenical structures have attempted both to bring about reconciliation and even union among likeminded denominations and to contain the effects of controversies that might further split the churches.

Through the twentieth century, the ecumenical movement assumed a significant role in healing many of the disruptions of the nineteenth century, especially those caused by sectionalism. The primary remaining task before all segments of American Christianity is the continued destruction of the remaining structures erected by slavery, segregation, and racism. As will be seen below, racism remains a significant force dividing Christians into denominations populated by African Americans who do not feel welcome in predominantly white settings and denominations created by whites wanting to exist apart from any integrated fellowships.

Approaching America's Denominations

It is the attempt to make sense of this immensely diverse and complex Christian community that has called forth this volume, *Nelson's Guide to Denominations*, designed as a concise and convenient overview of the basic structures of America's Christian religious community. The primary section of the handbook sorts out America's denominations, grouping them into their families—placing each individual church community beside the denomination from which its comes and which it most closely resembles. (To find any particular church group, look at the alphabetical index at the end of this volume.)

Following the chapters on the different denominational families, a chapter is given over to the various cooperative structures by which these different denominations relate to each other—the several councils, associations, and fellowship groups through which more or less closely related denominations affirm their common heritage.

To begin, however, we enter the world of American Christianity through one of its common denominators—the acceptance of the authority of the Bible. Thus we begin this exploration of America religion with a set of essays in which the authors, all from diverse backgrounds and different church communities, state their belief in the Bible and its message for today.

Throughout the twentieth century, church leaders have fought what has been called the "Battle for the Bible." In the process, we discovered on the one hand that allegiance to the most conservative views of the Bible did not prevent people from wandering off into the most blatant heresies. On the other hand, we have noted that toying with radical criticisms of the biblical text has not weaned the larger mainstream churches from their continued affirmation of the Bible as the Word of God or their need to return to the text for its message of salvation, inspiration, and guidance. Church leaders today are now asking the text for direction as a new generation grows up in not just the global community but the virtual community, a time in which feminism has been discarded for woman's equality, and a world still housing racist notions.

Your attention is invited to the five Bible essays. They are, firstly, not so much systematic statements of our theological understanding of the nature of the Bible as they are five contemporary probings, each somewhat personal and confessional, of the relevance of the Bible to our contemporary existence. Then, secondly, they are thought-provoking essays, not really calling for immediate assent but offering multiple starting points for discussion. Their success will be judged not by how much you agree with them but by the extent to which they lead to your own further exploration of the Bible and its role in shaping our lives.

Then, in turning to the actual denominations, *Nelson's Guide to Denominations* invites your attention to an understanding of some larger global trends into which American Christianity fits. In the nineteenth century, American and European Christians engaged in the vast missionary movement that spread Christianity worldwide, especially in Africa and Asia. While remnants of that missionary activity remain, its success was acknowledged in the mid-twentieth century by the complete reorganization of the world missionary endeavor. The former missionary-sending churches stepped back and the former mission churches assumed a new role as equal partners in the global task of carrying out the great commission. The changing nature of the missionary enterprise surprised and even bewildered the last generation of Western Christians, and the cultural shock continues as we cope with the further implication of our immediate ancestors' accomplishment, namely the shift of the center of world Christianity from Europe and North America to the lands south of the equator.

In his essay "The Changing Face of American Religion, A.D. 1900–2050," Todd Johnson, the emerging dean of Christian demographics, presents the best data we have on what is happening to the Christian community and its implications for American Christians.

Next, the *Guide* turns to its major task, presenting an overview of America's Christian denominations. In developing the *Guide*, the major questions to be resolved were, first, how to present the great diversity of American churches in the space allotted and in such a way as to provide a meaningful explanation of the origins of the different denominations and the rationale for their existence. Second, a decision had to be made as to how far afield the guide would reach in its coverage. As it turned out, the answer to the initial question provided much of the answer to the second.

It was decided to present the different churches relative to their heritage and to the historical development of the different denominational families. Thus, we begin with those churches that trace their organizational existence into the ancient past, that is, the Roman Catholic and Eastern Orthodox churches and the various modern organizations that attempt to carry on their tradition in the United States. There is some additional logic to this starting point, as the Catholic Church has for the last century and a half been the largest single denomination in the United States. We next move to the Reformation and the several Protestant traditions that emerged—Lutheran, Anglican, Reformed, and Radical Reformation—in the sixteenth century. With apologies to the Presbyterians, whom we recognize as rooted in the Reformed tradition of the sixteenth century, we next highlight the traditions that came to prominence in Great Britain in the seventeenth century, the Puritans—Presbyterians, Congregationalists, Baptists, and free churches such as the Quakers.

The eighteenth century was dominated by the rise of Pietism and the churches of the Evangelical Awakening—Moravians and Methodists being most prominent. And as one cannot understand the Reformation churches without understating the Catholic Church to which they reacted, and one cannot understand Puritans without a grasp of the Reformation, so one can only understand the eighteenth-century groups by comparing them with the Puritan and Reformation churches against which *they* reacted.

By the nineteenth century, America had been established as a nation. Along with the flourishing of Reformation, Puritan, and Evangelical groups came the new burst of free-church groups, church fellowships that developed in Europe in reaction to the weakening of the continuing religious establishments and in America in the free religious climate produced by the separation of church and state. The primary development in American Christianity was the emergence of the movements—the Restoration movement, Adventism, the Plymouth Brethren, and the Holiness movement.

In the free religious climate, besides the new Christian movements, a number of new movements developed, not just on the edge but well beyond the pale of Christianity—most prominently Spiritualism, the Latter-day Saints, Theosophy, and Christian Science. While these new movements cannot be understood apart from the Christian milieu in which they emerged, they were all deemed as beyond the boundaries of what Christians could accept as just a new, if fringe, branch of the Christian church. On the other hand, although most American Christians rejected the Restoration movement, Adventism, the Plymouth Brethren, and the Holiness movement, the church mainstream saw their differences as similar to the theological differences that already divided Lutherans from Presbyterians and Methodists from Baptists.

In the case of Spiritualism, the Latter-day Saints, Theosophy, and Christian Science, however, the differences went far deeper. These groups had not simply diverged on a few secondary theological points (ecclesiology, evangelism tactics, eschatology), but had created whole new theologies, however much they utilized Christian symbols (especially in the case of Christian Science and the Latter-day Saints), and offered a range of primary affirmations that took them beyond what could legitimately be called Christianity.

In the twentieth century, the additional esoteric groups appeared, many offering what they saw as an esoteric or metaphysical Christianity. The number of these groups has greatly expanded since the 1980s with the coming of the New Age movement and its most recent expression, Gnostic Christianity. The great majority of Christian leaders judged these new religious movements as taking Christian words and symbols and pouring very different meaning into them. At their heart, they replace the Christian message of salvation with one of religious enlightenment.

That these groups have been judged as something other than Christian in any traditional sense, has placed them beyond the scope of this *Guide*, which has limited itself to the Christian church community. In choosing not to include these groups, we are merely making the observation that they represent a very different religious reality than that presented by the Christian faith groups listed below.

Finally, we come to the twentieth century. This period has been marked by the emergence of three related movements: Pentecostalism, which primarily derived from a Methodist/Holiness context; Evangelicalism, which has its roots first and foremost in the Puritan churches (Presbyterian, Baptist, and

Congregationalist); and the Plymouth Brethren, whose leadership reacted to the British Anglican establishment. Pentecostalism can be seen as a revitalization movement that continues a Methodist emphasis on religious experience, though it would be wrong to simply reduce it to that. Evangelicalism was the product of the modernist theological conflict in the Puritan churches, further acerbated by the injection of the Brethren's dispensational theology. All three movements have been major forces creating the ferment driving the American church through the century.

Once you have located any particular church group (denomination) in the guide below, the introductory material in the chapter it is in will provide information on its origin and the theological context into which it fits. In reading the earlier chapters, a more comprehensive picture emerges of exactly where any particular group is located on the larger Christian landscape.

Parachurch Groups

The *Guide* also includes a section on what are termed parachurch organizations. Since the eighteenth century, the work of denominations has been supplemented by the important work of organizations that attempt to accomplish tasks that denominational bodies alone cannot or will not do. Many early organizations pioneered areas that denominational bodies were slow to recognize as important areas of church life—foreign missions, Bible publication and distribution, urban ministries, Sunday schools, etc. Additional organizations promoted different forms of spirituality and piety, while others became advocates of various causes from the abolition of slavery to the curtailing of alcohol consumption.

The number of new parachurch organizations expanded greatly in the nineteenth century. In America in particular, church leaders founded a host of new organizations to spread Christian values into what was seen as a decidedly secular and irreligious society. At the same time, a variety of new congregationally oriented denominations (especially the Baptists and the Disciples of Christ) grew but were reluctant to establish all the denominational machinery of the older hierarchical denominations. Many parachurch organizations (schools, missionary societies, evangelistic associations, social service agencies) formed to extend the ministries of these denominations.

Especially since World War II, the number of parachurch organizations has grown geometrically. Many of the most popular parachurch groups continue their traditional pioneering role, most noticeably in their move into religious radio and television broadcasting. Others have picked up the desire of nineteenth-century church leaders to undergird secular society and the public square with Christian values (and behavioral norms). Still others have established their role in carrying out certain activities that benefit all denominations.

In this first edition of *Nelson's Guide to Denominations,* we have chosen to emphasize the Bible to some extent, and amid the thousands of parachurch organizations that now exists, we have chosen to highlight the various groups engaged in the translation, publication, and dissemination of the Bible. All of the denominations have recognized this effort as vitally important and overwhelmingly have seen the task of Bible publication as one best done by cooperative parachurch organizations (including Christian publishing houses) that exist apart from any one denomination's hegemony.

One special type of parachurch organization are those cooperative councils and associations that bring members of different denominations together to learn about each other and cooperate with each other on mutually agreeable tasks. Two types of such organizations exists—those that attempt to bring together denominations from a variety of denominational families (such as the National Council of Churches of Christ in the U.S.A., the National Association of Evangelicals, the American Council of Christian Churches) and those that seek to provide fellowship for closely related denominations of a single family (Lutherans, Baptists, Presbyterians, etc.). These multiplied in the last half of the twentieth century and have taken on increasingly important functions as the public face for their member organizations.

Finally, this *Guide* makes note of the changes in Christian education for clergy that have occurred in the last half-century. While there is a very real, if minority, anti-seminary trend in American religion—some church groups feel that education hurts more than it helps pastoral performance—most denominations have to deal with the problem of providing ministerial leadership for their congregations and have discovered that some form of seminary training is the best method of accomplishing that task. As denominations have grown, they have formed new seminaries, while independent seminaries have grown up to serve congregationally oriented denominations. At the same time, cooperative ecumenical groups have prompted older denominational schools to open their doors to students from a greater variety of denominational backgrounds.

In the last chapter of this *Guide* we provide a listing of all the ministerial training schools, both those with official denominational ties and those that exist independent of any specific denomination. The list has been limited to those schools that remain campus-based and primarily offer a traditional classroom setting, as opposed to the newer distance learning schools. In making this distinction, we mean to make no value judgment about distance learning, which has become an increasingly important part of Christian higher education. In future editions of this *Guide*, we hope to include them.

Christian Pluralism in Perspective

This quick summary of the outline of this *Guide* brings us back to our opening observation about the American Christian community (which is equally true now of any country where even a modicum of religious freedom exists), namely a pluralistic setting exists and will continue to exist for the foreseeable future. Americans have created a religiously pluralistic society, and we all have been caught up in the ongoing process of negotiating our levels of acceptance of it. As Christians and as pluralists, we disagree not only on which community to attend and support, but on the range of acceptable divergence we can feel comfortable with, both as believers and as citizens.

Affirming the pluralistic nature of the modern Christian community does not mean that we can or should accept all of the variety of theological divergences or acknowledge the truth of other theological opinions. Most certainly, it does not mean that all the differences are unimportant. Rather, it means that we affirm the fact of our many divergences—that having separate denominations is the way that religion structures itself in a free society. For the past two hundred years we have been founding new denominations for a variety of reasons, and, in spite of the ecumenical movement, no noticeable counterforce has appeared on the scene. Even though American religion will continue to be dominated by the relatively small number of larger Christian churches, it is reasonable to expect that ever more new denominations will continue to arise, and a few of these may grow into substantial communities.

Christian pluralism exists not only as observable fact but as political reality. The American experiment in religious freedom resulted from the desire of the Founding Fathers to unite the thirteen colonies while confronting the fact that no one of the seventeen religious groups in the new country commanded the support of more than a small minority of the population. At the same time, many of the leading framers of the Constitution were, relative to the time in which they lived, outspoken religious skeptics (deists). The political reality of the lack of religious consensus forced Jefferson, Madison, Franklin, et al to guarantee all of the churches (and the small Jewish community) the government's religious neutrality.

In the end, America's pluralism comes home to us in our own neighborhoods, where we are likely aware of the existence of churches about which we know very little. Some have a denominational name we cannot identify, others have a name that carries little information about what goes on inside week to week and what the congregation's adherents actually believe and do. Thus while providing an overall picture of American Christianity, it is hoped that this *Guide* will also give you an initial introduction to some of your neighbors. Possibly it will offer some initial understanding about that church you have seen while driving around town and about which you reflected, "I wonder who those people are?"

J. Gordon Melton
2006

I

THE BIBLE TODAY

INTRODUCTION—
THE BIBLE: OUR AUTHORITY

By J. Gordon Melton

Among the most pervasive beliefs shared by Christians is an affirmation of the role of the Bible as the ultimate authority for our faith and life. From the Bible we come to know Jesus Christ, the nature of salvation, and what is expected of us as Christians concerning how we should live. Thus it seems only natural that for the first symposium in this first edition of *Nelson's Guide to Denominations* that we should focus on the Bible. Below we present five essays written from a variety of perspectives on the Bible and some of the basic questions that we are putting to the Bible about itself at the beginning of the twenty-first century.

Without attempting a complete and systematic lecture on biblical authority, let us briefly review some of the implications of our affirmations about the Bible. In positing the Bible as the authority of our faith, we are first and foremost witnessing to our relationship to Christ. Like Paul, we walk in the world and meet in fellowship with our Christian sisters and brothers, determined to know nothing but Jesus Christ and him crucified. For those of us who have not lived at the time and place of Christ's resurrection, the Bible has been the instrument of introducing us to the object of our faith. Facilitating our relationship with Christ is reason enough for us to keep the Bible close to us and make its words the keystone of our Christian life.

But let us probe a little more deeply and ask about the implications of our peculiar and special affirmation of the Bible's authority. What does it mean to say that the Bible is the Word of God, and why do we want to hear our fellow Christians verbalize that affirmation? To some extent, it provides us with a basis for discussing various issues with each other, but more to the point, it serves to relativize any other authority we might place beside the Bible. I enjoy reading the church fathers and find valuable insights in their words, but their words always stand under the judgment of the biblical text. The church had the role of assembling the canon and preserving the Bible to the present, but the church cannot assert its own authority over the Bible; rather it must be the Bible's faithful servant. Science has provided us with a picture of the way the natural order operates and how we might manipulate it. It is the Bible that gives us a set of values in approaching the world and that guides us in our manipulation of it.

In relativizing all other authorities, the Bible has somewhat contributed to our present state of relativism. We find it hard to put down an anchor in a fast-moving culture, a government system continually being hammered out in the give and take of the democratic process, and the daily pressure of vivid, attractive media images of a reality without real substance. With so many Christian denominations and local congregations from which to choose, even our church life takes on some of the characteristics of the omnipresent relativism. But each time one of the little anchors we set in pace to structure our lives is taken away, it serves to bring into ever clearer focus the one big anchor we have in the Christ who is presented to us in the Bible. The government asks for our patriotic allegiance, but it quickly loses its appeal when it deviates from New Testament affirmations.

We live in a rather remarkable time. Throughout the twentieth century, the Bible was put to the test as never before in history. Early in the century, theologians questioned its authority, biblical critics questioned its historicity, and archeologists questioned its accuracy. The Bible survived that era because of its life-giving power, and we have now entered a new century in which even the most liberal of theologians have gained a new appreciation of the Bible's importance: biblical scholar-historians have come to understand how the Bible illuminates the past, and archeologists are using the Bible to locate the remnants of ancient sites. Even as we develop a more sophisticated understanding of the process that produced the Bible, as with many other aspects of twentieth-century culture, we have moved on beyond those issues that so agitated us through much of the last century.

That is not to say that the challenges to the Bible have ceased, merely that they have changed, and in some cases moved from scholarly circles to the public forum. For example, in the last half of the twentieth century our understanding of the world of the early church was considerably broadened by the discovery of the Dead Sea Scrolls and the Gnostic texts at Nag Hammadi. After a generation of primary consideration of the importance of these texts largely within the scholarly community, now popular editions of these texts have been widely circulated and we are undergoing a popular appropriation of the knowledge derived from them, including a repetition of some of the wildest theories of what these texts might imply about Christ, the church, and biblical authority. The current debate over the *Da Vinci Code* is but one fallout of that popularization of knowledge.

Having been taught as a youth to adhere to the Bible as the source of my church's teachings, in my seminary years I developed a very different additional appreciation of the Bible. While studying the global missionary movement of the eighteenth and nineteenth century I came to appreciate the amount of time and effort expended by pioneer missionaries to learn new languages, reduce them to a written form, and produce a first dictionary—just so the Bible could be translated and given to a people. These pioneer missionaries not only presented many of the world's peoples the gift of literacy, but published the Bible as the first book the new readers could use as they began to read and write their own tongue.

I was still in graduate school in the early 1970s when I first met David B. Barrett, then on his way to becoming the dean of religious demographers, who drew my attention to the role that Bible translation played in the life of different African peoples. There was a direct relationship between the translation and publication of the Bible into a native tongue and the first large-scale movement by the people toward the Christian faith—a relationship that operated somewhat independently of missionary activity. That is, the Bible often speaks to people directly even when we as missionaries, with all good intentions, obscure the text by confusing the Bible's message with our own cultural renderings of it.

The study of the missionary movement gave me a deeper personal belief in the power of the Bible as a tool in the advancement of Christianity and has led to my advocacy of the work of such organizations as the American Bible Society, the Gideons, and the Wycliffe Bible Translators. From the latter's website (www.wycliffe.org) we can derive some interesting facts about the present progress in translating the Bible. We learn, for instance, that there are 6,912 languages spoken in the world—each language being spoken by a group of people most of whom know only that language. Of the world's languages, only 422 have a copy of a complete Bible translation, but these languages are the ones most widely used. The great majority of the world's peoples, those who speak the more popular languages—Chinese, English, Spanish, French, German, Arabic, etc.—have multiple translations. Our concern in their case is that those languages, which participate in the modern fast-moving world, are changing rapidly, and thus for them the Bible is in need of regular retranslation.

That being said, we turn to the remaining languages—1,079 languages have at least the New Testament and 876 more have at least one New Testament book. That means that a written form of these 1,955 languages exists and that someone (usually a small dedicated team) has produced a basic working dictionary. The same can be said of the 1,640 language groups for which a translation is in progress. But for the remaining 2,895 languages, the basic work remains to be completed, if it has even started. This work stands before the church as a high calling.

The imperative to get the Bible into the hands of those who do not have it eventually leads us back to the questions now before those who have had the Bible for centuries. The Western culture that has through the last two centuries done so much to translate, publish, and disseminate the Bible is the same culture that at the same time put the Bible to the test. The same culture that built the educational system that makes massive translation possible has also applied the range of modern critical interpretive tools to try better to understand the meaning of the text while at the same time making every effort to make it a more reader-friendly volume. While searching the world for every remaining scrap of ancient copies of the Bible in order to arrive at a text as close to the original as possible, scholars have also at one time or another raised serious questions about every biblical book. In the end, the Bible has stood up quite well, though some of the more naïve and extreme forms of interpreting it have suffered.

All of the major Christian communities, from Eastern Orthodox to liberal Protestant and from Roman Catholic to Evangelical, have within them a core of people who have devoted their lives to the mastering of the Scripture and who after decades of study remain devoted advocates of the Word and champions of the value of its study. These are the people who have examined the variant ancient texts, who know how to apply the many historical methodologies to tease meaning from texts originating almost two millennia ago, who understand the principles of biblical interpretation (hermeneutics), who have listened to all the Bible's critics, who also come forth to affirm the Bible's nature as the Word of God for the world today, as much as at any time.

It is from the perspective of the tests the Bible endured in the last century that we offer below a set of essays that reflect the current status of the Bible in the church. Each author is the heir of all the study of, controversy about, and reflections upon the Bible through the last century. The first two essays, by Samuel J. Mikolaski and Michael H. Reynolds, in their own way summarize what we can affirm in light of all that happened in the last century. They take us through some of the highlights of the past and provide convincing arguments for the contemporary trustworthiness of the Scripture.

The next essays, by Mimi Haddad and Mozella G. Mitchell, update us on several issues in modern biblical studies. Haddad reconsiders the questions of women's role in the church in the post-feminist world of the twenty-first century. Having put behind us the often anti-family rhetoric of feminism, how do we in fact treat women in the new world of gender equality into which we are moving? Mitchell then takes the issue one step further by asking the question initially raised by liberation theologians a generation ago about the cultural factors in our appropriation of the biblical text. In a very personal essay, she shares the problems that she has faced, as first a scholar in a modern secular university and then as an African American woman, in interpreting and appropriating a text whose interpretation has been dominated by European males. As one of those European males, I find the two essays by Haddad and Mitchell the most challenging to my reading of the Bible, and while I do not agree with everything they say, they are the kind of church leaders I want in my worshiping community as teachers to constantly remind me not to become complacent in my reading of the Bible and to make me aware of the personal cultural factors that repeatedly block my hearing God's Word in the text.

In the final essay, James C. Browning brings before us what is already emerging as one of the prime challenges of this century, rereading our Bibles in a religiously pluralistic world. In the last century, the other world religions established themselves in the West. We now read the scripture with Jews, Muslims, and Hindus (not to mention Buddhists, Jains, Sikhs, and Taoists) as neighbors who, as new members of a Christian culture, also read the Bible, but understand its words out of quite different faith commitments. We have a number of choices in how we respond to this new context, the most fruitful seeming to be an engagement in a creative and confessional dialogue that provides us the opportunity to affirm in a practical setting the inherent power in the Bible to speak and transcended culture.

In no case are the essays below, given their brevity and the broadness of their subject, meant to be the final word on the topics presented. Rather, they are meant to be cogent statements of important and immediate issues before the church, and they are offered in the hope that they will be received as an initial statement on the issues raised and then become the basis of many conversations and some future study of those questions. To take the next steps in expanding your study of the Bible and the issues these essays raise, all the authors would agree that you should equip yourself with:

1. A good one-volume Bible commentary,
2. A good one-volume Bible dictionary,
3. A good Bible atlas, and
4. A subscription to an archaeology magazine such as *The Biblical Archaeology Review.*

In closing I want to acknowledge the several authors of the essays who each did such a good job of responding to the topic placed before them and stuck to the accompanying guidelines they were supplied. Each of the authors brought the proper educational credentials, which I hope they will forgive me in skipping over as I introduce them to you. You can follow up on these all-too-brief acknowledgements of them by surfing the Internet for a more complete picture.

Samuel J. Mikolaski, now retired after a lengthy career in both academia and journalism, formerly served as president of Atlantic Baptist University in Moncton, New Brunswick, and Pioneer McDonald Professor at Carey Theological College and Regent College in Vancouver, British Columbia. Now residing in southern California, he is occasionally cajoled into teaching at Fuller Theological Seminary and Golden Gate Baptist Seminary/Saddleback Church Seminary.

Michael H. Reynolds is the president of The Lighthouse Group, a consulting organization that assists churches to become more effective in carrying out their mandates as Christian congregations.

Mimi Haddad, president of Christians for Biblical Equality, is a founding member of the Evangelicals and Gender Study Group at the Evangelical Theological Society, which she currently co-chairs. She teaches at North Park Theological Seminary in Chicago.

Mozella G. Mitchell is the chair of the Department of Religious Studies at the University of South Florida in Tampa. She is best known as one of the premier voices of Womanist theology, which speaks to the church from the experience of African American women.

James Browning is an assistant professor of religion at Pikeville College in Pikeville, Kentucky.

The Bible in Evangelical Faith and Life

By Samuel J. Mikolaski

The Bible is supposed to be at the center of evangelical faith and life. In what ways is this apparent confessionally, in the life-style of Christians, and in behavior? What should be the place of the Bible in evangelical life today?

As I think about it, the Bible in the hands of dedicated lay Christians was the crucial factor in the conversion of my parents, then in my own conversion and re-orientation in life as a young teenager. The turn of the wheel in attitudes toward the Bible during the past hundred years (my life encompasses most of those years) has been remarkable.

In the early 1900s the Modernist theological impulse, particularly from Europe, undermined confidence in the Bible and its key doctrines and resulted in rupturing most of the major Christian denominations. The reaction to this was swift, in the formation of new evangelical denominations and the development of the Bible School and Christian College movements. Through all of this, the *King James Version* (KJV) was the text in the hands of most Christians. It furnished a sense of common heritage and internalized language of faith.

Meanwhile in Britain, Modernism intruded only on the fringes of traditional theological commitment. From the 1920s through the 1950s new biblical scholarship emerged which trumped the theologically liberal ethos. I can easily list over one hundred names of prominent British biblical scholars from this period. These generated the impetus and furnished literature that fostered interest in biblical studies and new translations of the Scriptures in America as well as the emergence of new scholarship.

In America strong defense of Scripture during the rise of attacks on the Bible included B. B. Warfield's essays (later published as a collection in *The Inspiration and Authority of the Bible,* 1948), and the subsequent work of evangelical scholars such as those compiled by Carl F. H. Henry in *Revelation and the Bible,* 1958. Along with the rapid development of missionary outreach within America and overseas, the demand for the Bible and for new translations increased exponentially.

The Bible is the book of the people. Putting the Bible in the hands of the people in the language of the people began with John Wycliffe in England (1320–1384), long before the Protestant Reformation. The most lasting influence was that of William Tyndale, who is the father of English Bible translation. His work emerged publicly in 1523 and his complete Bible was published in Cologne in 1534. In 1536 he was arrested in Brussels, strangled and his body burned. His translation served as the foundation of the King James Version, which became the standard English-language text until modern times.

Meanwhile Baptists in Europe in 1529 completed the first German-language version, the *Worms Bible* (by the Anabaptists Ludwig Hetzer and Hans Denck), which quickly went through seventeen editions and was commended by Luther. Luther himself completed his New Testament translation by 1522 and the complete Bible by 1534, which became standard use among German-speaking Protestants.

The first Bible printed in America was the Eliot Bible (1623), an Algonquin Indian language translation, long before an English language Bible was printed in the American colonies.

After World War II, public demand and the new scholarly resources which were becoming available in the United States led to the current plethora of new Bible translations, the sale of which has massively increased English language Bible circulation worldwide, and has stimulated the production of hundreds of new language translations.

The *Revised Standard Version* (RSV: N.T. 1946, O.T. 1952; revised 1989) was well received at first, but circulation decreased when many readers felt that the Old Testament renderings published later tended to diminish or sidestep messianic implications of Old Testament texts as traditionally understood by Christians (I continue to use the complete 1952 RSV as a basic study tool). The *New International Version* (NIV 1978, revised 1984) is probably the most widely circulated translation among evangelicals and conservative Christians. I use it regularly as a study text, though I feel that neither the RSV nor the NIV approach the elegance or literary and liturgical value of the KJV.

The Bible is fundamentally a "people's book." Before we can address its place in modern evangelical life, we must consider some other issues.

What Is the Bible?

The Bible comprises the thirty-nine books of the Old Testament (the books of the Hebrew Scriptures) and the twenty-seven books of the New Testament (the writings which derive from Christ's apostles and their associates).

Fundamentally, Christians accept the Old Testament to be God's Word because these are the Scriptures handed down from generation to generation in the life of Israel. The word "Testament" is used in the sense of "Covenant"; the Old

Covenant of God with his people Israel, and the New Covenant with God's people in Christ (Luke 16:17).

Jesus identified the Old Testament as sacred Scripture comprising the Law, the Prophets, and the Psalms or Writings (Matt. 5:17-18; 11:13; Luke 24:44). The customary arrangement of the Old Testament was:

(1) The Law:
Genesis, Exodus, Leviticus, Numbers, Deuteronomy
(2) The Prophets:
(a) The Former Prophets: Joshua, Judges, 1 and 2 Samuel, 1 and 2 Kings
(b) The Latter Prophets: Isaiah, Jeremiah, Ezekiel, and the twelve minor prophets
(3) The Writings:
Psalms, Proverbs, Job, Song of Solomon, Ruth, Lamentations, Ecclesiastes, Esther, Ezra, Nehemiah, 1 and 2 Chronicles

Jesus affirmed this scope and limit of the Hebrew Bible when, in speaking of the Old Testament martyrs in Luke 11:51, he said "from the blood of Abel to the blood of Zechariah," which encompasses the first martyr (in Genesis) to the last. In the order of books in the Hebrew Bible, Zechariah is the last martyr to be identified in the last book of the Hebrew Bible, 2 Chronicles 24:21.

Subsequent to the resurrection of Christ, the apostles, either directly or through those associated with them, transmitted the story of Jesus' life and his teachings, and the significance of the events surrounding his birth, life, ministry, death, resurrection, their commissioning to mission, the promise of his return, and his ascension.

The key criterion which determined what was included in the canon or excluded from the canon was the concept of Holy Scripture: the Old Testament comprised the received Scriptures of the Hebrew Bible, and the New Testament comprised apostolic writings, or writings attributed to those associated with the apostles, and so acknowledged by their use among the early Christian churches.

Early Christian writings are replete with such data. To be sure, the writers were in many cases well educated and cite texts and practical wisdom from pagan sources, but their citation of the Scriptures stands on a higher plane: these are the authoritative Word or Oracles of God.

Thus Clement of Rome, when writing from the congregation at Rome to the congregation at Corinth about A.D. 96 concerning dissension in their ranks, cites or alludes to more than 180 biblical references, from both Old Testament and New Testament writings, to buttress his argument—a remarkable display of biblical literacy. The authority to which he appeals is not that of the church at Rome, but the wisdom that comes from Holy Scripture.

Similarly, in the latter part of the second century A.D. Irenaeus, who led in the rapid expansion of Christian witness in Gaul, emphasized that the truth the church preached was conserved by the prophets, fulfilled in Christ, and handed down by the apostles.

Along with the books of the Old Testament, the completed canon included writings by an apostle or apostolic man, and writings the early church found useful in congregational life.

The content of the canon was not a mechanical process, nor did any one church council decree its final shape. It was, I believe, the on-going action of the Holy Spirit to conserve Holy

Scripture: the books of the Old Testament and authentic apostolic writings.

Whether in classical studies or biblical studies, we all must deal with received texts. It is amazing that new discoveries relating to biblical studies have for over a century tended to push the dating of received texts closer and closer to apostolic times. Textual studies such as those published and ongoing at Tyndale House, Cambridge, England, have tended to reinforce confidence in the authenticity of the texts we have.

We have far more texts, and older texts, for Old Testament and New Testament studies than we have for studies in the classics. My love of study of Plato, Aristotle, the Stoics, and Epicurus and his heritage (which reached into apostolic times and called for rejoinder by the apostle Paul) is not diminished by the fact that most of our sources originate from mid- or late-medieval times.

My experience and suggestion is to follow the advice of the University of Virginia philosopher and educator E. D. Hirsch (*Validity in Interpretation,* 1967) that we accept a received text, confident that future work will gradually refine it, and work toward grasping its meaning not tearing it apart. Tearing apart does not educate. Give credence to authorial intent, Hirsch urges. To grasp the sense is to educate oneself.

A Universe of Meaning: The Bible's Transforming Paradigm

The failure of modern critics, in contrast to Christianity's antagonists when the apostles carried the gospel into the ancient world, is that they and the media who mindlessly feature them are nitpickers. They are too shallow. They don't get to the essentials. And the essentials embrace key elements of human existence and of life in this universe. The Bible presents a worldview; its message comprises a transforming paradigm for modern human beings and society.

This is true in two important practical respects: First, the Bible furnishes a set of guidelines for personal behavior—standards which define good and evil, right and wrong. Second, the Bible sets forth a set of practical guidelines for society, for governance—a set of standards for public policy.

Consider first biblical guidelines for personal behavior.

While the Bible is replete with ethical teaching, the Decalogue as a set of standards and the Book of Proverbs as a set of maxims embrace what I mean. At Sinai the Israelites were brought into a covenant relationship with God, which the "Ten Words," the Ten Commandments, epitomize. Idolatry of whatever kind is proscribed. They must worship the one and only true God of the universe whose covenant with them entails concrete ethical and moral precepts (Ex. 34:6-7).

Thus the Bible conveys this seminal truth: that in the universe which God has created, right and wrong stand for objective characteristics which attach directly and inalienably to acts and their consequences. Moral judgments are more than culturally fashioned and biologically induced responses, defined situationally as that which is right in any one person's eyes. They relate to the rightness or wrongness of acts that are normed by what God wills, neither capriciously nor arbitrarily, but reflecting God's own nature as holy, just, and good.

From many sources in Israel's life, the Book of Proverbs presents practical maxims on how to live morally, in harmony with others, a life pleasing to God. It is a manual for living that praises the surpassing worth of wisdom and highlights the tragedy of folly. These are basic principles to guide the prudent person who has a powerful sense of dependence upon God

(Prov. 3:5–12). The good life is the moral life, which contrasts with a life geared purely to amoral behavioral responses. Wisdom leads to pursuit of that which is good (Prov. 6:20–23). Rejection of moral standards opens one to the pitfalls of moral impurity, violence, dishonesty, duplicity, deviousness, and insincerity.

In the past men like Benjamin Franklin taught America practical morality, though today's ethos eschews criticism of anyone's behavior. But what is wrong with the following from Proverbs: be concerned for the poor (22:22–23); avoid violent persons (22:24–25); retain society's landmarks (22:28); avoid covetousness (23:4); guide and discipline children (19:18); refrain from drunkenness and gluttony (23:20–21); honor parents (23:22); flee immorality (23:26–28); seek good friendships and shun bad ones (24:1–2, 19–20)?

Second, what about matters of public policy?

On this matter the message of the prophet Amos is pivotal. Bear in mind that, as Amos prophesied in the mid-eighth century B.C.E., his fundamental public policy thesis is "Let justice roll down like waters, and righteousness like an everflowing stream" (Amos 5:24 NASB), which was uttered centuries before the Milesian philosophers speculated about the nature of reality, or Athenians such as Plato and Aristotle debated the nature of justice.

While Amos urges compassion for the poor and oppressed, he argues that the fundamental issue concerning social evils is not inequality. Inequality is the result; injustice is the cause. If there were justice, freedom, and opportunity there would not be so many poor.

His list of evils is astounding: genocide, barbarism, ethnic cleansing, judicial bribes, excessive penalties, arbitrary government, extortion, fraud, perjury, exploitation, fraud, moral and religious corruption, curtailing freedom of speech, and, generally, subversion of justice.

In Amos, justice, righteousness, and that which is right are correlatives. Justice (*mishpat,* 5:7, 15, 24; 6:12) is that which is one's due. Righteousness (*tsadaq,* 5:7, 24; 6:12) is that which is equitable or right; in societal matters it identifies that which is due, equitable, or right in the execution of social, judicial, and political obligations. Right (*nakoach,* 3:10) means that which is right, straightforward, upright. It is our obligation (5:14-15) to seek good (*tubh*) not evil (*ra'a*).

Amos was a keen observer of human affairs and well informed about evils within the life of his own people the Israelites and in surrounding nations. His indictment was unsparing, especially about the fraud of celebrating religious festivals while exploiting the oppressed. Amos was a tract of the times for many centuries in the rise of Christian Europe which helped move Europe from barbarism to civilized societies. Later it helped America to develop a constitution that honored the dignity of humans created in the image of God.

Further, Amos is among the first of the prophets to say that God is not only Lord of Israel but also of history. All nations are shown to be responsible to God. Thus the teleological character of history is declared. God is not removed from the movement of history and he will achieve his purposes. And though Amos sounds solemn warnings, his final word is one of hope based on God's unchanging justice and unending love (9:11–15).

Unlike their forebears, modern American evangelicals have been pushed to the fringe of American culture. Early- and mid-nineteenth century evangelicals in Britain had the strength to disestablish the Church of England if they had so desired, but instead of pursuing political power they devoted themselves to abolishing slavery, caring for the sick and widows and orphans, feeding the hungry, sheltering the homeless during the social and economic upheavals associated with the Industrial Revolution, and working to abolish the abuse of women. Our American evangelical predecessors were part of the mainstream of American culture.

Today's evangelicals, who are simultaneously despised by left-wing progressives who enjoy the social benefits of past evangelical compassion and cynically pandered to by politicians on the right, ought to renew their God-given mandate to create a revolution against today's cultural evils. But this can best happen not by political clout in Washington or in the courts. Acquiring political power does not equip one to change America morally and spiritually.

The philosophical materialists and transcendentalists have not and, indeed, cannot produce moral change in America. Only the willfully blind fail to see in our world that religious terrorism, mafia-type economies, repression and exploitation of women and girls, ethnic cleansing, caste systems, and transcendentalist myopia in the midst of unspeakable poverty and suffering, walk hand-in-hand with religious, economic, and metaphysical systems that America's cultural and academic secular reactionary elite like to play with but do not comprehend. Absorption with comparative religion has become a variegated quilt that hides a multitude of sins.

Change can come about only by seeding the main segments of American culture with key biblical ideals and values. If Mel Gibson can roil and challenge thinking in Hollywood with his film *The Passion of the Christ,* even temporarily, then others can do it in politics, business, education, the media, science, medicine, the judicial system, and social services. Abortion and divorce are receding in numbers, but the rate of change in these and other social evils could quicken if evangelicals again enter the mainstream of American life, exhibiting lives of goodness, intelligence, balance, and compassion—in short, Christ-infused principles—and then slowly by give and take, and by judicious compromises, seek to turn America toward higher ideals.

But there is more to the transforming biblical paradigm, beyond distinctive personal moral teaching and the concept of justice in regard to public policy: it is philosophically distinct and, in my judgment, the paradigm of choice for the future of humanity.

That we are now supposed to be in the post-Christian era suggests the loss of the biblical hermeneutic; we are witnessing a massive demonstration of unbelief the spirit of which is self-conscious use of power without faith. And anyone who proposes to limit power in line with faith is mocked. Despite secular rejection of them, it is time to ask whether biblical categories are in fact the viable intellectual alternative for the future.

Christianity's "way of arranging the world" is what overtook the ancient worldviews, and it is instructive to note parallels with today's mind-set.

In apostolic and post-apostolic times during the inception and rapid expansion of the Christian faith, Christians were confronted by two large philosophical traditions: Transcendentalism and Materialism.

First, Transcendentalism characterized the religions of the Empire, but was centered chiefly in the Idealism of the ancient philosophical schools. These tended to denigrate the empirical world and sought release from earthbound existence to behold the divine (Platonists, Gnostics, Manicheans, Neo-Platonists, among others). Fundamentally their views were *inimical to full-blown individual personhood.* For them, God was impersonal reason. Human personality was a transient epiphenomenon which would soon be cured by death and re-absorbed into infinite transcendent reality. Freedom was an illusion. In modern times, the parallels include various forms of Panentheism (Paul Tillich) and Process Philosophy (A. N. Whitehead).

The other major ancient philosophical tradition was the materialistic atomism of Leucippas, Democritus, and Epicurus: all that exists was matter in motion. This yielded a philosophy that was totally deterministic and fatalistic and, when put into psychological and ethical forms, totally hedonistic. Its exact parallel in our time is the Behaviorism of Ivan Pavlov and B. F. Skinner. For them, as well, human freedom is an illusion. This view denies the existence of the soul or spirit and views the termination of human life as the end of everything. The hedonist model of the good life is, "eat, drink, and be merry, for tomorrow we die." (see Eccl. 8:15) This is what the media in America foster today.

Karl Marx created a parallel economic and social theory out of the traditional materialist categories and, while he rejected teleology in favor of historical determinism, he nevertheless espoused a gospel of the inevitable movement of human history toward a classless society.

It is time to draw the contrast between these two deterministic models—Transcendentalist and Materialist—and the biblical model.

The biblical model is indeed a manifesto: it rejects determinism, whether metaphysical, psychological, or economic. God is the creator of the universe. Human beings have a spiritual nature. They are created for freedom and are responsible to God for their actions and their stewardship of the world.

The Christian view centers on the important points that the nature of reality derives from the creative act of God. It is essentially moral and spiritual in nature, fashioned for persons and interpersonal relations. The whole world is the object of God's love and concern. Its genius is not the behavioristically conditioned ant-heap, but the creation of free human beings in Christ who will know and serve God righteously.

In other words, conservation of humanity and stewardship of the created order is inherent in the biblical model, but has no intellectual foundation in either Transcendentalism or Materialism. Thomas Kuhn, physicist and philosopher of science, has said that science proceeds by occasional paradigm shifts. It is time for the West to shift away from the reductionist tendencies of the modern materialist view of human nature and re-affirm the truth of the biblical model: that each human being has a spiritual nature which is created in the image of God, and that recognition of this truth affords the best protection of human beings as free persons from modern manipulators who propose re-fashioning humanity biologically, psychologically, and socially into their motor-affective response reconstruction of human nature.

Enhancing the Role of the Bible in Modern Evangelical Life

The most important factor regarding the Bible in evangelical life is its use privately and in public worship *in the hands of the people.* At issue are four key factors: how to facilitate the internalization of the content of Scripture, how to affirm key Scripture doctrines, how to conserve faith in the authenticity of the Scriptures and in their being the norm of the Christian faith, and how to best propagate the biblical message.

Habits of private use are mostly shaped by the role of the Bible in public worship. One can register concern about aspects of modern evangelical worship practices.

To begin with, which Bible (translation) to use? This is a most perplexing question. Currently there is no resolution in sight, given the number of translations and paraphrases available. I will by-pass paraphrases, the use of which I discourage whether for private or public use. These often reflect the ideological slant of the paraphraser, and in use they often reflect the predilections of the reader who is looking for the rendering of a text to confirm a previously formed opinion.

As to translations, the NIV is the most commonly used modern version. Though the *New American Standard Bible* (NASB) often yields a more literal translation, it has not enjoyed the circulation of the NIV. The same can be said for the *New King James Version* (NKJV). The use of the RSV and its successor, the NRSV, and the *New English Bible* (NEB) among evangelicals is limited.

The many available translations inhibit the internalization of Scripture. An important aspect of the KJV heritage was its *common use* during public worship. The many translations now in the hands of the congregation militate against congregational responsive reading. Projecting the reading onto a screen or printing it in the church bulletin does not create familiarity with the pages of the Bible.

Internalization of Scripture happens best by repeated exposure to a commonly used translation. And the translation must be lyrical enough to facilitate memorization, as well as accurate enough to merit memorization. In my judgment modern translations are not designed as literature for oral reading and easy memorization. That was a key aspect of the private and public use of the KJV. I cannot imagine memorizing the twenty-third psalm or 1 Corinthians 13 in anything but the KJV.

At this point I offer a personal anecdote: I was ten when my parents came to a personal Christian faith. I remember the first day I was taken to Sunday school. For two years the leaders of the Sunday school sponsored a Memory Work Contest, and since my parents were new converts, it appeared to them that the only thing to do was for their children to enter the contest and win! So my sister and I spent each Saturday morning memorizing twelve to twenty verses of Scripture to recite the next day.

During those months I committed about a thousand verses of Scripture to heart. This created a reservoir of instruction on the back shelves of my mind that has proved to be life-directing. Included were the Ten Commandments, many of the psalms (including the entire 119th Psalm), Isaiah 53, the Beatitudes, parts of the Gospel of John, and many parts of the Epistles, including 1 Corinthians 13.

Consider Acts 2: 42: upon their conversion and baptism, new converts "devoted themselves to the apostles' teaching and to the fellowship, to the breaking of bread and to prayer." Add to this Ephesians 5:19 and Colossians 3:16, where Paul speaks of addressing one another "with psalms, hymns and spiritual songs." Liturgical practices not only reinforce faith in one's head, they deposit a rich store of truth in the heart.

Such worship practices were common in the evangelical tradition of recent generations, whether Baptist, Methodist, Congregationalist, Presbyterian, Reformed, Christian and Missionary Alliance, Pentecostal, or Independent churches. The Bible was not detached from worship, such as a text thrown up on a screen to reinforce the point of a topical sermon. It was integral to all that went on in worship as reflected in prayers, responsive readings, and expository sermons. The hymns, especially, reflected biblical language and motifs, without unseemly familiarity with God, such as some who today refer to God as "the Guy upstairs."

What I speak of embraced many differing liturgical patterns, whether that of Baptists and others who for generations used the Ira D. Sankey collection of hymns *Sacred Songs and Solos,* which originated with the Dwight Moody revivals, or more traditional denominational hymn books, or other traditions of music such as black gospel music or bluegrass. Worship had its confessional base, which emphasized the greatness of God, the divinity and saving work of Christ on the cross, the fellowship of the saints, and the call to holy living and committed Christian service. It must be, as Rick Warren warns in the *Purpose Driven Life,* "not about you, but about God."

Here are suggestions on how to increase the use of the Bible in public worship:

1. Use biblical sentences as a call to worship: Psalm 1:1–2; 8:1, 3–4, 9; 19:1–4; 23:1–3; 24:3–5; 32:1–2, 11; 34:1–3; 40:1–3; 89:1–2; 100; Isaiah 40:28–31; 45:5–7; 55:1, 3; 61:1–2a; 66:1–2; 1 Corinthians 1:3.
2. Use biblical benedictions and blessings at the end of the service: Numbers 6:24–26; Psalm 4:6b, 8; 73:23–26;

John 14:27; Romans 1:7b; 11:33–36; 16:20b; 1 Corinthians 16:23; Galatians 1:3-5; Ephesians 1:2, 17–20a; 6:23-24; Philippians 4:4–7.

3. A congregation should be trained to know the books of the Bible and be able to find them quickly. It should not be thought undignified from time to time to recite jointly the OT books and the NT books as an exercise, or have young children lead the congregation in such a recitation. While identifying the page number of a passage in the Bible may be helpful to persons totally at sea on how to find the passage for a point in the sermon or for a congregational reading, that should be a muted announcement. Congregations should develop familiarity with the Bible so that they can instinctively and quickly find the passage in the Bible.
4. Re-emphasis of at least the two key Christian annual festivals is in order, namely, Christmas to celebrate the birth of Christ, and Easter to celebrate Christ's resurrection. In some churches these have become so muted that traditional, biblically based Christmas carols and hymns concerning Christ's passion and resurrection are unfamiliar. I recommend also extensive use of biblical passages in the church services and sermons associated with these festivals. It seems in recent years that other special observances, such as women's events, men's events, youth events, social service events, and many others, have taken precedence over those of the traditional church year.
5. Brief expository series and Bible biography series, along with informing historical and geographical references, are splendid aids to increase Bible literacy.

6. I recommend that the church decide on a translation that will be placed in the pews or hymnbook racks behind the chairs. Whatever translation or paraphrase people use as a personal Bible is not at issue. Joint congregational use is important in conveying solidarity as to what the Bible means to Christians as joint members of Christ's body.

Whether one of the newer Bible translations will become dominant to most Christians in the English-speaking world remains to be seen. For biblical teaching to embed itself in the minds and hearts of the people, a church ought to settle on one translation and use it regularly in all the venues of worship and teaching so that its language becomes "second nature" to the people. The Bible in the hands of the people is its best defense, conservation, and propagation.

How can we maximize Bible teaching in church life? Small groups do not reach most people in any given congregation. The decline of Sunday school in many churches and the loss of expository preaching in favor of topical preaching has been disastrous for levels of biblical knowledge among many in modern times. This is true despite the enormous increase in the circulation of new translations and paraphrases of the Bible and the publication of some Christian books that have reached the best-seller lists.

The cure for absorption with pet themes, narrow-mindedness, and tunnel vision as to grasping the message of the Bible is canon-wide study and appreciation of the plenary scope of the teaching of the Scriptures. Systematic book-by-book study sets the message of the Bible in its historical contexts and makes the application to today all the more incisive, and is the best cure for narrow, mind-shackling, brainwashing obsession.

But what should be one's attitude to the Scriptures in light of the modern tension between scholarly and devotional uses of the Bible? It is quite remarkable how derisively dismissive secularists are in academic circles whenever the word "Bible" is heard. This attitude is simply proof of widespread ignorance of one of the most potent intellectual and cultural influences in the history of mankind. No one can think of himself or herself as an intellectual who does not know the contents of the Bible. To be an educated person, the study of the Scriptures purely as classical literature that has profoundly affected the development of western civilization is mandatory.

My advice: take the biblical texts as we have them and study them with care. Give even a modicum of credence to authorial intent. Leave the weightier academic questions about manuscripts, variant readings, source criticism, or form criticism in abeyance. This is no different from my taking Plato's *Republic,* or Aristotle's *Metaphysics,* or Marcus Aurelius' *Meditations* at face value and then striving diligently to grasp what the author has written in the text I have(or, for that matter, what the editors of the text have compiled). Bear in mind that in the case of the canonical scriptures, we have manuscript copies which extend the range of likely early textual authenticity far beyond anything available in classical studies. Give credence to the text, and diligently search out its sense in the form in which we have it.

Along with other teaching programs, I urge return to a canonical curriculum strategy. By this I mean that each minister, each lay person, resolves that at some point in life he or she will make a serious study of each book of the Bible. And, for each Bible book, one should prepare a "book report" consisting of several pages of notes on the historical background of the book and author, an outline of the literary and story structure of the book, and notes on its major themes and permanent values.

I have found this to be a rewarding aspect of church ministry. If you log in to my website [www.drsamstheology.com] you will find a BIBLE tab. Under that tab are files named Canonical Curriculum where there are notes on each book of the Bible. These were developed in connection with pastoral ministry in an attempt to convey the structure and content of the Bible. If I were to teach such a series today, would I revise them? Of course! It takes hours and hours of study to prepare such material, but it is eminently profitable to do so both for the doer and the listener.

Can We Trust the Bible?

By Michael H. Reynolds

It has been almost 3,500 years since the first book of the Bible was written. Yet Christians the world over believe that the Bible is reliable and accurate in its claims about God, the world, man, and his relationship with God. In recent years words such as "infallible" and "inerrant" have become buzzwords for those who claim to believe wholeheartedly the Bible as opposed to the rest of Christianity who, for the most part, simply trust the Bible as truth.

On the other hand there are plenty of critics who attack the Bible's accuracy and reliability. They cite the multiple authors, age, claimed language difficulties, alleged contradictions, and a host of other objections. Some critics even express the opinion that the Bible has been altered over the centuries since it was originally written.

The nineteenth-century Baptist preacher, theologian, and educator, Charles H. Spurgeon is reported to have said, "The Bible is like a lion; it does not need to be defended, but simply let loose. A lion can defend itself." It was Spurgeon's contention not to get into an argument about the reliability of the Bible but allow the book to stand on its own merits. If the same tests that are used to verify the authenticity and veracity of any other ancient book are applied to the Bible, how does it stand up? It was written over a 1,600-year time span, by more than forty authors from every walk of life.

Consider just a few of these men. Moses was a political leader educated in the schools of the Egyptian Pharaohs before becoming a shepherd; Joshua was a military general; Amos was a herdsman; Nehemiah, a cupbearer to the king of Persia;

Daniel, a prime minister in Babylon; Solomon, a king of Israel; Peter, a fisherman; Luke, the only Gentile, was a doctor; Matthew, a tax collector for the Roman Empire; and Paul was a Jewish rabbi.

The Bible was written on three continents: Asia, Africa, and Europe. It was written in three ancient languages: Hebrew, Aramaic, and Greek. Yet in spite of these factors there is continuity from the beginning to the end. From Genesis to Revelation it ultimately focuses on one subject and that is the redemption of man. Some would offer that the only explanation is God's protection of the entire process.

In the following paragraphs the very same tests applied to any other ancient text will be applied to the Bible to determine its reliability and trustworthiness. The historical record, languages used in the writing of the Bible, the manuscripts themselves, and the archaeological record will be the criteria that will determine if the Bible can be trusted or not. The book that claims to be the very Word of God will stand on its own merits.

Archaeological Evidence of the Trustworthiness of the Bible

Over the centuries since the time of the biblical writers there have been explorations, excavations, and discoveries. Yet the science of archaeology is relatively modern in its development and application.[1] It was only in the first half of the nineteenth century that archaeologists began to create what may now truly be called the science of archaeology. As the process turned from mostly trial and error to a defined process, special application was used in the realm of biblical archaeology. W. F. Albright said, ". . . from the chaos of prehistory the Bible projected as though it were a monstrous fossil, with no contemporary evidence to demonstrate its authenticity and its origin in a human world like ours."[2]

The term "biblical archaeology" refers to the branch of the science that has primarily to do with Bible lands, the geographical area extending from Mesopotamia to Egypt and from Asia Minor to the Red Sea, and reaching as far west as the Italian peninsula. Biblical archaeology adds to its authenticity by not restricting itself to the areas expressly mentioned in the Bible. By looking at other places and sites in the same general region, light has been shed on biblical history in matters such as customs in general and languages.[3]

Despite the fact that biblical archaeology is such a recent development, the application of it has located almost every city mentioned in the Bible. Most of the locations, events, and persons mentioned in this book spanning over 1,500 years can be located and placed with accuracy. The critics of the late nineteenth and early twentieth centuries alleged that new archaeological discoveries would surely prove the Bible inaccurate in matters of history and thus make it unreliable. Yet after a hundred years of such discoveries, Nelson Glueck, the renowned Jewish archaeologist, wrote: "It may be stated categorically that no archaeological discovery has ever controverted a biblical reference."[4] It was Glueck's conclusion that the archaeological record fortifies the historicity of the Bible. This is true of both the Old and New Testaments.

The archaeological record of the Bible adds to its reliability as the Word of God because no other ancient book has such evidence. Biblical archaeology provides a physical context for the times, places, and environment of the people who produced the Bible or are mentioned in it. Eminent archaeologist and biblical theologian Millar Burrows declared that the Bible needs not necessarily to be defended but to be understood. When real understanding of the times and lives of those who contributed to the Bible occurs then the Bible becomes even more reliable. This is the contribution of biblical archaeology.[5]

The archaeological evidence of the Bible is of great value because, as stated above, it places the people and events of the Bible in historical context. It places men like Abraham, Moses, David, Paul, Peter, and Jesus in the realm of history and not just in the areas of theology and philosophy. Archaeology is also important because the Bible is not a complete record of the times and lives of those it mentions in it. Not even a whole library could give a complete account of every experience of God's people. Those writing the books we now know as the Bible were not intent on giving their future readers the entire picture. They wrote about things that were important to their purpose. Biblical archaeology has allowed students of the Bible to fill in the gaps in the historical record and allows for a deeper understanding of those things mentioned in these ancient writings.

The languages of the Bible are ancient and sometimes difficult to understand because translators may not understand the idioms and fine nuances of the Hebrew, Aramaic, or Greek. Another important contribution of biblical archaeology is that it helps to explain some of these difficulties. This is done by locating a similar word or phrase in a language related to those of the Bible. With that understanding applied to the biblical languages, it makes the translation clearer and the meaning more relevant.

Prior to the twentieth century many biblical scholars were having a problem with some of the chronology of the Bible. This historical record outside of the Bible itself was of doubtful trustworthiness in many places. This was simply because there was no verification in other records and there was a lack of other written materials from the same period. However, with the advent of biblical archaeology the history and chronology of the Bible became verifiable.[6]

A tourist to Israel today would be presented with a number of locations for Golgotha, Jesus' empty tomb, the actual birthplace of Jesus, and other significant landmarks. One tour guide remarked that the traditional baptismal site of Jesus used to be in one location but was moved because it was more convenient for the tourists. From a variety of sources this seems to have been going on since the days of the late Roman Empire. While there is no doubt about the location of Bethlehem, the Jordan River, or many other major places in the Bible, some of the exact locations of the events are traditional and often unsupported by authentic biblical archaeology. Most people are unaware that the ancient walled city is not entirely the same city that David and Solomon built, Nehemiah rebuilt, and Jesus walked in. Most of the "ancient" walled city was built during the crusades, many of the places where Jesus actually walked are thirty feet under where the city now resides. Yet, in spite of these and tourist "points of interest," biblical archaeology brings an authenticity to the story that is hard to deny. Below are some selected examples from both the Old and New Testaments. Space does not allow for an extensive review of both testaments; these examples will suffice to make my point that the archaeology of the Bible is both reliable and verifiable.

Numbers 20:21 says, "Since Edom refused to let them go through their territory, Israel turned away from them." Later this refusal was repeated by the King of Moab in Numbers

21:22. In the 1940s Glueck's explorations revealed the existence of fortresses along the borders of both ancient Edom and Moab. It would have been practically impossible from a military point of view to force a passage through those territories by Israel or anyone else.[7]

Second Samuel 2:13 mentions the pool of Gibeon. Excavations in 1956–57 and later in 1959–1960 have uncovered this pool along with a hydraulic system in connection with it.[8]

The ancient city of Jebus or the Jebusite Jerusalem David captured and made his capital is mentioned in 2 Samuel 5:9 and many other places in the Bible. It has, since ancient times, been located on the southeastern hill of the city. Since 1867 a number of excavations have been made in and around Jerusalem. The most important of these were carried out in the years between 1961 and 1967. The oldest ruins discovered during those digs belong to a Jebusite wall dating to 1800 B.C., thus authenticating the statements of the Bible.[9]

As Nehemiah began to rebuild the city of Jerusalem following the exile he ran into opposition in the persons of Sanballat and Tobiah. These two local officials did all they could to hamper and oppose the rebuilding of the city. In 1962 in a cave north of Jericho a seal from the forth century B.C. was located. On that seal is mentioned a "son of Sanballat, governor of Samaria."[10] According to the biblical record in Nehemiah, Tobiah may have been a Jew who also served as some kind of local functionary of the Persian kingdom. In modern-day Iraq, close to the ruins of an ancient palace, a tomb was excavated which bears the name "*Tobiyah*" carved in the rock in Aramaic letters. While there is some disagreement as to whether this is the Tobiah of Nehemiah or not, most archaeologists do agree that the tomb is dated from the time of Nehemiah.[11] While it may well be that both Sanballat and Tobiah may have been family names or even the rank of their office, it is concluded by the evidence that these two minor biblical characters lived at the time of Nehemiah and the rebuilding of Jerusalem.

Today, modern-day Nazareth occupies the same location of the town where Jesus grew up. In the days when Jesus lived there it was a minor town and not well thought as a place to live. It probably would not have made the tourist list of the first century A.D. When Nathanael was invited by Philip to come and meet Jesus of Nazareth he replied, "Nazareth! Can anything good come from there?"[12] Archaeological remains of human settlement in the area of Nazareth can be dated to the sixth century B.C.[13]

John 19:13 records, "When Pilate heard this, he brought Jesus out and sat down on the judge's seat at a place known as the Stone Pavement (which in Aramaic is *Gabbatha*)." Excavating under the Convent of Our Lady of Sion in Jerusalem a stone paved courtyard has been located. Its location in reference to other known places, its shape and construction lead archaeologists to the conclusion that this is the place where Jesus stood and was presented to the people: "Here is your King."[14]

Philip was one of the original seven men chosen to serve the early church in Jerusalem to alleviate some of the early problems. He later became an evangelist in a variety of places. According to an ancient tradition, Philip spent the last part of his life in Hierapolis and in that city it has been possible to identify the remains of four early churches. In one of them the following inscription was found, "Eugenius the least, archdeacon who is in charge of (the church of) the holy and glorious apostle and theologian Philip."

In the book of last things, Revelation, we are told that the last living apostle, John, lived out the remainder of his days on the island of Patmos. It was there that God gave him a glimpse of heaven and the things that were to come. While some of the sites on the island are traditional and of modern origin, the island itself is without a doubt the place that John identifies as the location where he wrote The Revelation. This places the last events recorded in the New Testament squarely in the realm of history.[15]

Space simply does not permit us to review the sheer volume of archaeological evidence that supports the historicity of the Bible. However, the examples given from both the Old and New Testaments should serve as evidence of the reliability of the Bible from an archaeological viewpoint.

Historical Evidence of the Trustworthiness of the Bible

Very closely associated with the archaeological evidence of the Bible is the external historical evidence. By the end of the first century A.D. Christianity had spread throughout the Roman Empire and beyond and within a short span of time the Christian faith had firmly entrenched itself into western culture and philosophy. Christianity as a philosophy and worldview was in many ways opposite of the culture of the west, but in short order this new faith moved in and reshaped western thought in a myriad of ways. As the first century drew to a close the Christian church was not only referring to the Old Testament as scripture but also to other books written by apostles, eyewitnesses, and early followers of Jesus of Nazareth.

Part of the external historical evidence of the reliability of the Bible is in comparison with other books. Professor M.

Montiero-Williams, former professor of Sanskrit, spent 42 years studying Eastern books and compared them to the Bible.

> Pile them, if you will, on the left side of your study table; but place your own Holy Bible on the right side—all by itself, all alone—and with a wide gap between them. For, . . . there is a gulf between it and the so-called sacred books of the East which severs one from the other utterly, hopelessly, and forever . . . a veritable gulf which cannot be bridged over by any science of religious thought.[16]

In spite of the historical reality of the rapid spread of Christianity and the development of the Bible as a whole there are always critics. The French philosopher, Voltaire, said in 1750 that in one hundred years Christianity would be swept from existence. The fact that it had existed and even thrived in many ways for 1,600 years before did not sway his assertion. Voltaire would have been astounded to see that Christianity survived his prediction and is still vibrant and alive today. About fifty years after Voltaire's death the Geneva Bible Society purchased his house for printing the Bible. Later it became the Paris headquarters for the British and Foreign Bible Society. Today, the Bible is still a best-seller. It has been reprinted in more languages than any other book, it can be found in almost every inhabitable place in the world. It was the first book to be carried into space. While in space orbiting the earth one of the astronauts read from Genesis 1:1, "In the beginning God created the heavens and the earth. . . ." This is a book that Voltaire said would be extinct by 1800, along with the movement that professed faith in its words.

One of the external historical evidences for the reliability of the Bible is time. This is a small part of the manuscript evidence of the Bible that will be discussed later but this evidence is also of historical nature. The time interval between the original writing and the earliest manuscripts is incredibly short in the case of the Bible compared with other ancient literature. Sir Fredric G. Kenyon, who was the director and principal librarian of the British Museum, said that the interval between the dates of the original composition and the earliest extant evidence becomes so small as to be negligible. He relates that this removes any doubt that the Scriptures have come down to us substantially as they were written. It was Kenyon's conclusion that the general integrity of the books of the New Testament as well as the whole Bible was well established.

Writing shortly after A.D. 70 the Jewish historian, Josephus, wrote in his *Antiquities of the Jews*:

> Now there was about this time Jesus, a wise man, if it be lawful to call him a man, for he was a doer of wonderful works, a teacher of such men as receive the truth with pleasure. He drew over to him both many Jews, and many of the Gentiles. He was [the] Christ. And when Pilate, at the suggestion of the principal men amongst us, had condemned him to the cross, those that loved him at first did not forsake him; for he appeared to them again on the third day; as the divine prophets had foretold then and ten thousand other wonderful things concerning him. And the tribe of Christians, so named from him, is not extinct at this day.

Cornelius Tacticus, a Roman historian born between A.D. 52–54, twice referenced Christianity in his writings. He was a governor of Asia, and when he wrote of the reign of Nero in his *Annals* he referenced the death of Christ and existence of

Christians at Rome. Later in a fragment of his *Histories* he mentions the burning of the temple in Jerusalem in A.D. 70. Since there are not many books or writings that survive to today intact from ancient times, these two works along with the archaeological evidence and from what will be demonstrated from the archaeological evidence, attest to the trustworthiness of the Bible.

Being written on material that is easily destroyed over time such as papyrus, parchment, vellum, and others, it would be easy to assume that the Bible's reliability would be compromised. However, even though it had to be recopied for hundreds of years prior to the invention of the printing press, the accuracy of the text was not compromised. In comparison with other documents of classical antiquity none are as well attested bibliographically as the New Testament.[17]

Another piece of historical evidence for the reliability of the Bible is that throughout time it has withstood the attacks of its enemies as no other book. Some have tried to ban it, burn it, and outlaw it from the days of the Roman emperors to modern day dictatorships. Yet, it remains in print, is read worldwide, and influences lives time and time again.[18]

In the days that the New Testament was written very few books or writings were actually translated from one language to another. Since its inception Christianity has been a missionary faith and for this reason the New Testament, for the most part, was written in the common everyday language of Koine Greek. It was then translated to Syriac, sometimes called Christian Aramaic, Latin, and Coptic.[19] Syriac and Latin translations were made as early as A.D. 150. This puts them within a generation of the original manuscripts. The number of these different translations and the fact that they differ very little from one another is another strong support for the textual evidence and accuracy of the Bible used today.

As the early church fathers began to write about their faith in the second century A.D. they gave a great amount of credibility to the text of the Bible. J. Harold Greenlee says that the quotations of the early Christian writers are so extensive that the New Testament could almost be reconstructed from them without manuscripts.[20] Consider that Ignatius (A.D.70–110), the Bishop of Antioch, knew well the apostles and in his writings he quotes from fifteen different books of the New Testament. Polycarp (A.D. 70–156), martyred at 86 years of age, was Bishop of Smyrna and a disciple of the apostle John and he quoted from the New Testament writings. Clement of Alexandria, Tertullian, Hippolytus, Origen, and Justin Martyr were all born in the second century and were only one generation removed from the New Testament era. Their writings all show extensive quotations from the books that were part of the New Testament and these quotes reflect a textual accuracy that is not evident in other ancient writings. An inventory of the quotes by the early church fathers will reveal some 32,000 citations from the writings included in the New Testament prior to the Council of Nicea in A.D. 325.[21] This once again demonstrates the reliability of the Bible used today.

Another piece of external historical data that supports the trustworthiness of the Bible is the 2,000-year-old Dead Sea Scroll text known as 4Q521 discovered in 1946. In the scroll a five-line fragment referred to a Hebrew prophet who shared an ancestry with King David and was put to death. The scrolls are dated between 250 B.C. and A.D. 68. This indicates that just prior to the time of Jesus and certainly during his life writers belonging to a Jewish sect believed in a Messiah who would suffer and be put to death.[22]

Manuscript Evidence for the Trustworthiness of the Bible

The manuscript evidence for the Bible is a bit overwhelming when compared to other ancient writings. No one seriously doubts the authenticity or reliability of the works of Plato, Aristotle, Herodotus or Tacitus, but as it will be demonstrated shortly, the Bible's manuscript evidence far outweighs anything that supports those works.

Some critics of the Bible have argued that through the centuries it has been altered and had its message changed. Yet, as it will be clearly demonstrated below, this is almost impossible. The Bible has always been a very public document and widely disseminated. It would be almost as impossible to alter the message of the Bible as it would be to change the words of the Constitution of the United States. While different translations abound, the meaning of the translations are essentially the same. If the Bible had been privately altered in such a way as to change its message, I suspect there would have been a very public outcry.

One piece of evidence to the reliability of the manuscripts themselves is the interval between the dates of the original composition and the earliest extant evidence. The time between the two becomes so small as to be negligible. The interval of time between the origin and the earliest existing manuscripts of the above-mentioned classical writers is between 900 and 1,300 years. By contrast, the "John Rylands" fragment of the New Testament containing John 18:31-33 has been dated as early as A.D. 115. "Entire manuscripts of the New Testament can be dated within 300 years of its completion.

Virtually complete New Testament books, as well as extensive fragments, can be dated within 100 years of its close."[23]

No case examining the manuscript evidence of the Bible can ignore the sheer number of manuscripts of the New Testament in comparison to other ancient works. To date there are over 24,000 manuscripts of the New Testament alone. They are in various versions and ancient languages. Over 5,500 of those ancient manuscripts are Greek, and while it was very rare that any ancient writing was translated into another language, the New Testament was. These translations were made as early as A.D. 150 and were in Syriac, Latin, and Coptic.[24] In addition to these ancient manuscripts, others exist in Armenian, Gothic, Georgian, Ethiopic, and Nubian. These date from as early as the fourth century and no later than the sixth century.

For the sake of argument one could ignore all of the manuscripts save those written in Greek and still outweigh any other ancient work. Homer's *Iliad* is second to the New Testament in the number of ancient manuscripts and it only has 643. Even then, the interval between the time it was written and the date of the earliest existing manuscript is far greater than that for the Bible. The *Iliad* was originally written approximately 800 B.C. and the earliest manuscript dates from the thirteenth century A.D. All of the other ancient writings of the world fall way behind even the *Iliad*, much less the New Testament.

When one looks at the evidence of the manuscripts available for study, the uniqueness of the New Testament textual witnesses becomes apparent. Compared to the other writings of antiquity, the New Testament stands alone in the weight of evidence supporting it. The thinnest possible thread preserves the works of several ancient authors. Dr. Bruce Metzger,

Emeritus Professor of New Testament Language and Literature at Princeton Theological Seminary, gives three pertinent examples. First on the list is *The History of Rome*, by Vellius Paterculus. It survived to modern times through only one incomplete manuscript, and it was subsequently lost in the seventeenth century after being copied by Beatus Rhenanus. A second example is the *Annals* of the historian Tacitus. The first six books of this work are in a single manuscript dating from the ninth century. And the only known manuscript of the Epistle of Diognetus, an early Christian composition that many editors include in the corpus of the Apostolic Fathers, perished in a fire at the municipal library in Strasbourg in 1870. Among the world's scholars who study ancient documents there is very little doubt about the origin, authorship, and date of the examples given above, and they have very little manuscript evidence for support. In light of this Dr. Metzger states, "In contrast with these figures, the textual critic is embarrassed by the wealth of his material."[25]

Critics of the Bible's reliability will often point to the variations in the New Testament manuscripts. In the thousands of extant manuscripts there are some 150,000 variants. To the uninformed this seems like a staggering number to be sure until it is taken into account that every one of them was hand-copied. However, to those who study the issue the numbers are not so damaging as they may at first appear. A careful study of the manuscripts and the variants contained in them will demonstrate that the New Testament is accurate and trustworthy. Out of 150,000 variants that exist, 99 percent hold virtually no significance whatsoever. Many of them simply involve a missing letter in a word; some involve word reversal such as "Christ Jesus" instead of "Jesus Christ." Some of the variants involve the absence of one or more insignificant words. All total there are only about 50 of the variants that have any real significance, and even then, no doctrine of Christianity or any moral commandment is affected. Because of the sheer number of manuscripts to use as a comparison for more than 99 percent of the cases, the original text can be reconstructed with a practical certainty. The study of the ancient manuscripts is known as textual criticism, and by using this science and comparing all of the manuscripts with each other it can be concluded that the document known as the New Testament is reliable and trustworthy.[26]

Where the Old Testament is concerned there are currently more than 1,000 known manuscripts. Until 1947 and the discovery of the Dead Sea Scrolls, the oldest complete text of the Old Testament was the Aleppo Codex. It is dated around A.D. 1008 and is one of the extant manuscripts that constitute or support the Masoretic text. With the discovery of the Dead Sea Scrolls the oldest existing manuscript of the Old Testament predates the Masoretic text by 1,200 years. There are some minor scribal variants between the two manuscripts but no significant differences.

One of the major reasons for so few variations in the Old Testament manuscript was the method of transmission of the ancient documents of the Old Testament. As each scroll wore out another would be painstakingly copied to replace it. Every line and every page of material would be scrutinized and compared to the previous copy. If there were any abnormalities or differences the copy would be destroyed and the scribe would start over. This led to very few variations in the text of the books of the Old Testament. "The consonantal text of the Hebrew Bible which the Masoretes edited had been handed down to their time with conspicuous fidelity over a period of nearly a thousand years."[27] This meticulous method of transmission is one of the reasons that there are not nearly as many manuscripts of the Old Testament as the New, and this is additional proof for the reliability of the entire Bible.

By applying the same criteria to the Bible that are applied to any other ancient literature the evidence is clear and plausible enough to declare the Bible authentically trustworthy. Based on the normal uses of historical research it can be concluded that Moses was a real man and led Israel from Egypt to Palestine. It can be said with reasonable certainty that David was king of Israel and established his monarchy just as the Old Testament book of Second Samuel states. Using the exact standards applied to any other historical situation it can be concluded that the baby born in Bethlehem, attended by angels and shepherds alike, occurred just as Luke recorded it. Further, the Gospel accounts of the life of Jesus, his death, and resurrection are vindicated and declared true. The missionary journeys of the apostle Paul and his companions are authenticated and thus his letters can be trusted as authentic instructions to the church. There is no real evidence yet discovered in literary sources, epigraphy, or archaeology that would discount the veracity of the Bible.[28]

The Bible Speaks to Its Own Trustworthiness

Based on the above-stated evidence the manuscripts and texts of the Bible are authenticated and thus the Bible's testimony of itself has bearing on the question of its veracity. As stated previously the Bible was written over a span of 1,600 years, by forty authors, using three different languages, and yet there is one consistent, non-contradictory theme that runs through it all: God's redemption of man. Taking in the entire context of the Bible from Genesis forward it is apparent that God is preparing Israel and the world for the angel's announcement to the shepherds concerning the birth of Jesus and his coming to save mankind from sin.

The authors of the New Testament over and over again claimed to be eyewitnesses to the events they recorded. Although Luke was an eyewitness to much of the Book of Acts he did not witness the events of the Gospel. Yet in Luke 1:1–3 Luke tells his readers that he sought to investigate those events in the Gospel by talking to eyewitnesses and investigating their words and the events surrounding them thoroughly.

In Second Peter 1:16 the apostle Peter says, "We did not follow cleverly invented stories when we told you about the power and coming of our Lord Jesus Christ, but we were witnesses of his majesty." John states emphatically in First John 1:3, "We proclaim to you what we have seen and heard." In John 19:35, John declared himself again to be an eyewitness telling the truth so his readers would believe.

In Acts 2:22 Peter reminds his listeners, the masses of people gathered in Jerusalem for the feast holidays, that they were eyewitnesses to the miracles and wonders performed by Jesus. Often the writers in both the Old and New Testaments gave dates, times, and other historical information to corroborate their eyewitness testimony. In the Book of Isaiah the prophet dates the time of his call in the "year that King Uzziah died." Several times early in his Gospel Luke documents the historical reality of the events. In Luke 1:5 he dates the birth of John the Baptist during the reign of Herod, king of Judea. In Luke 2 he tells his readers that Jesus was born during the time that Caesar Augustus issued a decree for a census to be enacted.

Further, in Luke 3:1 he dates the beginning of the ministry of John the Baptist and Jesus in the fifteenth year of the reign of Tiberius Caesar.

Over and over in the Old Testament the prophets declared that the message they proclaimed was directly from God. They met with resistance to their message while at the same time they were understood to be mouthpieces for God. Referring to that very concept, Peter said in 2 Peter 1:20-21 that no prophecy had its origin in the mind or will of man, but was given by God through the Holy Spirit.

Another powerful statement on the reliability of the Bible is found in 2 Timothy 3:16: "All scripture is God-breathed and is useful for teaching, rebuking, correcting and training in righteousness." Although there is some indication that some of the early New Testament writings were being regarded as Scripture, for the most part the "scripture" referred to by the New Testament writers was the Old Testament. Yet an application of that principle can certainly be made to the writings of the New Testament as well, because by the end of the first century A.D. Christians did begin to accept the writings known as the Gospels and the letters of Paul, Peter, and John as Scripture. They attached as much authority to those writings as they did to the Old Testament.

Then there are the words of Jesus himself. In Matthew 5:18 Jesus said in the Sermon on the Mount, "I tell you the truth, until heaven and earth disappear, not the smallest letter, not the least stroke of a pen, will by any means disappear from the Law until everything is accomplished." Jesus often quoted Scripture as the final authority. Over and over again Peter, James, Stephen, and Paul declared with Jesus the Scriptures to be oracles of God which cannot be set aside.[29] The Bible declares itself to be the Word of God—truthful, reliable, and trustworthy.

Conclusion

Most evangelical Christians will agree that due to the overwhelming archaeological, historical, and manuscript evidence available the Bible can indeed be trusted in its content, message, and claims. If the ancient classics can be trusted to have been written by their alleged authors and the message contained therein considered to be trustworthy, then by the same token the reliability and trustworthiness of the Bible is likewise assured.[30] In fact, the sheer weight of the evidence in favor of the Bible more than assures its readers that its message is trustworthy.

The evidence presented herein certainly does not prove the Bible to be the Word of God but it does demonstrate the Bible to be unique among the world's literature. However, the span of time covering the books of the Bible, the continuity of its message, and care of its preservation in a variety of cultures and historical situations does lead many to conclude that it has been preserved and protected by God because it is what it claims to be—the Word of God. The same criterion used to substantiate any other literature demonstrates that the Bible is trustworthy as literature that occurred in its historical setting. With that being the case then the Bible's own claims about it being the Word of God need to be seriously considered. An intelligent person will certainly give consideration to the one book that has drawn more attention than any other as he searches for the truth.

This article began with a question: "Can We Trust the Bible?" Based on the evidence presented it can be said with reasonable certainty that the Bible is a trustworthy document. When the words of the angel declare, "Do not be afraid, for I know that you are looking for Jesus, who was crucified. He is not here; he has risen, just as he said. Come and see the place where he lay,"[31] those who read these words can rest assured that the tomb is empty and Jesus is alive! Since that is true the Bible is proven trustworthy in every other area of life as well.

Gender, Reform, and Evangelical Feminism

By Mimi Haddad

Evangelicals have been called a Bible-centered people. Scripture, for evangelicals, is the primary guide for faith and practice, and the principal source of authority when addressing theological and social issues.[32] Moreover, evangelicals acknowledge that the Holy Spirit guides the interpretive process whereby we address the concerns of each age.[33] Our interpretation of Scripture is also shaped by an exchange of ideas with others who share our exegetical commitments. Evangelicals frequently engage in dialectic through publishing, participation in professional organizations, or at conferences and denominational meetings. Admittedly, our dialogue on social and theological issues occurs with some acrimony as we seek biblical clarity on pressing issues.

In proposing that Scripture guides our faith and practice, do evangelicals advance a "plain reading of the Scriptures"? No. Interpreting Scripture means entering into a five-thousand-year dialogue, and thus the interpretive process is assisted by attending to the wisdom of previous generations. To discern God's revelation in Scripture, evangelicals also seek to understand the historical context of the Bible.

Recently, the Bible-centricity of evangelicals is noted most acutely in our exploration of the status of women in the church and the home. Evangelicals have, for nearly three decades, debated Scripture as a primary voice of authority on this topic. It is through the gender debate, and as an egalitarian, that I will consider the way evangelicals engage Scripture in bringing reform to the church.

Reform and the Church

The church continues to undergo renewal and reform throughout its earthly journey. Evangelicals assert that authentic church reform is always Bible-centered. The egalitarian reform in the church is no exception. Here we will highlight the ways in which reform movements resemble each other, particularly as they engage the biblical text to address theological error and prejudice. Church reformers endeavor to bring greater biblical clarity in addressing sin, deceit, and oppression that seek shelter in the teachings and authority of the church. Their challenges are often directed at long-held teachings of the church.

Reform movements are never without conflict because they address error woven into the fabric of the church. Reformers serve as prophets, and through their moral dissent they "clean house" from time to time.

God provides church reform initially through biblical debate and dialogue. Here are a few examples. Protestant reformers returned to the biblical text to argue that souls are redeemed through Calvary, rather than through indulgences sold by the church. Abolitionists opposed slavery, insisting that the law of love, as found throughout Scripture, calls us to treat others as we wished to be treated.

In both the Protestant Reformation and the Abolitionist Movement, Christians heartily debated the biblical texts. As a result, there was a flowering of scholarship and a vigorous exchange of ideas. The debate over reformist ideas becomes heated at times primarily because reformers challenge sin and institutional abuse of power.

Like reformers from previous generations, egalitarian reformers rigorously engage the biblical material related to women's authority in the home and church structure. In advancing women's equality, egalitarians challenge theological error and unbiblical social practices, and by doing so they restore justice and a gospel witness. Like other reform movements, gender equality in the church is a biblical and moral challenge to church leadership that has failed to engage consistently the biblical texts related to men and women's spiritual service. As a result, the male-only leadership model has undergone rigorous critique by scholars, leaders, and reformers.

As we consider reform movements throughout history, similarities emerge. First, reformist movements appeal to reason. There is a burgeoning of biblical scholarship, beginning first in the academy. In both the Protestant Reformation and the Abolitionist Movement, Christians considered the biblical texts anew with great vigor. The growth of scholarship usually is led by key proponents who serve as spokespersons for the reform. These individuals often become founders of their own reform organizations. They are visionary and articulate and they develop strategic networks with other like-minded leaders.

A second characteristic of reform movements is the way in which the watershed of scholarship captures the attention of the global church. Christians from different traditions and from around the globe discuss, debate, and eventually reach consensus on an issue. This agreement or consensus is often hard won. In the case of the Protestant Reformation, many lost their lives. In releasing the slaves, the U.S. fought a bloody Civil War while Great Britain emptied the national treasury.

Reformist ideas are hard to ignore, and though God-given, they disrupt the status quo.

Once the case has been made for reform, and after key reformers articulate their arguments, others find ways of making these biblical ideas accessible through the arts, music, literature, cartoons, etc. Why art? Art enables the average person to feel the injustice that the reform addresses. The Protestant reformers, for example, harnessed the printing press and music (often beer drinking songs, e.g. "A Mighty Fortress"), which historians tell us rapidly generated a broad base for their ideas. The Abolitionists engaged slave narrative, music (African spirituals), and literary works to impart the pathos of their biblical ideals. For example, *Uncle Tom's Cabin, Huckleberry Finn,* and the *Narratives of Sojourner Truth* were used to popularize the Abolitionist ideals. These stories and the African American spirituals helped people feel the injustice of slavery. The popularization of reformist ideas is a third quality of reform movements.

As reformers raise the consciousness of the church, there is a backpedaling of the position under critique. For example, during the Abolitionist Movement, the proslavery camp insisted that it was the abuses of slavery that needed addressing, not the institution itself. Slavery, they argued, was necessary because without it, slaves would never have an opportunity to learn the gospel message. Yet, rather than overturning slavery as an institution, they called upon slave owners to be kind and gentle to their slaves. Similarly, in the gender debate, those insisting upon male leadership are vocal in their opposition to the abuses of patriarchy. For example, a 2003 article in *Christianity Today* entitled "Headship with a Heart," called upon husbands to remain in authority, but to do so with empathy.

Finally, once reformist ideas have been discussed and roundly debated among academics, and once the average person has been prompted to feel the injustice of the issue, real change ensues. It is as if the Holy Spirit drags the church kicking and screaming into the Bible anew. What was once the perspective of a few individuals eventually leads to global church reform, through a rigorous engagement with the Bible, and through venues that are both academic and popular. Let us now turn to an evangelical approach to biblical reform and gender.

Radically Traditional: Gender and Bible-Centered Reform

Evangelical egalitarians are radically traditional. They are radical because their support for women's equality is relatively new. Egalitarians are also traditional in suggesting that their position arises from the biblical text, so that Scripture (rather than church tradition) informs their faith and practice.

Therefore, as we reflect upon the historical context of Scripture, as the Holy Spirit guides our reading, and as we listen to those who share our interpretive methods, we also deliberately reconsider longstanding assumptions regarding women's authority within the church and home. This has resulted in a growing number of evangelicals who support an egalitarian view of ministry and marriage. Like the abolitionists who had a biblical basis to oppose slavery, egalitarians find their support for mutual service and submission of men and women in the biblical text. Egalitarians assert that the whole of Scripture teaches that men and women *equally*:

- Bear the image of God
- Share in the divine mandate
- Are responsible for sinning against God and one another
- Are redeemed by Christ's death on Calvary
- Are gifted by the Spirit
- Are held responsible for using their God-given gifts in service to Christ

An egalitarian reading of Scripture suggests that what is true of one member united to Christ is true of all members united to Christ. Union with Christ therefore imparts an equality of being and service. This led to practices in the early church that were in conflict with cultural expectations. For example, slaves comprised nearly two-thirds of the population of the Roman world in the first century. The status into which one was born was relatively fixed. It was a world deeply divided by ethnicity, and a culture in which women had little social cachet. Into such a world Paul suggested that our status is defined not by our gender, but by our identity in Christ. Union with Christ completely redefines, and ultimately realigns our status in relationship to God and to one another. While Paul did not overturn slavery or release women from cultural bondage during his lifetime, he did plant the seeds of emancipation, both in his writings and in his dealings with the women with whom he worked.

As we reconsider the biblical texts, we discover the message of mutuality between men and women flashing from the pages of the Bible. Consider, for instance, the birthday of the church—Pentecost. Parthians, Medes and Elamites, Arabs, slaves, and women were among those who received the Holy

Spirit's empowering for ministry. The gifts of God's Spirit were given without regard to ethnicity, class, or gender. This diverse group of women and men preached and prophesied as the Spirit enabled them.

After his miraculous conversion Paul became one of the greatest preachers and evangelists in the Bible. He set aside Jewish male privilege to work beside slaves, Gentiles, and women. Apart from the empty tomb, the conversion of Saul of Tarsus and the life he lived as the apostle to the Gentiles are among the most astonishing facts in all of history. Why?

Saul the Pharisee had excelled in his observation of Jewish law, which held a very restrictive view of women. Women could not learn the Torah; they were silenced and excluded from priestly roles. But Paul also realized that, like the women, Parthians, Medes, and Elamites, he was grafted into Christ and was part of the new covenant that extended power and spiritual gifts to diverse members of Christ's body, the church.

Paul sets forth the foundations of the new covenant throughout his epistles, particularly in Romans 6, where he says that the basis for our new life in Christ comes through a baptism into Christ's death and resurrection. The fruits of union with Christ established a harmony between all people, and a mutuality between men and women, which Paul summarized by Galatians 3:28, a passage F. F. Bruce believed to be the eye of the New Testament. Therefore all of Paul's work must be considered through Galatians 3:28. While we live in a culture where sin creates barriers according to ethnicity, gender, and class, in Christ these are irrelevant and ultimately impotent in determining our worth and service. More important, Paul's own Christian service demonstrates that cultural restrictions held no authority in the body of Christ. Unless we embrace the full significance of Paul, and the centrality of Galatians 3:28, we will fail to observe the egalitarian impulse of Paul.

Consistent with his teachings in Galatians 3:28, Paul worked beside women leaders such as Priscilla, Lydia, Phoebe, Junia, Lois, Euodia and Syntyche and the elect woman. Sadly, as Christianity became established after the time of Constantine, women's leadership was systematically suppressed.

Consider Lydia (Acts 16:13–15, 40) who established the first church in Philippi—the first church in Europe. In Acts we are told that Paul encountered a group of women praying. Here Paul meets Lydia, a wealthy merchant of purple and a woman of faith. "The Lord opened her heart. . . . She and the members of her household were baptized." Her home became a house church, and the Scriptures suggest she was its leader. In Paul's letter to the Philippians we find the great affirmation and love he had for this church. We are told that the church in Philippi was the only church that regularly contributed to Paul's support, and the only church from which Paul accepted support. Paul's letter to the Philippians was one of his most affectionate and personal letters.

The church at Philippi grew out of three conversions:

1. A businesswoman (Acts 16:13–15) Lydia, probably a wealthy Jewish woman.
2. A slave girl (Acts 16:16–18), a young Macedonian slave afflicted with an evil spirit.
3. A jailor (Acts 16:19–34), a Roman man, probably middle class.

In the fourth chapter of Philippians, Paul mentions two women, Euodia and Syntyche, who struggled beside Paul in the work of the gospel. Paul affirms these women as co-laborers in building the church. Rather than silencing women, we note that in the first church in Europe, Paul affirms and extols the gospel-ministry of women.

Lydia was not the only woman leader of a house church. Nor was she the only woman who co-labored with Paul in the gospel. There was the "elect lady," mentioned in Second John 1:1, 11, and Priscilla and Aquila. Priscilla and Aquila represent a profound example of Galatians 3:28, for Priscilla was likely Roman and free, while Aquila was Jewish and a freed slave. We learn from Luke that Priscilla is married to a Jew named Aquila, and is perhaps herself a Roman Gentile (Acts 18:2). We assume Aquila is a freed slave because his name means eagle's feather. Slaves were often given silly or insignificant names. When the Jews were banished from Rome by decree of Claudius, Priscilla and Aquila left Italy, reaching Corinth before Paul, in A.D. 51. Paul visited Priscilla and Aquila because they were tentmakers, a trade he knew well. They invited Paul to live with them, and because Paul does not mention leading them to faith, we presume they were Christians at the time of Paul's visit, or became so before all three relocated to Ephesus eighteen months later.

While in Ephesus, Priscilla and Aquila gained prominence not only through the church they established in their home (1 Cor. 16:19), but also because they risked their lives for Paul (perhaps during the riots mentioned in Acts19:23–41), a deed for which the Gentile churches gave thanks (Rom. 16:4).

Scripture recognizes Priscilla and Aquila as skilled teachers for having instructed Apollos—an eloquent teacher who was himself well versed in the Scripture—though he lacked some theological insights that Priscilla and Aquila provided. Apollos received Priscilla's instruction without reservation. Far from condemning her for having taught a man, both Luke and Paul praise Priscilla.

Priscilla's authority in the early church is highlighted by Paul who calls her his "co-worker" (Rom. 16:3), a term he uses to identify leaders such as Mark, Timothy, Titus, Philemon, Apollos, and Luke. Moreover, her name is mentioned ahead of her husband in four of the six references to the couple, suggesting she was the more distinguished of the two. Both Luke and Paul honor her in this way. Some scholars suggest that Priscilla may have been the author of the Book of Hebrews.

Consider also Phoebe, mentioned in Romans 16:1. Paul calls her a deacon in the church in Cenchrea. Commentators suggest she was responsible for carrying Paul's letters between Rome and Greece, a hazardous stretch across rough waters and a hundred miles of rocky terrain. Phoebe had to be strong and Paul had to trust her. The word deacon was used of Apollos, Timothy, and Phoebe. It would have been difficult to be a deacon if silence were a requirement.

In the case of Phoebe, Paul also refers to her as *prostates.* This literally means "one who is in authority or one who presides".This is the only place in the New Testament where this noun appears. Paul uses the verb form of *prostates* in 1 Thessalonians 5:12, where it means exercising leadership.[34]

In Romans 16, Paul provides an astonishing list of women who served as co-workers, deacons, and even an apostle. Paul identifies the woman Junia as an apostle. Moreover, Paul offers support of women in ministry in the leadership of Chloe, Nympha and the "elect lady."

Then there is the motherlode of all passages, Paul's teachings on the spiritual gifts. If Paul intended women to be silent or subordinate, his teachings on the spiritual gifts would have been the perfect place to state this. Yet in the passages exploring the spiritual gifts, in 1 Corinthians 12:7 ff, Romans 12:6-8, and Ephesians 4:11, not once does Paul suggest or state that the spiritual gifts are given along gender lines. The spiritual gifts, used to build up and edify the church, include evangelists, prophets, pastors, teachers, and apostles. And, we can identify women who engaged these gifts as evangelists, prophets, pastors, teachers, and apostles.

Despite these many examples of Paul's support for women in ministry, we have three passages to consider in determining whether Paul requires the silence or subordination of women in the churches at all times. Or, is Paul calling for specific women, in specific churches, to be silent due to a specific problem? The three passages include: 1 Corinthians 14:34-36, 1 Timothy 2:11-15, and Ephesians 5:21 ff. Let us consider each one in turn.

1 Corinthians 14:33-36 (NRSV)

> *As in all the churches of the saints, women should be silent in the churches. For they are not permitted to speak, but should be subordinate, as the law also says. If there is anything they desire to know, let them ask their husbands at home. For it is shameful for a woman to speak in church. Or did the word of God originate with you? Or are you the only ones it has reached?*

Paul's letter to the church in Corinth reveals a troubled and struggling church. Corinth was one of the richest, most decadent cities in the ancient world. It is the location of the temple of Aphrodite—a temple that boasted of 1,000 prostitutes. Sailors, when nearing the port city of Corinth, often burst into song about the great temple in Corinth and the prostitutes who served the goddess Aphrodite.

The letter to the Corinthians was written about A.D. 55, and is an occasional letter directed to a set of difficulties. Writing from Ephesus, Paul was addressed those specific problems.

- Divided loyalties. Some claimed to belong to Paul, some to Peter, some to Apollos, and some to Christ.
- Sexual immorality within the church. Corinth was a center for sex with temple prostitutes who served the famed Aphrodite.
- Conflict over food taboos, and eating food sacrificed to idols.
- The actions of women—how they should dress when praying or prophesying. Paul seems equally concerned with men's apparel. Men, Paul claims, should pray with their heads uncovered.
- Disorderliness and confusion during worship.

Paul asks women to be silent in the church in Corinth (1 Cor.14:34). This must be viewed in light of his comments three chapters earlier, when he tells women how to dress when speaking: "But any woman who prays and prophesies with her head unveiled disgraces her head" (1 Cor.11:5). Here, Paul instructs women how to dress when praying and prophesying. They could not prophesy while being silent. Clearly, Paul's instruction to silence women appears at the end of his extensive exhortation on orderly worship. Orderly worship makes it possible for others to hear and understand the gospel (1 Cor.

14:1–36). It is probable that women were speaking in a manner that Paul considered disorderly and inappropriate (perhaps similar to the way women worshiped in the Greek cults with uncovered heads, yelling, etc.). Paul asks these women to cover their heads. Because these (married) women are proving disruptive, Paul instructs them to bring their questions to their husbands at home so that their concerns might be addressed. Paul's priority, however, is for orderly teaching. He is eager that women's questions not disrupt the learning of others. This passage works to address a specific problem in Corinth, and should not be viewed as universal in application.

The point is that Paul wishes for the teaching to occur in an orderly, non-disruptive manner, to maximize the learning of all people. Thus, the trouble was not women speaking, but that women's speaking was disruptive. After all, three chapters earlier, Paul tells women how to dress when speaking in public; in chapter 11, the women were speaking in a way that was not disruptive, as long as their heads were covered.

1 Timothy 2:11–15 (NRSV)

> *Let a woman learn in silence with full submission. I permit no woman to teach or to have authority over a man; she is to keep silent. For Adam was formed first, then Eve, and Adam was not deceived, but the woman was deceived and became a transgressor. Yet she will be saved through childbearing, provided they continue in faith and love and holiness, with modesty.*

First Timothy 2:11–15 is perhaps the most frequently quoted passage used to prohibit women from using their leadership and teaching gifts. Paul raises three significant issues which may be summarized by three questions. (1) Does Paul suggest that women shall never exercise authority or to speak in the church? (2) What is the significance of Eve in the above passage? (3) Why would Paul argue that women are saved by childbirth? We shall answer each question in turn. But first, let us consider the historical background of Paul's letter to Timothy.

Paul's personal letter to Timothy (not addressed to the church) is a tender and personal message from Paul, written to his loyal and trusted coworker. Paul's letter to Timothy seeks to help him deal with a troubled church in Ephesus, which, like Corinth, was a center of debauchery. Ephesus was the location of the temple of Artemis said to be one of the seven wonders of the ancient world. Artemis (Romans called her Diana) was a fertility goddess who had many worshipers throughout Asia, especially in Ephesus (Acts 19:24, 27–28, 34–35). According to legend, Artemis attended the birth of Alexander the Great, and she promised to protect her female worshipers in childbirth. Moreover, because Artemis was able to procreate without the assistance of a male consort, she was thus independent and even superior to men, a superiority she extended to the women who worshiped her.

Paul's letter to Timothy concerns false teaching in the church at Ephesus. In the first chapter, Paul defines the faulty teachings as myths and endless genealogies, whereby some have shipwrecked their faith (1 Tim. 1:3–7, 19–20). False teachers, perhaps some of whom were women, were clearly leading the church away from the gospel.

In the context of false teaching, we observe Paul requesting women to learn in silence or quietness. He goes on to limit women's domineering authority over men, as perhaps the worshipers of Artemis might be tempted to do. And he reminds women that their life is to be characterized by faith and submission (all Christians are called to exhibit a character of mutual submission [Eph. 5:21]), exhibited by living holy and quiet lives which included marriage and the rearing of children.

Would Timothy have understood Paul as silencing all women for all time? Hardly. Timothy was acquainted with the success Priscilla and Aquila had in instructing Apollos in Ephesus, and also in building house churches. Paul's last letter to Timothy, just before his execution in Rome, instructs Timothy to greet Priscilla and Aquila, as they had apparently returned to Ephesus to help Timothy (2 Tim. 4:19). Paul would not have instructed Timothy to receive help from Priscilla and Aquila if silence had not been required, or if leadership were the privilege of men rather than women. Paul would not ask Timothy to involve Priscilla in a teaching, mentoring, or leadership position if he believed this was not God's intention for women. Because Paul engages Priscilla's gifts of teaching and leadership, this is therefore Paul's implied commendation of women's ministry of leadership.

It is important to note that Paul prefaces his request for women's silence with a call for women to learn. Possibly the women advancing myths regarding Artemis had not been educated. Clearly, they were unschooled in the truths of Christ. To suggest that women should learn was radical! Rabbis were said to learn in silence. This would hardly be Paul's approach if his goal were to ensure their continued silence in public meetings.

Moreover, in the twelfth verse Paul employs a very rare Greek verb, *authentein,* and though translated as "authority" in many Bibles, *authentein* means "to usurp or to dominate." Some scholars say it can mean to behave in a violent way.[35] This unusual verb appears only this once in the Bible. The common word for authority is *exousia*. It is clear from Jesus' instructions to the disciples that those who exercise authority should never domineer, and so Paul forbids women to exercise abusive authority, as indicated by this unusual verb.

Another dynamic of this passage concerns Paul's reference to the deception of Eve. There appears to be a parallel between Eve who received the prohibitions of Eden from Adam (whereas Adam was given the rules of Eden directly from God)[36] and the women whose lack of education makes them vulnerable to the treachery of false teachers in Ephesus. Thus Paul asks women to learn so they will not be deceived nor exercise abusive authority over men.

Last, we should not underestimate the influence of Artemis, who was widely worshiped in Ephesus. Remember, Artemis promised to rescue women, especially in childbirth. In confronting false teaching in Ephesus, perhaps Paul is suggesting that women are not saved by Artemis, but through a life of faith, holiness, and by living godly lives as women should, which included bearing children. In 1 Timothy 5:14 (NIV) Paul says that "I counsel younger widows to marry, to have children, to manage their homes and to give the enemy no opportunity for slander. Some have in fact already turned away to follow Satan," as Eve had turned to follow Satan's deception in Eden.

Therefore, we can conclude that women were involved in false teaching, perhaps by incorporating not only the teachings of Artemis but also by exercising abusive authority, and Paul asks them to learn, to live respectable lives that do not abuse authority but reflect a life of service to Christ and their families.

Ephesians 5:21–22 (NRSV)

> *Be subject to one another out of reverence for Christ. Wives, be subject to your husbands as to the Lord. For the husband is the head (*kephale*) of the wife just as Christ is the head (*kephale*) of the church, the body of which he is the Savior. Just as the church is subject to Christ, so also wives ought to be, in everything, to their husbands.*

Many Bibles (including the TNIV) begin the paragraph with verse 21 where the verb "submit" first appears. In Greek, this passage literally reads: *Submit yourselves to one another in deference to Christ. Wives to your husbands as to the Lord.* One notices that verse 22 lacks a verb. Translators place the verb from verse 21, into verse 22, which is proper, grammatically. However, this means we should begin the paragraph where the verb appears, in verse 21. By doing so, we more clearly understand Paul's emphasis on mutual submission. Paul argues that all Christians should submit to each other. Wives, he repeats in verse 22, should submit themselves to their husbands. Does rehearsing the call for wifely submission negate his earlier request that all Christians submit to one another? No. According to Paul, Christians are to be known by their mutuality and deference. Remember the verb is submit, *not* obey. Submission is the call for voluntary deference.

The thrust of Ephesians 5:21 and following concerns unity, oneness, and mutuality, noted in the husband and wife relationship, but also between members of Christ's body, the church. In Ephesians 5:28–33 Paul refers back to the one-flesh relationship of Adam and Eve, described in Genesis 2. "In the same way, husbands should love their wives as they do their own bodies. He who loves his wife loves himself. For no one ever hates his own body, but he nourishes and tenderly cares for it, just as Christ does for the church, because we are members of his body. For this reason a man will leave his father and mother and be joined to his wife, and the two will become one flesh. This is a great mystery, and I am applying it to Christ and the church. Each of you, however, should love his wife as himself, and a wife should respect her husband."

In Genesis, God creates woman from the man's body. Likewise, Christ is the origin or source of the church. Christ died to bring others to life. In the same way, husbands are to love their wives sacrificially—as their own flesh. This underscores the idea of oneness, of intimacy. The one-flesh relationship is an image of intimate communion, of mutuality and sacrificial love that prompts us to submit to one another, the emphasis of Ephesians 5. All Christians are to be characterized by their mutual submissiveness, for that is how the church and marriage work best. It is the same intimacy and mutuality that operates within the Godhead, between members of the Trinity (1 Cor. 11:3).

All Christians are to submit themselves to one another (Eph. 5:21). Wives are to submit to their husbands, and husbands are to love their wives as they love their own bodies. The language is not a military type of authority, but the language of love and intimacy, of the one-flesh relationship. Ephesians 5:21 and following is not intended to place wives in a position subordinate to their husbands. Ephesians 5 seeks to establish Christian marriage upon the foundation of love, unity, and oneness.

In Ephesians 5 Paul states that Christ is head of the church, as the husband is head of the wife. However, given the context of Ephesians 5, with its emphasis on unity and oneness, the word "head" here is best translated "source" or "origin." That is why Paul selected the Greek word *kephale,* rather that the Greek word for boss or authority, which is *arcon. Kephale* is best translated source, beginning, or origin.

The only place where Paul talks exclusively about marriage is 1 Corinthians 7, where Paul gives the same instructions to husbands and wives regarding sex and the responsibility for maintaining the marriage. If Paul had intended that husbands rule their wives, we would expect to find some indication in this text on marriage. What we find, however, is complete mutuality.

Again, it is best to read Paul through the main stream of his thought, most clearly articulated in Galatians 3:28. The thrust of Paul's teaching is that men and women are equal heirs of God's promises, equally gifted by God, and equally called to service in building the church, according to their spiritual gifts. Paul prohibits the public ministry of specific women in Corinth and Ephesus because they were exercising abusive authority and advancing false doctrine in Ephesus, and because of their disruptive behavior in Corinth. However, Paul makes it clear that women should learn correct theology (1 Tim. 2:11), so that their behavior might be consistent with correct doctrine. Finally in Ephesians 5:21 Paul calls all Christians to submit to one another. He also asks husbands to love their wives sacrificially, just as Christ loved the church. To ask first-century husbands to love their wives, and to love them as they love their own body, was most radical indeed.[37]

In building the early church, Paul dealt with many challenges, which at times meant he limited for a season the expression of women's freedom in Christ. Yet, in the absence of these struggles, men as well as women enjoyed the freedom of mutual service in which both men and women use their God-given gifts to advance the gospel.

This brief survey suggests that the main thrust of Paul's thought supports rather than opposes women's equal service in gospel work. Here I have briefly presented the argument of egalitarians, and we see ourselves as part of the great reforming work of God within the church. Women's equal service in the church is, I believe, a Reform Movement, as the Holy Spirit returns the faithful to our biblical moorings, allowing us to embrace the full equality and service of women whose biblical status has been recovered.

Text and Context: Approaching Scripture as an African American Woman Minister and Scholar

By Mozella G. Mitchell

I was the first woman and the first African American faculty member joining the Religious Studies Department at a major university in the early 1980s, and, needless to say, I faced many challenges and hurdles that had to be met and overcome. I was accustomed to such challenges, for I had for years encountered much opposition and difficulty in finding myself in situations and contexts wherein I was the "only" or "first" of my kind to be so placed. During my graduate study in English at one of the then top ten universities in the North in the 1960s. I was always the only one of my race in our literature and philosophy classes. Having up to that point attended only all-African American grade schools, high schools, and an all-African American college in the South, I was then encountering this experience of the "only" of my race for the first time. And while I strongly appreciated of the opportunity and privilege of such circumstances, I was struck rather unpleasantly by the fact and reality that it all came with a price of uneasiness and burden. There were many hurdles to overcome.

Some years later I found myself, in the Civil Rights and Black Power era of the 1970s, the only African American woman member of a small Black caucus of seminarians at a renowned Northern seminary. There was also a women's caucus on campus struggling, as we were, with the social and religious issues facing all of us as so-called minority groups. This was a religious context, different, of course, from the secular educational setting at the university where I did my M. A. in English. Here we had the Bible, theology, and all the sainted religious traditions to either help or inhibit our handling of and struggles with the issues facing us. Added to this was and still is my involvement both as a student/scholar and my preparation for and participation in the ministry of the African American Methodist church, where I was often the "first" or "only" woman facing almost insurmountable obstacles stemming from Scripture, theology, and church traditions, as well as social mores and folkways, or just plain politics that were put in my pathway by adamant Christian believers and officials. And when I received my Ph.D. from a major university in the South—being the only minister serving the church in my particular communion with a Ph.D.—I had the dubious distinction of being a woman religious scholar and minister who it was thought could be of much help and enhancement to the work and affairs of the church but who also posed a possible threat to the church's stability.

Although being the "only" and the "first" in both gender and race in the Religious Studies Department at my university of employment mentioned earlier, while at the same time serving as pastor of a small Methodist congregation, here in the department I faced a different ball game. It was a place of teaching, scholarship, and academic achievement. Our department was and is unique in that, while certainly aware of race and gender differences, we did not let those cloud our vision for the department and the struggle for equal recognition and opportunity for advancement both as individual members and as a department. Thus, it was quite gratifying to me when one of our top professors and scholars in the department, commenting on my scholarly publication, teaching, and ministry in the community, asserted, "You are indeed both a minister and a scholar." He was expressing in his own way his pride in my achievements and my contributions to the department, the university, and the community. After years of struggle in these areas as a pastor, professor, writer, scholar, and community leader, this was the only place I heard such a compliment. And it has left an indelible impression on me.

This background leads me to my central focus in this essay: out of my own experiences and context as an African American woman serving in many roles and capacities I have been able to use the Bible both as a minister and a scholar in such a way as to allow it to inform and enrich my spiritual journey. In serving both the university and the Christian church, or one might say, serving both academia and ecclesia, I have had to meet the challenges of intellectual, objective, and theoretical study and examination of religion and Scripture among students and faculty and in scholarly research and writing, while at the same time studying, analyzing, and interpreting the Bible within a particular Christian perspective in sermonizing, teaching, and writing for and among congregants of the particular Christian faith. In short, mine has been a journey of balancing objective/theoretical study and examination and practicing a particular faith grounded in the very Scripture examined and critiqued in academic settings and contexts of which I am also an intimate participant.

In order not to become schizophrenic, I have had to adopt a broader and more or less detached stance in the academic setting and a more personal spiritual attitude and state of mind in the ecclesial context. This in itself has been an interesting career-long challenge, but the challenge does not end there at all.

There is much more to it when we look at the challenges that come with being an African American woman Christian minister preaching from a mainly androcentric and patriarchal Scripture to a Christian community (predominantly African American) among whom are many members, perhaps even a majority, who use that very Scripture (the Bible) to "prove" that God has not called women to clergy roles. We add even more to the picture and the challenge when we take into consideration the facing of an academic community that is unaccustomed, to say the least, to having women and African Americans teaching, doing research, writing, and publishing in the highly competitive upper echelon of religious studies, which has long been the arena of mainly European or Euro-American men.

Fortunately for me, the university where I have been serving in religious studies for over two decades has been somewhat of a haven, where I have been able to retreat from the harsh realities of rather unpleasant encounters and blatant attacks on me in my role as a practicing minister in the church and the Christian community and sort through, intellectually analyze, and come to terms with as well as heal emotionally from such situations. So while the academic setting was not free of challenges for me as an African American woman scholar in religious studies, it was for me more subtle in its unpleasantries, as it were. Establishing myself as a competent professor and scholar in this setting was less stressful than establishing myself as a competent and reliable minister in the African American Christian church. Although many times I found sources of healing in reading the Bible and sacred texts of other religions, as well as Christian theological writings, private prayer, and the like when I encountered rough spots in academia, the challenges of the academic setting have been by comparison much easier for me to meet and overcome in establishing myself as a colleague among my peers.

Let me explain one of the main reasons I see for this. And this has to do with the narrow perspective and interpretation of the Bible that tends to drive the Christian community with which I am associated and carry out my ministry. To be precise, that perspective and interpretation is literalist and fundamentalist. There is no openness to women's participation in all roles in the church, and it is beset by all manner of prejudices, predispositions, and presuppositions in regard to women in ministry.

I will go more into this later in talking of my use of the Bible in my scholarship and ministry. But for now, I want to say that the lack of racial, gender, ethnic, and intellectual diversity in the church in contrast to the existence of such diversity in the university setting where I serve is definitely a factor in this equation. While the university is becoming more and more diverse with African Americans, Hispanics, East Indians, Chinese, Euro-Americans, British nationals, French nationals, Latin Americans, Caribbean nationals, and numerous other racial, ethnic, and religious (Hindu, Christian, Buddhist, Jewish, Muslim, Indigenous American, African Traditional, and other varieties of religious) groups interacting and competing for attention and consideration, the churches remain fairly narrow and undiversified in their congregational make-up, as well as predominantly male in their ministerial leadership. And while the university is struggling to meet the challenges of such diversity in terms of equality and justice in representation and leadership (especially in regard to race, gender, ethnic group, and sexual orientation, and the like), the church, guided by its narrow biblical perspective and its narrow ethnic group composition, appears comfortably aloof from the social demands of modern-day living. Thus, for me as a liberal (in terms of open-mindedness) scholar and minister of the gospel, my approach to the Bible in my journey of faith—which includes teaching, preaching, writing, and research—is of crucial import.

First I want to speak of this in the context of teaching courses at the university with the great variety of students (and faculty, of course) of numerous racial, ethnic, and religious backgrounds and practicing faiths. While at a state university such as ours we cannot teach any religion as such, we teach *about* religions, all religions. From the historical, analytical, critical, literary, sociological, political, archeological, anthropological, psychological, and spiritual perspectives, among others, we teach about all religions, including examination and interpretation of sacred texts, such as the Christian Bible, the Jewish Bible, the Qur'an, the Bhagavad Gita, and the like. With such a diversity of students of various religious backgrounds and orientations in all classes, there has to be equal respect and regard for all religions and their sacred scripture, as well as unbiased presentation, examination, and analysis of all religions. In such a setting I have learned to appreciate other religions and to see and engage their truths deeply. I have learned through analytical and critical analysis and interpretation to discern the biases and prejudices of particular content and perspectives in sacred scriptures, including the Christian Bible, and I am able to engage and discuss these comparatively and freely with the students in class. Since the religious background of students in almost any religious studies class is usually overwhelmingly Christian (predominantly Catholic at that), any objective scholarly/critical examination of the Christian Bible may be met with resistance and often sharp disagreement by those students who have been instilled with the absolutist Christian perspective and literalist biblical stance throughout their religious orientation. Notwithstanding, I, as a Christian scholar (and minister, of course), must deal with Christian scripture as one of the many revelations of truth in the world and transmit this perspective to students in the class. Kwok Pui Lan of the Chinese University of Hong Kong expresses well this particular scholarly stance toward the Bible:

> Once we recognize the Bible is one system of language to designate the "sacred," we should be able to see that the whole biblical text represents one form of human construction to talk about God. Other systems of language, for example, the hieroglyphic Chinese which is so different from the Indo-European languages, might have a radically different way to present the "sacred." Moreover, once we liberate ourselves from viewing the biblical text as sacred, we can then feel free to test and reappropriate it in other contexts.[38]

Viewing the Bible within this broader and more wholistic perspective is highly revealing and enriching rather than, as some may think, destructive, as some may think. My discovery has been that when one is able to see the truths represented in competing spiritual visions represented in different religious texts comparatively, then one develops a deeper appreciation for all religions and gains greater understanding and deeper enrichment in the religious tradition of one's upbringing. If we take the Bible, for instance, as the source of revealed truth for all Christians and examine it within the perspective of the sacred texts of other religions we examine closely such as the Jewish Bible (and the Talmud, etc. of Judaism), the Vedas, Bhagavad Gita, the Upanishads, and the Qur'an, we surprisingly discover that divine revelation has not occurred only in one culture and among only one religious tradition but rather that God is revealed in many different ways everywhere.

We find that all of these religions have something to contribute to the inclusive spiritual vision of life and that none expresses the whole truth to the exclusion of all the others. We find furthermore that the Creator God is not fully revealed in any book of writings, no matter how sacred they are considered to be, but rather that to really come to know God and all sacred reality, we must seek our own personal encounters within human experience and the natural world, among many other sources. Our sacred books are starting points in the direction of exploring and discovering and encountering God wherever God may be found or decides to reveal Godself to us. As the great twentieth century mystic Howard Thurman said of his own spiritual quest in regard to his own inner and outer quest for God, "I must be at home somewhere before I can feel at home everywhere."[39]

In my own quest for truth and spiritual encounter, I learned to appreciate what Thurman was saying. For instance, he asserted that in his quest he discovered for himself that the truth is found in every religion, "And it is not truth because it is found in those religions but rather it is found in those religions because it is truth."[40] To me this is a profound way of recognizing God's choice of making known divine truth without being restricted by our own narrow exposure to the partial divine revelation to which we have been exposed and which we have a tendency to claim as absolute. To me this is rich and rewarding and in no way destroys my own appreciation for the Bible. Finally, Thurman clarifies another mystery that confronts us all in relation to religious identification. His life-long journey of spiritual quest led him to the stunning conclusion that:

"God bottoms existence; therefore, the deeper down I go, the more into Him I find myself. None of the categories of classifications—of faith, belief, etc.—have any standing in the presence of this transcendent experience, because I think that whether I'm Black, White, Presbyterian, Baptist, Buddhist, Hindu, Muslim, that in the presence of God, all these categories by which we relate to each other fade away and have no significance whatever. For in God's presence I am a part of Him being revealed to Him."[41]

I use these references from Thurman to show one of the types of influences that have informed me and led me on my own spiritual journey to the point where I can experience the Bible and its teachings and indeed all of Christian theology and tradition from an inclusive rather than an exclusive standpoint. For instance, I have no problem with seeing Jesus from the inclusive perspective from which one can relate to and find meaning in all the religions of the world. And this brings into the picture what I have come to understand from liberation theology.

In order to preach and teach in Christian ministry as an African American woman, I have had to come to terms with my role and significance as a human person in a profession wherein the Bible is used and interpreted, if not entirely constructed in its textual representation, by Western theologies and religious exegetes as condoning and upholding only male (often only white male) leaders and practitioners as legitimate and divinely sanctioned participants. In other words, along with Black theologians, Feminist theologians, Womanist theologians, and Two-Thirds World theologians, I have had to confront and dispel the negative and destructive and oppressive realities that inhibit non-white or non-European or non-Euro-American males and females in Christian ministry and biblical interpretation.

We have had to use the Bible itself to counter and destroy the misconceptions and misinterpretations that have long persisted in denigrating peoples in these categories. Cain Hope Felder refers to this as "troubling Biblical waters." In introducing his book by that title, Felder asserts that the almost exclusive European and Euro-American biblical scholarship and exegesis has thus far traveled on rather calm waters, asking questions and shaping answers "within the framework of the racial, cultural, and gender presuppositions they hold in common." And he rightly points out that "This quiet consensus has undermined the self-understanding and place in history of other racial and ethnic groups."[42] In later sections Felder adds the gender and class perspectives and makes clear his intentions of troubling "the placid waters of Eurocentric historiography, exegesis, and hermeneutics on questions of race, class, and family," taking inspirations from the African American spiritual, "Wade in the water, children, wade in the water, children, Wade in the water, God's a gonna trouble the waters."[43]

Felder's stance has been extremely helpful to and affirmative of me in developing my own perspective on biblical interpretation, as I am sure he has influenced other scholars in coming to terms with biblical interpretation within their own contexts. In fact, whether influenced by Felder or not, there has been a steadily increasing growth of biblical scholarship and interpretation devoted to contextual understanding of scripture far beyond the quiet confines of Western scholarship. To be sure, the same year as Felder's book was published, Katie G. Cannon and Elisabeth S. Fiorenza jointly edited the 1989 edition of *Semeia 47*, titled *Interpretation for Liberation*, for the Society of Biblical Literature. It contained a number of articles by highly acclaimed scholars (biblical and theological) of ethnic and feminist perspectives: "Slave Ideology and Biblical Interpretation," by Katie Cannon; "Historical/Cultural Criticism as Liberation," by Vincent L. Wimbush; "Discovering the Bible in the Non-Biblical World," by Kwok Pui Lan; "'Mother to the Motherless, Father to the Fatherless': Power, Gender, and Community in Afrocentric Biblical Tradition," by Cheryl Townsend Gilkes; "Gomer: Victim of Violence or Victim of Metaphor," by Renita Weems; "A Chamberlain's Journey and the Challenge of Interpretation for Liberation," by Clarice J. Martin; and "Can an Enslaved God Liberate? Hermeneutical Reflections on Philippians 2:6-11," by Sheila Briggs.

The titles of these essays reflect the depth of thought and analysis and interpretation attempted "different from those of Euro-American Christian biblical scholarship."[44] Since the publication of these and other works in African American and womanist and feminist biblical interpretation and theology within the same period, there has been an explosion of works in this area of biblical interpretation from the liberation standpoint. Cain Hope Felder's edited collection, *Stony the Road We Trod: African American Biblical Interpretation*,[45] includes works by some of the same scholars included in the Cannon and Fiorenza *Semeia* edition, as well as others with articles under the headings: "The Relevance of Biblical Scholarship and the Authority of the Bible," "African American Sources for

Enhancing Biblical Interpretation," "Race and Ancient Black Africa in the Bible," and "Reinterpreting Biblical Texts." The scholarly enthusiasm and the depth and breadth of research in this area is astounding, and the discoveries made are extremely revealing and encouraging to students of the Bible and preachers and teachers such as myself who have been confronted and attacked by biased believers and interpreters who have only been exposed to a narrow interpretation and application of biblical truths.

I should mention a few other highly influential works of womanist biblicists and theologians that are quite effective in bringing into significant focus the vital role of Black women in Bible and theology. These works have influenced me greatly and helped me in coming to terms with my Blackness and femaleness in the ministerial and scholarly contexts. Delores Williams's brilliant and in some ways shattering work, *Sisters in the Wilderness: The Challenges of Womanist God-Talk,*[46] brought about a profound awakening of scholars and ministers in all areas of theology and biblical interpretation (traditional, liberationist, womanist, feminist, mujeristic—Hispanic feminist, and others) to the more thorough and penetrating aspects of biblical and theological interpretation with respect to African American women. Jacqueline Grant's work, *White Women's Christ and Black Women's Jesus: Feminist Christology and Womanist Response,*[47] is a meticulous and insightful historical analysis and interpretation of the distinctions of white feminist and black womanist theological perspectives, focusing specifically on and defining the contextual variations of biblical and theological understanding and interpretations of Black women from the standpoint of their particular racial and class context. Cheryl Sanders has edited yet another work giving expression to womanist scholars of church and society who have done even further research and study on the subject. Her work is titled *Living the Intersection: Womanism and Afrocentricism in Theology*[48] and is divided into three parts: Experience, Interpretation, and Learning. One of her own contributions to the collection is titled "Black Women in Biblical Perspective: Resistance, Affirmation, and Empowerment,"[49] which offers a supportive view of Black women from the biblical perspective. In addition to her many other works, especially her pioneering one in womanist theology, *Black Womanist Ethics* (1988), Katie Cannon has published a penetrating interpretive and analytical work on understanding Black women and their roles and contributions in the society, the church, preaching, and ministry that is quite supportive of Black women's self-understanding in all areas of life. This book is titled, *Katie's Canon: Womanism and the Soul of the Black Community,*[50] and as the title suggests, the author is taking a supplemental route clarifying and interpreting Black women's ministry, scholarship, social functions, and the like that is not confined to the biblical perspective but is inclusive of her own historical and contemporary research and study from the Black womanist perspective. History, literature, experience, and society in general are a part of the context out of which Black women may view their significance and functions in the world.

Speaking of texts and contexts, prominent Old Testament scholar Renita Weems has some excellent insights into this view of biblical interpretation. And what she has to say is highly pertinent to my own perspective of biblical usage and interpretation. She points to the growing attention in recent years to the influence that readers themselves exert in interpreting texts and asserts:

> Meaning is no longer seen, as it has been in formalists circles, as the sole property of the text, and the reader is no longer viewed simply as one who is to perform certain technical operations (literary analysis, lexical studies, etc.) upon the text in order to extricate its carefully guarded, unadulterated message. Rather, meaning in contemporary discussions is viewed as emerging in the interaction between reader and text; that is, the stimulus of the text (language, metaphors, literary form, historical background, etc.) interacts or enters into exchange with the stimulus of the reader (background, education, cultural values, cosmology, biases, etc.).[51]

This text/context interactive process is very close to ways that I have come to read and interpret, and make use of the Bible and its content. And this is something I have noticed taking place with other teachers, preachers, and Bible exegetes in their own presentations wherein they were claiming sacred authority for their social contextually conditioned perspectives on particular texts. Weems further explains the subtlety of this practice by acknowledgment in this perspective of reading as a "social convention, one that is taught, reinforced, and when 'done properly,' rewarded." And this means, she says:

> What is considered the appropriate way to read or interpret literature is dependent upon what the dominant reading conventions are at any given time within a culture. Indeed, it should be added, the dominant reading conventions of any society in many instances coincide with the dominant class's interests in that society. In fact, one's sociocultural and economic context exerts enormous influence upon not only how one reads, but what one reads, why one

> reads, and what one reads for. Thus, what one gets out of a text depends in large measure upon what one reads into it.[52]

This is basically what happens in Euro-American biblical interpretation, either purposefully or subtly.

Weems has more clarification in regard to textual authority: "When we consider more specifically the matter of the Bible's status as an authoritative text, again the histories of both African Americans and women in this country show rather clearly that it is not texts per se that function authoritatively. Rather, it is reading strategies, and more precisely *particular* readings that turn out, in fact, to be authoritative."[53]

And she rightly concludes in a note that, "In other words, even if one concedes that the Bible is authoritative, one still has not said anything about how the Bible should be interpreted. For example, the Bible can be read figuratively or literally, from a christocentric or theocentric perspective, from a historical-critical or fundamentalist point of view, and still be viewed as an authoritative book."[54] What this clearly indicates, and I fully agree, is that when one is confronted with biblical prescriptions as to what is right, wrong, appropriate, or divinely sanctioned, one needs to analyze the perspective from which the person is speaking and the basis on which the person is claiming biblical authority. That's one thing that needs to be taken into account. This sort of problem with the claim of biblical authority has led me to embrace what some scholars in liberation theology have referred to as a "hermeneutic of suspicion," which I interpret as investigating any truth claim or authoritative assertion for its inherent social and cultural bias.

I am at a point where I can state in summary form my overall approach to the Bible in Christian ministry, that is, in preaching, teaching, writing for the church, and in Christian counseling. The process is complex because the Bible itself is a complex book consisting of many peoples and cultures, histories, experiences, literary genres, books, problems, issues, positions, and viewpoints. As we have often been told and truly know for ourselves, the Bible is a book of books with innumerable authors from the most ancient of times and spanning numerous cultural settings and geographical areas, and the like. So it becomes highly problematic as to how we are to approach such a book and seek in it answers to our most searching human questions of meaning and destiny, as well as ways of living a wholesome, productive life in today's world so far removed from the contexts found in these ancient writings. How are we to apply what we learn from this definitive and descriptive source?

Certainly, there are numerous methodologies for doing biblical studies, and we must choose one of the many or develop our own if we would be productive and resourceful in our biblical exploration. I must say that I am a constant and perennial student when it comes to biblical interpretation and understanding. I bring to bear on my Bible reading all that I am as a person, all that I have experienced, all that I have been exposed to in my training and education, reading of numerous books, and exposure to various religions of the world, including African traditional religions, African-derived religions of the Americas, indigenous religions of the Americas, Australian Aboriginal religions, in addition to the so-called major world religions. And I view the Bible and its message within the context of all religions and cultures to which I have been exposed and to which I am constantly being exposed through either reading of texts or interactions with practitioners of such religions. Certainly the Bible is the scripture most native to my growing up in the Black church tradition, but in my learning and spiritual journey I have grown to extend my vision far beyond a mere book and church tradition into the realm of actual spiritual encounter and interaction with spiritual realities, which is a part of my African religious background. Having developed what may be termed an inclusive spirituality, I simply must see the Bible-content within that context.

For example, I do biblical exegesis (historical-critical, lexical, literary, etc.) for any writing, teaching, or preaching task. But I do not stop there. I must trouble the text of scripture for its ancient contextual bias and for its possible meaning in a modern setting in reference to particular peoples and cultures. To whom might it be applicable and to whom might it not be applicable at all? I know that there are universal truths in the Bible just as there are sacred texts of other religions of the world. But I cannot for the life of me do as some Bible-pushers do, and that is to take Bible passages and beat people over the head with them out of context as though the words of such ancient writings spoke directly to them in their particular situations without regard for time and social, political, cultural location, and most of all, for the present-day ways in which the God of the universe wants to speak and is indeed speaking to human beings in their particular complex situations.

I am fully convinced that the Bible is an invaluable guide to lead people to direct encounter with God, with the divine reality, to what may be called salvation (liberation, peace, harmony, love, wholeness, completeness, freedom, hope, integration of self and reality, individuation, etc.). And this cannot be done sufficiently by beating people over the head with it and condemning them to hell if they don't listen to us and our interpretation and presentation of the Bible.

When I am conducting Bible study in my church, I sit in a circle with congregants and we read the Bible together, and as we do we allow individual responses to Bible passages. Each individual is allowed to respond experientially. If there are historical and cultural contextual problems within the texts we will bring them out and deal with them honestly and openly. If there are inapplicable viewpoints or contradictory issues in relation to our time, we deal with those honestly as well. If there is anything in the scriptural passages that would be divisive of the people in their freedom and equality in participation in the community and in life, such as in Romans 1:18-27, 1 Timothy 2:8-15, or Ephesians 5:21-24, we investigate thoroughly its applicability, contextual significance, authorial authority, divine source, and significance for the salvation (freedom, liberation, wholeness, etc.) of God's people, as well as its relevance for how God is speaking to God's people today. This is simply a slight recognition of the numerous trouble spots in the Bible for people today in their quest for meaning and wholeness, and my stance toward such is to advise love for the word of God that is found in the Bible, not in every passage, but throughout the whole. And most of all, my advice is to counsel all to be led and served by the love of Christ, which is exhibited in his teachings, actions, and way of living. For if we examine Christ's life as told to us through the four Gospels, we find the example to follow in regard to scripture, laws, and doctrines. He makes it clear that it is living and actualizing the God-encounter and God-reality that counts, not the following of certain prescriptions in books and scrolls. He stated that one will *know* the truth and the truth will make one *free*. And to know is to experience. Freedom is also a key word here, because, for me, it sums up the whole Bible from beginning to end. From Genesis to Revelation, the most important theme is God's pursuit of freedom for God's creation, and especially human beings.

Let me explain this by way of conclusion. In the Book of Genesis we find that all, including humans, was created to serve and glorify God in freedom, to live, flourish, enjoy life in goodness and peace. (And this is a universal theme, the finding of peace, freedom, and happiness in existence, *shalom*.) But this freedom did not continue. Disharmony, destruction, death, and vileness came into the picture, and God wiped out everything in the deluge and started over with Noah and his crew of animals and people. There is a quest that God pursues in a sort of partnership with humans, according to the patriarchal narratives, although the full story is not told because of the lack of inclusion of a wholesome and equal presentation of women. And this quest involves the search for freedom and peace of God and the creation. The most salient feature of this quest is the great liberation, the deliverance of the people of Israel from Egypt, from bondage under Moses' leadership. (This theme is here, whether every scholar and critic will agree on whether the liberation was intended for all peoples, as one recalls the criticisms and theses of Delores Williams in *Sisters in the Wilderness*, with which I resonate fully.)[55] I am merely calling attention to the peace and freedom paradigm, if I may, which I see running through the Bible. And I believe that this is the divine desire for all creation, and it is not limited to the biblical content, though it is found there, but found in all religious visions. It is expressed in the Prophets, the Psalms, and other biblical books. I am reminded of its expression in Micah 6:8,[56] as well as its full reflection in the birth, life, and ministry of Jesus Christ.[57] (It is also exhibited in other spiritual leaders and figures both in the Bible and in other religions, such as the case of the Buddha, Mohammed, the Dalai Lama, etc.). But the point is that this is for me the major theme of the Bible, and anything we encounter in this great book that contradicts this purpose and inhibits the present-day readers and interpreters, believers, etc., from pursuing and achieving its goal is not of God. This is where I stand.

The Bible Through Many Eyes: How Jews, Muslims, and Hindus Read the Bible

By James C. Browning

Christians view the Bible through eyes of faith in Christ. The Bible also is read through many other eyes, eyes focused by the world's religions. While the Christian Bible is not central to other faiths, it may be read and interpreted for a variety of reasons. Jews affirm the Old Testament as Scripture, but have concerns about the New Testament's portrayal of Jewish people. Muslims affirm that God has revealed many scriptures, but interpret the Christian Bible through the eyes of the Qur'an. Hindus see in the Bible a Jesus who is an ethical model and a guru.

This essay examines representative examples of how Jews, Muslims, and Hindus interpret the Christian Bible, with the hope of helping Christians understand how other faiths view the Bible. While the essay does not give a detailed Christian response to the issues raised, the notes provide resources that address these issues from a Christian perspective. The method is descriptive, relying on primary sources from the faiths represented. Since no religious tradition speaks with one voice, the positions described are selected examples and are not exhaustive. This discussion is intended as a basic overview, so the notes provide resources for further study.

Jews and the Bible

Jews stand in a unique relationship with Christians because of the Bible. On the one hand, they share belief in the Old Testament (Hebrew Bible) as Scripture. On the other hand, the New Testament involves the Jewish people in its story and teachings.

Christians and Jews share a scripture, the Old Testament, but they see this shared scripture through different eyes. As Jewish philosopher Michael Wyschogrod notes:

> Both Judaism and evangelical Christianity hear the Hebrew Bible as the Word of God. . . . Because the Christian canon includes the New Testament, the Christian reads the other 80 percent of his canon differently than does the Jew. For the Christian, the content of the New Testament sheds a totally new light on the content of the Old Testament, and he therefore reads the Old Testament from the vantage point of the New. The events of the Old Testament are taken to foreshadow those of the New; moreover, the significance of the Old Testament events would remain shrouded without the vantage point of faith in Jesus as Christ and God. Jews, of course, have traditionally resisted such a reading of the Jewish canon as a retroactive revision of the true meaning of the text, while Christians have accused Jews of misunderstanding (willfully or otherwise) their own Scriptures.[58]

Jewish commentators differ from Christians in interpretation of many key Old Testament passages, such as Genesis 3, Jeremiah 31, and Isaiah's Suffering Servant Psalms.

Christian interpreters, following Augustine and Calvin, see in Genesis 3 a fall of humankind. While Jewish writers note the sin of Adam and its consequences, they do not see any basic change in human nature in this passage. Humans possess both a good and a bad inclination (*yetzer ha-tov* and *yetzer ha-ra*) and are responsible for their own actions before God. One Jewish writer explains: "'The Fall' and 'original sin' are difficult concepts for Jews. Even though Jewish tradition speaks of Adam's sin and punishment, the idea that we are still somehow involved in this very ancient sin and punishment offends basic Jewish ideas of justice."[59] From a Jewish perspective, the story of Adam and Eve in Genesis 3 illuminates the difficult choices that face all people, but does not teach a fundamental Fall.

Christians, following Hebrews 8, interpret the promise of a new covenant in Jeremiah 31:31–34 as being fulfilled in Jesus. Jewish commentators see Jeremiah's call for a new covenant as a renewed covenant. Rabbi Leon Kleniki writes: "The call for a new covenant is the prophetic advice to renew the living experience with God, to implement it under new horizons." He sees three aspects to this renewed covenant. First, it is a new understanding of the covenant produced by the Babylonian Exile. Second, it is the discovery of new meanings of the covenant by the rabbis in their commentaries on the biblical texts that were incorporated into the Talmud. Third, it is "a living reality in the life of the people, a spiritual obligation honoring the binding relationship with God."[60]

Christians, following the New Testament writers, interpret the Suffering Servant psalms in Isaiah 42:1–9, 49:16, 50:4–9 , and 52:13—53:12 as fulfilled by Jesus. In particular, Isaiah 53 has been crucial since the first century in shaping the Christian understanding of Jesus' death (see Acts 8:26–40). In general, Jewish interpreters understand the Suffering Servant to be Israel or a righteous remnant of Israel (Isa. 49:3). Others believe that the Suffering Servant is the prophet Isaiah. Finally, some maintain the figure of the Suffering Servant is an individual who stands for the whole community.[61] Jews do not identify the Suffering Servant with the Messiah, since they understand that suffering is not a part of the vocation of Messiah. The Messiah will be a victorious figure who liberates people and establishes an era of peace. Jews do not believe Jesus is the Messiah because he did not perform the mission of Messiah as Jews understand it. Jesus did not restore Jerusalem, did not establish a renewed Jewish nation, and did not inaugurate the Messianic age.[62]

While the Old Testament is shared by Jews and Christians, the New Testament sharply separates them. "Since Judaism does not hear the New Testament as the Word of God, a deep division between the two faiths becomes apparent," notes Wyschogrod.[63] While Jews do not accept the New Testament as Scripture, they are still concerned with the content of the New Testament. Many of the texts in the New Testament were written by Jewish Christians. The New Testament quotes extensively from the Old Testament, uses imagery from the Old Testament, and continues the Old Testament narrative. Thus Jews find themselves a part of the story of the New Testament, even though it is not their scripture.

Rabbi Yechiel Eckstein outlines the basic Jewish view of the New Testament in his book *What Christians Should Know About Jews and Judaism.*[64] From a Jewish perspective, the New Testament is not scripture and was written by people biased against Judaism. Jesus was largely in agreement with the Pharisees and is not the Messiah. He is, however, "a great moral teacher who was kind, loving, and compassionate toward others."[65] Paul reinterpreted Jesus and the Law, thus leading to a break between Judaism and Christianity. Finally, Jews are concerned with Christian interpretations of the New Testament that Jews find anti-Jewish.

First, Jews view the New Testament as a secondary source written by Christians, rather than as a scripture that continues the story of the Hebrew Bible. Eckstein writes:

> From a Jewish perspective, the New Testament is neither inspired nor Holy Writ, but rather, an indirect source written by people with a definite bias against the established Jewish community at a time when Jewish-Christian relations were shrouded in polemic. Thus Jews would tend to regard the various gospel proof-texts of Jesus' messiahship as having been written *ex post facto*, to concur with prophetic messianic predictions. In their eyes, early Christians read into the Hebrew Bible their *a priori* viewpoints and reinterpreted events in that light. Similarly, they would tend to submit that when the prophesied messianic peace never materialized even after Jesus' coming, the early church conjured up the notion of a second coming.[66]

Rather than fulfilling the Old Testament story, the New Testament departs from the story of the Hebrew Bible. As the Christian church became increasingly Gentile, the earlier connection with Judaism became severed.

Second, Jesus was fundamentally in agreement with the Pharisees, says Eckstein. Most of the disagreements between them were on secondary matters that were still under discussion in the Jewish community, such as Sabbath regulations. Jews object to the Gospels' portrayal of the Pharisees as self-righteous and hypocritical. They point out neglected passages that cast the Pharisees in a more positive light and show their harmony with Jesus, such as Luke 7:36 and 11:37 and John 7:50.[67] Jewish concern with the portrait of the Pharisees in the

New Testament stems from history: after the destruction of the Temple in 70 C.E., "Pharisaic Judaism became normative Judaism. . . . All Jewish life today, therefore, stems from the Pharisaic tradition and derives its central religious characteristics from it."[68]

Third, Paul and later Gentile Christians reinterpreted Jesus, leading to a decisive break between Jews and Christians. Jesus never broke with the Jewish religion and never desired to form another religion, according to Eckstein. Matthew 5:17-18 demonstrates that Jesus never abrogated the Law as Paul later did.[69] Isodore Epstein describes the earliest Christians as faithful Jews who differed only in their belief in Jesus as Jewish Messiah. The split came later, when "the Christian church under the influence of Paul was altering its conception of Jesus in a way that meant he was no longer thought of as merely human and implied that he was in fact a second God—a belief that was a denial of the unity of God as Jews understood the term."[70]

Finally, Jews are sensitive to New Testament teachings that, in their eyes, cast Jews as evil and that denigrate Judaism. A particularly sensitive issue is the role of Jews in the crucifixion of Jesus. Eckstein maintains that Jesus was a martyred Jew who died like other Messianic claimants such as Bar Kochba (135 C.E.). The Romans executed Jesus as a political act, but the Gospel writers shifted the blame to the Jews. This reflects both later tensions between Jews and Christians, as well as a practical need to avoid Roman persecution.[71] Jewish commentators also denounce the New Testament portrayal of the trial of Jesus before the Jewish court, the Sanhedrin. Since the proceedings described in the New Testament are in gross violation of correct procedure, and since the Sanhedrin could not hear capital cases at any rate, Jewish writers believe that the New Testament accounts are inaccurate.[72] One writer declares: "The entire trial business is legendary and tendentious."[73]

Jewish interpretations of the New Testament are framed by the larger issue of Jewish-Christian relationships. Centuries of oppression and persecution shape the concerns illuminated above. Christians can be sensitive to such concerns and engage in sympathetic dialogue with Jews, while at the same time maintain their fundamental belief in Jesus Christ and their faith in the Bible. In particular, many Christians believe that a proper interpretation of the New Testament involves appreciating its Jewish background, and that avoiding anti-Judaic interpretations is possible without sacrificing the integrity of the gospel story.[74]

Muslims and the Bible

Islam, which began with Muhammad in the seventh century C.E., has a distinctive view of the Christian Bible. The Islamic understanding of the Bible is based primarily on the Qur'an and the Hadith (stories about Muhammad's sayings and deeds), along with later teachings based on these two sources. Muslims also have long experience of contact with Christians and have developed a sophisticated apologetic.[75]

Muslims interpret the Bible through the eyes of their own faith, producing unique Muslim views. According to Muslims, Christians are a "people of the book" who posses a scripture revealed by God. Christians share in the history of prophets sent by God. The Christian scripture has been corrupted, so that the current New Testament is not the original gospel given by God to Jesus. There is an extensive "Jesus-ology" in the Qur'an, which both connects and contrasts with orthodox Christian Christology. Contemporary Muslims also read prophecies of Muhammad in the Bible. Finally, Muslims offer an alternative text for the original gospel.

Islam teaches that God has been revealed through written scriptures throughout history. "People of the book" (*dhimmi*) hold a special place in Islam because they have been given a scripture by God. This means that the Christian religion is recognized and that Christians are tolerated and given special protection under Islamic law.[76] The Qur'an states: "And do not dispute with the followers of the Book except by what is best, except those of them who act unjustly, and say: We believe in that which has been revealed to us and revealed to you, and our God and your God is One, and to Him do we submit" (Qur'an 29:46).[77]

The Qur'an teaches that God has revealed scriptures through prophets, including Jesus: "And in their footsteps We sent Jesus the son of Mary, confirming the Law that had come before him: We sent him the Gospel (*Injil*): therein was guidance and light, and confirmation of the Law that had come before him: a guidance and an admonition to those who fear Allah" (Qur'an 5:46). Other revelations to prophets include the Torah given to Moses and the Psalms given to David. All these prophets proclaimed the same message of worshiping the one God and provided the same guidance for people. The Qur'an states: "Say ye: 'We believe in Allah, and the revelation given to us, and to Abraham, Isma'il, Isaac, Jacob, and the Tribes, and that given to Moses and Jesus, and that given to (all) prophets from their Lord: We make no difference between one and another of them: And we bow to Allah (in Islam)'" (Qur'an 2:136).

The one message of the prophets was eventually corrupted in each instance prior to Muhammad, according to Muslims.

This means that the current scriptures of Jews and Christians contain an admixture of truth and error. According to one Muslim scholar: "Islam asserts that the Holy Qur'an is the only divinely revealed scripture that has been preserved in its exact form throughout history. . . . Concerning early revelations, Islam states that parts of such divinely revealed scriptures as the Torah (*Taurat*) given to Moses, the Psalms (*Zabur*) revealed to David, and the sayings of Jesus (known as *Injil*) remain, other intermixed with human additions and changes."[78]

Thus the definitive revelation for Muslims in understanding the Bible, Jesus, and Christianity is the Qur'an.

Jesus is mentioned more times in the Qur'an than any figure other than Muhammad.[79] Thus a well-developed "Jesus-ology" emerges from the Qur'an. Jesus is a prophet, born of a virgin, a miracle worker, and a servant of God. Jesus is not the Son of God, not a part of the Trinity, and was not crucified.[80]

In the Qur'an, angels announce the birth of Jesus to his mother, Mary: "Behold!" the angels said: "O Mary! Allah hath chosen thee and purified thee—chosen thee above the women of all nations" (Qur'an 3:42). When Gabriel appears to her and announces the gift of a holy son, Mary is puzzled, since she is a virgin: "How shall I have a son, seeing that no man has touched me, and I am not unchaste?" (Qur'an 19:20). The angel responds that God has said: "'that is easy for Me: and (We wish) to appoint him as a Sign unto men and a Mercy from Us': It is a matter (so) decreed" (Qur'an 19:21). When Mary gives birth to Jesus, the child speaks from the cradle and says: "I am indeed a servant of Allah. He hath given me revelation and made me a prophet" (Qur'an 19:30).

Jesus is given a variety of honorific titles in the Qur'an, including Al-Masih (Messiah), son of Mary, servant of Allah, prophet, messenger, and blessed one.[81] Jesus led a sinless, righteous life. He worked miracles by the power of God. He was saved from crucifixion, although in the Qur'an the exact nature of this deliverance is unclear. The Qur'an says: "but they killed him not, nor crucified him, but so it was made to appear to them, and those who differ therein are full of doubts, with no (certain) knowledge, but only conjecture to follow, for of a surety they killed him not: Nay, Allah raised him up unto Himself" (Qur'an 4:157-158). Various Muslim traditions expand on this statement, such as the teaching that someone was crucified in Jesus' place.[82]

Although it is not of major theological concern to Muslims, they generally believe that Jesus will return at the end of time. There is no clear statement about Jesus' return in the Qur'an. Some take the following passage to teach the return of Jesus: "And [Jesus] shall be a Sign [for the coming of] the Hour [of Judgment]: therefore have no doubt about the [Hour], but follow ye Me: this is a Straight Way" [Qur'an 43:61]. Some Hadith also refer to Jesus' return, such as this one: "God's Messenger said: By him in whose hands my soul is, [Jesus] son of Mary will descend amongst you shortly as a just ruler."[83] While the exact nature of Jesus' return is unclear in these sources, it is clear in Muslim sources that Jesus will return as a Muslim and will teach Islam.

Muslims reject Christian teaching on the Trinity. The Islamic understanding of God's absolute oneness prohibits God from having a partner and eliminates the possibility of God taking on human form. For example, the Qur'an says: "He to whom belongs the dominion of the heavens and the earth: no son has He begotten, nor has He a partner in His dominion" (Qur'an 25:2). The Qur'an specifically condemns belief in the

Trinity: "They do blaspheme who say: Allah is one of three in a Trinity: for there is no god except One Allah" (Qur'an 5:73). The emphasis in Islam is upon God, so God's prophets manifest a message, but they do not embody God.

Some Muslims have read prophecies of Muhammad in the Bible. One such passage in the Old Testament is Deuteronomy 18:18: "I will raise them up a Prophet from among their brethren, like unto thee, and will put my words in his mouth; and he shall speak unto them all that I shall command him" (KJV). Muslim commentators indicate that Muhammad is the fulfillment of this prophecy.[84] They interpret "brethren" as the Ishmaelites (Arabs). They further claim that "like unto thee" means Muhammad, since he is the prophet most like Moses. Sometimes this passage is linked with Qur'an 46:10, which says that "a witness from among the Children of Israel" testifies to the similarity of Muhammad's message with earlier scriptures.

In the New Testament, the Gospel of John's promise of the coming paraclete (understood by Christians to be the Holy Spirit) mentioned in John 14:16, 15:26, and 16:7 is seen as a prophecy of Muhammad. One Muslim scholar provides a typical commentary on this passage:

> It was Prophet Muhammad (peace be upon him) who was the Paraclete, Comforter, helper, admonisher sent by God after Jesus. He testified of Jesus, taught new things which could not be borne at Jesus' time, he spoke what he heard (revelation), he dwells with the believers (through his well-preserved teachings). Such teachings will remain forever because he was the last messenger of God.[85]

In both the Deuteronomy and John passages, Muslims read the Bible through the eyes of their own faith, seeing Muhammad where Christians do not.

Some Muslim apologists claim the Gospel of Barnabas is the original Gospel given to Jesus. In this pseudepigraphical work, Jesus is described as a prophet, denies being the Messiah, predicts the coming of Muhammad, and is raised to heaven without being crucified. The Gospel condemns the doctrine of the Trinity and is critical of Paul. On the basis of manuscript evidence, most scholars regard the Gospel of Barnabas as a medieval work, perhaps produced or edited by a Muslim writer.[86]

Just as Christians interpret the Old Testament through the eyes of the New Testament, Muslims interpret the Bible through the eyes of the Qur'an. Christians can engage in loving dialogue with Muslims while maintaining their belief in the authority and reliability of the Bible and the centrality of Jesus for their faith.[87]

Hindus and the Bible

Asian religious traditions generally have large, flexible canons of scripture. These scriptures are not read in a literalistic fashion, but are plumbed for their deeper, symbolic significance. They are sources of inspiration, objects of meditation, manuals for practice, and symbols of universal truth.[88] When Hindus consider the Bible, they use eyes trained to see many scriptures as valid and minds accustomed to seeking deeper truths. The literal message of the Bible is less important than its ethical precepts and its models of devotion. Jesus, reinterpreted as yogi (practitioner of yoga) and as guru (teacher), is particularly compelling to Hindus.

Vivekananda (d. 1902) is one Hindu interpreter of the Bible. Vivekananda was a missionary who popularized Hinduism in the West. His perspective was shaped by the Vedanta school of Hindu thought, which emphasizes non-duality, or the elimination of all distinctions in the One ultimate reality, Brahman. He reinterpreted Jesus as a guru who taught the same universal message found in Hinduism, as an appearance of God, and as a yogi who was adept in all forms of yoga.

Vivekananda expressed disdain for literal and doctrinal interpretations of the Bible, calling them "intellectual gymnastics" and "text-torturing." He saw Jesus as a practical teacher who modeled and taught a life of the spirit and thus was a "true son of the Orient." To the uneducated masses, Jesus taught simple prayers like the Lord's Prayer. To the more advanced seekers, he taught the connection of all people to God. Finally, to the most advanced, he taught oneness with God: "As the New Testament says, 'Blessed are the pure in heart, for they shall see God.' And they found at last that they and the Father are one."[89] Vivekananda summarizes:

> It is the Man who said, "I and my Father are one," whose power has descended unto millions. For thousands of years it has worked for good. And we know that the same Man, because he was a non-dualist, was merciful to others. To the masses who could not conceive of anything higher than a Personal God, he said, "Pray to your Father in heaven." To others who could grasp a higher idea, he said: "I am the vine, ye are the branches," but to his disciples to whom he revealed himself more fully, he proclaimed the highest truth, "I and my Father are one".[90]

This oneness is not the unique communion of Father and Son, but the universal truth of Oneness with ultimate reality.

The spiritually advanced discover that they and the Father are one. This notion of three stages of spiritual development allows Vivekananda to reinterpret the New Testament along Vedanta Hindu lines.

Jesus taught a life of purity and renunciation, according to Vivekananda. The story of the rich young ruler (Matt. 19:16–30; Mark 10:17–31; Luke 18:18–23) illustrates these twin themes. Jesus challenged the rich man to renounce his wealth and lead a life of simple purity. Vivekananda believed this simple story embodied a universal message: "'Give up all that thou hast; give it to the poor and follow Me.' This is the one great ideal he preaches, and this has been the ideal preached by all the great Prophets of the world: renunciation."[91]

Vivekananda also interprets Jesus through the Hindu idea of avatars, or appearances of God.[92] Jesus is another instance of God appearing in human form to help people advance spiritually. Jesus is not the unique Son of God, but one of many manifestations of God, in the same manner as Krishna. He says: "Let us, therefore, find God not only in Jesus of Nazareth, but in all the Great Ones that have preceded him, in all that came after him, and all that are yet to come. . . . They are all manifestations of the same Infinite God. They are all pure and unselfish; they struggled and gave up their lives for us."[93] All the avatars were examples of purity and renunciation, according to Vivekananda.

Vivekananda also interprets Jesus as a practitioner of yoga: "The powers and works of this meek, gentle, and self-sacrificing Divine man, who is worshipped throughout Christendom as the ideal Incarnation of God and the Savior of mankind, have proved that he was a perfect type of one who is called in India a true Yogi." While Christians maintain Jesus is unique,

Vivekananda asserts that Jesus is better understood through a Hindu lens: "Therefore if we wish to understand the character and miraculous deeds of Jesus of Nazareth, the surest way open to us is the study of the Science of Yoga and the practice of its methods." Vivekananda examines the life of Jesus in order to demonstrate that he was adept at types of Hindu yoga. He then concludes by urging Christians to understand Jesus through the teaching of Vedanta Hinduism:

> Let him study the character of Jesus through the Philosophy of Vedanta and I am sure that he will understand Him better and be a truer Christian, a more genuine disciple of the Son of Man than ever before. Let him follow the teachings of Yoga and he will some day become perfect like Christ. It is through the teachings of Vedanta that the Hindus have learned how to glorify the character of Jesus; so also it is through Vedanta that a Christian will learn to adore the great Yogis like Krishna, Buddha, Ramakrishna, and others. It is through Vedanta that a Christian will be able to see how Divinity dwells in all animate and inanimate objects, and thus comprehending the true relation of the individual soul to the Supreme Spirit.[94]

Thus Vivekananda asserts the primacy of a Vedanta Hindu interpretation of the New Testament over a historical and traditional Christian interpretation.

Vivekananda's view of Christ is still taught by the Vedanta Society. This teaching of Jesus as guru, yogi, and exemplar of universal truth is translated into art and practice. A striking example is the painting "Christ the Yogi," which portrays Jesus meditating in the half-lotus position. Commissioned by Swami Trigunatita, this portrait is popular among American Hindus.[95] Another example is the Christmas Eve service held each year at the Ramakrishna Vedanta Society of Boston. Worshipers place garlands on a statue of Jesus and Mary, read the story of Jesus' birth from the King James Bible, listen to the Sermon on the Mount, sing carols, and hear a talk on the life of Jesus.[96] Through these teachings and practices, Jesus becomes Hindu.

Mohandas K. Gandhi (d. 1948) is another Hindu interpreter of the Bible. He was interested primarily in the ethical teachings of Jesus, in particular the Sermon on the Mount. Gandhi relates reading the Bible while studying in England. He was bored with the Old Testament, but had a more positive reaction to the New Testament: "The New Testament produced a different impression, especially the Sermon on the Mount, which went straight to my heart." He was delighted with Matthew 5:38-40, in which Jesus says to turn the other cheek.[97] Gandhi said: "The gentle figure of Christ, so patient, so kind, so loving, so full of forgiveness that he taught his followers not to retaliate when abused or struck, but to turn the other cheek—it was a beautiful example, I thought, of the perfect man."[98] The Sermon on the Mount's emphases upon love of enemy and upon non-retaliation impressed Gandhi. He called Jesus "the greatest non-resister the world has ever seen."[99] Despite his respect for Jesus, Gandhi did not regard the Bible as authoritative and objected to the exclusive claims of Christianity. He also criticized Western Christianity as a "negation of Christ's Christianity."[100]

Christians may appreciate the positive understanding of Jesus' character and ethics by these two Hindu figures. At the same time, Christians will note that the reinterpretation of Jesus as guru and yogi goes beyond the New Testament portrayal of Jesus and is based on a Hindu worldview rather than the historical meaning of the text.[101]

Conclusion

Christians need not be defensive or feel threatened by the alternative interpretations of the Bible offered by Jews, Muslims, and Hindus. After listening in love, Christians are challenged to read the Bible through the eyes of faith in Christ, to interpret it faithfully and honestly, to bear witness to its truths, and to take its message seriously in their lives.

II

The Church in North America—Trends and Prospects

By Todd M. Johnson

The Changing Face of American Religion, A.D. 1900–2050

In the past two decades, data on American religion have become increasingly accessible through articles, encyclopedias, books, surveys, and, more recently, online.[102] As a result, a comprehensive view of religious adherents in the USA is emerging. The approach of this article is to present data that has been analyzed, collated, and reconciled to United Nations demographic data.[103]

The Global Context Comes First

One of the most significant observations about American religion is that it can no longer be discussed in isolation but requires an understanding of global religious realities. This is true with an increasing number of religionists emigrating from nearly every country in the world to the USA. And since Christianity is the religion of the majority of Americans, trends within global Christianity are likely to impact the American religious landscape.

Map 1. Trajectory of the center of gravity of global Christianity, AD 33–AD 2100

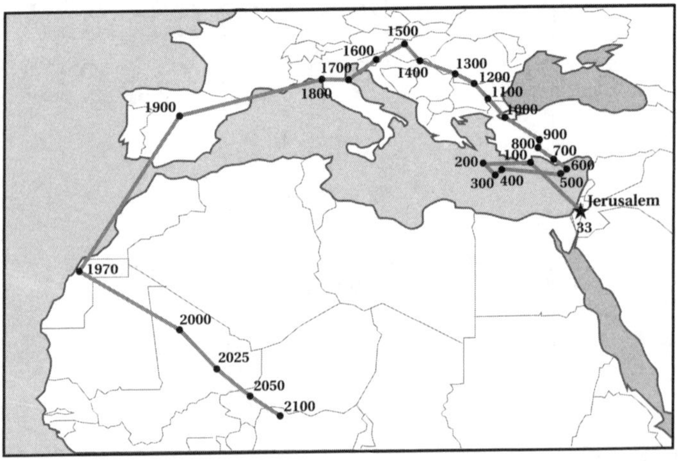

Graph 1. Christians, North and South by Percentage, AD 33–AD 2100

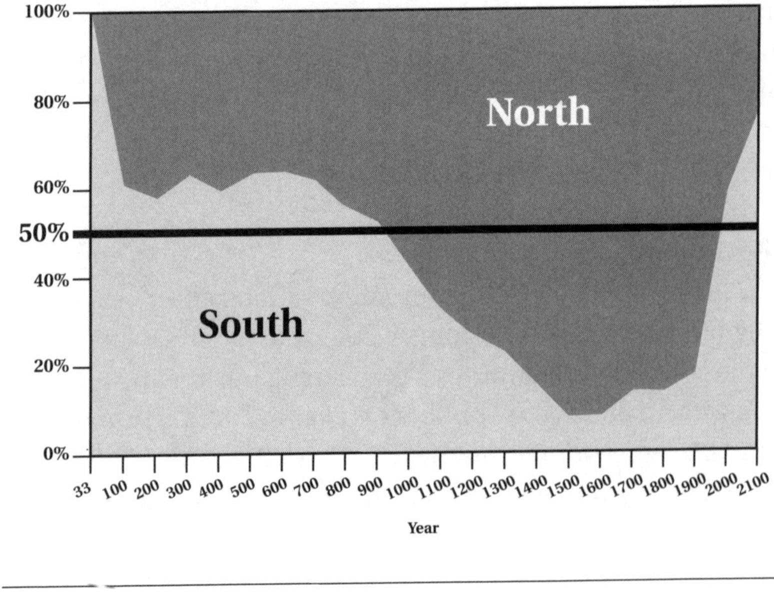

Map 1 locates the statistical center of gravity[104] of global Christianity across its entire history.[105] The statistical center was located in Asia and Africa for the first thousand years and in Europe for the next thousand years. Since 1900, there has been a profound shift to the Southern Hemisphere. Graph 1 tackles the same data in slightly different form by dividing all Christian followers into North (Europe, North America)[106] and South (Latin America, Africa, and Asia).[107] Southern Christians represented the majority of Christians for the first 1,000 years of Christian history. But with the eclipse of Christianity in Asia and Africa by 1500,[108] 92 percent of all Christians were Europeans. Since 1900, the balance of Christianity has shifted radically in the direction of the Global South. Even though Christians have represented about one-third of the world's population for the past hundred years, Graph 2 reveals the massive internal changes being wrought in global Christianity from an ethnic perspective. These changes are readily seen in Graph 3 (Top 10 Christian countries) where over this same period one can observe European countries gradually falling off of the list, replaced by African, Asian, and Latin American countries. Of the top 10 in 1900 only one (Brazil) was found in the Global South. By mid-2005, the situation had reversed, with only three Northern countries (USA, Russia, and Germany) in the top 10. By 2050, if current trends continue, only the USA represents the North. Yet it is significant to note that throughout this entire period the USA is at the top of the list! To this we now turn.

Graph 2. Global Ethnic Background of Christians, AD 1900–AD 2025

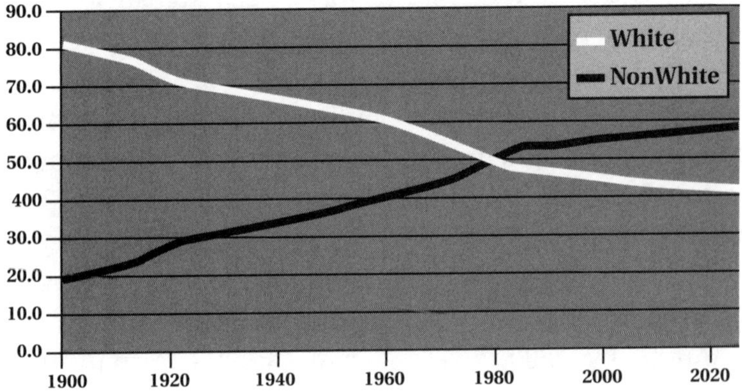

Graph 3. Countries with a Top 10 ranking of Christians, AD 1900–AD 2050

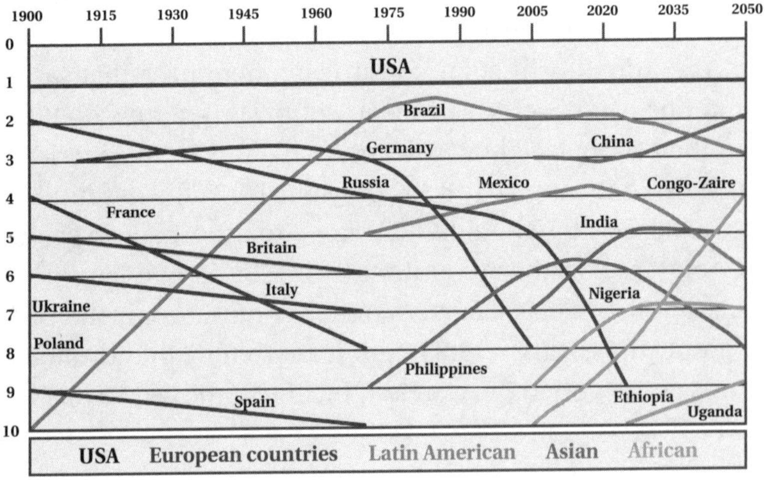

Trends in American Religion

Table 1 looks specifically at the changing religious demographics in American religion from 1900 to 2050 (projected). What is most striking about this analysis is the overwhelming Christian character of the USA. One might expect secularization and immigration to have a more significant impact on American religious demographics. Graph 4 presents estimates on the religious demographics of legal immigrants from 1989 to 2004.[109] This picture reveals one of the most significant drivers of change in American religion. While 84 percent of American identified themselves as Christians in mid-2005, only 68 percent of immigrants are identified as such. Note that percentages of Muslims, Hindus, Buddhists, and even ethnoreligionists (tribal religionists) are much higher than the current percentages found in Table 1 in mid-2005. One would expect then for the USA to become less Christian over time. Why then do we project a decline to only 80 percent by 2050? One of the answers is found when illegal immigrants are included. Recent studies indicate that there are equal numbers of illegal as legal immigrants coming into the USA every year. The vast majority of these (95 percent) are Latin American Christians. This means that the percentage of legal and illegal Christian immigrants is closer to 81.5 percent. If this continues into the future, immigration, by itself, would have little effect on the overall percentage of Christians in the USA.

Table 1. Religious adherents in the USA, AD 1900-AD 2050

Religion	Pop 1900	%	Pop 2005	%	Pop 2025	%	Pop 2050	%
Christians	73,270,200	96.4%	249,390,000	83.6%	287,291,000	82.1%	315,983,000	80.0%
Nonreligious	1,000,000	1.3%	28,829,000	9.7%	36,000,000	10.3%	44,000,000	11.1%
Jews	1,500,000	2.0%	5,729,000	1.9%	6,200,000	1.8%	6,800,000	1.7%
Muslims	10,000	0.0%	4,752,000	1.6%	6,900,000	2.0%	9,500,000	2.4%
Buddhists	30,000	0.0%	2,703,000	0.9%	5,000,000	1.4%	8,000,000	2.0%
Neoreligionists	10,000	0.0%	1,483,000	0.5%	2,000,000	0.6%	2,600,000	0.7%
Atheists	1,000	0.0%	1,479,000	0.5%	1,850,000	0.5%	2,250,000	0.6%
Ethnoreligionists	100,000	0.1%	1,294,000	0.4%	1,350,000	0.4%	1,500,000	0.4%
Hindus	1,000	0.0%	1,137,000	0.4%	1,550,000	0.4%	1,850,000	0.5%
Baha'is	2,800	0.0%	818,000	0.3%	1,150,000	0.3%	1,500,000	0.4%
Sikhs	0	0.0%	268,000	0.1%	400,000	0.1%	500,000	0.1%
Spiritists	0	0.0%	148,000	0.0%	175,000	0.0%	200,000	0.1%
Chinese universists	70,000	0.1%	86,000	0.0%	120,000	0.0%	150,000	0.0%
Shintoists	0	0.0%	60,000	0.0%	70,000	0.0%	85,000	0.0%
Zoroastrians	0	0.0%	17,000	0.0%	20,000	0.0%	20,000	0.0%
Taoists	0	0.0%	12,000	0.0%	15,000	0.0%	20,000	0.0%
Jains	0	0.0%	8,000	0.0%	12,000	0.0%	18,000	0.0%
Total population	75,995,000	100.0%	298,213,000	100.0%	350,103,000	100.0%	394,976,000	100.0%

Source: World Christian Database, www.worldchristiandatabase.org, accessed December 2005

Graph 4. Religion of Legal Immigrants to the USA, 1989-2004

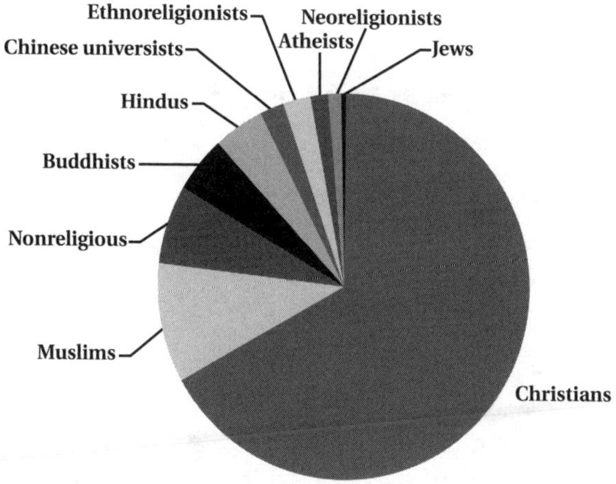

However, the second force at work is secularization. Not so long ago leading sociologists predicted that by A.D. 2000 there would hardly be any Christians left in the USA.[110] This trend has turned out to be less pronounced and far more complex than social scientists first predicted. Although there is still not a clear agreement on these trends today, one has to be extremely careful in projecting the decline of Christianity due to secularization. We cautiously project that the nonreligious will continue to grow over the next 45 years (from 9.7 percent of the population in 2005 to 11 percent by 2050). Nonetheless we are keeping an eye on some interesting countertrends to secularization in the USA, such as the rise of postdenominationalists, renewal movements within mainline churches, and experimental forms of Christianity.

Another way to try to understand the future of religion in the USA is to examine the current ethnic background of religionists (and nonreligionists). What follows are a series of pie charts derived from an ethnolinguistic analysis of the USA and its intersection with religion.[111] Taking these one at a time, one can make the following observations:

Graph 5. Ethnic Background of Atheists in the USA.

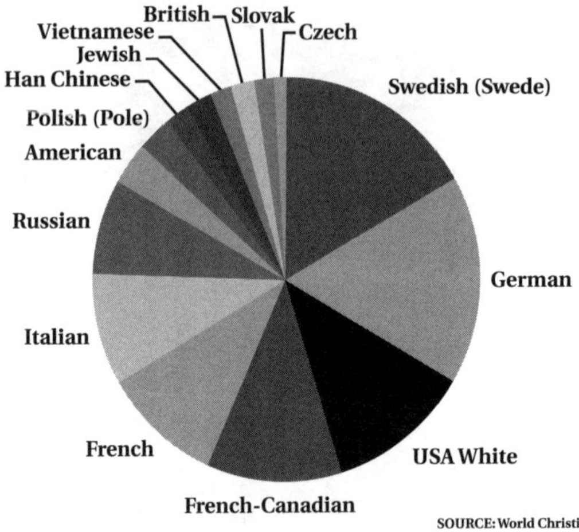

SOURCE: World Christian Database. October 2005

Graph 5 illustrates how atheists are made up primarily of European peoples (with low birth rates). In a postmodern climate it is difficult to predict the appeal of atheism to the general population. We project a slight increase of atheists to 0.6 percent of the population by 2050. One wildcard: a sudden influx of Chinese atheists could have a profound effect on the future of atheism in the USA.

Graph 6. Ethnic Background of Buddhists in the USA.

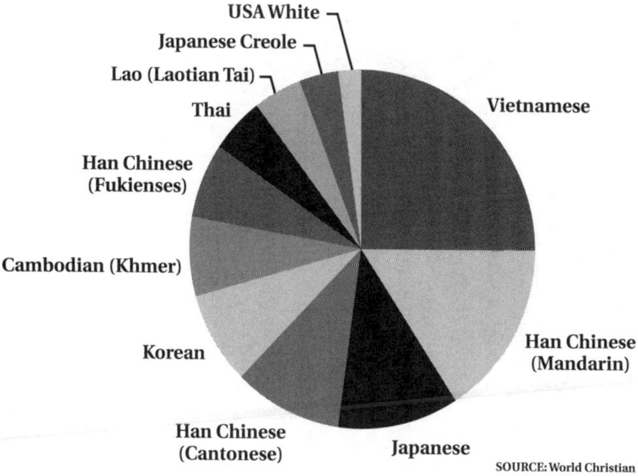

SOURCE: World Christian Database. October 2005

Graph 6 shows that Buddhists are primarily found in the Asian immigrant communities. Buddhism, like Hinduism, has a wider impact on American culture than the number of adherents might reveal. Many Americans of varying religious stripes are borrowing spiritual techniques from Buddhism.[112]

Graph 7. Ethnic Background of Christians in the USA.

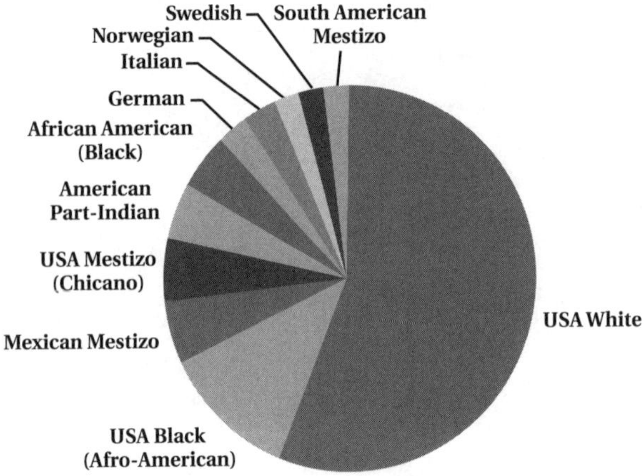

SOURCE: World Christian Database.
October 2005

Graph 7 examines the ethnic background of Christians in the USA. Christians in 1900 would have been found largely in European immigrant communities and in the amalgam of these under the rubric of USA White. This appears to be gradually changing through immigration, with Hispanics in particular taking an increasing share of American Christianity. If current patterns of illegal immigration continue over the next 45 years, by 2050 Hispanic Christians (Roman Catholic and Protestant) could represent over 25 percent of all Christians in the USA.

Graph 8. Ethnic Background of Hindus in the USA.

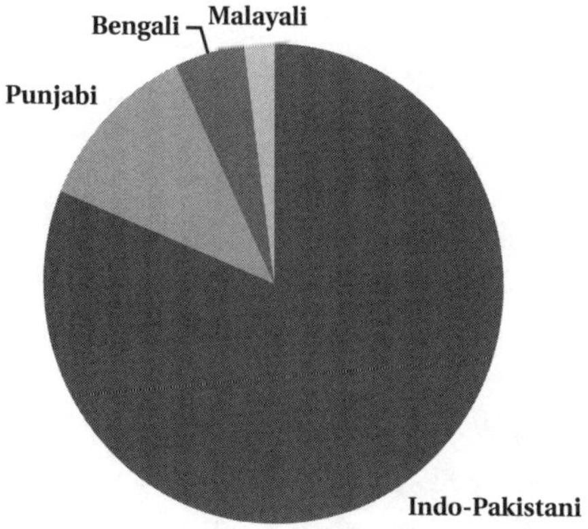

SOURCE: World Christian Database. October 2005

Graph 8 illustrates how Hindus are largely found in immigrant communities from India. A small but significant number of Americans are converting to Hinduism through intermarriage and through defection from other religions. Nonetheless, Hinduism has had a wider impact through the New Age movement and through postmodern spirituality.

Graph 9. Ethnic Background of Baha'is in the USA.

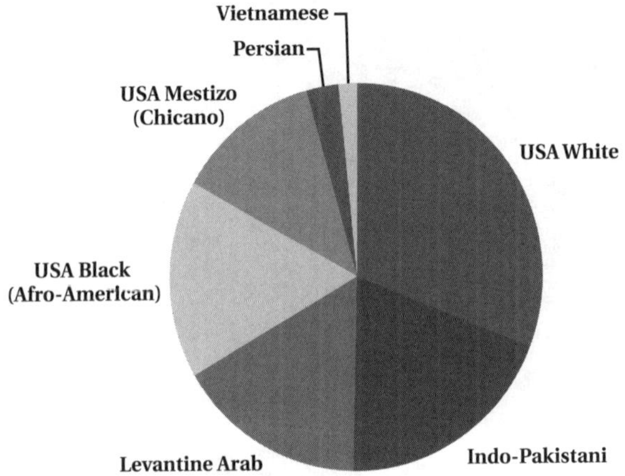

SOURCE: World Christian Database. October 2005

Graph 9 highlights the success Baha'is have had in integrating into many American ethnic communities. Baha'is are projected to nearly double in size between 2005 and 2050.

Graph 10. Ethnic Background of Muslims in the USA.

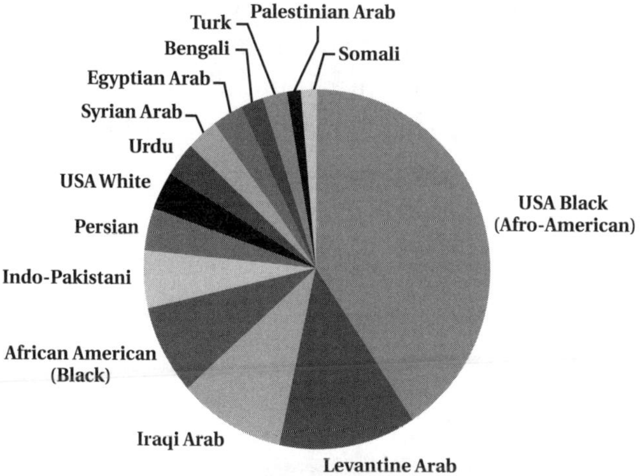

SOURCE: World Christian Database. October 2005

Graph 10 shows the three major components of Muslims in the USA. First, Muslim immigrant communities make up the largest component and have been largely Arab but are increasingly of Asian origin. The second piece is found among African Americans, primarily in the form of the Nation of Islam. The third, and smallest portion, are USA Whites who have converted to Islam, predominately through intermarriage. Though estimates for Muslims in the USA vary widely, it is likely that before 2025 Muslims will pass Jews in numerical size.

The ethnic diversity of each religious community is complemented by an increasing diversity within each of the religious traditions in the USA. For example, in 1900 there were 175 Christian denominations in the USA. By mid-2005 this had increased to 5,000. The same could be said for large numbers of new religious movements, some as small as a single family! Thus, a country that will likely be 80 percent Christian in 2050 bears almost no resemblance to one that was 96 percent Christian in 1900. How Americans respond to this diversity will largely determine whether the future of American religion is one of peace and harmony or one of confrontation and conflict.

III

A Guide to America's Christian Churches

Introduction: Making Sense of Christian Pluralism

1. Ancient Catholic and Orthodox Churches

A. Roman Catholic Church
B. Eastern Catholic Churches
C. Old Catholicism
D. World Marian Movement
E. Eastern Orthodoxy
F. Non-Chalcedonian Orthodoxy

2. The Reformation Churches of the Sixteenth Century

G. Lutheran Churches
H. Reformed Churches
I. Mennonite Churches
J. Anglicans

3. Puritanism

K. Congregational Churches
L. Presbyterian Churches
M. The Baptists
N. The Society of Friends

4. **Evangelical Pietism**
   - O. German Baptist Brethren
   - P. Methodism
   - Q. Moravians

5. **Nineteenth-Century Free Churches**
   - R. Restoration Movement
   - S. Adventism
   - T. Brethren (Christian Brethren; Plymouth Brethren)
   - U. Holiness Movement
   - V. Additional European and American Evangelical Churches

6. **Contemporary Evangelical Movements**
   - W. Independent Fundamentalist and Evangelical Churches
   - X. Pentecostalism/Charismatic Movement

7. **Parachurch Organizations**

8. **Christian Cooperative Organizations**

Introduction: Making Sense of Christian Pluralism

The Christian community of the United States of America has emerged over the last five centuries with a distinct shape and structure, largely determined by the unique moment when Europeans discovered the existence of the North American continent, and the particular condition of religious freedom under which it developed. Columbus' travels made all of Europe aware of North America during the generation immediately prior to the disruption of Western Christianity's organizational unity. Amid all the battles undertaken by European nations for control of North America, the British American colonies inadvertently became home to all the losers in Europe's religious wars. Then, increasingly, through the nineteenth century, when space for the survival of minority groups disappeared in Europe, they were able to survive and even thrive in the United States.

The relative freedom permitted to religious expression permitted in the British American colonies and later the United States became a magnet drawing religious people in general and Christian people in particular from around the world seeking a place to worship apart from situations that threatened life and limb. The result was the creation of a Christian community that largely recapitulated Christian history. All the issues that initially gave birth to the hundreds of different Christian churches resurfaced in America as each church's members and leaders gave them voice, in part as a rationale for continuing the old group in a new home. The government proved itself uninterested in punishing believers who adhered to a slightly different (or even radically heretical) theology or organized their communal life in a slightly different manner.

Once the United States was formally constituted at the end of the eighteenth century, the new nation became a religious pressure cooker into which new groups from elsewhere in the world were continually added and where new groups were continually being produced. Year after year the number of new Christian churches grew, from less than twenty at the time of the American Revolution to some three hundred by the end of the nineteenth century, and to nearly a thousand today.

In the midst of a fast-moving society so exemplified by the modern West, churches emerged as the most conservative of institutions. Each one originally appeared at one point in history when certain issues were at the forefront. Decisions made at the time of a group's founding gain a certain sanctity and are difficult to change. Commitments made in the beginning become a reason to exist, and become hard to move beyond. The conservative nature of American religions is nowhere so clearly manifest as in the continuation of churches that originated among immigrants who did not speak English, but which continue as ethnic fellowships long after the old language and old patterns of behavior have been discarded.

In this guide to America's Christian churches we look successively at the periods of history that gave birth to the larger Christian bodies in America. The early church emerged as a movement out of the eastern Mediterranean that for several centuries fought for its very existence and then for some kind of recognition by the powers that ruled the Roman Empire. That recognition came during the rule of the Emperor Constantine at the beginning of the fourth century. In the new situation, now aligned to the ruling secular forces, the church emerged around the older traditional urban centers—Jerusalem, Antioch, Alexandria, Rome, and Constantinople, whose bishops attained immense power. In the several centuries after Constantine (through a series of international councils) church leaders shaped the rapidly expanding Christian community. These decisions represented the consensus of beliefs and practices that defined the Christian faith and set some boundaries as to differences that would be allowed to coexist. One landmark in the work of the councils was the agreement upon the text of the Nicene Creed that to this day still serves as the most pervasive symbol of Christian unity.

In the eleventh century, the Latin-speaking Western church and the Greek-speaking Eastern church went their separate ways. The continuing conflicts between them, occasionally heightened by an Islamic catalyst, produced an additional set of new churches through the centuries. However, in the West, the Roman Catholic Church reigned supreme with only minimal competition for almost a millennium. The hegemony came to an end in the sixteenth century with the emergence of Protestantism. By the end of the century, Europe was divided into five religious camps—Catholic, Lutheran, Reformed, Anglican, and Anabaptist/Mennonite.

The divisions produced in the sixteenth century set the stage for proliferation that increased century by century. From the time of the Reformation, a set of issues emerged and continually reappeared to vex Christians. Among the first was the nature of Christian worship. The Catholic Church had developed an elaborate ritual, the mass, which used Latin as its major language. Reformers attacked its contents, argued for the replacement of Latin with vernacular languages, and attempted it in varying degrees. While Anglicans kept most of the traditional service, one would hardly recognize any remaining elements of the traditional mass in the simplified worship service of the Mennonites.

Over the next centuries Christians argued about the nature of the sacraments, the relation of church and state, the identification of a particular church with a particular ethnic group or nation, the organization of the church, the importance of religious experience, the nature of the authority of the Bible and creeds, and the details of Christ's promised return—to name but a few of the more prominent issues. The variant answers given to each issue—and every church had to reach a conclusion on all of the important issues—provided numerous possibilities for new churches.

In the vast majority of cases new denominations arose from dissent within an older group over a relatively small number of issues and the new group is readily identified as a child of its parent body. Periodically, dissenting leaders have attempted a radical reappraisal of the theological position of the group such as the Mennonite and Baptist dissent on sacraments, state-church relations, and church organization. In some cases, the reappraisal of basic theology by a new Christian movement—as for example in the Pentecostal movement at the beginning of the twentieth century—led to widespread controversy.

On occasion, the revision of Christian theology offered by a new group goes beyond what the Christian community as a whole deems acceptable. Thus, while the community will accept the variant opinions that, for example, divided Lutherans, Presbyterians, and Pentecostals from each other, they have been much less accepting of the Church of Jesus Christ of Latter-day Saints and the Jehovah's Witnesses, to name two of the more successful of the dissenting denominations. Thus, while Baptists and Methodists might argue about their various points of theological differences, they do so recognizing each other as members of the larger community of Christians. The same recognition is not extended to the Jehovah's Witnesses and the Mormons. Among the groups that might appear to an outsider (say a Buddhist or Hindu or an atheist) as clearly "Christian" groups but are not viewed as such by mainstream Christian groups, are the Church of Christ, Scientist; the Unity School of Christianity; and the Church of Jesus Christ Christian, Aryan Nations (and other British-Israelism groups). In addition, there are a variety of esoteric-Christian groups, churches that pour esoteric Christian interpretations into Christian symbols and liturgies, the most notable being the several Liberal Catholic Churches that attempt to interpret the Christian tradition through Theosophy.

Although all of these groups have a place in the American religious scene, and certainly groups like the Church of Jesus Christ of Latter-day Saints and the Jehovah's Witnesses have assumed a most important place in American's contemporary religious life, they fall outside the scope of this volume and have therefore not been included as objects of attention in the directory below.

The exact boundaries of church communities are continually being negotiated. The most prominent recent example of the reconsideration of the status of a denomination was the case of the Worldwide Church of God. In the 1980s, this was among the most controversial groups, but internal changes in the 1990s led to its acceptance into the National Association of Evangelicals, clear evidence of its recognition as a church within the Christian consensus. Earlier in the twentieth century, the Non-Chalcedonian Orthodox churches (such as the national Orthodox churches of Armenia, Egypt, and Ethiopia) were invited to join the World Council of Churches (and a variety of similar regional and national church councils). As these councils also included the larger Eastern Orthodox churches as members, the invitation was a clear sign that their long-standing alienation from the larger Christian community was undergoing a major reassesment.

An equally interesting situation has arisen around the Apostolic or "Jesus Only" Pentecostals churches. An early break within the Pentecostal movement occurred over the proper mode of baptism and the variant understanding of the Trinity it implied. Apostolic Pentecostals emphasized the oneness of God over against the belief in the essential trinitarian nature of God that has been a bedrock of Christian belief over the centuries. An orthodox doctrine of the Trinity has also been most frequently cited as a fundamental standard of Christian belief. That being said, Trinitarian Pentecostal churches, while withdrawing formal fellowship from Apostolic Pentecostals, have been less willing to distance themselves from the Apostolic churches in the same manner as they have from other less-than-orthodox Christian-inspired groups.

In spite of any contested status, both the Non-Chalcedonian Orthodox and the Oneness Pentecostals are included in this Directory.

American Christianity in the Twenty-first Century

Here at the beginning of the twenty-first century, there are more than a thousand different Christian denominations operating in the United States. They vary in size from some fairly small groups measured in the hundreds to the Roman

Catholic Church with an excess of sixty million members. In addition, there are thousands of independent Christian organizations, generally called parachurches, that perform some functions usually handled by denominations.

This situation would seem to present a chaotic picture, and in many ways the Christian community exists in some chaos, but it is not nearly as confusing as it might initially appear.

First, an increasing number of Christians have found their way into the more than twenty denominations that have a million or more members. Together, these twenty-plus churches include approximately half of the American population. Also, most of these larger groups are members of the two large Christian cooperative groups, which bring them into fellowship with a number of the other larger groups (whose membership is in the multiple hundreds of thousands). These larger Christian bodies represent the Christian consensus that still dominates the debates on spiritual and moral issues in the United States.

The larger Christian denominations in the United States include:

Roman Catholic Church	67,200,000
Southern Baptist Convention	16,400,000
United Methodist Church	8,200,000
The Church of God in Christ	5,400,000
National Baptist Convention, U.S.A., Inc.	5,000,000
Evangelical Lutheran Church in America	4,900,000
National Baptist Convention of America, Inc.	3,500,000
Presbyterian Church (U.S.A.)	3,200,000
Assemblies of God	2,700,000
African Methodist Episcopal Church	2,500,000

National Missionary Baptist Conv. of America	2,500,000
Progressive National Baptist Convention	2,500,000
Lutheran Church-Missouri Synod (LCMS)	2,400,000
Episcopal Church	2,300,000
Churches of Christ	1,500,000
Greek Orthodox Archdiocese of America	1,500,000
Pentecostal Assemblies of the World, Inc.	1,500,000
American Baptist Churches in the U.S.A.	1,400,000
The African Methodist Episcopal Zion Church	1,400,000
Baptist Bible Fellowship International	1,200,000
United Church of Christ	1,200,000
Christian Churches and Churches of Christ	1,000,000
The Orthodox Church in America	1,000,000

(Please note that the membership figures have been rounded off to the nearest 100,000 members.)

Besides the twenty-plus Christian groups with over a million members, there are more than fifty with more that 100,000 members, a few of which, like the Church of God (Cleveland, Tennessee), are approaching a million members.

In addition to the Christian denominations considered in this directory, there are several additional religious groups with more than a million adherents, including the Christian-inspired Church of Jesus Christ of Latter-day Saints (5,500,000 members) and the Jehovah's Witnesses (with approximately 1,000,000 members). Of the thirty or more Jewish "denominations," three groups generally referred to as the Orthodox, Conservative, and Reformed have more than a million members. The synagogues of these three groups are represented by the Union of Orthodox Jewish Congregations of America, the United Synagogue of Conservative Judaism, and the Union of

American Hebrew Congregations. Other Jewish groups of note include the Lubavitcher Hassidic community and the Sephardic community.

There are between three and five million Muslims in the United States, the lower number representing those who have made their presence known at one of the functioning mosques. The largest number of these, though figures are estimates, are Sunni (with a number of Shi'a and Sufi groups also represented). Mosques are organized congregationally, but are related to each other in a number of associations, the most prominent being the Federation of Islamic Associations in the United States and Canada and the Islamic Society of North America. The Washington-based Council on American-Islamic Relations attempts to represent the Muslim community in the public sphere and works for a more positive image of Islam in the non-Muslim community.

There are more than a million Buddhists and a million Hindus in the United States, but both communities are divided into many small groups. The majority of the Buddhist community resides on the West Coast. The largest single Buddhist group in America is Soka Gakkai International, a Japanese-based Nichiren Buddhist groups that reports a membership in excess of 350,000. The Buddhist Congress of America, based in Los Angeles, represents many of the non-Japanese Buddhist groups.

What Is a Denomination?

This guide is a directory of American Christian denominations. By denomination we mean an organized group of affiliated congregations that hold the primary religious membership/affiliation of their adherents and whose congregations are the places where the members receive their regular ongoing weekly Christian nourishment and make their regular religious expression. On a practical level, the fact that most Christian churches have their primary worship hour at the same time (on Sunday morning) makes it difficult if not impossible for an individual to be active in a second church. Thus while a person may support a variety of different Christian parachurch organizations (which as a whole avoid any regular Sunday meetings), s/he will pick one congregation of one "denomination" as the place to attend weekly worship. That same congregation will normally be the recipient of the bulk of their financial contributions to support Christianity.

In creating this directory, the compiler is quite aware that the term "denomination" is a highly contested term. There are groups included in this list that eschew the term in the extreme. For example, one church group states on its web site that it "... is not a denomination, but a fellowship of churches. Each [local congregation] is governed by its own leadership, and financed by the contributions of its members. Our connection with each other is for the purpose of fellowship, encouragement, and accountability."

However, this use of the term denomination here is an extremely limited one, which suggests that the term denomination is to be used only for groups that have a centralized hierarchy or governance. The particular "fellowship of churches" described above is a denomination by our definition—a denomination with a congregational (rather than an episcopal or presbyterian) polity.

The term denomination originally indicated that different groups had a distinctive name (either asserted by the group or given to its by others), indicating its beliefs. Today, especially among some of the smaller and newer groups, names merely designate one group of congregations from all the rest while carrying little if any information about the beliefs or practices of the group itself.

Each distinctive fellowship of congregations must make some choices about the grounds of fellowship, which may be minimal or quite extensive. The older the fellowship, the more extensive the grounds of affiliation tend to be. But minimally, even the more loosely organized groups must make decisions about who holds ownership of local church property (which may be the local church, the fellowship as a whole, or an individual leader, such as the bishop). It must make a decision about what beliefs it shall require those who hold responsible positions within it to adhere to and/or teach, and what level of deviance from those teachings will be allowed. It must, in the case of Christian churches, make a decision on how it will administer the sacraments (or ordinances), how many there will be, and what is believed to happen when they are administered. It must make a decision about how ministers are selected and what qualifications they must have. It must make a decision as to the qualifications of a non-member to join. These issues are but a few each fellowship, even the most disorganized, must rule upon.

Each fellowship of congregations is defined by the decisions it makes on those issues minimally necessary for it to exist and by any additional issues it chooses to address.

While few individuals may attempt to keep a double denominational affiliation (a most difficult activity if more than one affiliation is maintained more than in name only), in practice, each denomination becomes an exclusive realm unto itself, with its membership not affiliated with another denomination. Thus while an individual (or congregation) may relate to and support any number of missionary, advocacy, educational, or special ministries, as a whole, they do not relate to two or more denominational fellowships.[113] There are individual congregations that attempt to remain free of any denomination, and although a few have been able to survive, most will affiliate after a few years, often occasioned by the need of a new pastor. Given the many ways in which congregational fellowships now operate, there is almost always a denomination with which any given congregation may affiliate.

Included in this guide are all of the denominations in the United States with more than a few congregations. Each denomination is listed with others that share a similar heritage and affirm similar beliefs. Among American churches, most denominations fit into one of a dozen or so denominational family groupings. As may be seen from the list in chapter 6, the number of Pentecostal/charismatic denominations has grown significantly in recent decades, while a few of the older Pentecostal groups have grown in numbers.

1. Ancient Catholic and Orthodox Churches

Background

Though the United States is usually seen as a Protestant country, the largest single religious group is the Roman Catholic Church. It attained that status in 1844 when the Methodist Episcopal Church, then the largest religious group in the country, voted to divide into two regional jurisdictions over the same issues that would eventually lead to the American Civil War. Bolstered by immigration from Catholic countries (Italy, Ireland, Poland, etc.) through the rest of the century, the Catholic Church has remained the largest church while Protestant churches have continued to fragment.

The Catholic Church places the American Christian community in touch with the seminal events that reshaped the church in the years of the Emperor Constantine (r. 306–337) and his immediate successors. Following three hundred years as a marginalized and persecuted religious community, the Christian church was suddenly the privileged group. The change began with the granting of Christians religious freedom in 312 C.E. Constantine then moved to adopt Christianity as the religious unifying force in his empire. Christianity could function openly and increasingly exercise a degree of power. The change set the stage for Christian leaders to make a variety of decisions of immense consequence for the shape and structure of Christianity.

Among the first decisions was a ruling against the Donatists, a Christian group in North Africa perceived to be heretical. Constantine used state force, the beginning of a new mode of operation, to back the decision of clerics in Constantinople.

More important than the distraction of the Donatists, however, was the challenge posed by the Arians. Throughout this period Christian theologians struggled with the dilemma of how to affirm Jesus' divinity without loosing the monotheistic heritage the church had inherited from Judaism. The Arians solved the problem by backpeddling on Jesus' divinity. Unwilling to follow such an approach, the orthodox clergy met at Nicea (outside Constantinople) in 325. At that meeting, the bishops condemned Arius' views and issued a creedal statement that resolved the dilemma by affirming Jesus Christ as being of one substance with God the Father. This creed underwent some additional changes as the battle between the Arians and the Orthodox continued; the evolved version was reaffirmed in 431 at the church council in Ephesus. It subsequently was inserted into the liturgy of both the Western Catholic and Eastern Orthodox churches, and remains the most popular statement of orthodox Christian belief. It was, for example, placed in the *Book of Concord* of the Lutheran Church in Germany and acknowledged in various ways by the other Protestant and post-Protestant churches. It states:

> I believe in one God, the Father Almighty, Maker of heaven and earth, and of all things visible and invisible.
>
> And in one Lord Jesus Christ, the only Begotten Son of God, begotten of the Father before all worlds; God of God, Light of Light, very God of very God, Begotten, not made, Being of one substance with the Father; by whom all things were made; who for us men, and for our salvation, came down from heaven, And was incarnate by the Holy Ghost of the Virgin Mary, And was made man. He was crucified for us under Pontius Pilate; And suffered and was buried; and the third day he rose again According to the Scriptures; And ascended into heaven, and sitteth on the right hand of the

> Father; and he shall come again, with glory, to judge the quick and the dead; whose kingdom shall have no end.
>
> And I believe in the Holy Ghost the Lord, and Giver of Life, who proceedeth from the Father [and the Son]; who with the Father and the Son together is worshiped and glorified; who spake by the Prophets. And I believe in one holy catholic and apostolic Church; I acknowledge one baptism for the remission of sins; and I look for the resurrection of the dead; and the life of the world to come. Amen.

As the Nicene Creed was being hammered out, so too the lengthy process of deciding on the canon of the New Testament Scripture proceeded. While most of the books accepted as canonical, hence authoritative, had been decided in the second century, controversy remained concerning other books, with the Book of Revelation or Apocalypse being the last to receive widespread approval.

Also, in the post-Constantinian era, the church continued to develop the episcopal polity that had emerged in the second century, but which now took on an increasingly monarchial appearance. Bishops were acknowledged as the power in their diocese, and the bishops of the large urban dioceses as having some authority over the nearby adjoining dioceses. The bishops of the ancient cities of Jerusalem, Antioch, and Alexandria were acknowledged as Patriarchs. They would be joined by the bishop of the new city of Constantinople, the capital of the empire, and Rome, the one major urban center left in the Western church after the empire shifted to the east.

Over the centuries of the first Christian millennium a division began to manifest itself between the East and the West. First and foremost this division was one of language, with Greek predominating in the East and Latin in the West. It was also one of liturgy—with slightly different liturgies being installed in the two regions, and subsequently evolving somewhat independently of each other. A real difference arose with the existence of one key patriarchal bishopric in the West, and four competing Patriarchs in the East. In the West the church's organization became increasingly centered on Rome.

The diocese of Rome was headed by the bishop of Rome, the pope. He was assisted by the cardinals—the priests of the cardinal parishes of Rome, the deacons of the primary charitable districts, and the bishops of the nearby dioceses. As the pope became not only the leading ecclesiastical figure in the West, but the ruler of central Italy, the cardinals became government officials of the Papal States. Beginning with Leo IX (r.1049–1054), prominent church leaders from outside Rome began to be appointed to a cardinal's position. The cardinals assumed additional authority as the electors of future popes, who were usually chosen from among the members of the college of cardinals.

At the same time that the Western church was reorganizing around papal authority, competing concepts of authority between Rome and Constantinople led to increasing tension between the two most powerful figures in Christendom. Differences between the two reached a significant point in the so-called *filioque* controversy. A relatively minor point in Trinitarian theology, the word *filioque* is Latin for "and the son." In the West it began to be inserted in the Nicene Creed so that the last section of the creed read, "And I believe in the Holy Ghost, the Lord and Giver of Live, who proceedeth from the Father [and the Son]." Generally in the East, the phrase "and the Son" was rejected. In 1054, when the pope and the archbishop of Constantinople mutually excommunicated each other, the *filioque* clause was cited as a key issue.

The possibility for healing the breach between the Western Roman Church and the Eastern Orthodox Churches was open for several centuries. However, in the meantime, Islam had arisen, and in the seventh century overrun three of the ancient Greek Patriarchates (Antioch, Jerusalem, and Alexandria) and moved across North Africa. Not challenged immediately, Islamic rule became a problem in the eleventh century when Constantinople was threatened. The emperor appealed to the West for help, resulting in the first of several Crusades to reclaim the Holy Land. The first Crusade met with relative success and a Christian kingdom was established in Jerusalem that lasted for some ninety years.

Subsequent crusades had mixed results, but they proved disastrous for East-West relations. Western churchmen took advantage of relatively successful periods to proselytize among the residents of the formerly Islamic lands, but had their most notable success in converting groups of dissatisfied Orthodox believers who reoriented their life around communion with Rome. Thus emerged the first of the Eastern Catholic churches, who followed a liturgy of the Orthodox tradition but made the necessary changes to satisfy Rome. The most egregious action of the Crusaders, however, occurred in 1204 when they overran Constantinople, sacked the city, and made it the capital of a Latin empire for the next half-century.

In spite of the significant issues between the East and West, new hope for resolving the problem emerged in 1438, when under renewed pressure from the Ottoman Empire, Constantinople again appealed for help against the Turkish Muslims about to take the city. Catholic Church leaders convened a council to attempt to resolve the differences and made significant headway on everything except the *filioque* clause, the item that stalled any final resolution. Negotiations came to an end with the fall of Constantinople in 1453.

A. Roman Catholic Church

From its name, the Roman Catholic Church affirms itself as continuing the church (Greek, *ecclesia*), the body of followers of Jesus Christ sent out to bring the gospel (good news of Jesus Christ) to the world (Matt. 28:18-20). As a catholic or universal body, it claims jurisdiction throughout the world. It is Roman in that it traces its authority from Peter, the chief of the apostles, who is acknowledged as the first bishop of Rome. Membership in the church is defined as being in communion with Peter and his successors, the lineage of the bishops of Rome (the popes) to the present-day (cf. Matt. 16: 13-20).

Today the Catholic Church numbers slightly more than one billion faithful. It has established worshiping communities in more than two hundred of the world's countries, and is the majority or largest religious body in many of them. The great majority of church members adhere to a Western Latin liturgy, but the faithful also include a number who follow various Eastern liturgies and exist in semi-autonomous churches—the Eastern Catholic or Uniate churches (described separately below). Its pervasiveness, and the fact that the great majority of presently existing Christian churches that do not acknowledge Roman authority nevertheless ultimately trace their history to their split from Rome, gives the Catholic Church an additional role. It is often the Christian body over against which other churches define themselves. Important in understanding the Catholic Church is some comprehension of its teachings and beliefs, it organization, and it life of worship and devotion.

Teachings

The Roman Catholic Church, as the continuation of the apostolic church, perpetuates the apostles' assignment of preaching the message of salvation in Jesus Christ. It sees itself as the faithful and authoritative transmitter of the message of Christ. Catholic teachings are thus rooted in God's revelation in the Bible and in the tradition of the church. At the most recent official gatherings of the church's leaders, the second Vatican Council, the church's bishops affirmed, "The books of Scripture must be acknowledged as teaching firmly, faithfully, and without error that truth which God wanted put into the sacred writings for the sake of salvation." Tradition consists of truth believed handed down by the apostles and transmitted through the church beside the Scripture. Most important, tradition includes the progressive development of doctrine through the living experience of the church.

The individual believer may gain some knowledge of God through the use of reason, but ultimately, it is through the revelation of God in Israel and finally in Jesus Christ, to which one responds in faith, that the fullness of the divine mystery is appropriated. The church calls all of humanity to respond to the gospel through faith. Along with calling people to faith, the church also has the task of faithfully passing along the correct teachings that inform faith—the doctrines, formal teachings of the church, amid which appear the dogmas, those teachings which form the heart of the church's belief and to which ascent must be given by a faithful Catholic Christian.

The Catholic Church affirms belief in the One Triune God who is Father, Son, and Holy Spirit—God as three divine persons united by a common nature or essence. The doctrine of the Trinity, although not explicitly found in the Scriptures, was developed as the church reacted to a series of heresies. The nature of the relationship of the Father, Son, and Holy Spirit is stated in the Nicene and other creedal statements, though theologians have expounded it in a variety of ways through the centuries. In attempting to understand the Triune God, a distinction is drawn between the essential Trinity (God as mysteriously existing in the godhead) and the economic Trinity (God as active in the world and with humanity), though both refer to the same Triune God.

Catholic theology holds that God created the cosmos out of nothing (*creatio ex nihilo*), and in so affirming denied that God created out of some pre-existent matter or that creation was accidental. What God created is good. Of particular importance in the contemporary church is the affirmation of the role of human reason in the development of science and the effort to reconcile fundamental affirmations about creation with modern scientific discoveries and their impact on human life in technology. Periodically, the church speaks to a range of modern concerns such as evolution, ecology, abortion, and euthanasia.

The church also affirms the saving action of God toward a humanity fallen into sin. Jesus Christ, the second person of the Triune God, incarnated in a human body to facilitate humanity's salvation and creation's renewal. The incarnation is described by St. Paul as a *kenosis,* which is literally a self-emptying or condescension of God's becoming human without thereby ceasing to be God.

Basic to understanding Jesus Christ and salvation is the belief that He has two natures—divine and human—united, without change, confusion, separation, or admixture, into one person. As God he can save; as fully human, he can accept the offer of salvation for humanity. Christ is considered to be like human being in all things, except sin.

The events of Christ's life—incarnation, death, resurrection, and ascension to heaven—provide the content of our understanding of salvation (soteriology). Because of these acts, Christ stands as the sole mediator between God and humanity. He is also head of the church, which is seen as his body. Individual Christians participate in Christ's body. Christ's presence in the church is seen in the actions of the Holy Spirit, who allows Christ to become actualized in each Christian's life, both individually and communally.

Rounding out Christian theology is the affirmation of the Holy Spirit, the third person of the triune God. The Spirit is active in creation, descended upon Jesus at his baptism, and comes to the church to give life and power for its mission to spread the gospel.

The Spirit endows the church and its members with numerous gifts to aid their life in the church and in the world. The vitality of the church is based upon the Holy Spirit's indwelling.

The Church

The church, that community of believers called together and sent on mission by Christ, has traditionally been seen to have four primary characteristics: unity, holiness, catholicity, and apostolicity. The church is also seen to exist in both a visible and invisible aspect and to have both a universal and local presence. It is most visible in its institutional incarnation and its ordained ministerial leadership of bishop, priest/presbyter, and deacon. Deacons, traditionally appointed to serve the temporal needs of the local church and oversee its charitable operations, evolved into assistant priests and now as priests in training. Priests oversee local parishes and preside over their sacramental life. The bishop is a priest set aside to oversee a local area of multiple parishes and the priests within that area, called a diocese. The bishop also has a responsibility for the whole church and serves in the episcopal college headed by the pope. This episcopal college meets periodically in synods or councils.

The bishops have an essential and unique role in the church. Catholics assume, for example, that collectively they have been entrusted with continuing the teachings of the apostles. They possess the teaching authority (magisterium), which they exercise in two ways: extraordinary and ordinary. The ordinary magisterium refers to the ongoing role of transmitting the church's beliefs and practices essentially on matters of faith and morals. They exercise the extraordinary magisterium when, for example, they gather in a council and proclaim a doctrine to be a dogma, hence infallible and a matter to which the faithful must give their assent. Acting in such an extraordinary manner is relatively rare. In 1870, the bishops gathered for the First Vatican Council and there decreed that the pope, when speaking *ex cathedra*, that is as the bishop of Rome from the chair of St. Peter on matters of faith and morals, speaks infallibly in defining a belief to be universally held by the entire church. Since 1870, the pope has exercised his extraordinary magisterium only once, in 1950, in defining the doctrine of Mary's Assumption into heaven.

In contrast to the very rare definition of a new dogma, the numerous papal encyclicals, statements issued by the international church offices (the Curia), and statements of individual bishops (often taking the form of pastoral letters) are not seen as having the gift of infallibility. They are, however, seen as authoritative and deserving of respect as an exercise of the ordinary magisterium, and hence an exposition of the traditional teachings of the church.

The most visible recent event in which the Catholic Church exercised its ordinary magisterium was the Second Vatican Council. Over a three-year period (1962–1965), the bishops collectively attempted to provide the church with a modern restatement of traditional theological emphases and offered new directions for action for both clergy and laity. The council did not change traditional dogmatic perspectives but was seen as offering a new more positive relationship with the larger Christian world, other religions, and the secular realm. Its tone stood in sharp contrast to the promulgations of the two other most recent councils, Trent (1545–1563) and the First Vatican (1869–1870). In its many statements, Vatican II influenced the themes of contemporary theology, reemphasized the role of the laity, and remade its relations with other Christians and other faiths. It also spoke on a variety of secular issues relative to social, political, and economic justice, the role of the social and natural sciences, and the need of moral decision-making. The significant changes awaiting the Christian world as the many documents issued by the council were reread, absorbed, and acted upon were heralded by the replacement of the Latin liturgy with a new liturgy translated into the many languages of the worshipers.

Much of the authority of the church is based on the notion that it carries on not only the teachings of the apostolic church but its ministry. The authority of the apostles was, it is believed, passed to the church's bishops and by the bishops delegated to the priests and deacons. That authority has been passed from generation to generation by the sacrament of ordination, and there exists an unbroken chain of ordinations that tie each priest backward through the laying-on-of-hands to the apostles in general and Peter in particular. Apostolic succession is passed from one bishop to the next and each bishop is able to trace a lineage from the bishop who consecrated him in office backward to the apostles. As only bishops may ordain priests, the apostolic succession is passed through bishops, another aspect of their essential role in the life of the church. The protection of the church's apostolic succession and the evaluation of such claims of succession in other churches (Eastern orthodoxy, Old Catholicism, Anglicanism) is an important aspect of the church's magisterium.

The ministry of the church occurs primarily through local churches regionally gathered into dioceses. However, it greatly benefits from and is extended by a host of religious orders, special communities within the church whose members commit themselves to a life of ministry and service, take vows of total commitment to their mission through a life of poverty, chastity, and obedience, and enter a life in community with fellow members. Religious orders usually have overarching ministries in which they engage such as education, evangelism, missions, publishing, service to the poor, care of the ill, or a life of prayer and contemplation. Of the hundreds of ordered communities, a few have become global institutions, well known for their work (Jesuits, Dominicans, Franciscans), though most remain rather small and obscure.

Worship through a Sacramental Life

The Catholic Church is a sacramental church. Sacraments are means of mediating divine grace and as acts of worship provide a means for individuals to encounter the ultimate mysteries of God in Christ. In the sacraments, preeminently the Eucharist, participants experience the presence of God, which comes to them freely by virtue of Christ's suffering, death, and resurrection. The number of formal sacraments is seven: baptism, confirmation, Eucharist, reconciliation (penance), anointing of the sick, matrimony (marriage), and holy orders (ordination).

The act of baptism incorporates the individual into the church, and has the sacramental effect of restoring to that person the image of God that had been distorted by the fall of humanity. At the same time, all sins that have occurred since birth are forgiven. Baptism usually occurs shortly after birth, but may occur at any time in a person's life.

Confirmation is an anointing with the holy oil of chrism whereby the baptized person is sealed with the gift of the Spirit. Confirmation now usually occurs as children reach what is considered an age of reason (know good from evil) and have received and understood (at least in a rudimentary sense) the teachings of the church. Today, confirmation usually occurs just prior to a young person's admittance into the major ongoing sacrament of the church, the Eucharist. Participation in their First Communion is a high moment in the life of a young Catholic.

In the Eucharist (also known as Communion and the Lord's supper), the believer is seen as participating in the mystical body and blood of Christ, sacramentally presented in the bread and wine. The Eucharistic service is seen as a reenactment of Christ's sacrifice on the cross, during which time the bread and wine are changed substantially into the body and blood of Christ. This central event of the Eucharist is termed transubstantiation. The essence or substance of the bread and wine are believed to change during the service, though the outward characteristics of the elements (appearance, texture, taste, etc.) remain the same.

The regular reception of the Eucharist is seen as essential to the ongoing life of the Christian who is engaged in a pilgrimage toward sanctification or holiness. The individual falls into sin and needs regular forgiveness, reincorporation into communion with the faithful, and the continued experience of the presence of God assisting their efforts to live the Christian life.

Operating with the Eucharist, most often as preparation for participation, is the sacrament of reconciliation (previously called penance), a formal ritual in which a priest pronounces the forgiveness of sin. Forgiveness has two aspects. First, God forgives the sinner unconditionally out of His grace. However, it is also recognized that sin has consequences, so in receiving forgiveness the individual also agrees to take actions that manifest their repentance of past sins, usually the performance of a penitential act assigned by the priest with whom they have discussed their recent sins. The sacrament of reconciliation now exists in a spectrum of formats, both private and communal.

Anointing of the sick is a sacrament of prayer, which for many centuries was largely limited to those believed to be dying (and known as extreme unction). Today it is offered to many who are ill or suffer from the ravages of aging.

The sacramental life may be punctuated by the sacraments of marriage and/or ordination. In general these are mutually exclusive acts, as in most Catholic settings priests may not be married. In most female religious orders, the act of joining the order (which includes a vow of chastity) includes a marriage ceremony in which one is seen as becoming a bride of Christ.

The object of engaging in the sacramental life of the church is the movement toward the sanctified or holy life, the life of sainthood. Few reach sainthood in this life, but some have and have been formally recognized as saints. Such saintly individuals are seen as still alive in their heavenly existence and maintain their concern for life in the earthly church. They are a vital element in the communion of saints, the relationship that exists between all Christians, both dead and alive.

The church recognizes a saint in a formal process that begins with an initial determination that a person is a worthy candidate for formal sainthood, after which the investigation of the person's life, one element of which includes the occurrence of miracles associated with him/her. Following such investigation, the person may be beatified (after which public veneration of the person may occur), and at a later time canonized, named a saint. Saints may be venerated, but not worshiped (a distinction often lost in practice). Worship (adoration) is to be given to God alone, but it is believed that veneration leads to worship.

Among all the saints, the Blessed Virgin Mary, the human mother of Jesus, holds a special place. Mary's particular importance may be traced to the debates on the nature of Christ in the ancient church and the designation of Mary as the mother of God (*Theotokos*). The veneration of Mary has been a part of the church's life for many centuries, but has received a new emphasis and attained a new significance through the nineteenth and twentieth centuries.

From the biblical narrative, Mary attained initial attention as the virgin who conceived Jesus by the Holy Spirit, not by human procreation, and the woman who stood by him as he died on the cross. Consideration of Mary over the centuries led to the formulation of two additional ideas about Mary, the Immaculate Conception and the Assumption. The Immaculate Conception, formally promulgated in 1854, asserts that Mary, from the moment of her conception, by the grace of God and the merits of Christ's saving work, was free from original sin, and thus a fitting vessel for Christ's incarnation. The Assumption holds that at the end of her earthly life Mary did not die but rather was taken up to heaven in body and soul.

While not part of the dogmatic teachings of the church, the role of Mary in the last centuries has grown appreciably due to the many claims of her appearances to individuals. While there have been hundreds of such apparitions, a relatively small number have attained a status whereby the church authorities permit the veneration of Mary in the form of a particular appearance. Examples are the appearances that occurred at Lourdes, France, in the 1850s and at Fatima, Portugal, in 1917. Papal visits to the sites of different apparitions have added to their prestige.

In the wake of the new emphasis on the role of the Virgin Mary, a worldwide movement has emerged within the Catholic Church that promotes Marian devotion in all its aspects, has introduced new forms of devotion into the church's life, and emphasizes specific teachings and issues based upon their mention during an apparition.

The Catholic Church in the United States

Roman Catholic presence in what is now the United States is usually traced to the founding of the first parish in St. Augustine, Florida, in 1565, though there had been a Catholic presence since the arrival of the first Spanish and French explorers in the previous century. Spanish settlement had its most lasting effect in California and the southwest and the French in the Mississippi River Valley and the Great Lakes region. Most determinative for the future nation, however, was the establishment of Maryland as a haven for Catholics, who in the seventeenth century suffered a variety of problems in England. Maryland attained notoriety for its promulgation of religious toleration, over against the religious establishments in most of the American colonies.

Interestingly, the French Revolution played a significant role in the development of American Catholicism, as Catholic priests fleeing the post-revolutionary secular government founded the first Catholic seminary in America in 1791 in Baltimore. Baltimore had also become the residence of the John Carroll the first bishop (1789), who later became the first archbishop (1808) in the United States.

The church expanded swiftly through the nineteenth century, due in large part to the immigration of millions of people from predominantly Catholic countries in Europe. It faced challenges from the desire of immigrants, most of whom did not speak English as a first language, to keep their ethnic and linguistic heritage, the education of children in a predominantly Protestant land, and hostility from nativists. The church responded by creating an Americanized church and developing a system of parochial schools that took their place as an important facet of America's educational system.

While remnants of anti-Catholicism remain to the present, the absence of anti-American attitudes and actions coming from the Catholic community and the integration of Catholics into American economic, political, and social life powerfully refuted any anti-Catholic prejudices. Recognition of Catholicism's full integration into American life was signaled most forcefully by the election of John F. Kennedy as president of the United States in 1960.

Catholics began the twentieth century embroiled in a major controversy over how American they might become. The desire to adapt to democracy and life in a nation without a religious establishment and a need to respond to emerging intellectual currents ran headlong into the problems caused by the rise of modern Germany and Italy in Europe, the loss of the Papal States (the land ruled by the pope in central Italy), and some hesitancy to meet the challenges posed by the advent of the new sciences. Papal pronouncements against what was seen as a too-optimistic Americanism slowed the progress of Catholic participation in American life until World War II.

The mobilization of the country during World War II and the full Catholic participation in the war effort changed the church. Catholic leadership came out of the war with a new sense of belonging and a readiness to fully participate in public life. Already structures had been set in place to speak to a wide variety of moral and social issues, and two decades of significant post-war growth gave the church new clout in the secular world.

The role of Catholicism in America life was given another significant boost by Vatican II and the new openness shown by Pope John XXIII to the Protestant community. Protestants embraced Pope John and the new era of good feeling he brought, and Vatican II permanently changed the manner in which Catholics interacted with both their Protestant and Orthodox neighbors.

As the twenty-first century began the Catholic Church in America reported an excess of 66 million members in a country of 293 million residents; approximately 23 percent of the American public now identifying themselves as Catholic. National leadership for the church is provided by the National Conference of Catholic Bishops and the United States Catholic Conference, both organized in 1967.

Coming to the fore in the 1990s, the Catholic Church in the United States faced its most important challenge in decades when widespread charges of sexual abuse of children in Catholic parishes and parochial schools were made public. As the stories of abused children appeared in the public media, the church faced additional charges that its leadership had been aware of the problem and had systematically tried to cover it up. Under tremendous pressure, slowly the hierarchy confronted the problem, including the complicity of individual bishops in covering it up, and took action to respond to those hurt by the abuse of priests and to develop structures to prevent any further reoccurrence of the problem. [As this volume goes to press, negotiations that will put this issue behind the church continue.]

Contacts:

The international headquarters of the Roman Catholic Church is located in the Vatican, the smallest country in the world, a remnant of the former Papal States. Each year, the church's press issues the *Annuario Pontificio,* which includes the address of all of the bishops worldwide, the headquarters of the major religious orders, and the curial offices. Also annually, P. J. Kenedy & Sons, a Catholic publishing house, issues *The Official Catholic Directory* with contact information for all 208 dioceses and archdioceses in the United States and the American headquarters of all of the religious orders operating in America.

For Internet users, the Saint Ambrose Foundation sponsors the Catholic Internet Directory, found at www.catholic-church.org/cid.

United States Conference of Catholic Bishops, Washington, D.C. www.usccb.org/index.shtml

For further reading:

Broderick, Robert C. *Catholicism A to Z.* Nashville: Nelson Reference, 2006.

Carey, Patrick W. *The Roman Catholics.* Westport, Conn.: Greenwood Press, 1993.

Dolan, Jay P. *The American Catholic Experience: A History from Colonial Times to the Present.* Garden City, N.Y.: Doubleday & Company, 1985.

Ellis, John Tracy. *American Catholicism.* Garden City, N.Y.: Doubleday, 1965.

Flinn, Frank. *Encyclopedia of Roman Catholicism.* New York: Facts on File, 2006.

Foley, Leonard. *Believing in Jesus: A Popular Overview of the Catholic Church.* 4th ed. Cincinnati, Ohio: St. Anthony's Messenger, 2001.

Foy, Felician A. *A Concise Guide to the Catholic Church.* Huntington, Ind.: Our Sunday Visitor, 1984.

Gillis, Chester. *Roman Catholicism in America.* Columbia Contemporary American Religion Series. New York: Columbia University Press, 2000.

Hennesey, James. *American Catholics.* Oxford: Oxford University Press, 1981.

McBrien, Richard P. *The HarperCollins Encyclopedia of Catholicism.* San Francisco: HarperSanFrancisco, 1995.

B. Eastern Catholic Churches

As the church took shape around the Mediterranean basin, the Eastern and Western branches developed distinctive ecclesiastical styles. Some of these derived from the two dominant languages (Greek used in the Eastern church and Latin in the West). In the East, there were multiple sites that emerged as important urban centers from which the church spread regionally—Jerusalem, Antioch, and Alexandria. These were given a place of honor and their bishop designated as a patriarch. Each bishop's realm of influence was termed a patriarchate.

When the headquarters of the Roman Empire moved to Constantinople, the bishop of the new city quickly attained a status equal to and eventually above that of the other patriarchs, and over time Constantinople was recognized as a fourth patriatrchate. Constantinople assumed even more important status after the land overseen by the three other patriarchates fell under Muslim control. In the West, only one bishop attained the status of the Eastern patriarchs, the bishop of Rome. The absence of competing patriarchates was a key factor in the development of the Roman Catholic Church.

The Roman Catholic Church established a presence in the eastern Mediterranean as a result of the First Crusade. Over the next centuries, various attempts were made to heal the rift between the Catholic and Eastern Orthodox communions, but hope for any reconciliation waned considerably after the council of Florence, which met in the years immediately before Constantinople's fall to the forces of the Ottoman Empire in 1453. From that time, the Orthodox patriarchs had to operate in settings in which the secular rulers and the majority of the population were Muslim.

In the years after the fall of Constantinople, the Roman Catholic Church initiated a missionary policy toward Orthodox communities in the Middle East and other locations where the two churches co-existed. Over the years, often following the political changes that placed a Roman Catholic ruler over a land with a significant Orthodox population, efforts were made to change the allegiance of the Orthodox and bring them into communion with Rome. In most cases, this transition required little of the Orthodox apart from their bishops acknowledging Rome and a few changes in the liturgy. Thus in such faraway places as India, Ukraine, and Greece, new Catholic churches that followed an Eastern rite emerged. One practice of interest that continued in the Eastern churches was allowing married men to be priests, while a celibate priesthood continued among those who follow the Latin rite.

As the Eastern rite churches grew, a question of leadership emerged. The Eastern Orthodox churches were organized around leading bishops known as patriarchs, and their area of authority designated a patriarchate. Patriarchs are deemed to have a certain autonomy and authority above that of the average archbishop, and the leader of the Eastern Catholic Churches was seen as operating in a position parallel to the ancient Orthodox patriarchs. Over the years, the heads of six of the Eastern Catholic Churches have been recognized as patriarchs—Armenian, Chaldean, Coptic, Maronite, Melkite, and Syrian. Interestingly, the two largest of the Eastern churches—the Syro-Malabar and Ukrainian churches—have yet to attain that status. In 1992 the papacy granted the Syro-Malabar and Syro-Malandara rites (both based in India) the status of a major archepiscopy, a rank slightly beneath that of patriarchy. In 2002, the Ukrainian synod requested patriarchal status. The Second Vatican Council's "Decree on the Eastern Catholic Churches" asserted the autonomous patriarchal structure of the churches and the integrity of their liturgical worship.

The existence of Eastern Rite Catholic churches has become one of the most important issues to be resolved as the post-Vatican II Catholic leadership seeks to revive cordial relationships with Eastern Orthodoxy. In the late twentieth century, the spread of Soviet Marxism and the attempts of Communist governments to interfere with the Catholic presence in Ukraine and Romania created new tensions now manifest in local property disputes that have international repercussions. In the meantime, Pope Benedict XVI, elected in 2005, has made reconciliation with Eastern Orthodoxy a top priority of his papacy.

As one might expect, the eastern churches are strongest in their traditional homeland, but in the nineteenth and twentieth centuries, human mobility has affected them as it has most other older churches. Members of the larger bodies have spread globally and may now be found in Australia, Europe, and South America.

Members of the several Eastern Catholic Churches began migrating to the United States and Canada in the later-nineteenth century. As parishes emerged they were initially incorporated into the Latin rite dioceses. Early in the twentieth century, separate diocesan structures began to appear. The first to organize were the Ukrainians, who were able to establish an initial exarchate in Philadelphia in 1907. As additional dioceses were established, Philadelphia became an archeparchy. A parallel structure developed simultaneously in Canada.

Through the twentieth century, almost all of the Eastern Catholic churches have attained at least a minimal presence in the United States. Joining the Ukrainians, the Marionites, the Chaldeans, Melkites, Romanians, Ruthenians, and the Syro-Malabaans have established dioceses. Others have parishes currently operating within Latin rite dioceses. The Italo-Albanian Catholic Church, one of the smallest of the Eastern Rite churches, has no parish, but has established the Italo-Albanian Byzantine Rite Society of Our Lady of Grace, based on Staten Island in New York City. It sponsors services using the Italo-Albanian liturgy in several New York area churches on a monthly basis.

Contacts:

Chaldean Catholic Church
c/o St. Thomas the Apostle Chaldean Catholic Diocese Chancery
25603 Berg Rd.
Southfield, MI 48034

Italo-Albanian Byzantine Rite Catholic Society of Our Lady of Grace
51 Redgrave Ave.
Staten Island, NY 10306
www.byzantines.net/OurLadyofGrace

Maronite Catholic Church
c/o Eparchy of St. Maron of Brooklyn
109 Remsen St.
Brooklyn, NY 11201
www.bkerke.org.lb

Melkite Catholic Church
c/o Eparchy of Newton
3 VFW Parkway
Roslindale, MA 02131
www.melkite.org

Romanian Greek Catholic Church
Eparchy of Canton
Chancery Office
1121 44th St., NE
Canton, OH 44714
www.romaniancatholic.org

Ruthenian Catholic Church
c/o Eparchy of Pittsburgh
Chancery Office
66 Riverview Ave.
Pittsburgh, PA 15214-2253
www.archeparchy.org

Syrian Catholic Church
c/o Our Lady of Deliverance Syriac Catholic Diocese in the United States and Canada
Chancery Office
502 Palisade Ave.
Union City, NJ 07087-5213

Syro-Malankara Catholic Church
c/o St. Thomas Syro-Malabar Catholic Diocese of Chicago
717 Eastland Ave.
Elmhurst, IL 60126
malankara.net

Ukrainian Catholic Church
c/o Archeparchy of Philadelphia
Chancery Office, 827 N. Franklin St.
Philadelphia, PA 19123
www.ugcc.org.ua/eng

For further reading:

Attwater, Donald. *The Christian Churches of the East.* Milwaukee: Bruce, 1961.

Pospishil, Victor J. *Eastern Catholic Church Law.* Staten Island: Saint Maron, 1996.

Roberson, Ronald G. *The Eastern Christian Churches—A Brief Survey.* 5th ed. Rome: Edizioni Orientalia Christiana, 1995.

C. Old Catholicism

In 1869–70, the Roman Catholic Church called the first church council since the sixteenth-century. It became known as the First Vatican Council and was focused upon the dramatic changes that had overtaken the church, including the threat posed to the Papal States—the land in central Italy that the pope had ruled for many centuries—which were being lost by the unification of Italy into a modern secular state.

Reacting against the loss of temporal power, the council's main action became one of bolstering the pope's power within the church. This elevation was accomplished through the declaration of the doctrine of papal infallibility. Actually, the council's understanding of infallibility was very narrowly defined. It applied only to the core teaching of the church on matters of faith and morals. The council asserted, "The Roman Pontiff, when he speaks *ex cathedra*—that is, when in discharge of the office of pastor and teacher of all Christians, by virtue of his supreme apostolic authority, he defines a doctrine regarding the faith or morals to be held by the universal church, by the divine assistance promised to him in Blessed Peter—is possessed of that infallibility with which the divine redeemer willed that his Church should be endowed in defining doctrine regarding faith and morals; and therefore such definitions are irreformable of their own nature and not in virtue of the Church's consent."

The Council's action proved quite acceptable to the great majority of Catholics. However, in Europe, a variety of somewhat prominent leaders such as German church historian J. J. I. von Döllinger, saw the council's action as a significant departure from and innovation in Catholic tradition. These dissenters made common cause with several dioceses in the Netherlands that had a century-old unresolved disagreement with Rome. Early in the eighteenth century, the pope had deposed Peter Codde (1656–1710), the bishop of Utrecht. However, he failed to appoint a replacement and for many years no bishop existed to perform ordinations and confirmations. In 1824, Bishop Dominique Marie Varlet agreed to consecrate a bishop for the diocese of Utrecht and the neighboring dioceses of Deventer and Haarlam, which had sided with Utrecht. The Dutch had appealed their situation to a church council and existed in their unusual status until Vatican I, which did not deal with their situation. However, in light of their action on papal infallibility, there was every reason to believe that the council would have sided against the Dutch dioceses.

Immediately after the issuance of the pronouncement on infallibility, a conference held by those in opposition organized the Old Catholic Church. A widespread response did not emerge, but enough people supported the idea to form national churches in Germany, Switzerland, Austria, and several other countries. The dioceses in Holland then reorganized as the Old Catholic Church of the Netherlands and passed episcopal orders to the other Old Catholic churches. (The Roman Catholic Church considers the Old Catholic Church's episcopal orders valid but irregular.) The action by the dissenting Catholics was supported by the Church of England, whose episcopal orders had been called into question by Rome.

In 1874–1875, the Old Catholics held two Union Conferences in Bonn, Germany, but made no administrative moves toward closer alignment until 1889, when the Old Catholic bishops created the Union of Utrecht, which carried provisions for an annual bishops' conference and promulgated principles to guide their common life. The Union later reached out to include some parallel groups, most notably the Polish National Catholic Church and its European affiliate, the Polish Catholic Church. In 1931, the Church of England signed the Bonn Agreement, creating full sacramental intercommunion between the Church of England and the churches of the Union of Utrecht.

Over the years, the Old Catholics began making a variety of changes, many of which could be seen as a move toward Anglican practice. Among others, they dropped the private confession of sins to a priest, requirements for priestly celibacy, and the Latin Mass, in favor of a liturgy in the vernacular. In 1925, the Old Catholics formally recognized the validity of Anglican orders.

The relationship between the Old Catholic and Anglican communions was briefly disturbed when the latter began to admit women to holy orders, but in the 1990s the Old Catholics dropped their barriers to female priests. The first Old Catholic female priest was ordained in Germany in 1996. In 1985 the Old Catholic Church in Germany reached an intercommunion agreement with the (Lutheran) Evangelical Church in Germany.

In the twentieth century, Old Catholicism split into two very different strains. One, described above, occurred largely in Europe with the establishment of a stable if relatively small ecclesiastical body that has taken its place within the larger non-Roman Christian community. The several Old Catholic Churches in Europe are members of the World Council of Churches and remain in communion with the Anglican Communion worldwide. The only church representative of this strain of Old Catholicism in North America is the Polish National Catholic Church (PNCC).

The Polish National Catholic Church emerged out of the larger controversy that occurred in various Catholic ethnic communities in America as the Roman Catholic leadership attempted to create a single national church as opposed to a set of ethnic churches in the American context. To carry out their policy, bishops assigned priests to ethnic parishes without reference to the priests' ethnicity. Thus an Italian or French priest might be assigned to a predominantly Polish parish while Polish priests could be assigned to a Portuguese- or German-speaking parish.

Fr. Francis Hodur (1866–1953) took the lead in mobilizing the dissent from the bishops' policy among Polish American Catholics, resulting in the formation of the PNCC at Scranton,

Pennsylvania, in 1897. Hodur went on to become the church's first bishop (1906), receiving his consecration from the Old Catholics. Beginning in 1919, the church spread to Poland, where it eventually evolved into the Polish Catholic Church (PCC). Like the Old Catholics, the PNCC dropped the Latin liturgy in favor of one in Polish and in 1954 its General Synod decreed that henceforth Polish would be the sole language of the liturgy (a reaction to the gradual replacement of Polish with English as the everyday language of the membership). The church has also renounced the idea of papal infallibility, and in 1921 dropped requirements for clerical celibacy.

With some 265,000 members (2001), the PNCC continues as a substantial body, though the great majority of Polish Americans remain in the Roman Catholic Church. The PNCC's 144 parishes are organized into four dioceses. Its headquarters and the Savonarola Theological Seminary are in Scranton, Pennsylvania. Like the Old Catholics, the PNCC is a member of the World Council of Churches and remains in communion with the Church of England and other Anglicans worldwide.

A second strain of Old Catholicism dates to 1908. Arnold Harris Mathew (1852–1919), a former Anglican priest, convinced the bishop of Utrecht that he was the leader of a substantial body of British Christians who wanted to be neither Anglicans nor Roman Catholics, but Old Catholics. With little investigation of the substance of his claims, the Dutch Old Catholic bishops consecrated Mathew. When the following he thought he had did not materialize, Mathew set about the task of growing one, but it never materialized. In this endeavor, he broke his promise to the Dutch that he would not consecrate any bishops without their advice and consent. He actually went on to consecrate a number of bishops who in turn consecrated still more bishops, all of whom founded churches/dioceses in the hope that a lay membership would be drawn to them. In no case did that happen to any great degree.

Among Bishop Mathew's most significant consecrations were those of Prince de Landas Berghes et de Rache, Duc de St. Winock, an Austrian nobleman, who by the accident of being caught in America during World War I established Mathew's succession in the United States, and Frederick Samuel Willoughby, who founded the Liberal Catholic Church, which applied an esoteric interpretation to Christian doctrine and worship. While in America, the Duc de Landas Berghes consecrated W. H. Francis Brothers (1887–1979) and Henry Carfora (1895–1958), who became the ultimate source of most Old Catholic bodies in America because of the many men that they consecrated as bishops.

Today, more than fifty Old Catholic jurisdictions trace their orders to Mathew through Brothers or Carfora. They range from churches with membership in the thousands to others that are little more than paper organizations. Hindering the development of any substantial organization has been the absence of the substance of an episcopal organization, though all the outward trappings are present (parish churches, priests, bishops, archbishops, etc.). Very early in the movement, the ideal of the worker-priest was adopted, thus the bishops and priests usually made their living in a secular job thus limiting their efforts to grow a diocese or parish in after-work hours. While this allowed the movement to exist and perpetuate itself, it did not lend itself to the development of strong parishes and viable dioceses. When, on occasion, parishes did develop, the congregation owned the property (rather than the bishop), which meant that the bishop had little real authority should a dispute arise. In addition, without educational facilities under the diocese's control, it was difficult to demand high educational standards for the priesthood.

The Old Catholic movement in the Mathew tradition has had little to offer Catholics dissatisfied with the Roman Catholic Church. Few responded to the issue of papal infallibility. For a period, Carfora had modest success building ethnic parishes, but these were eventually lost to Americanization. The movement suffered greatly from the very positive response that the Catholic Church received in the wake of the changes initiated by Vatican II, especially the vernacular mass.

Recently, Old Catholics have emphasized their openness to those who have been denied communion in the Roman Catholic Church, especially divorced people who have remarried. Many of the Old Catholic churches have opened holy orders to females, and some of the most successful Old Catholic bodies have been started by gay priests and have presented their jurisdiction as an inclusive church that opens all levels of church life to people regardless of their race, gender, or sexual orientation.

Through the twentieth century, the holders of the several Old Catholic lineages developed relationships with independent bishops operating from the Eastern Orthodox and Anglican traditions. Often, as an act of intercommunion, they have held ceremonies in which they reconsecrate each other to episcopal orders so that all participating bishops come to possess multiple apostolic lineages. In this manner, some bishops have acquired a dozen or more episcopal lineages, some representing churches quite different in belief and practice from that of the lineage holder.

In the last generation, in response to Vatican II, a new reaction to the Roman Catholic Church developed among very conservative Catholics who rejected the many changes initiated by the church, especially the dropping of the Latin Mass, the loosening of rules for those in religious orders, and changing theological emphases that created the new openness to Protestants and non-Christians. The most prominent dissenting voice from Vatican II was Archbishop Marcel Lefevre, who after many years of negotiation with Rome finally broke with the church and consecrated a set of bishops to perpetuate pre-Vatican II Catholicism. The major new jurisdictions to emerge from this latest traditionalist movement are the Society of St. Pius X and the Society of St. Pius V.

Lefevre was not the only Catholic bishop to break with Rome. Vietnamese archbishop Pierre Martin Ngo-Dinh-Thuc, living in retirement in Italy, also rejected Vatican II, and became the source of a variety of new churches from his several consecrations. The most extreme branch of the post Vatican II traditionalists are the sedevacanists, those who do not merely disagree with the stance of Vatican II but who have argued that since Pope Paul VI began the implementation of the council's decrees, the papal office has been without a properly elected pope. In several cases, people have claimed the vacant papal office and begun building followings of people who accepted them. Among the people Archbishop Thuc consecrated was Clemente Dominguez Gomez of Palmar de Troya, Spain, who later emerged as Pope Gregory XVII and leader of the Holy Palmarian Church.

Contacts:

African American Catholic Church
c/o His Holiness, George Augustus Stallings, Jr.
5000 Pennsylvania Ave., Suite E
Suitland, MD 20746-1062
imaniaacc.org/clergy.htm

Since his initial consecration to the episcopacy and founding of the church, Archbishop Stallings has founded more than a dozen congregations primarily serving African Americans.

Christ Catholic Church
c/o Most Rev. Karl Pruter
Box 98
Highlandsville, MO 65669

Old Roman Catholic Church in North America
c/o Most Rev. Francis Facione
1207 Potomac Place
Louisville, KY 40214
www.orccna.org/index.htm

Archbishop Facione's jurisdiction has emerged as one of the most stable of the several churches in the lineage of Archbishop Carmel Henry Carfora (d. 1958), one of the founders of Old Catholicism in the United States.

Polish National Catholic Church (U.S.A.)
1002 Pittston Ave.
Scranton, PA 18505
www.pncc.org

With congregations across the United States serving primarily believers of Polish dissent, the PNCC is the only American-based church in communion with the European Old Catholic churches.

Society of St. Pius V
8 Pond Place
Oyster Bay Cove, NY 11771

The Society is one of two organizations serving traditional Catholics who continue to practice the Latin mass and have an episcopal lineage through Archbishop Marcel Lefevre.

Society of St. Pius X
c/o Regina Coclihouse
2918 Tracy Ave.
Kansas City, MO 64109
www.sspx.org

The Society of St. Pius X is the American affiliate of the international organization founded by Archbishop Marcel Lefevre (1905–1991) to protest changes initiated by Vatican II, especially the discontinuance of the Latin Mass. In general it continues traditional pre-Vatican practices.

United Catholic Church
Most Rev. Dr. Robert M. Bowman
5017 Bellflower Ct.
Melbourne, FL 32940-1200
united-catholic-church.org

Since his consecration in 1996, Archbishop Bowman has led a growing movement targeting former Roman Catholics who have been alienated by various Vatican policies.

For further reading:

Anson, Peter F. *Bishops at Large.* London: Faber and Faber, 1964.

Fox, Paul. *The Polish National Catholic Church.* Scranton, Penn.: School of Christian Living, [1955].

Kubiak, Hieronim. *The Polish National Catholic Church in the United States of America from 1897 to 1980.* Warsaw-Kraków: Panstwowe Wydawnictwo Naukowe, 1982.

Moss, C. B. *The Old Catholic Movement.* Eureka Springs, Ark.: Episcopal Book Club, 1977.

Plummer, John P. *The Many Paths of the Independent Sacramental Movement: A Study of its Liturgy, Doctrine and Leadership in America.* Dallas: Newt Books, 2005.

Pruter, Karl, and J. Gordon Melton. *The Old Catholic Sourcebook.* New York: Garland Publishing, 1983.

Ward, Gary L. *Independent Bishops: An International Directory.* Detroit: Apogee Books, 1990.

D. World Marian Movement

Over the last two centuries, the Roman Catholic Church has become home to a significant new movement centered on the veneration of the Blessed Virgin Mary, the Mother of Jesus. The special place of Mary in Catholic theology and worship has grown slowly since the fifth century, when Mary was initially designated as *Theotokos* (the mother of God) by the Council of Ephesus. The special veneration of the Blessed Virgin has received renewed emphasis at sporadic moments following reported apparitions of Mary. For example, in 1208, St. Dominic had a vision of the Virgin while preaching in southern France. That vision not only led to the formation of the Dominican order but to the promotion of the rosary as a prominent tool for prayer within the church.

In 1830, the Virgin appeared to Catherine Labourne, a nun then residing in Paris. Not known at the time of their occurrences, these several appearances of the Virgin became the first of a dozen or so similar apparitions reported around Catholic Europe over the next century. All of the apparitions called Catholics to a life of greater devotion, and some, such as the Paris appearances, which led to the striking of what was termed the Miraculous Medal, initiated new ways to show one's devotion. As the apparitions continued to occur, a manuscript written by a Marian devotee, Louis Grignon de Montfort (1673–1716), *True Devotion to Mary*, was rediscovered and published. It became a bestseller.

The growing devotion to Mary occurred as bad times fell on the papacy. Its influence appeared to be on the wane as European governments moved toward democracy and the separation of church and state. A movement began to unify the Italian Peninsula as a single modern state, the completion of which required the dissolution of the Papal States, over which the pope reigned as a monarch. As these temporal powers diminished, a succession of popes asserted renewed powers within the Catholic Church. Successive popes have frequently used new statements about and actions concerning Mary (such as visiting sites where apparitions occurred) to assert their ecclesiastical powers. The initial act tying Marian devotion to papal authority was the definition in 1854 of the Immaculate Conception (the belief that the Virgin Mary was born without original sin) as dogma (a doctrine to which the Catholic faithful were required to assent).

As each apparition has occurred, organizations have been formed to promote the forms of devotion advocated in the apparition. Often, the site of the apparition was turned into a shrine and place of pilgrimage. Among the most important and well known, the apparition to Bernadette Soubirous at Lourdes, France, led to the grotto where Mary appeared becoming one of the most popular European pilgrimage sites, as many came in search of healings from contact with the spring water that had appeared. The appearance of the Virgin to three children in Portugal in 1917 turned the small town of Fatima into a site rivaling Lourdes in popularity.

The frequency of apparitions has grown through the twentieth century to the present. They also are no longer confined to Europe, but have occurred around the world—Asia, Africa, and North and South America. Most of the nineteenth-century appearances were relatively short-lived events, the Virgin appearing just once or several times over a relatively short period. The twentieth century was marked by a number of examples in which the claimed apparition of the Virgin continued with some regularity over a number of years or even decades. These apparitions were frequently accompanied by lengthy discourses that would be relayed to the faithful by the few privy to the Virgin's appearances.

The Catholic Church takes reports of apparitions very seriously, especially if they appear in public. If people begin to gather around the site of an apparition and promote devotion based upon it, the church will investigate. It will ask if the messages being received in the apparition are aligned with Catholic doctrine. It will look into the life of those receiving the apparition and examine them while they are in the act of seeing the Virgin. If it reaches the conclusion that nothing contrary to Catholic teachings is being received and that the visionaries appear genuine, the church may remove any obstacles to the development of piety around any given apparition. However, the church is much more likely to speak clearly when there appears to be a flaw in the apparition.

In the face of the large number of apparitions reported through the twentieth century, the Catholic Church has expressed some uneasiness, and it has been increasingly reluctant to clear away the obstacles to the Catholic faithful who wish to associate themselves with particular apparitions. Moreover, though the study of the significance of Mary has become a recognized specialty in Catholic theology, the bishops at Vatican II refused to promulgate a separate document on the Blessed Virgin and kept its consideration of her as a safe topic within its consideration of the church.

At the same time, recent popes, especially Pope John Paul II, have promoted Marian devotion, even devotions associated with the recent apparitions. On May 13, 1981, the anniversary of the first apparition at Fatima, John Paul II was making a public appearance when he turned and bent down to look at a picture of the Virgin as she appeared at Fatima. As he turned, an assassin's bullet barely missed its target. The pope credited Our Lady of Fatima with saving his life. He later visited Fatima on two occasions and participated in the canonization of two of the three seers as saints. In 1987 he proclaimed a Marian year and in his encyclical *Redemptoris Mater* he called for a revival of Marian spirituality.

The words spoken by the Virgin in the more accepted apparitions, along with the appearance and gestures of the Virgin on the different occasions, have become a body of material that many who participate in Marian devotion look to as a particular message from God for this modern age. That message has assumed an apocalyptic tone, with many warning of disaster if piety and morality are not revived and modern movements from secularism to Communism overcome.

The promotion of Marian devotion is based in two sets of groups. One, headed by several Catholic orders, consists of international organizations devoted generally to the Virgin Mary. Typical of them are the Servants of Mary (the Servites), the Militia of the Immaculata founded by St. Maximilian Kolbe, the Legion of Mary, and the Marianists (a term referring to a set of related organizations: the Society of Mary, the Daughters of Mary Immaculate, the Lay Marianists, and the Alliance Mariale). By far the greatest number of organizations, however, are focused on promoting the piety surrounding a single Marian apparition such as the Blue Army of Our Lady of Fatima or the Association of the Miraculous Medal. Besides the several large international organizations are hundreds operating locally. In the case of the more popular apparition sites, or those where regular apparitions are continuing, local organizations promoting devotional activities are generally set up to assist pilgrims in making a visit.

In addition to those organizations mentioned above which operate informally within the larger structure of the Catholic Church are a number that operate on the church's fringe or beyond it. Most of these organizations, such as Our Lady of the Roses, Mary Help of Mothers shrine in Bayside, New York, or For My God and My Country in Necedah, Wisconsin, promote apparitions about which the church has specifically pronounced its disapproval.

Contacts:

Association of the Miraculous Medal
1811 West St. Joseph St.
Perryville, MO 63775
www.amm.org

The association promotes the veneration of Mary with special emphasis on the message of the Miraculous Medal given to St. Catherine Labouré in Paris in 1830.

The Blue Army (World Apostolate of Fatima)
Mt. View Rd.
P.O. Box 976
Washington, NJ 07882
www.bluearmy.com

The Blue Army is the largest organization promoting the messages received by the three children at Fatima, Portugal, in 1917.

Congregation of the Daughters of Mary Perfect
251 W. Ligustrum Dr.,
San Antonio, TX 78228
www.marianistsisters.org

Also known as the Marianist Sisters, the Congregation is an ordered community, with a special veneration of the Blessed Virgin, founded in post-revolutionary France and active in rebuilding the French church. Its programs aimed at assisting women, the poor, and building an inclusive church have led to its international expansion.

Legion of Mary
P.O. Box 1313
St. Louis, MO 63188
www.legionofmary.org

The Legion is the largest Catholic lay organization. Its members operate at the parish level to extend the pastoral services of congregations to members in need.

Militia of the Immaculata
1600 W. Park Ave.
Libertyville, IL 60048
www.consecration.com

The Militia, founded by St. Maximillian Kolbe (1894–1941), killed by the Nazis at Auschwitz, seeks to develop the spirituality of its members through their devotion to the Blessed Virgin and her Son Jesus.

For further reading:

The primary center for the study of devotion to the Virgin Mary is the Marian Library and International Marian Research Institute located at the University of Dayton (Ohio), an institution sponsored by the Marianists. It has an expansive website, www.udayton.edu/mary/, reflective of the central core of Marian devotion.

Ashton, Joan. *Mother of All Nations: Visions of Mary.* San Francisco: Harper and Row, 1989.

Attwater, Donald. *A Dictionary of Mary.* New York: Kenedy, 1956.

Garvey, Mark. *Searching for Mary: An Exploration of Marian Apparitions across the U.S.* New York: Plume, 1998.

O'Carroll, Michael. *Theotokos: A Theological Encyclopedia of the Blessed Virgin Mary.* Wilmington, DE: M. Glazier, 1983, 1982.

Pelikan, Jaroslav. *Mary Through the Centuries.* New Haven, Conn.: Yale University Press, 1996.

Perry, Nicholas, and Loreto Echeverría. *Under the Heel of Mary.* London: Routledge, 1988.

Warner, Marina. *Alone of All Her Sex: The Myth and Cult of the Virgin Mary.* New York: Alfred A. Knopf, 1976.

Zimdars-Swarts, Sandra L. *Encountering Mary: Visions of Mary from La Salette to Medjugorje.* New York: Avon Books, 1992.

E. Eastern Orthodoxy

The Eastern Orthodox churches, based in the Eastern Mediterranean, share a common history with the Roman Catholic Church in the centuries immediately before and after the Emperor Constantine, but even as the major decisions were being made on the canon of Holy Scriptures and the basic doctrines that defined orthodox Christian teachings, Eastern and Western Christianity were developing distinctive emphases. In the years between the Council of Nicea (324) and the formal break between Rome and Constantinople (1054), the differences were largely a matter of language (Greek versus Latin) and some liturgical and devotional emphases. The Eastern approach to theology and worship was more mystical and the themes concerning the eventual deification of the saved in Christ gained a certain precedence.

Of primary importance in the East, the church developed around four centers of authority—the three ancient patriarchates of Jerusalem, Antioch, and Alexandria, and the new patriarchate at Constantinople, the headquarters of the Roman Empire since the days of Constantine. While the church in Rome became a powerful religious organization working in the vacuum created by the loss of the center of the Roman Empire, the church in the East operated in a context with a strong government, first with the Roman Empire and then with the Islamic rulers in the Holy Land and Egypt. The existence of strong governments prevented the development of understandings of the church that saw it as equal to or even superior to the secular government as was seen in the medieval papacy.

From Antioch and Jerusalem the church spread eastward to places such as Armenia, Mesopotamia (Iraq), Persia, and even, some say, to India, and south from Alexandria to Ethiopia. From Constantinople it pushed northward into Slavic lands. This new territory lay beyond the reach of the Roman Empire. The initial problem faced by the Eastern churches came as theologians and church leaders advocated divergent views on the nature of God, Christ, and salvation. It was, in fact, in responding to these new ideas that the Orthodox position on the Trinity and two natures of Christ (human and divine) were hammered out. However, as the majority of the church reached the consensus that became orthodoxy, various branches of the church were lost as different bishops refused to accept the council decisions. Eventually, theologically distinct churches arose in Armenia, Persia, and lands to the east. The most important loss was Egypt. These churches refused to accept the final Orthodox solution to the Trinitarian question promulgated by the Council of Chalcedon in A.D. 451 and have come to be known as the Non-Chalcedonian churches, though their positions vary considerably. The Non-Chalcedonian churches are discussed separately below.

In the seventh century, the development of the Eastern churches took a decided turn with the rise of Islam, which quickly overran the Holy Land. The establishment of Islam in the land previously dominated by Orthodoxy not only swept many Christians into the Islamic community but placed the Christian bishops in a subordinate position and stopped any efforts to missionize outside of the surviving Christian community. It also placed severe limitations on future theological creativity.

The most dramatic break in the church came in 1054 with the growing split between Constantinople (still outside the expanding Muslim Empire) and Rome. That split was given theological sanction by a technical theological disagreement concerning the place of the Holy Spirit in the Trinity. Eastern Orthodox churches, following the traditional text of the Nicene Creed, state "the Holy Spirit, who proceeds from the Father." The Roman Catholic Church added a phrase "and the Son," so that its version of the creed reads, "the Holy Spirit, who proceeds from the Father and the Son." The Eastern church leaders rejected that phrase, believing that it suggested an undue subordination of the Holy Spirit.

The real split between East and West did not rest on the added phrase; it rested on political differences. Efforts to heal the East-West schism were attempted for several centuries, but largely came to an end after Constantinople was overrun by Muslims in 1453 and became the new capital of the Ottoman

Empire. Until the twentieth century, Roman Catholics classified Orthodox Christianity as suitable for missionary activity, and attempts were made to bring Orthodox believers under papal authority. These efforts resulted in the establishment of a number of Eastern-rite Catholic churches, churches that followed a slightly altered Orthodox liturgy, but recognized the supreme authority of the pope.

The Orthodox Church has been tied together by a shared faith and liturgy and a communion of the patriarchs. The archbishop of Constantinople (now Istanbul) over several centuries emerged as the symbolic focus of the unity of Eastern Orthodoxy. He is now referred to as the Ecumenical Patriarch. His jurisdiction, the Ecumenical Patriarchate, includes Turkey (the former base of the Byzantine Empire), parts of Greece, all of Europe not specifically assigned to other jurisdictions, and the Greek-speaking Orthodox in North and South America. Early on, Syria, Palestine, and lands to the east were assigned to the Greek Orthodox Patriarchate of Antioch and the Greek Orthodox Patriarchate of Jerusalem, while the continent of Africa was assigned to the Greek Orthodox Patriarchate of Alexandria and All Africa.

Through the centuries a variety of autonomous Orthodox jurisdictions have been recognized. The taking of Constantinople by the Ottoman Turks caused the assertion of patriarchal status by the Russian Orthodox Church, whose leader is now recognized as the patriarch of Moscow. More recently patriarchal status has been granted to Serbia, Bulgaria, Romania, and Georgia. Autonomy (but not patriarchal status) has been granted to a variety of national churches as they have grown in size and their countries asserted their national prerogatives. For example, the Church of Greece (which includes that part of Greece not directly under the jurisdiction of the Ecumenical Patriarch), is an autonomous church, but its leader is not designated as a patriarch. Other autonomous churches are found in Cyprus, Albania, Finland, the Ukraine, Poland, the Czech Republic and Slovakia, and Japan. One of the smaller autonomous churches is the Church of Sinai, whose primary territory is the isolated monastery of St. Catherine in the Sinai Desert and the uninhabited lands immediately adjoining.

The Eastern church differs from the Roman Catholic Church in several respects. It did not adopt the idea of a celibate priesthood, though it requires those priests who wish to marry to do so prior to receiving holy orders. Bishops, however, are chosen from unmarried priests, meaning that most come from the ranks of the monks who reside in ordered communities. The church also makes extensive use of icons, holy pictures believed to provide a particular representation of holy realities. In Orthodox churches a panel of icons, the *iconostasis*, divides the area where the eucharistic ceremony is performed (the *bema*) from the area where the congregation gathers.

The twentieth century has seen the rise of a new set of Orthodox churches that are completely orthodox in belief and practice but are not in communion with the ecumenical patriarchate. Among the largest and most important of these is the Russian Orthodox Church Abroad, formed by Russian bishops residing outside of Russia at the time of the Russian Revolution (1917) and who decided that the Russian bishops inside the Soviet Union had become subservient to and corrupted by an atheist government. As other countries came under Marxist governments, additional anti-Communist churches emerged. Also, through the century, some of these churches assumed a very conservative stance and opposed changes in the larger Orthodox churches, such as the acceptance of the modern calendar (which led to a movement of the date on which Orthodox feasts were celebrated). They also sharply opposed the alignment of Orthodox churches with Protestants in the World Council of Churches and the movement toward reconciliation with Rome made by the Ecumenical Patriarchate. The fall of Communism has led to the merger of some of the independent churches, but the churches emphasizing the "old calendar" have tended to remain separate.

In America

Orthodoxy made its initial move into what is now the United States in 1741 when the Russian Orthodox Church established a mission in Alaska. The first church was consecrated in 1794 in Paul's Harbor and a seminary established in the 1840s. A diocese, created in the 1860s, was moved to San Francisco in 1872. In Orthodoxy, the movement by a church into a new land not previously home to an Orthodox church gives that church primacy. Thus the Russian Orthodox Church assumed hegemony over the Orthodox community in America, and most Orthodox groups formed their first parishes as ethnic parishes within a Russian Orthodox diocese. Immigration to America from predominantly Orthodox countries increased greatly in the 1880s and continued until the radical changes in the immigration laws in the 1920s. During this period, the road to forming an independent Orthodox church occasionally involved the establishment of an ethnic-based diocese within the Russian church.

The emergence of viable communities of Orthodox believers of different ethnic backgrounds led to the call for the creation of a multi-ethnic American Orthodox Church. This idea gained significant support within the Orthodox community, but was blunted by the Episcopal Church, which saw itself as holding the place that would be assumed by an American Orthodox Church and was, at the time, heavily subsidizing the Orthodox Church in the United States. More recent attempts to merge the various Orthodox jurisdictions and form an American church have been blocked by disagreements between the Greeks, who currently form the largest Orthodox community in America, and the Russians, who by protocol assume that they would have a primary role in any new church. In 1970, the Russians created a merger of several of the different splinters that had been formed because of the events in Russia and created the Orthodox Church in America. The patriarch of the Russian church in Moscow granted the American church an autonomous status.

The Orthodox Church in America's hope to become a focal point for Orthodox unity in America has not been realized. Churches attached to the ecumenical patriarchate and a number of the other autonomous Orthodox churches now exist in the United States. In 1960, the American branches of the established Orthodox bodies formed the Standing Conference of the Canonical Orthodox Bishops in the Americas (SCOBA). Its membership includes the presiding bishops of the Greek Orthodox Archdiocese of America, the Orthodox Church in America, the Antiochian Orthodox Christian Archdiocese of North America, the Serbian Orthodox Church in the USA and Canada, the Romanian Orthodox Archdiocese in America and Canada, the Bulgarian Eastern Orthodox Church, the American Carpatho-Russian Orthodox Diocese in the USA, the Ukrainian

Orthodox Church of the USA, and the Albanian Orthodox Diocese of America.

Independent Orthodoxy

Apart from the several large Orthodox bodies in SCOBA, whose membership includes the great majority of Orthodox believers, there are more than fifty other Orthodox churches that exist in North America. Several of these are remnants of the Communist era, the most prominent being the Russian Orthodox Church Abroad, that have been unable to resolve the issues and hard feelings generated during that period. Several of the churches derive from the attempt of Syrian Archbishop Aftimios Ofeish to build an American Orthodoxy early in the twentieth century. Originally backed by the Russian bishops, Ofeish continued independently after they withdrew their blessings on his work. The African Orthodox Church was formed by African Americans under the leadership of George McGuire, formerly in the Episcopal Church, who were seeking equality in the ecclesiastical realm.

The largest number of different Orthodox churches derive from the ministry of independent Catholic bishop Joseph Rene Vilatte. In 1892, Vilatte was consecrated by the Non-Chalcedonian Bishop Antonio Francisco-Xavier Alvarez (Mar Julius I), bishop of the Syrian Jacobite Orthodox Church and metropolitan of the Independent Catholic Church of Ceylon, Goa and India. Though Vilatte seems to have considered himself an Old Catholic bishop, he joined Ofeish as a major source for independent Orthodox episcopal orders. As occurred in the American Old Catholic community, a variety of independent bishops have formed churches and attempted to grow memberships, some emphasizing ethnic heritage and others emphasizing the American context. As the major Orthodox bodies have resolved many of the issues that affected them over the twentieth century, the independent churches, who, like the Old Catholics, often have a part-time worker-priest leadership, have found it difficult to develop any substantial following. Among the Independent Orthodox churches, the American World Patriarchs, the Catholic Apostolic Church in America, and the Orthodox Catholic Church of America appear to have more than local support.

Contacts:

The Orthodox Church Institute in Regensburg, Germany, annually publishes *Orthodoxia*, a detailed directory of Orthodox churches and bishops around the world.

Jurisdictions associated with the Standing Conference of the Canonical Orthodox Bishops in the Americas:

Albanian Orthodox Diocese of America
6455 Silver Dawn Lane
Las Vegas, NV 89118
www.orthodoxalbania.org/English/MainMenu.html

Founded in America at a time (1950) when Albania was under Communist control and the Christian church suppressed, the small diocese is in communion with those churches affiliated with the Standing Conference of the Canonical Orthodox Bishops.

American Carpatho-Russian Orthodox Diocese in the USA
312 Garfield St.
Johnstown, PA 15906
www.acrod.org

The diocese had its origin among Roman Catholics of southwestern Ukrainian heritage who decided to adhere to Eastern Orthodoxy and were organized into a separate Orthodox jurisdiction.

Antiochian Orthodox Christian Archdiocese of North America
358 Mountain Rd.
Englewood, NJ 07631
www.antiochian.org

The archdiocese is the American affiliate of believers who come from the territory in the Middle East served by the ancient Greek Orthodox Christian Patriarchate of Antioch (Syria).

Bulgarian Eastern Orthodox Church
550-A West 50th St.
New York, NY 10019
bulch.tripod.com/boc

The church serves primarily Orthodox Christians of a Bulgarian heritage.

Greek Orthodox Archdiocese of America
10 East 79th St.
New York, NY 10021
www.goarch.org

The Greek Archdiocese, serving a million and a half Greek Americans, is the largest of the Eastern Orthodox bodies in the United States.

Orthodox Church in America
P.O. Box 675
Syosset, NY 11791
www.oca.org

The Orthodox Church in America, which emerged from the Russian Orthodox community in the United States, continues the oldest Eastern Orthodox work established in what is now the United States.

Romanian Orthodox Archdiocese in America & Canada
5410 N. Newland Ave.
Chicago, IL 60656-2026
www.romarch.org/eng

The archdiocese was founded by Romanian Orthodox believers who migrated to the United States beginning in the late nineteenth century.

Serbian Orthodox Church in the USA and Canada
P.O. Box 519
Libertyville, IL 60048
www.westsrbdio.org

The Serbian Church serves believers of southern Balkan heritage in communion with the patriarch who resides in Belgrade.

Ukrainian Orthodox Church of the USA
P.O. Box 495
South Bound Brook, NJ 08880
www.uocofusa.org

The Ukrainian Orthodox Church has played a key role in Ukrainian history as the bearer of independent Ukrainian aspiration through the period of Soviet domination and the suppression of the Ukrainian Church and its merger into the larger Russian Orthodox Church based in Moscow.

Independent Orthodoxy

African Orthodox Church
c/o Right Reverend Donald A. Smalls
3010 NW 211st St.
Miami, FL 33169

The African Orthodox Church was founded by Archbishop George McGuire (1866–1934) in protest of the racism he encountered in the Episcopal Church.

American World Patriarchs
c/o Most Reverend Emigidius J. Ryzy
19 Aqueduct St.
Ossining, NY 10562
members.aol.com/amworldpat

The American World Patriarchs organization has attempted to provide a meeting ground for independent Orthodox bishops of a variety of ethnic backgrounds.

Catholic Apostolic Church in America
c/o The Most Reverend Anthony Santore
Holy Trinity Cathedral Parish
P.O. Box 8631
Reston, VA 20195
www.cacina.org

The Catholic Apostolic Church is the most successful of several churches to grow out of the Brazilian work begun by former Roman Catholic Archbishop Carlos Duarte Costa (1888–1961).

Greek Orthodox Missionary Archdiocese of Vasiloupolis
44-02 48th Ave.
Woodside, NY 11377
netministries.org/see/churches.exe/ch04350

The Archdiocese of Vasiloupolis is one of several Greek Orthodox jurisdictions that protested the adoption of the Gregorian calendar by most Greek Orthodox and continues to use the Julian calendar.

Orthodox Catholic Church of America
c/o Most Rev. E. Paul Brian Carsten, Metropolitan Archbishop
Crosswood Centre
5355 County RD. #35
Auburn, IN 46706-9717
www.orthodoxcatholicchurch.org

The Orthodox Catholic Church continues an effort initiated early in the twentieth century to build an American Orthodoxy that transcended the ethnic-based life of much of the Eastern Orthodox community in North America.

Russian Orthodox Church Abroad
c/o Metropolitan His Eminence Laurus
75 E. 93rd St.
New York, NY 10028
www.russianorthodoxchurch.ws/english

The Russian Orthodox Church Abroad emerged in the years after the Russian Revolution by bishops operating beyond the hegemony of the Soviet government. They initially opposed the Russian church's subservience to Communist authorities and more recently what it sees as it modernist changes and compromising ecumenical relationships.

For further reading:

Fitzgerald, Thomas E. *The Orthodox Church.* Westport, Conn.: Greenwood Press, 1995.

Meyendorff, John. *Orthodox Church: Its Past and Its Role in the World Today.* Trans. by John Chapin. Crestwood, N.Y.: St. Vladimir's Seminary Press, 1996.

Prokurat, Michael, Alexander Golitzin, and Michael D. Peterson. *Historical Dictionary of the Orthodox Church.* Metuchen, N.J.: Scarecrow Press, 1996.

Roberson, Ronald G. *The Eastern Christian Churches.* Rome, Italy: Pont. Institutum Studiatorum Orientalium, 1988.

Schmemann, Alexander. *The Historic Road of Eastern Orthodoxy.* New York: Holt, Rinehart and Winston, 1963.

Serafim, Archimandrite. *The Quest for Orthodox Church Unity in America: A History of the Orthodox Church in North America in the Twentieth Century.* New York: Saints Boris and Gleb Press, 1973.

F. Non-Chalcedonian Orthodoxy

Beginning in 325 C.E., the bishops of the Christian church gathered at Nicea (now called Iznik), a town east of Constantinople (Istanbul, Turkey) to begin work on a set of issues before the church concerning basic beliefs about God, Christ, and salvation. The first council of Nicea and the six councils that followed it were prompted by controversies over the attempt of different bishops and theologians trying to state how the church could affirm one God while claiming Jesus Christ as divine, how Jesus Christ could be both God and human, and how God saves us. The first council, for example, argued about the position of Arius, who had suggested that Christ was not God but merely like God. The council issued a creedal statement affirming that the Lord Jesus Christ was "very God of very God."

In 428 C.E., a bishop named Nestorius attained the all-important post of patriarch of Constantinople. Subsequently he suggested that Christ was not properly seen as the Son of God, rather, it was the case that the one God was living in him. Thus it was improper to speak of Mary as the God Bearer or mother of God, *Theotokos*. The divine and human in Jesus were separable and when Jesus died, God did not bear the suffering. A mere three years after Nestorius entered into his new office, a council was called to deal with his views. It met at Ephesus in 431. The council ruled against Nestorius and deposed him from office. It spoke of Mary as *Theotokos* and affirmed that the two natures in Christ were inseparable.

Nestorius was banished several years later, but did not fade into oblivion. Along with his supporters he moved beyond the ears of the Roman Empire's rulers and spread his doctrines through Mesopotamia and Persia. He followers eventually introduced Christianity into China. The Holy Apostolic Catholic Assyrian Church of the East, now centered in Iraq, is the major remnant of the Nestorian movement, and the first of the churches to dissent from the decisions of the main body of

Christian leaders. Its designation as a Non-Chalcedonian church derives from the nonparticipation in the 451 Council of Chalcedon at which a more detailed version of the Nicene Creed was issued.

The opposite of Nestorius' position was that of the Monophysites, who argued that Christ had only one (*mono*) nature (*physis*), as his divine nature absorbed and hence obliterated his human nature. This position was put forward by one Eutyches, the head of a monastery in Constantinople in the 440s. It was also later identified with teachings offered by Cyril of Alexandria. After the 451 Council of Chalcedon ruled that Christ had two natures, the position of Alexandria seemed to be refuted. However, upon reflection, it appears that Cyril and his followers were affirming something different from what the Council refuted. However, the political differences between the different church leaders of the day worked against any reconciliation of the different views.

As a result of Chalcedon's ruling and the continuing polemics over the next half-century, the church in Egypt, much of Syria, and later Armenia, began to pull away from the rest of Christendom and organize separately. In Egypt, the dissidents took the see of Alexandria, one of the ancient patriarchal centers of the church (though an Orthodox bishop was later installed there and recognized by the Orthodox Church).

Today there are six main "monophysite" churches: The Coptic Orthodox Church of Egypt, the Ethiopian Orthodox Tewahedo Church, the Syrian Orthodox Patriarchate of Antioch and All the East, the Malankara Orthodox Syrian Church (the Indian Orthodox Church), the Armenian Church, and the Armenian Apostolic Church. It should be noted that the majority of the members of the Syrian Orthodox Church are in India.

The several Indian churches claim an independent origin from the work of the apostle Thomas in the first century, however; their episcopal orders come from Syria. Today these churches claim that they were not monophysite and were not opposed to the Chalcedonian Creed. They suggest instead that they simply never affirmed the creed and because of the break in church relationships did not continue to participate in the work of the later ecumenical councils.

The Non-Chalcedonian churches continue to exist separate from the Eastern Orthodox churches, but in the modern world have initiated conversations with them through a shared membership in ecumenical bodies, notably the World Council of Churches. The Armenian Church, the Armenian Apostolic Church, the Coptic Orthodox Church, the Ethiopian Orthodox Tewahedo Church, the Holy Apostolic Catholic Assyrian Church of the East, and the Syrian Orthodox Patriarchate of Antioch and All the East are all members of the council.

In America

Members of these churches, like those of the Eastern Orthodox churches, began to migrate to the United States in the late nineteenth century. Unlike the Orthodox churches, there was no ecclesiastical body to receive them and organizing turned into a slow process beginning with the sending of priests, the association of isolated parishes, and finally the development of a diocesan structure. The Syrians organized first, following the arrival of a priest sent to America in 1907. A bishop arrived in 1947. That bishop, Mar Athanasius Y. Samuel, later attained some fame when he purchased a set of materials found along the Dead Sea that turned out to be the Dead Sea Scrolls.

The Ethiopian Church was granted full autonomy by the Coptic Church in 1959. That same year a group of seminary students studying in the United States organized an initial parish in Brooklyn, New York, of the Ethopian Church in America. From that effort, other parishes were organized among Ethiopian expatriates who had settled in cities across the United States.

Contacts:

The Orthodox Church Institute in Regensburg, Germany, publishes *Orthodoxia,* an annual directory of Orthodox churches (including the Non-Chalcedonian churches) around the world.

Apostolic Catholic Assyrian Church of the East, North American Diocese
c/o H. H. Mar Dinkha, IV, Catholicos Patriarch
7201 North Ashland
Chicago, IL 60626

The Assyrian Church continues the Orthodox tradition as found in the modern state of Iraq.

Armenian Apostolic Church of America
138 E. 39th St.
New York, NY 10016
www.armenianprelacy.org

The Armenian Church split following the incorporation of Armenia into the Soviet Union. The Armenian diocese based in Lebanon at Cilicia sanctioned the dissidents.

Coptic Orthodox Church
c/o Bishop Moussa
5 Woodstone Dr.
Cedar Grove, NJ 07009
www.ecucopt.org

The Coptic Orthodox Church continues the ancient Egyptian Christian community that broke relations with the rest of the Christian world in the fifth century.

Diocese of the Armenian Church of America
c/o His Eminence Khajag Barsamian
630 Second Ave.
New York, NY 10016
www.armenianchurch.org

The Armenian Church is the American body in communion with the Armenian patriarch residing in Etchmiadzin, Armenia.

Ethiopian Orthodox Church in the United States of America
c/o His Eminence Abuna Yeshaq, Archbishop
140-142 W. 176th St.
Bronx, NY 10453
www.angelfire.com/ny3/ethiochurch

The Ethiopian Orthodox Church, for many centuries in close connection with the Egyptian Orthodox community, became jurisdictionally autonomous in the twentieth century.

Malankara Orthodox (Syrian) Church
His Eminence Zachariah Mor Nicho-lovos
Indian Orthodox Church Center
Bellerose, NY 11426
www.malankara.com

The Malankara Church is one of several Orthodox churches in India with orders derived from the Syrian Orthodox Church.

Syrian Orthodox Church of Antioch (Patriarchal Vicariates of the United States and Canada) (Jacobite)
Eastern U. S. Vicariate
260 Elm Ave.
Teaneck, NJ 07666

or
Western U. S. Vicariate
417 East Fairmount Rd.
Burbank, CA 92501
www.syrianorthodoxchurch.org

The Syrian Orthodox Church continues the ancient Christian church centered in Antioch, which has existed independently of the larger Eastern Orthodox community due to an unwillingness to accept the creedal formulas proposed by the early church councils in the fifth century.

For further reading:

Elmhardt, William Chauncey, and George M. Lamsa. *The Oldest Christian People.* New York: AMS Press, 1970.

Issac, Ephraim. *The Ethiopian Church.* Boston: Henry N. Sawyer Company, 1968.

McCullough, W. Stewart. *A Short History of Syriac Christianity to the Rise of Islam.* Chico, Calif.: Scholars Press, 1982.

Meinardus, Otto, F. A. *Christian Egypt Faith and Life.* Cairo: The American University in Cairo Press, 1970.

Moffett, Samuel Hugh. *A History of Christianity in Asia. Vol. I: Beginnings to 1500.* San Francisco: HarperSanFrancisco, 1992.

Ramban, Kadavil Paul. *The Orthodox Syrian Church, Its Religion and Philosophy.* Puthencruz, Syria: K. V. Pathrose, 1973.

St. Mark and the Coptic Church. Cairo: Coptic Orthodox Patriarchate, 1968.

Sarkissian, Karekin. *The Council of Chalcedon and the Armenian Church.* New York: The Armenian Church Prelacy, 1965.

__________. *The Witness of the Oriental Orthodox Churches.* Artelias, Lebanon: The Author, 1970.

2. The Reformation Churches of the Sixteenth Century

Background

In the second decade of the 1500s, the Western world was shaken at its foundations by the demand that the Christian church headquartered in Rome reform itself. Calls for reform were nothing new, but this time the demand for reform got out of hand. The success of the Reformation must be attributed to a variety of causes, including widespread perception that there were serious problems in the church, the distraction of Catholic resources to handling the invasion of Islamic forces up the Danube Valley, and the political base Luther was able to command, beginning with the ruler of Saxony, one of the people charged with selecting the new Holy Roman Emperor whenever the office became vacant.

While the secular support that Luther received certainly contributed to the Reformation, if he had not made the theological case for his cause, it would likely have not led to any systemic change.

Luther launched his critique of the Catholic Church with a challenge to the practice of selling indulgences. In Christian thought, God forgives sin, but as part of the repentance of the sins that God has forgiven, the repentant believer attempts to make recompense for those sins. The repentant sinner attempts in part to make right what s/he has done wrong and in the process learn something of the way of holiness. Thus, if one has stolen money, one might repay the money and go through the process of asking forgiveness from those hurt by the original theft. Such actions recognize the social consequences of sin and prevent the cheapening of grace. To deal with the personal consequences of sin, the church suggests a variety of actions that engage the repentant sinner in various acts of piety and/or charity.

As Catholic thought developed, it was understood that for most people recompense for sin and the adoption of a holy life would not be completed in this life. The idea of purgatory was posited as a place where Christians could complete the process of purging oneself of sin. In purgatory one experienced some of what the damned experience in hell.

Indulgences emerged as a means by which one could do a special act that would be counted as the equivalent of full recompense for specific sins or for all the sins one had committed to date. During the Crusades, an indulgence was part of what one might receive for participation. In an interesting twist, indulgences were also given to those who could not go on crusade, but who financially supported it. Thus began the practice of purchasing indulgences. In 1506, the Catholic Church in Rome initiated the building of St. Peter's Basilica, a project that continued for many decades and at times drew heavily upon the Vatican's coffers. Thus it was that in 1517 the pope authorized the selling of indulgences to raise money to continue the building program.

In Germany the indulgence program met some resistance, as it would take significant amounts of money out of the German states and send it to Italy. For Luther, however, the program offered a variety of offenses, not the least being the manner in which it was carried out—playing on people's fears and concern for deceased loved ones. John Tetzel, who sold the indulgences in Luther's region, appealed to people to buy indulgences to obtain release of their loved ones from their suffering in purgatory.

In October 1517, Martin Luther, a professor of theology at Wittenberg, Saxony, posted a list of debating point (theses) that he was prepared to defend in a public disputation. As a result of the ensuing discussions, in order to defend his position Luther had to take a further step and assert the authority of the Bible over that of the church and pope. Luther's attack on papal authority led to the issuance of a papal bull denouncing Luther. He answered with three essays that outlined a more comprehensive stance relative to changes he saw necessary for the reformation of the church.

Luther now openly attacked the Roman Catholic doctrine of transubstantiation (the means by which the church explains how the elements of the eucharist become the body and blood of Christ), called for limiting the number of sacraments to two (baptism and the Lord's supper) rather than seven, and began to promote the concept of the priesthood of all believers. He elaborated on his basic principle of scriptural authority (*sola scriptura*) and, possibly his most important insight, that salvation is by grace through faith alone.

Luther's understanding of salvation went far beyond the earlier call for reform and struck at the very heart of sacramental theology. Catholic theology certainly taught that God's grace was the central element in salvation, but it ascribed a role to one's lifelong participation in church and sacrament and to the development of holiness as part of one's preparation for heaven. Luther asserted instead that God freely justified and sanctified the individual Christian by his grace. The resultant life of good works and piety was an effect of gratitude over one's salvation vouchsafed in Christ, not a means of preparing for it. This view of salvation would effectively throw away the entire system of piety that included not only indulgences but pilgrimages, relics, and austerities that had become popular in the medieval church.

In 1521, Luther defended his views before the Diet (Parliament) of the Holy Roman Empire that met at Worms, a German city on the Rhine south of Mainz. The Diet condemned him and a permanent break was created between church authorities and reformers. Luther's speech before the Diet, reportedly concluding with the famous words, "Here I stand, I can do no other," can rightly be seen as the beginning of the Protestant Reformation.

Meanwhile, as Luther moved toward Worms, in the Swiss canton of Zürich a parallel development was occurring. In 1518, Ulrich Zwingli was selected as the main priest at the Grossmünster (Great Church). The people of Zürich, a German-speaking part of Switzerland, were quite aware of Luther's early activity, and Zwingli had independently come to the conclusion that church reform was needed. Shortly after his arrival in Zürich, he put his ideas on reform before the congregation in a series of sermons preached on the Gospel of Matthew. He called for a more simplified worship, which included the removal of a spectrum of items from the church buildings (including statues) for which he could find no biblical justification. He emphasized the sovereignty of God and the doctrine of election—the belief that God had chosen the elect to salvation even before the creation of the world. Most crucially, he followed Luther in limiting the sacraments to baptism and the Lord's supper. He then went far beyond Luther in denying the real presence of Christ in the Lord's supper and developed the view that it was merely a celebration and remembrance of Christ's death and resurrection. He did believe that during the meal Christ was spiritually present, not in the elements, but in the congregation, uniting the believers.

Zwingli initiated real reform in Zürich with his issuance of his own debating points, the 67 Theses, and convincing the city council of Zürich to hold a public debate in which the Bible would be the authority cited. The debate occurred on January 29, 1523. The council disallowed the arguments used by Catholic supporters that referenced the church's teachings and tradition. Zwingli was seen as the winner and the council gave him authority to pursue his proposed reforms. Among the first to be implemented was the discarding of the practice of priestly celibacy. Zwingli married in 1524. The next year, the Catholic mass was discontinued and replaced with a service of the Lord's supper as a memorial feast.

Through the 1520s, Zwingli's approach to reformation was established in the Swiss cantons. It found strong support in Berne and Basel. At the same time, he drew sharp criticism from Luther for his low-church approach to the Lord's supper. While denying transubstantiation, Luther held to a doctrine of the real presence of Christ. In 1529 Luther and Zwingli met at Marburg, Germany, and attempted to work out their differences. Their failure to reconcile their positions on the Lord's supper left the reform divided, with the Swiss by far the smaller camp.

While negotiations continued to resolve the problems with Luther, war broke out in Switzerland. In a relatively short time, the small Protestant force was defeated. Zwingli died as a result of wounds received at the second battle of Kappel, on October 11, 1531. His death ended the first phase of the Swiss Reformation. During the 1530s, attention shifted to French-speaking Geneva and a new leader, John Calvin.

Prior to Zwingli's death, he attracted a wide spectrum of followers, among whom was a small group that included former-monk Georg Blaurock and laymen Conrad Grebel and Felix Manz. Meeting together in 1524, the three concluded that the baptism of infants was nowhere justified in scripture. The baptism of infants had become the common practice in the Catholic Church and served as one means of integrating the next generation into the church and society, which were at the time co-terminus with each other. The three dissidents saw the logic of their opinion, that the church should include only baptized adults. However, a public discussion of the new ideas about baptism and the church were held in Zürich in January 1525, and the city council decided to continue as before. The rejection served to confirm the three in their opinion and, subsequent to the event, Blaurock had himself rebaptized. Then he in turn rebaptized Grebel, Manz, and the other members of the small group.

This act of rebaptism is generally seen as the date of the founding of the Anabaptist movement. Those baptized on this occasion immediately began to press their opinions among their neighbors. Their activities soon brought the authorities into the picture, and they were forced to flee. The desire of the authorities to apprehend them was only heightened by events in Germany later that year when one Thomas Müntzer gathered an army and attempted to radicalize the Reformation by force. Many died before his effort ended.

The fleeing of the Anabaptists from Zürich had the effect of spreading their perspective through Austria and Germany. Thus it was that in 1527 a group of Anabaptist leaders met at Schleitheim, Switzerland, to formulate a statement concerning their position. A need had arisen to defend themselves in the eyes of the authorities from identification with the violence of Müntzer as well as a strain of apocalypticism that had crept into the movement.

Those gathered at Schleitheim produced a short document, the "Brotherly Union of a Number of Children of God concerning Seven Articles." Generally termed the Schleitheim Confession, it spoke of baptism, the ban, the breaking of bread, separation, pastors, the sword, and taking an oath. It called upon the rather small Anabaptist community to affirm believer's baptism for adults only; advocated the banning of members of the fellowship who go astray; limited the sharing of the Lord's supper to those in the fellowship; advised separation from, among other things, "all popish and antipopish works and church services, meetings and church attendance, drinking houses, civic affairs, the commitments [made in] unbelief"; declared that pastors had to be men of good report; moved toward pacifism in noting that the Christian should not take up the sword (or the office of magistrate); and concluded by calling upon Christians to refrain from swearing an oath, even in legal matters.

In spite of the circulation of the Schleitheim Confession, Anabaptists were identified with apocalyptic notions and violence through the 1530s, especially after the events at Munster, Germany, where some reformers attempted to establish a commune into which a number of radical and even bizarre ideas were introduced. The experiment was finally ended by a Catholic force laying siege to the town. Across Europe, both Protestant and Catholic authorities arrested, tortured, imprisoned, and executed Anabaptist leaders. Threatened with complete annihilation, the Anabaptists were saved by the emergence of a new leader, former Roman Catholic priest Menno

Simons. Working primarily in the Low Countries and Germany, Simons called together the scattered Anabaptist communities, found a haven from the persecution for them, and argued effectively for their cause. They would eventually take his name, the one by which they are still known, Mennonite.

As Menno Simons appeared on the stage of history, back in Switzerland, the Reformation was in some disorder following the death of Zwingli. However, William Farel had convinced an influential majority to move Geneva into the Reformation camp. He saw in John Calvin, who had recently arrived in the city from France, the leader who could carry out the reform he envisioned. After a rocky start, in 1541 Calvin was installed in office in Geneva ready to make the city the center of the Reformed faith he had defined in his *Institutes of the Christian Religion,* the basic document of what would become the Reformed church.

As the Reformation spread across Europe, its ideas spread to but received little support in England. The country's ruler, King Henry VIII, had a cordial relationship with Rome and had written a book attacking Luther, for which he had been awarded the title "Defender of the Faith" by the pope. He had no issues with Catholic thought or worship, and no plans to become a Protestant. However, he had another problem. As the ruler of England, he saw among his primary duties the production of a male heir to assume the throne when he died. But Catherine of Aragon, his wife, had mothered only one child, Mary, a female. He sought a means of acquiring another wife who would be more fertile.

He turned to his ecclesiastical advisor, Thomas Wolsey. When he failed, Henry pushed him aside and found two new advisors who could find a way. Listening to Thomas Cranmer and Thomas Cromwell eased Henry down a slippery slope that led to his break with the papacy, administratively if not ideologically. He put Catherine aside, married Anne Boleyn, and when she failed to have a male child, had her executed. He finally married Jane Seymour, who in 1537 gave birth to Edward VI.

By 1537, Henry had taken a number of steps that forced a separation of England from Rome. During this time, both of his main advisors had become Protestants, a fact that became evident in 1539 when Cranmer published a Protestant manifesto, the "Ten Articles." As archbishop of Canterbury, he had already begun to institute reforms. Henry opposed the "Ten Articles," but did not move against Cranmer, who remained in office through the remainder of Henry's reign. The reformation Cranmer had come to envision really begins with the accession of Edward to the throne in 1547. Then, during the reign of Edward's sister and successor Elizabeth, a new form of the Christian faith arose. By the end of the sixteenth century, the Church of England had carved out a distinct niche for itself, not quite Protestant, but certainly no longer Catholic.

At the end of the sixteenth century, Europe looked considerably different in its religious life than it had at the beginning. The visible unity of the religious community had been destroyed and in its place Lutheran, Reformed, and Anglican establishments had arisen in different countries, and the Mennonites were filling in the small spaces that existed on the margins. Over the next centuries, all found their way to the New World, and all became the basis of a worldwide communion of like-minded churches.

G. Lutheran Churches

In the several decades following the beginning of the Luther Reformation, the various German states had to choose between Lutheran Protestantism and Catholicism. Through the 1530s, the Scandinavian countries aligned themselves with the Protestant cause, and Lutheran ideas found support in the Baltic states. Much of the rest of the century was spent attempting to reconcile the reform demands within a Catholic consensus, war, and temporary peace treaties. The Augsburg Confession, largely shaped by Luther's colleague at Wittenberg, Philip Melancthon, was an attempt to affirm Lutheran allegiance to the Christian essentials and find a basic agreement with the church. When that effort failed, Lutherans became more assertive of their distinctives.

A crucial agreement was reached in 1555 with the Peace of Augsburg. The rulers of the German states agreed that each one could choose the religion of his own land. Admittedly somewhat limited, it nevertheless provided an initial legal recognition of Protestantism, though the Reformed church was not included in such recognition until 1648. The peace gave Lutherans some breathing space to consolidate their gains.

In the generation after the death of Luther and Melancthon, some disagreements arose on interpreting the Augsburg Confession. A consensus on these matters was handled in the Formula of Concord promulgated in 1577. Three years later a collection of confessional documents seen as defining Lutheranism were compiled in the *Book of Concord.* It contains three ancient creeds (the Apostles' Creed, the Athanasian Creed, and the Nicene Creed) and six items written in the sixteenth century (the Augsburg Confession, the Apology of the Augsburg Confession, the Schmalkald Articles, Luther's

Larger and Smaller Catechisms, and the Formula of Concord). There is also an appended optional collection of early church material. While the Augsburg Confession continued to be the most authoritative statement of Lutheran faith, the *Book of Concord* has served as a primary sourcebook defining Lutheran orthodoxy.

In Germany, as the country united, the Protestant areas consolidated into 24 states. In each state a Protestant (Evangelical) church was organized. In most of these states, the Protestant church was Lutheran. In one, Lippe, it was Reformed. Unique was Prussia, where the state church was Lutheran, but a tolerance of the Reformed church had led to the founding of many Reformed congregations. The two churches mixed in a rather friendly way through the seventeenth century, and in 1817 the king of Prussia ordered the two churches to unite in a single Evangelical Church, a union that had interesting consequences in the United States.

In America

Lutherans first arrived in what is now the United States from Sweden, an artifact of a Swedish attempt to colonize the Atlantic seaboard. Fort Christina (now Wilmington, Delaware) was founded in 1638. Later in the century, German Lutherans responded to William Penn's appeal for colonists to build Pennsylvania immediately to the north of the Swedish fort. Other Germans settled in Georgia in the 1730s. In 1742 Henry Melchior Muhlenberg arrived in America with the task of organizing the scattered congregations. Six years later he founded the Ministerium of Pennsylvania. One additional synod, the Ministerium of New York, was formed prior to the American Revolution. Then, through the first half of the nineteenth century, more than a hundred synods were founded across the expanding country.

The Lutheran synods, frequently with overlapping boundaries, were a result of immigration from the different countries of Europe. Synods followed linguistic boundaries—German, Swedish, Norwegian, Danish, Finnish, Slovakian, etc. During the last half of the century, synods began to merge with those who spoke the same language, while at the same time their members were learning English. World War I became a major impetus to adopt English.

Through the nineteenth century, Lutherans also realigned themselves theologically. Samuel S. Schmucker, the leading American Lutheran theologian, became known for his emphasis on piety and religious experience over a rigid doctrinal conformity. Schmucker was opposed by the likes of his student, Charles Porterfield Krauth, who championed what became known as confessional Lutheranism. Krauth advocated a strict adherence to the doctrines articulated in the Augsburg Confession and more generally the *Book of Concord.* As synods consolidated, they tended to align with one emphasis or the other.

Possibly the most important center of confessional Lutheranism was established in Missouri in the 1830s by immigrants from Prussia who rejected the Lutheran/Reformed union forced upon Protestants in 1817. They formed the Missouri Synod (and additional synods with which they would later merge). An even more conservative body, the Wisconsin Evangelical Lutheran Church, was founded by German immigrants in the upper Midwest.

Even as migration from predominately Lutheran countries grew in the late nineteenth century, a move to bring the many relatively small synods into larger church bodies began. The first mergers occurred along linguistic lines and saw the establishment of churches like the United Evangelical Lutheran Church (a Danish body), the Evangelical Lutheran Church (Norwegian), and the Augustana Synod (Swedish). The largest number of Lutherans were of German background and formed a number of different bodies. By 1920 almost all of the Lutheran groups had adopted English as their primary language, and future mergers tended to be along theological lines rather than linguistic or ethnic. The twentieth century saw the formation of new united Lutheran churches.

The largest number of Lutherans in America were involved in one of the two major church unions which led to the formation in 1960 of the American Lutheran Church (ALC) and in 1962 of the Lutheran Church in America. Both tended to identify with the Schmucker lineage of American Lutheranism, but the ALC was seen as slightly more conservative. These two churches merged in 1988 to form the Evangelical Lutheran Church in America (ELCA), the largest Lutheran body in the country. They were joined in that merger by a much smaller body, the Association of Evangelical Lutheran Churches, which had been formed by a group of more liberal leaders who had left the Missouri Synod in the 1970s.

Meanwhile, as American Lutherans were finding their way into union, the original home of Lutheranism was devastated by the rise of Nazism and World War II. Out of that war Lutherans worldwide came together in the Lutheran World Federation, initially to rebuild those countries ravaged by the war, but later to participate in a variety of cooperative activities around the globe. While a variety of American Lutheran groups initially participated in the LWF, all of the American groups eventually came together in the ELCA, which is today the only American Lutheran body that is a member of the LWF.

While the Wisconsin Synod has tended to remain aloof from any ecumenical contacts, the Missouri Synod was an active party in bringing together confessional Lutherans around the world in the 1960s. They engaged in a lengthy process that eventuated in the 1990s in the formal organization of the International Lutheran Council.

Contemporary American Lutheranism is dominated by the three large church bodies; the Evangelical Lutheran Church in America, with slightly more than five million members, the Lutheran Church—Missouri Synod, with about 2.5 million, and the Wisconsin Synod, with approximately a half-million members. These three churches all adhere to the Lutheran theological heritage and affirm the Augsburg Confession as their doctrinal standard. They can, however, be distinguished by the level of strictness in doctrinal conformity they demand of pastor and members. There are a number of other Lutheran bodies, most on the more conservative end of the theological spectrum, but all are relatively small. Many of these churches were founded in the twentieth century, formed by those who rejected one of the post-World War II Lutheran mergers. Others continue ethnic-based fellowships.

Today all Lutherans are characterized by their double emphasis upon Word and Sacrament, that is to biblical authority and preaching coupled with the celebration of the liturgy and the sacrament of the Lord's supper. Their understanding of the sacrament separates them from the Reformed churches.

The ELCA has emerged as a major participant with other Protestant churches in the ecumenical movement. They are members of the National Council of Churches in the U.S.A.

and the World Council of Churches. The Lutheran World Federation has its headquarters in the same building that houses the World Council of Churches. The Missouri Synod develops working relationships only with other confessional Lutheran churches, and generally considers the contemporary Evangelical movement as doctrinally suspect (deriving, as it does, largely from the Reformed tradition). It also is not welcoming to Pentecostalism.

Common to Lutherans is an emphasis on education. They have formed a number of colleges for the training of lay leadership and seminaries for the training of ministers. This heritage has placed them at the center in ecumenical theological discussion, in which their representatives tend to excel.

Contacts:

Evangelical Lutheran Church in America (1988)
8765 W. Higgins Rd.
Chicago, IL 60631
www.elca.org

Formally created in 1988, the formation of the ELCA culminated a process by which more than twenty synods that existed in the late nineteenth century merged into a single communion.

Lutheran Church—Missouri Synod
1333 S. Kirkwood Rd.
St. Louis, MO 63122
www.lcms.org

The major representative of confessional Lutheranism, the Missouri Synod was formally established in 1847.

Wisconsin Evangelical Lutheran Synod
c/o President of the Synod
2929 North Mayfair Rd.
Wauwatosa, WI 53222
www.wels.net

The Wisconsin Synod, founded in 1850, is considered the most conservative of America's major Lutheran bodies.

Additional Lutheran Churches

American Association of Lutheran Churches
801 W. 106th St., Ste. 203
Minneapolis, MN 55420-5603
www.taalc.org

Apostolic Lutheran Church of America
RR 1
Bentley, AB
Canada T0C 0J0
www.apostolic-lutheran.org

The Apostolic Lutherans primarily serve believers who trace their heritage to Lapland and a nineteenth-century pietist movement in the Lutheran Church led by Lars Levi Laestadius (1800–1861).

Association of Free Lutheran Congregations
3110 E. Medicine Lake Blvd.
Minneapolis, MN 55441
www.aflc.org

The association was formed in 1963 by conservative members of the Lutheran Free Church who did not wish to follow that church's merger into the American Lutheran Church (now an integral part of the Evangelical Lutheran Church in America).

Church of the Lutheran Brethren of America
1007 Westside Dr.
Box 655
Fergus Falls, MN 56537
www.clba.org

The church was formed in 1900 by several congregations in the Midwest who had roots in the Lutheran Free Church of Norway.

Church of the Lutheran Confession
501 Grover Road
Eau Claire, WI 54701
www.clclutheran.org

The Church of the Lutheran Confession was formed in 1960 by conservative congregations whose former denominations had participated in the Synodical Conference (an ecumenical body that existed from 1872 until the early 1960s). These denominations moved into the mergers that produced the American Lutheran Church (1960) and the Lutheran Church in America (1962).

Estonian Evangelical Lutheran Church
c/o Abp. Udo Peterson
383 Jarvis St.
Toronto, ON
Canada M5B 2C7
www.elca.org/countrypackets/estonia/church.html

This relatively small body was formed by exiles fleeing the Soviet takeover of Estonia during World War II. Originally formed in Sweden, it spread to North America with the movement of members in subsequent decades.

Evangelical Lutheran Synod
6 Browns Ct.
Mankato, MN 56001
www.evangelicallutheransynod.org

The synod was formed by some conservative pastors and lay people of Norwegian heritage who refrained from joining the mergers early in the twentieth century of the several regional Norwegian Lutheran synods looking to create a national Norwegian American Lutheran Church.

Laestadian Lutheran Church
10911 Highway 55, Ste. 203
Plymouth, MN 55441-6114
www.laestadianlutheran.org

The church is one of several churches rooted in the work of Finnish evangelist-pastor Lars Levi Laestadius (1800–1860).

Latvian Evangelical Lutheran Church in America
2140 Orkla Dr.
Golden Valley, MN 55427-3432

The church was formed by Latvian exiles following the takeover of their country by the Soviet Union during World War II.

Lutheran Churches of Calvary Grace
3531 S. Logan St., #D-239
Englewood, CO 80113-3700
thelutheran.net/open/in.htm

The Lutheran churches of Calvary Grace began as a set of missionary churches established by Dr. Roger Eyman in various foreign countries and in the United States among Native Americans in Arizona and Alaska. Today the church unites work in the United States, Canada, Singapore, Indonesia, and Malaysia.

Lutheran Churches of the Reformation
c/o Council Administrator
Pastor Kenneth K. Miller
4014 Wenonah Lane
Fort Wayne, IN 46809
www.lcrusa.org

The LCR was formed in 1964 in protest of liberal themes believed to be creeping into the Lutheran Church—Missouri Synod.

For further reading:

Bachman, E. Theodore, and Mercia Brenne Bachman. *Lutheran Churches in the World: A Handbook.* Minneapolis: Augsburg Press, 1989.

Bodensieck, Julius, ed. *The Encyclopedia of the Lutheran Church.* 3 vols. Minneapolis: Augsburg Publishing House, 1965.

Gassmann, Günther, with Duane H. Larson and Mark W. Oldenburg. *Historical Dictionary of Lutheranism.* Metuchen, N.J.: Scarecrow Press, 2001.

Luther, Martin. *Works.* Edited by Jaroslav Pelikan and Helmut T. Lehman. 55 vols. St. Louis: Concordia Publishing House/ Philadelphia: Fortress Press, 1958-67.

Mildenberger, Friedrich. *Theology of the Lutheran Confessions.* Philadelphia: Fortress Press, 1986.

Nelson, E. Clifford. *The Rise of World Lutheranism.* Philadelphia: Fortress Press, 1982.

Nichol, Todd W. *All These Lutherans.* Minneapolis: Augsburg Publishing House, 1986.

Schwarz, Hans. *True Faith in the True God: An Introduction to Luther's Life and Thought.* Trans. by Mark Williams Worthing. Minneapolis: Augsburg Publishers, 1996.

Stauffer, S. Anita, Gilbert A. Doan, and Michael B. Aune. *Lutherans at Worship.* Minneapolis: Augsburg Publishing House, 1978.

Weideraenders, Robert C., and Walter G. Tillmanns. *The Synods of American Lutheranism.* n.p.: Lutheran Historical Conference, 1968.

H. Reformed Churches

The Reformed churches trace a common history to the thought and ministry of John Calvin (1509–1564) and the Protestant Reformation of the sixteenth century. John Calvin, a Frenchman, assumed a leadership position among French-speaking Protestants following the publication of his watershed theological text, the *Institutes of the Christian Religion* (1536), and then took control of the Protestant cause in the Canton of Geneva in Switzerland, first for two years (1536–38) and then more permanently in 1541.

[Note: **Presbyterian Churches** are treated separately in the next chapter. While they certainly date to the Protestant Reformation in Scotland, they had their definitive development as the center of the Puritan movement in the seventeenth century.]

The *Institutes* laid out a Reformed theology and a presbyterian ecclesial organization. Theologically, Calvin was close to Luther, the primary disagreement concerning the nature of Christ's presence in the sacrament. In fact, Calvin's view of the sacrament can be seen as an effort to mediate the disagreement between Luther's affirmation of Christ's real presence in the sacrament and Zwingli's emphasis on getting rid of the magical elements that he felt had crept into the Catholic mass. In contrast to Zwingli's view of the Lord's supper as a memorial meal, Calvin affirmed Christ's real presence, but in keeping with Zwingli's concerns about magic, he suggested that the presence was purely spiritual (not substantial or working a change in the elements), and to be apprehended through faith. Unfortunately, by the time Calvin arrived on the scene, the Lutheran position had been hardened, the Augsburg Confession published, and Calvin's solution was never really considered by Luther and his closest associates.

Calvin's solution might not have been accepted even if proposed in the 1520s. Underlying his approach to the sacraments was a more secular worldview. It included Zwingli's very different stance toward reform. Lutherans tended to keep as much of traditional Western Christian practice as possible—all that was determined not to be in opposition to the Bible. The Reformed tended to discard anything that was not actually biblical. This more radical approach manifested itself most forcefully in the appearance of Reformed church buildings that were much more austere than their Lutheran counterparts.

Calvin's reformation found its first support outside of Geneva in the other cantons of Switzerland, but then came to dominate Protestantism in the French-speaking countries, spreading into France and the Low Countries. Once accepted in the German-speaking Swiss cantons, it found a home among German-speaking groups in Austria and Germany and lands to the east (as the Hapsburg family holdings expanded). It became established in Scotland and largely pushed Lutheranism aside in England.

In the generation after Calvin's death, the most definitive events in the life of the Reformed church occurred in the Netherlands, where the Reformed church became closely identified with the struggle for independence against Spain. In the Netherlands a major controversy developed around the understanding of predestination, an idea affirmed by Luther but emphasized by Calvin. At the beginning of the seventeenth century, a Dutch theologian offered a slightly different view of predestination that left a small but significant role for human response to God's grace. Whereas Calvinists had tended to affirm that God's will logically preceded his foreknowledge, Jacob Arminius suggested that God's foreknowledge came first (Rom. 8: 28-31). The argument affected a number of assumptions about the working of God's grace and the understanding of human nature. For example, Arminius said that humans were not totally depraved by sin, but only partially depraved. They retained enough of their original creation in the image of God as to be able to respond to the gospel.

The majority of the Reformed church leadership rejected Arminius' view and in 1618–19 held a council, the Synod of

Dordrecht, at which it condemned five positions attributed to Arminius (who had died in 1609) and his colleagues. The council affirmed what became known as the five canons of the Synod of Dort, namely that: (1) Christ died only for those elected to salvation; (2) predestination and election to salvation constituted an act of God's sovereign will (rather than being the natural result of his foreknowledge); (3) God's grace given to an individual is irresistible; (4) humans were so depraved that they could do nothing for their own salvation; and (5) God's elect will persevere to the end. In English, the affirmations of the Synod were presented in a shorthand fashion that recalled the Netherlands' identification with its national flower:

Total depravity
Unconditional election
Limited atonement
Irresistible grace
Perseverance of the saints

The canons of the Synod of Dort fit within a Reformed tradition of issuing statements of belief as a major act of confessing their faith. Through the sixteenth and seventeenth century, a set of such confessions were published, and all Reformed churches used one of these documents as their basic doctrinal standard. For Reformed churches, the most important of these confessions are the Gallican (1559), Belgic (1561), and Second Helvetic (1566). To these was added the Heidelberg Catechism (1563). Doctrinally, the three sixteenth-century confessions, the Heidelberg Catechism, and the canons of Dort defined the Reformed tradition. The centrality of these documents reflects the importance placed upon a theologically trained leadership within the Reformed church—an emphasis that carried over into the Presbyterian and Congregational churches that became so important for America in future centuries.

In America

The several churches that bear the name Reformed and are active in the United States today come primarily from Holland. The first Reformed church in what is now the United States was organized in 1628 in the New Amsterdam (now New York) colony by the Rev. Jacob Michaelius. That church, the Marble Collegiate Reformed Church, has the distinction of being the oldest continuously existing Protestant congregation in the country. The Dutch Reformed movement spread through the next centuries, and the American Revolution became the catalyst for its formal organization into what is now the Reformed Church in America (RCA).

The RCA received a boost in the 1840s when a new wave of immigrants arrived from Holland, many representative of a secessionist movement from the Reformed Church in the Netherlands that grew out of problems over the church's relationship to the Dutch government. The new immigrants settled in Michigan and aligned with the Reformed Church in America as its Classis Holland. All was well for a decade, but then some within Classis Holland began to accuse the RCA of being too lenient on doctrinal standards. As a result, some left Classis Holland and formed a separate organization, which in 1904 adopted the name Christian Reformed Church (CRC).

Through the twentieth century, the two larger Reformed churches went in quite separate directions. The RCA found common cause with the other large Protestant churches, became part of the ecumenical movement, and emerged as a member of the liberal Protestant establishment. Its ecumenical connections include the World Alliance of Reformed Churches, the World Council of Churches, and the National Council of the Churches of Christ in the U.S.A.

The CRC, on the other hand, continued a traditional conservative Reformed perspective that led it to reach out to similar churches and take the lead in the formation of the Reformed Ecumenical Council. It also became the site of a significant theological battle over the issue of what was called Common Grace. Those who represent the minority position withdrew and founded the Protestant Reformed Church in America. Some Korean members withdrew in 1991 after the CRC decided to welcome females to the ordained ministry. Both the RCA and the CRC have approximately 300,000 members.

Additional Reformed churches have been founded by immigrants who arrived at different times from Holland and other European countries. Among the most interesting are those of German Reformed background who moved toward Congregationalism and will be discussed in the next chapter. French Reformed congregations formed, but were absorbed by various Presbyterian bodies. A small Hungarian Reformed Church survives to the present.

Contacts:

Christian Reformed Church in North America
2850 Kalamazoo Ave. SE
Grand Rapids, MI 49560
www.crcna.org

Though tracing their roots to a disturbance in the Reformed Church of the Netherlands in the 1830s, the CRC was officially organized in the late1850s by members of the Reformed Church in America who withdrew over what were deemed irregularities in its beliefs and practices.

Reformed Church in America
475 Riverside Dr., Rm. 1811
New York, NY 10115
www.rca.org

The Reformed Church in America continues the Reformed church established in the Dutch colony of New Amsterdam (now New York) in the 1600s.

Additional Reformed Churches

Canadian and American Reformed Churches
Box 62053
Burlington, ON L7R 4K2
Canada
www.canrc.org

The Canadian and American Reformed Churches was formed in 1950 in Canada by conservative Reformed believers.

Christian Presbyterian Church (Korean)
4741 N. Glen Arden Ave.
Covina, CA 91724

The Christian Presbyterian Church (Korean) was founded in 1992 by Korean-American members of the Christian Reformed Church who opposed the ordination of females.

Federation of Reformed Churches
P.O. Box 1156
Williamsville, NY 14231-1156
www.federationorc.org

The federation was formed by a group of independent Evangelicals in 1997 to counter a perceived trend of movement away from scriptural standards.

Free Reformed Churches of North America
c/o Reverend P. Vander Mayden
950 Ball Ave., NE
Grand Rapids, MI 49503
www.frcna.org

The Free Reformed Church was formed in the 1950s by former members of the Christian Reformed Church who believed that the CRC had departed from its original doctrine and practice.

Heritage Netherlands Reformed Congregations
c/o Dr. Joel Beeke
540 Crescent St., NE
Grand Rapids, MI 49503
hnrc.org

The Heritage Netherlands Reformed Congregations resulted from a 1993 split in the Netherlands Reformed Congregations (see below).

Hungarian Reformed Church in America
c/o Bishop Andor Demeter
3921 W. Christy Dr.
Phoenix, AZ 85029
www.hrca.us

Netherlands Reformed Congregations
1255 Covell Rd., NW
Grand Rapids, MI 49504

The Netherlands Reformed Congregations were formed in 1907 by the affiliation of two independent Reformed congregations that had shared roots in an 1834 split in the state-supported Reformed Church in the Netherlands.

Orthodox Christian Reformed Church
For Information:
778 North Burlington Blvd.
Burlington, WA 98233
reformed.net/ocrc/index.shtml

The Orthodox CRC was formed in the early 1980s by congregations that had at various times left the Christian Reformed Church of North America.

Protestant Reformed Churches in America
4949 Ivanrest Ave.
Grandville, MI 49418
www.iserv.net/~prc

The Protestant Reformed Church formed in 1924 as a result of a doctrinal controversy over "common grace," a belief that had recently been accepted by the Christian Reformed Church.

Reformed Church in the United States
P.O. Box 486
Eureka, SD 57437
www.rcus.org/

In 1934, the Reformed Church in the United States, a body of German heritage, merged with the Evangelical Church to form the Evangelical and Reformed Church (now a part of the United Church of Christ). One classis (synod) refrained from participating in the merger and continues today as the Reformed Church in the United States.

United Reformed Churches of North America
c/o Mr. Bill Konynenbelt, Stated Clerk
5824 Bowwater Cr. NW
Calgary, AB T3B 2E2
Canada
www.covenant-urc.org/urchrchs.html

The United Reformed Churches grew out of dissention within the Christian Reformed Church at the end of the 1980s. As congregations disaffiliated, they began to meet initially as the Alliance of Reformed Churches, which matured into the URCNA in 1995.

For further reading:

Bauswein, Jean-Jacques, and Lukas Vischner, eds. *The Reformed Family Worldwide: A Survey of Reformed Churches, Theological Schools, and International Organizations.* Grand Rapids: William B. Eerdmans Publishing Company, 1999.

Calvin, John. *Institutes of the Christian Religion.* 2 vols. Philadelphia: Westminster Press, 1960. Various editions.

Cochrane, Arthur C., ed. *The Reformed Confessions of the Sixteenth Century.* Philadelphia: Westminster Press, 1966.

Leith, John H. *An Introduction to the Reformed Tradition.* Atlanta: John Knox Press, 1977.

Nichols, James Hastings. *Corporate Worship in the Reformed Tradition.* Philadelphia: Westminster Press, 1968.

I. Mennonite Churches

The Mennonite movement emerged in the 1540s as the more moderate and theologically sophisticated branch to the Anabaptist movement that had begun in Switzerland two decades earlier. The Anabaptists can be, and often are seen as presenting a fourth option beside the perspectives offered by Zwingli, Luther, and Calvin. They can thus be seen as picking up the Reformation's (particularly Zwingli's) ideas on biblical authority and the nature of the sacraments and pushing them to a logical conclusion. While much insight is gained with following that perspective, Anabaptists are best understood as presenting to Christians of the sixteenth century a radically different way of looking at themselves. They presented not just another theological variation, but a very different way of thinking about living the Christian life.

The Anabaptists suggested that the first-generation reformers had not gone far enough in questioning the Catholic Church. The primary reformers maintained the assumption that the church was and should be co-terminus with the society and that society should think of everyone as basically a Christian. In their examination of the Bible, Anabaptists saw no such church-state relationship. Rather, they saw a community that existed as an entity within a larger society that accepted into itself those who professed faith in Christ. Such a church stood over against the society's authorities. They also saw no precedent for baptizing children or infants or considering them church members.

The Anabaptists used the picture of the biblical church to critique what they saw existing around them. The biblical church, they claimed, would be exclusive—consisting only of those adults who had experienced salvation and were received into the church by baptism. Members of that church would distance themselves from the ruling authorities and would not participate in the governance of the world. They would not bear arms, swear an oath in legal proceedings, nor use secular authorities to back up decisions by church leaders. The church would discipline its own members for ecclesiastical infractions, its power being limited to disfellowshipping erring members.

Such a vision of Christianity and church life challenged both Catholics and Reformers who had no difficulty perceiving what the adoption of the Anabaptist vision would mean. Thus, even though the Anabaptists and Reformers shared most traditional Christian affirmations, the Reformers understood the threat. The Anabaptists were undercutting all of the structures of the stable Christian society that had been created over the previous centuries, and Protestants made common cause with Catholics against them. Hence the importance of Menno Simons.

Through the 1540s and 1550s, the former priest and Anabaptist convert Menno Simons articulated a centrist position that took away as many of the clubs being used against his fellow believers as possible. He pushed aside the apocalypticism of a few teachers and the overly mystical and doctrinally suspect teachings of others. He rallied the scattered and beleaguered Anabaptist faithful and found havens for them to survive the most difficult years. His guidance provided a pathway for them to survive until a few countries, for a variety of very different reasons, provided a place where Mennonites could live openly. By this time, most of the competing Anabaptist groups had disappeared.

In 1632, Mennonites in Holland, meeting in the same town where the Reformed leaders had met to discuss their response to Arminianism, published the Dordtrecht Confession. Building on the earlier Schleitheim Confession, the new statement covered key theological points in a more systematic manner. While affirming faith in a Triune God and salvation in Christ, it also outlined Mennonite distinctives such as the definition of the visible church, which consists of those who have been baptized and incorporated into the communion of saints on earth. It defined Christians as those who are obedient through faith and who follow the precepts of the New Testament. Baptism is for repentant adult believers. The church observes the Lord's Supper and the washing of the feet as ordinances (not sacraments).

By the middle of the seventeenth century, the major issue threatening the Mennonite community had shifted. Most no longer believed that they were destroying society. However, government leaders were most intolerant of their pacifism and refusal to serve in an army. In peaceful times, countries provided a haven for Mennonites to live, but those countries often turned against them when they failed to provide soldiers for the next war. The right to avoid serving in combat led a number of Mennonites to make the trek all the way to Russia, where they were able to live and even thrive for several centuries.

In America

The first Mennonites appear in America in the 1640s, but it was four decades later before the first congregation was organized. The founding of that congregation in Germantown (now a section of Philadelphia), Pennsylvania, is generally accepted as the beginning of the movement's American history. The group did not collect in the seaboard cities, however. Basically farmers, they spread to claim the relatively cheap farmland to the west.

The community grew quietly for a century, but reached an initial crisis when they were asked to choose sides during the American Revolution. One leader, Christian Funk, argued that the community should throw their support behind the Continental Congress, and since they could not fight, manifest that support by paying the war tax. The majority rejected his position, suggesting that any visible support of the congress would involve them in war. They excommunicated Funk, and with his supporters he organized the first dissident Mennonite Church.

Meanwhile, in Europe an even more important division was in the making. One Jacob Amman, a minister in Switzerland, called for a new emphasis on church discipline. He stressed the practice of avoidance of those the church placed under the ban, meaning that a member was to neither eat nor sleep with a person undergoing church discipline, even if s/he was a family member or spouse. Amman also emphasized the member's need to avoid worldliness. Those attracted to his teachings soon came to be identified by a distinctive dress. Men wore broad brim hats and coats and pants without buttons. They grew beards without mustaches. Women wore their hair in a bun under bonnets and aprons over their ankle-length dresses. The number of distinctives multiplied as new innovations in the larger culture were one by one rejected.

Through the eighteenth and nineteenth centuries, there was a continued immigration of Mennonites to North America. Most of these immigrants came from Western Europe. Then in 1870, the Russian czar moved to integrate the Mennonite colonies in Russia into the mainstream of Russian life. As a major point in his program, the czar insisted on replacing German with Russian in the Mennonite schools and colonies and the dropping of exemptions for Mennonites from military service. The Mennonite leaders saw this program as a threat to their very existence and began to plan immigration to North America. The thousands of Mennonites who came into the country settled in the middle of the continent from Oklahoma to Ontario, with the majority settling in Kansas.

Through the nineteenth century, the Mennonites slowly spread across America. They were an agricultural people who sought to live a simple, unassuming life. While they occasionally were beset by neighbors who resented their pacifism in times of war (the Civil War era being an especially troublesome time), as a whole, the greater problems emerged as they attempted to adjust to cultural changes. Their early refusal to adjust their clothing to new styles marked them as a separate group, the "plain people."

Slowly, the main body of Mennonites adapted to the changing world and adopted more sophisticated ways of distinguishing the biblical principles to which they were committed from those cultural artifacts that offered only to keep them attached to the seventeenth century. By the end of the nineteenth century, the real challenges came from the developing technology that made traditional farming uncompetitive and modern inventions (such as indoor plumbing) designed to made daily existence more comfortable. At various points, divisions occurred over the propriety of adopting such things as contemporary clothing, automobiles, or improved farm equipment.

While government pressure to participate in war occasionally reappeared, the rise of public schools and a growing body of law on the education of children also affected the Mennonites (and Amish). Those laws raised issues of the use of German versus English, the number of years of education (the Amish saw no need of high school), and the subject matters to be taught. The pressure to adopt English in order to conduct business also eventually led to changes in church services, where worship (including the hymns and sermons) were in German.

At the same time, Mennonites came into contact with the larger Christian community. They found themselves pulled on every side by Christian neighbors who wished to involve Mennonites in everything from the peace movements to ecumenical cooperation to Sunday schools. Revivalism and fundamentalism found a home in some quarters.

Given the relatively free atmosphere in the United States, and the large number of issues that were continually pressing upon the Mennonites as they attempted to define themselves as a people apart, it is not surprising that the movement splintered into a number of separate factions. Given the relatively small size of the total Mennonite community (which numbers only several hundred thousand), it is the most splintered segment of American Christianity.

The two groups that made the most concerted effort to accommodate to the culture while affirming their Mennonite heritage became the largest Mennonite bodies—the Mennonite Church and the General Conference Mennonite Church. In 1995, these two churches merged to form the Mennonite Church USA. With about 150,000 members, the new church includes about half of the total Mennonite-Amish community. As part of the merger process, both groups approved a new statement of belief, the "Confession of Faith in a Mennonite Perspective," which restates and reaffirms the Mennonite/Anabaptist distinctives.

The Old Order Amish Mennonite Church, the main Amish body, has about 60,000 members. With few exceptions, most of the additional Mennonite denominations have fewer than 10,000 members.

Contacts:

Mennonite Church USA
Great Lakes Office:
500 S. Main St.
P.O. Box 1245
Elkhart, IN 46515-1245

Great Plains Office:
722 Main St.
P.O. Box 347
Newton, KS 67114-0347
www.mennoniteusa.org

The Mennonite Church USA was formed in 1995 by the merger of the Mennonite Church and the General Conference Mennonite Church, two of the larger and more liberal of the Mennonite bodies.

Old Order Amish Mennonite Church
No central address. For information:
c/o *The Dairy*
P.O. Box 98
Gordonville, PA 17529.

The Old Order Amish continue the history of the first Amish migrants to America and are the largest of the several presently existing Amish groups.

Additional Mennonite groups

Alliance of Mennonite Evangelical Congregations
Box 97
Paradise, PA 17562
www.aemc2000.org/main/home.html

The alliance emerged in stages in the mid 1990s among conservative Mennonites who rejected the merger that produced the Mennonite Church USA.

Church of God in Christ, Mennonite
420 N. Wedel
Mountridge, KS 67107

The Church of God in Christ grew out of the religious awakening experienced by John Holdeman (1832–1900) in the mid-nineteenth century.

Congregational Bible Church
1185 River Rd.
P.O. Box 180
Marietta, PA 17547
www.cbcpa.org

The Congregational Bible Church was formed in 1951 by several congregations previously affiliated with the Mennonite Church.

Conservative Mennonite Fellowship (Non-Conference)
Box 36
Hartville, OH 44632

The fellowship resulted from a protest against previous accomodation of steps to American culture by the larger Mennonite Church in the 1950s.

Fellowship of Evangelical Bible Churches
5800 S. 14th St.
Omaha, NE 68107-3584
www.febcministries.org

The fellowship resulted from an 1889 merger of two Mennonite groups, one founded by Isaac Peters (1826–1911) and the other by Aaron Wall (1835–1905).

Mennonite Brethren Church of North America (Bruedergemeinde)
315 S. Lincoln
P.O. Box V
Hillsboro, KS 67063-0155

The Mennonite Brethren are the result of a revivalist movement among Russian Mennonites in the mid-nineteenth century. Members began to arrive in America in the 1870s.

Amish groups

Beachy Amish Mennonite Churches
9650 Iams Rd.
Plain City, OH 43064

Among the most liberal of the Amish, the Beachy Amish meet in churches, allow members to drive automobiles, and even use electricity.

Conservative Mennonite Conference
9910 Rosedale-Milford Center Rd.
Irwin, OH 43029
www.cmcrosedale.org

The Conservative Mennonite Conference was formed in 1910 by Amish Mennonites who rejected the organizational developments occurring within the Old Order Amish Mennonite Church.

Evangelical Mennonite Church
1420 Kerrway Court
Fort Wayne, IN 46805

The Evangelical Mennonite Church was formed by Henry Egly (1824–1890), an Amish bishop, and others who had been deeply affected by American revivalism.

For further reading:

The Complete Writings of Menno Simons, 1491-1561. Scottsdale, Penn.: Herald Press, 1956.

Dyck, Cornelius J. *An Introduction to Mennonite History.* Scottsdale, Penn.: Herald Press, 1967.

Kauffman, J. Howard, and Leland Harder. *Anabaptists Four Centuries Later: A profile of five Mennonite and Brethren in Christ denominations.* Scottsdale, Penn.: Herald Press, 1975.

The Mennonite Encyclopedia. 5 vols. Scottsdale, Penn.: Herald Press, 1955-59.

Mennonite World Handbook: Mennonites in Global Mission. Carol Stream, Ill.: Mennonite World Council, 1990.

Snyder, C. Arnold. *Anabaptist History and Theology. An Introduction.* Scottsdale, Penn.: Herald Press, 1995.

J. Anglicans

The Church of England traces its beginning to the emergence of Christian communities in the second century C.E. and the development of the first dioceses by the fourth century. The British church evolved as an integral part of Roman Catholicism. Then in the sixteenth century, it made its break with Rome in two stages. First, Henry VIII separated from

Rome administratively. He had himself declared the head of the British church, and blocked any acknowledgement of the pope's authority. The primary change, besides the redirection of any money traditionally sent to Rome to Henry's coffers, was also organizational—the dissolution of the religious orders and the confiscation of their property. Henry resisted, however, any attempt to adopt Protestant thought and institute more substantive reform, even though favored by some of his closest advisors and confidants. Such change awaited his death in 1547.

Henry was succeeded by his son Edward VI. Since he was a minor, real leadership of the country was placed in the hands of a Council of Regency. The Council moved to implement the suggestions of the now-Protestant Archbishop of Canterbury, Thomas Cranmer. The Protestantizing of the church proceeded quickly, anchored by a new *Book of Common Prayer*, which reordered public worship and offered a liturgy that replaced the Catholic mass. The future of England would probably have had a very different course had it not been for the short reign of Edward, who died in 1553.

Mary, his half sister, now came to the throne—with a vengeance. In the midst of all of Henry's maneuvers to father a male heir, Mary had been declared illegitimate. She moved quickly both to establish her legitimacy and undo all of her father's actions relative to the Catholic Church and the religious disaster she believed had been perpetrated during her brother's reign. She planned to return England to its traditional place in the Catholic fold. The formal changes occurred during her first year in office. She then turned on those who had led the Protestantizing effort, whom she had already imprisoned. Over the next few years hundreds were executed, while many fled to the continent. Protestants gave her the name "Bloody Mary" and enshrined her victims in one of the most famous and significant books in the English language, the *Book of Martyrs* by John Foxe. While Mary's actions formed the center of the book, subsequent editions through the ensuing decades documented any further Catholic actions against the Protestant community.

Mary's body, however, was little stronger than her brother's, and after a mere five years she died and was succeeded by her half-sister Elizabeth in 1558. Beset by both Catholic and Protestant supporters, but seeing her real job as building a strong country, Elizabeth set about the creation of a totally new entity, a church that drew upon the popular strengths of both communities. Her plan followed what was termed the *via media*, the middle way.

She revived the Supremacy Acts that had made the British sovereign head of the church, published a new edition of the *Book of Common Prayer* (with some of the most anti-Catholic elements removed), and moved to have vacant bishopics filled with her supporters. The most Protestant feature of her new church was a statement of belief, the Thirty-Nine Articles of Religion, which specifically condemned a number of Catholic beliefs such as transubstantiation. The pope countered by declaring Anglican episcopal orders invalid and excommunicating Elizabeth (1570). Elizabeth's position was solidified in 1588 by the destruction of the Spanish Armada, which had been paid for largely with papal funds.

Though the Catholic threat now moved into the background, Elizabeth had to contend with Protestants dissatisfied with her new church. The Protestant element was led by the so-called Marian exiles, those who had fled the country during

Mary's regime and spent their years absorbing Calvin's brand of Protestant thought. They began to demand the further purification of the British church. Their primary, though by no means only, issue was the episcopacy. They wanted a presbyterian (elder-led) church. Meanwhile, Elizabeth forced Protestantizing priests out of their parishes (and hence out of their livelihood).

The issues with Protestants continued into the next century when a set of rulers plainly favoring Catholicism came to the throne. Finally, in the 1640s, the Puritans rose up, executed King Charles I, and instituted a Protestant Commonwealth. The Church of England began its second era as a Protestant church. That experiment lasted for a decade, but failed for a variety of reasons. With the restoration of the monarchy in 1660 and especially the arrival of William and Mary to the throne in 1689, the place of the Church of England and the unique form of Christianity known as Anglicanism was firmly established.

The Church of England continued a three-fold ministry of deacon, priest, and bishop, with a staunch claim of apostolic succession for the later. While limiting the sacraments to but two, baptism and the Lord's supper, they retained a belief in the real presence of Christ in the Lord's supper. Biblical authority was affirmed, though a role for tradition remained.

During the seventeenth and eighteenth centuries, England developed a global colonial presence and the issue of establishing the Church of England in other lands came to the fore. Slowly, beginning with Canada following the American Revolution (1787), bishops were placed over significant Anglican communions internationally and a new definition of Anglicanism emerged; it included those in communion with the Archbishop of Canterbury,though, in fact, most of the foreign work initially fell directly under the bishop of London.

Anglicans in America

The settlement of the eastern seaboard of North America by British citizens created a new situation for the Church of England. Of course, many of the initial settlers were dissenters—people who wanted to have a land to establish their own form of Christianity, most notably the Puritans of New England. However, in most of British America (Pennsylvania and New England aside), a Church of England establishment prevailed. The attempt to create a colony dominated by Catholics (Maryland) proved too intimidating and was ended by colonists from neighboring Virginia.

The real difference between the American establishments and the homeland was the weakness of the church. Pastoral leadership was sparse and, with some notable exceptions, of inferior quality. Most important, it lacked episcopal oversight. In the Church of England, a significant task of the bishop (as in Roman Catholicism) is the confirmation of children as they come of age. Without a bishop no confirmations occurred, and the unconfirmed should not take communion (though many ignored this provision). Additionally, the lack of a bishop to ordain new ministers became an obstacle to the development of a native ministry. The weak American church left room for the growth of a host of competing churches to challenge Anglican privileges and hegemony.

The American Revolution became a crucial turning point for the Church of England in the former British colonies. The great majority of ministers returned to England, and the few who remained were left with the task of picking up the pieces and going forward. They were aided by the fact that many of the Revolutionary leaders, beginning with George Washington, were Anglicans, and thus they had an elite (and relatively wealthy) constituency. They also had a few worthy leaders, most notably, Samuel Seabury, Samuel Provost, and William White. Among their urgent challenges was the acquisition of valid episcopal orders. Seabury turned to the Anglican bishops in Scotland, but Provost and White worked their way through the obstacles in London (primarily a requirement that any bishops swear loyalty to the ruler of the country) and finally were granted orders in 1787. Upon their return to America they were able formally to organize the Protestant Episcopal Church in the U.S.A., now known simply as the Episcopal Church.

The Episcopal Church was able to shed its image as the faith of the Tories (those who opposed the Revolution) and though a relatively small body (less than one percent of the population) supplied an inordinate amount of the country's political and business leadership. More than a dozen presidents have been drawn from its lay ranks, the most recent being George W. Bush.

In the wake of the international growth of Anglicanism, American bishops played an active role in the Lambeth Conference, the decennial gathering of Anglican bishops from around the world. In the last half of the nineteenth century, they also became attuned to the nascent calls for Protestant unity. In 1886, the Episcopal Church's House of Bishops considered a suggestion of a platform for union with other churches that Anglican's could find acceptable. It offered four points around which they believed Christians could rally:

1. The Holy Scriptures of the Old and New Testaments, as "containing all things necessary to salvation," and as being the rule and ultimate standard of faith.
2. The Apostles' Creed, as the Baptismal Symbol; and the Nicene Creed, as the sufficient statement of the Christian faith.
3. The two Sacraments ordained by Christ Himself—Baptism and the Supper of the Lord—ministered with unfailing use of Christ's words of Institution, and of the elements ordained by Him.
4. The Historic Episcopate, locally adapted in the methods of its administration to the varying needs of the nations and peoples called of God into the Unity of His Church.

This proposal, which came to be known as the Chicago-Lambeth Quadrilateral, has subsequently hovered in the background of Anglican negotiations with other churches. While gaining consensus on the first three points proved relatively easy, especially with mainstream Protestant churches, the last point, so crucial to Anglican life, usually becomes the deal breaker with all but the Old Catholics and some European Lutherans. However, the Quadrilaterial has emerged as a ready statement of the unique position of Anglicanism amid the many ecclesiastical communities of contemporary Christianity.

Not mentioned in the statement is the *Book of Common Prayer*, the daily and weekly guide for the church's liturgical services. While the Quadrilateral defines the church relative to it neighbor, the *Prayer Book* defines church worship and establishes the format of Anglican appropriation of the faith. Early on it set them apart by their use of English (as opposed to Latin) in worship. More recently, it stands over against a whole range of nonliturgical forms of worship.

Contemporary Tensions

The Episcopal Church was able to withstand the pressure to divide (as the Baptists, Methodists, and Presbyterians did) at the time of the American Civil War. It faced its first problem after the Civil War when informal divisions appeared among members and priests who favored a high-church Romanizing approach to Anglican life, as opposed to those who favored a low-church approach more accommodating to the church's Protestant neighbors. In the middle was a large body of people opposing either extreme. Some low-church members pulled out in 1873 to create the Reformed Episcopal Church, but as a whole the internal tension did not lead to fractures.

The real problem for the Episcopal Church developed in the last half of the twentieth century. The church had a sophisticated theological apparatus and had been able to accommodate slowly to the new trends within theology—some British bishops such as William Temple and Charles Gore taking the lead. However, in the 1960s, demands that significantly affected church life ran into widespread dissent.

In the years after World War II, the Episcopal Church began to deal with demands for further change in response to intellectual and social developments in the larger culture. Several Episcopal scholars began to call for further developments in the church's ethical perspective in the light of the complexities of modern culture. Most notable was Joseph Fletcher, author of the best-selling *Situation Ethics*. Though he attempted to deal with a range of emerging ethical issues, conservative critics tended to reduce Fletcher's position to a tool for condoning extramarital sexual activity, which had traditionally been viewed as immoral. The arguments over ethics were then joined by the adoption of changes in the *Prayer Book,* the one book regularly used by all parishioners. Conservatives saw changes as an attack upon traditional theology and values. Then a decision to admit women into the priesthood was seen by conservatives as an attack on tradition and an open door to further unwelcome ethical changes.

An initial schism in 1964 (leading to the formation of the Anglican Orthodox Church) heralded the much larger revolt that came in 1976 following the first (if irregular) ordination of females, which became the catalyst for the Episcopal Church taking the lead in welcoming females to both the ministry and the episcopacy.

Since 1976, those who rejected the directions taken by the Episcopal Church have formed what is unofficially called the Continuing Church movement. They gathered in St. Louis in 1977 and issued a position statement called the "Affirmation of St. Louis." Those associated with the movement have argued that the Episcopal Church has itself departed from the Anglican tradition. Thus the dissidents saw themselves as in fact the continuing Anglican church in America. Churches related to the movement are generally identified by their continued use of the 1928 edition of the *Book of Common Prayer* and their refusal to admit women to the priesthood. The real problem that the movement has faced has been its inability to remain united. It initially divided theologically along high-church-low church lines and became a home to charismatic Episcopalians. It also has suffered from the desire of too many of its leaders for the episcopacy and their continued search for more acceptable episcopal orders. (The Continuing Church movement currently exists in more than fifty jurisdictions, though most of these have very few parishes. Only the larger jurisdictions are listed below in the directory section.)

The original new Anglican body, the Anglican Catholic Church, had its orders in part through the Philippine Independent Church, the representative Anglican church in the Philippines. However, those orders became suspect after the participating bishop, Francisco Pagtakhan, involved himself in a number of episcopal consecrations for leaders of different factions of the movement and then became involved in the splitting of the Philippine Independent Church back in his homeland. Through Pagtakhan, Anglican orders also became entangled with independent and Old Catholic orders.

Then in 2000, a new phase of the controversy was opened when two American priests were consecrated by two of the most conservative Anglican bishops, one from Rwanda and one from Singapore, for work in the United States. The act of setting up the Anglican Mission in America with support by two members of the Anglican Communion created a crisis within the Communion by invading the territory over which fellow bishops had hegemony, a severe breach of etiquette. In fact, however, the Anglican Mission in America remains small and has yet to draw many from either the Continuing Church movement or the Episcopal Church.

The latest issue before the Episcopal Church has been created by its condoning the consecration of Bishop V. Eugene Robinson as the bishop of New Hampshire. Robinson is a practicing homosexual in a long-term relationship with a male partner. While obviously acceptable to the majority of the church's leadership and tolerated by the majority of members (homosexual priests have operated as parish priests in the church quite openly for a generation), this action further infuriated conservatives. It has led to even stronger actions by third world Anglican bishops, the most conservative element of the church's leadership, and called into question the Episcopal Church's standing in the Anglican Communion. The nature of the eventual resolution of this situation is yet to be determined.

The worldwide Anglican Communion currently consists of more than forty independent church bodies that derive from the Church of England and are in communion with the Archbishop of Canterbury. Administratively, the concerns of the Communion are handled by the Anglican Consultative Council and the Anglican Communion Secretariat headquartered in London. The Continuing Church movement is based in some thirty distinct jurisdictions, most of which are quite small, the largest still counting its membership in the thousands. A few like the Anglican Catholic Church have been able to find some substantial support and have begun to create the institutions needed to support the church's ongoing life—seminaries, mission programs, and publishing houses.

Contacts:

Episcopal Church
c/o Episcopal Church Center
815 Second Ave.
New York, NY 10017
www.episcopalchurch.org

The Episcopal Church is the primary body carrying the Anglican tradition in the United States, and the only group in formal communion with the Church of England and the Archbishop of Canterbury.

Other Anglican Churches

American Anglican Church/Province of the Good Shepherd
680 Albany Post Rd.
Scarborough, NY 10510
www.americananglicanchurch.org

The American Anglican Church is a small jurisdiction headed by Rt. Rev. John A. Herzog.

Anglican Catholic Church
c/o Mt. Rev. Mark Haverland, Archbishop/Metropolitan
800 Timothy Rd.
Athens, GA 30606
www.anglicancatholic.org

The largest of the several traditionalist Anglican churches, the ACC grew directly out of the 1976 gathering in St. Louis in protest of the ordination of women to the priesthood (and other changes) in the Episcopal Church.

Anglican Church in America
c/o The Most Rev. Louis W. Falk, Primate
2365 NW 162nd Lane
Clive, IA 50325
www.acahome.org

The Anglican Church in America was founded in 1991 when a segment of the Anglican Catholic Church (which had rejected a merger agreement with the American Episcopal Church) withdrew from the ACC and proceeded with the merger.

Anglican Mission in America
National Mission Resource Center
P.O. Box 3427
Pawleys Island, SC 29585
www.anglicanmissioninamerica.org

The Anglican Mission in America is a traditionalist jurisdiction initiated by several conservative Anglican bishops (Rwanda, Singapore) who have been outspoken critics of the Episcopal

Church, especially its seeming acceptance of homosexuals in the priesthood and episcopacy. The mission was established to receive Episcopalians who wished to withdraw from the Episcopal Church but remain in communion with the Church of England and Anglicans worldwide.

Anglican Orthodox Church
c/o The Most Rev. Jerry L. Ogles
P.O. Box 128
Statesville, NC 28687
www.anglicanorthodoxchurch.org

The oldest of the traditionalist Anglican bodies, the Anglican Orthodox Church was founded by former Episcopal priest James Parker Dees (1915–1990), consecrated as an independent bishop in 1964.

Anglican Province of Christ the King
c/o Mt. Rev. Robert Sherwood Morse, Archbishop
2727 O St., NW
Washington, DC 20007

Bishop Robert S. Morse, one of the original bishops named for the proposed Anglican Catholic Church in 1977, disagreed with the jurisdiction's constitution and withdrew with his supporters and formed the Diocese of Christ the King. It evolved into the Province of Christ the King in 1991.

Charismatic Episcopal Church
c/o Mt. Rev. A. Randoph Adler, Patriarch
107 West Marquita
San Clemente, CA 92672
www.iccec.org

The Charismatic Episcopal Church is a traditionalist Anglican body that has aligned with the contemporary charismatic renewal.

Communion of Evangelical Episcopal Churches
5224 E. 69th Place
Tulsa, OK 74136-3407
www.theceec.org

Unique among the relatively new Anglican communions, the Evangelical Episcopalians see themselves as a product of the "converging" church as articulated by Swedish bishop/theologian Leslie Newbigin, who saw the church as one but with a variety of diverse emphases drawing on Catholic, Protestant, and Orthodox traditions.

Episcopal Missionary Church
National Office
c/o The Rt. Rev. William Millsaps, Presiding Bishop
P.O. Box 157
Monteagle, TN 37356
www.emchome.org

The Episcopal Missionary Church was founded in 1992 by former Episcopal Church bishop A. Donald Davies.

Episcopal Orthodox Christian Archdiocese of America
Chancery office:
464 County Home Rd.
Lexington, NC 27292
eoc.orthodoxanglican.net

In 1998, the Anglican Orthodox Church experienced a major schism with the majority withdrawing and forming the Episcopal Orthodox Christian Archdiocese. The archdiocese continues to play a leading role in the Anglican Orthodox Communion, an international fellowship of Orthodox Anglicans.

Reformed Episcopal Church
c/o Rt. Rev. Royal U. Grote
4142 Dayflower Dr.
Katy, TX 77449
rechurch.org

The Reformed Episcopal Church grew out of a controversy in the 1870s in which evangelical members protested the catholicizing tendencies of the Episcopal Church's leadership. One group of the evangelical members left in 1873 under the leadership of Bishop George David Cummins (1822–1876).

United Anglican Church
c/o Mt. Rev. Norman F. Strauss, Archbishop Primate
79 Kingsboro Ave.
Gloversville, NY 12078
www.unitedanglicanchurch.org

The United Anglican Church formed at the end of the 1990s following a merger of two older independent Anglican communions, the Traditional Episcopal Church and the Anglo-Catholic Church in the Americas.

United Episcopal Church of North America
Mt. Rev. Stephen C. Reber, Sr., Presiding Bishop
614 Pebblestone Ct.
Statesville, NC 28625
united-episcopal.org

The United Episcopal Church was formed in 1980 by Bishop C. Dale Doren, formerly with the Anglican Catholic Church.

For further reading:

Armentrout, Don S., and Robert B. Slocum, eds. *An Episcopal Dictionary of the Church : a User-Friendly Reference for Episcopalians.* New York: Calvary Publishing, 2000.

Clark, Ken, and Charlie Steen. *Making Sense of the Episcopal Church: An Introduction to Its History.* Harrisburg, PA: Morehouse Group, 1996.

Guelzo, Allen C. *For the Union of Evangelical Christendom: the Irony of the Reformed Episcopalians.* University Park, PA: Penn State Press, 1994.

Holloway, Richard, ed. *The Anglican Tradition.* Wilton, Conn.: Morehouse-Barlow, 1984.

Katerberg, William H. *Modernity and the Dilemma of North American Anglican Identities, 1880-1950.* Montreal: McGill-Queen's Univ. Press, 2001.

Kew, Richard, and Roger J. White. *New Millennium, New Church: Trends Shaping the Episcopal Church for the 21st Century.* Cambridge, Mass.: Cowley Publications, 1992.

Konolige, Kit, and Frederica Konolige. *The Power of Their Glory.* n.p.: Wyden Books, 1978.

Manross, William W. *A History of the American Episcopal Church.* New York: Morehouse-Gorham Co., 1950.

Neill, Stephen. *Anglicanism.* London: A. R. Mowbrays, 1977.

Prichard, Robert W. *A History of the Episcopal Church.* Harrisburg, Penn: Morehouse Group, 1999.

Sumner, David E. *The Episcopal Church's History, 1945-1985.* Wilton, Conn.: Morehouse Publishing, 1987.

Webber, Christopher L., and Frank T. Griswold, III. *Welcome to the Episcopal Church: An Introduction to Its History, Faith, and Worship.* Harrisburg, Penn.: Morehouse Group, 1999.

Whale, John. *The Anglican Church Today: The Future of Anglicanism.* London: Mowbrays, 1988.

Wingate, Andrew, et al., eds. *Anglicanism: A Global Communion.* London: Mowbrays, 1998.

3. Puritanism

Puritanism—frequently confused with the often stuffy etiquette and pedantic morality of late-nineteenth century Victorianism—has been a major theme in American culture as the ultimate source of the form of Protestantism that long dominated the religious community in the United States. However, more than anything, the "purity" being sought by the movement's founders was more theological and ecclesiastical than anything else. Puritanism emerged during the Elizabethan years, gained a popular following through the early decades of the seventeenth century, and finally seized its opportunity in the 1640s to take control of not just the Church of England, but of the country as a whole. The consequences unleashed by the formation of the Puritan Commonwealth under Oliver Cromwell would reverberate across the Atlantic and continues to make waves.

A number of British leaders had drunk deeply from the wells of Geneva during the years of Queen Mary's rule in England. They returned convinced Calvinists in theology and presbyterians in their understanding of church government. Among the Marian exiles was one John Knox, a Scotsman who had published an exhortation calling England to accept Calvin's version of reform just as Mary's reign came to an end. As soon as she died, he returned to Edinburgh and began an effort for reform. In Scotland, Anglicanism was not really an option, and Queen Elizabeth threw her support behind the Protestants against her rival, the Catholic Mary Queen of Scots. Thus, through the 1560s, Scotland became a Presbyterian land.

But England was another matter, and Elizabeth was intent on imposing her Anglican *via media.* While a number of Calvinist themes were integrated into Anglican theology, an episcopal hierarchy remained in place, and the church liturgy, although in English, still looked more like a Catholic mass than the worship prevalent in Geneva. The issue first surfaced soon after Elizabeth pushed through her Act of Uniformity in 1559. She demanded that parish priests continue to wear traditional vestments when leading worship. Protestants had already opted for a very simple gown. When some Protestants refused to adopt the "Catholic dress," Elizabeth had these nonconformists dismissed from their pulpits.

Cambridge University became the bastion of Protestant agitation. Here Thomas Cartwright advocated the Protestant cause and called for a further purification of the Church of England by its adoption of a Presbyterian form of church governance. While Elizabeth reigned there was little that could be done, but agitation continued and pockets of dissent formed around the country. In the midst of the polemics, a new option appeared among the Puritans: Congregationalism. Robert Browne, Cartwright's contemporary, is generally credited with initially advocating the transfer of church authority to the congregation.

By the time Elizabeth's successor James I (already the king of Scotland) came to the throne in 1603, Puritanism existed as a spectrum of options among critics of the Church of England. First, there were Anglicans who accepted the episcopal structure, but saw a need for reform of the spiritual life of the church. The second group, and seemingly the largest faction, were the Presbyterians who wanted to get rid of the bishops and replace them with a conference of elders (presbyters). And finally, a third group were Congregationalists who wanted to do away with the presbyteries and synods, in favor of allowing the local parishes to run their own affairs. However, there was now added a new factor, the independents who not only opted for a congregational form of church governance (polity) but wanted to separate from any entanglement with the state. Like the Anabaptists, they had come to the opinion that the church was only for believers, though they did not follow the Anabaptists on other issues such as pacifism. The independents, however, began a critique of the sacraments and finally agreed that they were also an adult matter. Baptism was for those who had come of age and professed faith, and the Lord's supper was for baptized church members.

On each end of the spectrum, Puritanism produced very different results. The Anglican Puritans generation by generation produced exemplars of piety. The independents were the least favored, and one group eventually left England for the relative freedom in Holland. In 1620 this group found its way to Plymouth, Massachusetts, and later became enshrined in history as the Pilgrims. This small group was shortly overwhelmed and eventually absorbed into the much larger groups of Puritan Congregationalists who followed.

With no real hope for success in England, beginning in 1630 a number of Puritans favoring a congregational polity left for Massachusetts. Here they created an experimental society to show the viability of their way. Often confused with the Pilgrims, who simply wanted a place to survive and freely practice the faith as they saw it, the congregationalists of New England had quite a different agenda. They wanted to build a society conforming to their dictates, and once established, they showed no tolerance for variation. Their intolerance of dissent led to their executing Quakers and banishing those offering differing opinions from within their own community, most notably Roger Williams and Anne Hutchinson. Their intolerance of Anglicans made the renewal of their colonial charter a matter of periodic anxiety, and they had to be forced by the crown to allow an Anglican church to be opened in Boston.

Meanwhile, in England, the Puritans scored an early victory through their participation in the new Bible translation completed and presented to King James in 1611. Biding their time, they were ready to seize power when King Charles I ran into problems with his efforts to reimpose Catholicism. The first step came in 1642, when a Parliament with a Protestant majority acted against the king's authority. Religiously, they dismissed the bishops, one of the steps leading to civil war. As the war proceeded, Oliver Cromwell led in the calling of the assembly of divines to meet at Westminster in 1646.

With Scottish church leaders looking over their shoulders, the Westminster clergy produced the four documents for the reform of the Church of England and in the process the four documents that came to define Presbyterianism—the Westminster Confession of Faith, the Westminster Catechism, the *Directory of Worship* (to replace the *Book of Common Prayer*), and the Form of Church Government, designed to reorder church life throughout England, Scotland, and Ireland. Published in 1648, these were given to church leaders in England and Ireland and formally adopted by the Church of Scotland.

The Westminster documents dictated church life for the next decade, but in 1660 the Puritan Commonwealth came tumbling down. The monarchy was restored and the Church of England returned to its Elizabethan form, complete with bishops, the *Prayer Book*, and the Thirty-nine Articles of Religion. But even during the Commonwealth, the Westminster documents were not fully accepted by the British Puritan leaders. In 1658, those who still favored Congregationalism issued the Savoy Declaration, which accepted the Calvinist theology of the Westminster Confession but rejected a Presbyterian polity.

To say the least, the Restoration of the monarchy had significant effects for the Puritan community. In England, Puritans survived as a set of minority groups—a minority faction in the

Church of England, a dissenting Presbyterian church, a dissenting Congregationalist church, and a dissenting Baptist movement. The fall of the Commonwealth in England, and its reverberations in Scotland, also spurred the migration of a new generation of Puritans—mostly Presbyterians—to America. Here they hoped to have the impact that they were denied in England.

K. Congregational Churches

Congregationalists were the first Puritans to migrate to the British American colonies. Congregationalists trace their history to the early independents in Elizabethan England who called for a congregational form of church governance; however they only gained real support in the first decades of the seventeenth century and only had a chance to test their approach in New England in the 1630s.

New England church life, of course, began with the Pilgrims, those independents who had left England for Holland and finally made their way to Massachusetts in 1620. The church at Plymouth remained somewhat aloof from the Puritan establishment (they gave aid and comfort, for example, to the banished Roger Williams) and eventually in the nineteenth century aligned with the Unitarians.

The Congregationalists really wanted the Church of England to become a Protestant church with Reformed theology and a congregational polity. In this system, the local churches should operate administratively as autonomous units, though they should keep their intimate connection with the state and maintain fellowship with each other through geographically based associations allowed to act when local disputes remained unresolved. They differed from the

Presbyterians (who wanted to establish the collective leadership of lay and clergy elders) and the independents (who wished to end the church's connection to the government).

Congregationalism was first established in Massachusetts and Connecticut. For a century and a half they had the opportunity to test their idea of church life. They controlled the religious realm and could count among their accomplishments the pioneering of American higher education (with the founding of Harvard University) and the launching of the American phase of the Protestant world missionary movement. Along the way they fought witchcraft and Quakerism and through the decades dealt with the problem of their increasing inability to pass the faith to the next generation. Their experiment came to an end with the disestablishment of the church after the American Revolution and the loss of many parishes to Unitarianism in the nineteenth century.

The dismantling of the Puritan establishment in New England was countered by the spread of Congregationalism across America—though that spread was somewhat blunted by what was known as the Plan of Union, a 1801 agreement with the Presbyterians that turned out to work in favor of the Presbyterians as the nation expanded westward.

With the loss of the unique structure of church and state in colonial New England, Congregationalists evolved as a loose association of parishes, tied together by their mutual missional programs and educational endeavors. Also through the nineteenth century, Congregationalism became the source for many voluntary associations (now called parachurch organizations) aimed at reforming society. In addition, before most other American denominations, the Congregationalists developed a global missionary program through the American Board of Commissioners for Foreign Missions. Meanwhile, its educational institutions have produced a steady stream of leaders both in the religious field and in the secular community.

Congregationalists assumed leadership in the emerging ecumenical movement at the end of the nineteenth century and joined in the forming of the Federal Council of Churches. Through the twentieth century, they followed a singularly unique program for church union, a program that requires the following background information to understand.

At the same time that Congregationalism was developing in New England, large numbers of German immigrants were pouring into Pennsylvania. Some of these immigrants brought with them the German Reformed tradition and, during the nineteenth century, the unique Prussian Evangelical tradition (mixing Lutheran and Reformed elements). A German Reformed Church was organized in 1747 and an American branch of the Evangelical Church emerged in 1840. In 1934 these two churches united to form the Evangelical and Reformed Church.

Also, in the years after the American Revolution, a number of independent congregations that simply called themselves Christian churches emerged on the American frontier. Beginning in 1833, representatives of these churches gathered to form a loose-knit association. They would henceforth be known as the Christian Church. In 1931, this group made common cause with the Congregationalists and merged to form the General Council of the Congregationalist Christian Churches.

In 1957, the General Council of the Congregationalist Christian Churches merged with the Evangelical and Reformed Church to create the United Church of Christ (UCC). The UCC emerged on the stage as the most impressive example of what could be done in uniting the scattered Protestant believers. The UCC immediately took its place as one of the leading bodies of mainstream liberal Protestantism, and in subsequent decades has become the most liberal of the larger Protestant churches in the United States.

Because of their congregational polity, the Congregationalists have allowed ministers with a variety of dissenting views to emerge, and their loose-knit structure provided little means to prevent its fellowship from becoming home to the broadest spectrum of theological perspectives. While traditional Reformed theology was in the majority, Unitarianism (which affirmed one Father God in distinction from the orthodox affirmation of the Trinity) grew strong and eventually the Unitarian congregations withdrew and formed a separate denomination. Through the twentieth century, as more liberal voices came to dominate the church, conservative ministers and congregations withdrew. As early as 1930, for example, a number of Congregational churches had joined in the formation of the Independent Fundamental Churches of America (discussed below in chapter 6).

Thus it was not surprising that a number of congregations with a Congregational or Christian background refused to join the UCC when it was founded in 1957. The more theologically conservative formed the Conservative Congregational Christian Conference. Others believed that the new church replaced elements essential to maintaining a congregational polity with presbyterian structures, and left to form the National Association of Congregational Christian Churches.

In spite of the dissent, the UCC remains by far the largest representative of the Congregational tradition in the United

States, with some 1.3 million members. It is a member of the World Alliance of Reformed Churches, the World Council of Churches, and the National Council of the Churches of Christ in the U.S.A. The National Association of Congregational Christian Churches has around 100,000 members and has affiliated with continuing Congregational churches around the world in the International Congregational Fellowship.

Meanwhile, a new denomination with a very different background has arrived at much the same position as the United Church of Christ. The International Council of Community Churches originated out of a vision of forming interdenominational local parishes across America, especially in communities that were too small to support several competing denominationally affiliated parishes. As the council (formed in 1946) attained some visibility in recent decades, it has welcomed more and more independent congregations, and a few small denominations of various backgrounds seeking a more stable denominational home have merged into it. The fellowship evolved into a liberal ecumenically minded Protestant communion and joined both the National Council of Churches and the World Council of Churches.

Contacts:

Conservative Congregational Christian Conference
c/o 7582 Currell Blvd.
St. Paul, MN 55125
ccccusa.ccccsitelaunch.com

The CCCC formed in 1935 to provide a home for theologically conservative Congregationalists who rejected the growth of liberal theological tendencies in the larger Congregational fellowship.

International Council of Community Churches
21116 Washington Parkway
Frankfort, IL 60423
www.icccusa.com

Emerging in stages as a fellowship of non-sectarian community churches, the International Council, formally established in 1946, has evolved into a congregationally organized association of liberal Protestant churches.

National Association of Congregational Christian Churches
8473 S. Howell Ave.
P.O. Box 1620
Oak Creek, WI 53154-0620
www.naccc.org

The NACCC is the major dissenting body representing Congregationalists who rejected the merger that produced the United Church of Christ. Members believed that the UCC's constitution departed from several important Congregationalist organizational principles.

United Church of Christ
700 Prospect Ave. E.
Cleveland, OH 44115-1100
www.ucc.org

The UCC, the major carrier of the Congregational tradition in the United States, was formed in 1957 by the merger of the Congregational Christian Churches and the Evangelical and Reformed Church.

For further reading:

Bauswein, Jean-Jacques, and Lukas Vischner, eds. *The Reformed Family Worldwide: A Survey of Reformed Churches, Theological Schools, and International Organizations.* Grand Rapids: William B. Eerdmans, 1999.

Von Rohr, John. *The Shaping of American Congregationalism, 1620–1957.* New York: Pilgrim Press, 1994.

Walker, Williston, ed. *Creeds and Platforms of Congregationalism.* New York: Pilgrim Press, 1991.

L. Presbyterian Churches

Presbyterians continue the history of the Reformed church and trace their history to Switzerland and the ministry of Ulrich Zwingli, though preeminence is assigned to John Calvin and the church life he established at Geneva in the 1530s. As such, Presbyterians share the history and theology of the Reformed Church (discussed in the previous chapter) and represent its development in the British Isles.

Calvin's ideas filtered into England in the last years of the reign of Henry VIII and found much favor during the brief rule of Edward VI. However, those who had openly professed Protestant ideas feared for their lives when Mary I ascended to the throne, and many fled England for Geneva once she began to return the country to Catholicism. These Marian exiles were deeply affected by Calvin, and returned to England only to be disappointed by Elizabeth's Anglican solution to the religious turmoil of the day. While having some appreciation of the rejection of Catholicism, they saw a real need to further purify the Church of England. A major issue was the replacement of the authority of the bishops with the leadership of elders (presbyters)—teaching elders (ministers) and ruling elders (laymen)—hence their designation as Presbyterians.

Presbyterianism scored its initial success in Scotland, where John Knox returned from his self-imposed exile in Geneva to rally Protestant forces. In 1560, the Scottish parliament voted to accept the confession of faith written by Knox, who subsequently put together a book of discipline for reforming the church. Work would be required for several decades to consolidate the gains, but the Church of Scotland was a constant reminder to the British of the possibility of further change south.

Through the first half of the seventeenth century, Presbyterianism steadily gained strength in England and found an opening during the reign of King Charles I, who sought a way to return the Church of England to Catholicism. Their chance came after Charles tried to force a new Prayer Book on Scotland and saw his army badly beaten in the attempt. Facing a financial crisis, Charles had to deal with a parliament dominated by Protestants that subverted his power. With neither side in a compromising mood, civil war erupted. As the war proceeded, the parliament assembled British Presbyterian leaders at Westminster to prepare the roadmap for reforming the church. Scottish leaders traveled to London to assist as was appropriate.

The Westminster assembly prepared summaries of the Calvinist faith they professed which found expression in the Westminster Confession of Faith and Westminster catechism. Instructions for public worship were embodied in the *Directory of Worship*, designed as a substitute for the Anglican *Book of Common Prayer*. Finally the reforming of the organization of the church was outlined in the Form of Church Government. When published in 1548, the Westminster documents were intended as authoritative in the regulation of church life across England, Wales, and Ireland. Scotland was the first to officially accept and approve them. There was an attempt to impose them in England and Ireland, but the short-lived nature of the Commonwealth and the vocal dissent of the Congregationalists limited their role in England. With the restoration of the monarchy and the return of episcopal leadership to the church in

1660, the Westminster documents became the sole possession of the surviving Presbyterians.

While a few Presbyterians had moved to America prior to the Commonwealth, it was after the Restoration that significant immigration occurred. The first synod was formed in 1706. Through the eighteenth and nineteenth centuries, Presbyterians in America became divided over several issues. First, Scottish immigrants, dissenters from the Church of Scotland over various polity matters, formed the Associate Presbyterian Church (1753) and the Reformed Presbyterian Church (1774). Meanwhile, in the middle 1700s, the British Presbyterians split over the issue of revivalism, as promoted by evangelist George Whitefield. A second split on the American frontier early in the nineteenth century led to the formation of the Cumberland Presbyterian Church. Prior to the American Civil War, both the British and Scottish Presbyterian churches split along regional lines.

Even as the Presbyterians were dividing into major factions, efforts were underway to reunite them. As early as 1782, the two main Scottish Presbyterian groups merged to form the Associate Reformed Presbyterian Church, though a faction of the Associate Presbyterian Church remained outside of the new body. In 1858, when the Associate Reformed Presbyterian Church separated into southern and northern factions, the continuing Associate church merged with the northern faction to form the United Presbyterian Church of North America.

The northern faction of the British Presbyterians first merged with the Cumberland Presbyterians in 1906 and then in 1958 with the United Presbyterian Church of North America to form the Presbyterian Church in the U.S.A. In 1983, the main body of southern Presbyterians, the Presbyterian Church in the U.S., merged with the Presbyterian Church in the U.S.A. to form the Presbyterian Church (U.S.A.), making it by far the largest Presbyterian denominational body in the United States. This church is one of the more important bodies of liberal Protestantism in America. It is a member of the National Council of Churches in the U.S.A., the World Council of Churches, and the World Alliance of Reformed Churches.

While most Presbyterians are members of the Presbyterian Church (U.S.A.), a variety of Presbyterian groups continue separate from it, most formed by more conservative factions of churches that participated in one of the mergers described above. The two largest independent groups are the Presbyterian Church of America, formed by the most conservative elements in the former Presbyterian Church in the U.S., and the portion of the Cumberland Presbyterian Church that stayed out of the 1906 merger.

During the 1920s and 1930s, the northern Presbyterian church became one of the main stages for the playing out of the Fundamentalist-Modernist controversy. Tensions within the church over new theological currents had been visible since the late-nineteenth century. They came to a head with the fight for control of the church's educational institutions, most notably Princeton Theological Seminary, and for the board that oversaw foreign missions. Through the 1930s, the more liberal faction in the church gained the upper hand over both the schools and mission board, and some fundamentalists left to form the Orthodox Presbyterian Church. The group that left then disagreed over whether they should continue to affirm the traditional a-millennialist Calvinist theology or the more recently popularized premillennial dispensational theology. The latter group left to form the Bible Presbyterian Church.

Among the most successful missionary efforts by Presbyterians occurred in Korea. Beginning in the years after the Korean War, a number of Korean Presbyterians moved to the United States. Once here, they aligned with the spectrum of theology that has become present in the several churches of British and Scottish heritage. The Korean Presbyterian Church in America is the more liberal of the Korean churches and is a member of the National Council of Churches. More conservative is the Korean American Presbyterian Church, which, along with the Orthodox Presbyterian Church, is a member of the North American Presbyterian and Reformed Council. Also on the conservative end of the spectrum is the General Assembly of the Korean Presbyterian Church.

Other Presbyterian churches include the Free Presbyterian Church, a conservative Presbyterian body of Irish heritage aligned with the dissenting Northern Ireland ministry of Ian Paisley. Paisley was at the center of much of the Protestant-Catholic tension in Northern Ireland in the last decades of the twentieth century. The Evangelical Presbyterian Church was founded in 1981 in anticipation of the merger that produced the Presbyterian Church (U.S.A.).

With approximately 3.4 million members, the Presbyterian Church (U.S.A.) is the largest Presbyterian church in the United States and one of the ten largest churches in the United States. Its major competition comes from the conservative Presbyterian Church in America, which has around 300,000 members and is found primarily in the American South. The remaining Presbyterian churches count their members in the tens of thousands.

Churches in the Presbyterian tradition have become known for their allegiance to the Reformed theological tradition and more than any other Christian tradition have divided over doctrinal questions. The strictness with which the theological tradition is affirmed has led to a variety of ecumenical alignments. The Presbyterian Church (U.S.A.) and the Cumberland Presbyterian Church have identified with the National and World Council of Churches. The Presbyterian Church in America is a member of the National Association of Evangelicals. The Orthodox Presbyterian Church and the Korean American Presbyterian Church are members of the International Conference of Reformed Churches. The Bible Presbyterian Church (General Synod) is a member of the World Council of Biblical Churches. The Bible Presbyterian Church (Collinswood Synod) and the Free Presbyterian Church of North America affiliated with the International Council of Christian Churches.

Contacts:

Presbyterian Church in America
c/o Stated Clerk
1852 Century Plaza, Suite 202
Atlanta, GA 30345
www.pcanet.org

The PCA represents the most theologically conservative faction of the former Presbyterian Church in the United States that declined to participate in the 1983 merger that produced the Presbyterian Church (U.S.A.).

Presbyterian Church (U.S.A.)
100 Witherspoon St.
Louisville, KY 40202
www.pcusa.org

The Presbyterian Church (U.S.A.) grew out of a series of mergers (the last being in 1983) that united the several branches of British and Scottish Presbyterianism that had formed in the United States.

Additional Presbyterian Churches

Associate Reformed Presbyterian Church (General Synod)
Associate Reformed Presbyterian Center
1 Cleveland St.
Greenville, SC 29601
www.arpsynod.org

The Associate Reformed Presbyterian Church, with roots in Scottish Presbyterianism, grew out of the Associate Church's South Carolina Synod, the only one to remain outside of the mergers in which the other synods joined. The church remains essentially a southern church.

Bible Presbyterian Church
P.O. Box 26164
5804 Hedgecrest Pl.
Charlotte, NC 28221-6164
www.bpc.org

The Bible Presbyterian Church is one of the several conservative fundamentalist groups to break with the larger Presbyterian Church in the 1930s over its modernist tendencies.

Cumberland Presbyterian Church
Cumberland Presbyterian Center
1978 Union Ave.
Memphis, TN 38104
www.cumberland.org/

The Cumberland Presbyterian Church continues the original revivalistic Presbyterian thrust on the early nineteenth-century American frontier. In 1906 the majority of the church merged into what became the Presbyterian Church (U.S.A.).

Cumberland Presbyterian Church in America
226 Church St.
Huntsville, AL 35801
www.cumberland.org/cpca

The Cumberland Presbyterian Church in America is a predominantly African American church that continues the original revivalistic Presbyterian thrust on the early nineteenth-century American frontier.

Evangelical Presbyterian Church
17197 N. Laurel Park Dr.
Suite 567
Livonia, MI 48152
www.epc.org

The Evangelical Presbyterian Church was formed by conservative Presbyterians in 1981 as the two major branches of American Presbyterianism prepared to merge (1983). The founders rejected the theological liberalism they found in their parent bodies.

Free Presbyterian Church of North America
209 N. Newtown St. Rd.
Newtown Square, PA 19073
www.freepres.org

The Free Presbyterian Church has its roots in Northern Ireland and is identified with the ministry of Ian Paisley and his opposition to Roman Catholic influence and attempts to reunite Ireland into a single national entity.

General Assembly of the Korean Presbyterian Church on America
17200 Clark Ave.
Bellflower, CA 90706
www.kpcaem.com

The General Assembly is a conservative Presbyterian church primarily serving Korean Americans.

Korean American Presbyterian Church
1901 W. 166th St.
Gardena, CA 90296
www.kapc.org

The Korean American Presbyterian Church is a fundamentalist church primarily serving Korean Americans.

Korean Presbyterian Church in America
P.O. Box 457
280 Fairfield Pl.
Morganville, NJ 07751
www.kpca.org

The Korean Presbyterian Church is the most liberal of the spectrum of Korean Presbyterian denominations established by Korean immigrants to the United States in the last half of the twentieth century. It is a member of the National Council of Churches and in communion with the Presbyterian Church (U.S.A.).

Orthodox Presbyterian Church
607 N. Easton Rd.
Bldg. E, Box P
Willow Grove, PA 19090-0920
www.opc.org

The Orthodox Presbyterian Church dates from the 1930s protests of fundamentalist Presbyterians over the liberal drift of the Presbyterian Church. Theologian J. Gresham Machen (1881–1937) was the leading figure in the church's formation.

Presbyterian Reformed Church
2107, 320 St.
Madrid, IA 50156
www.presbyterianreformed.org/

The Presbyterian Reformed Church is a very conservative Presbyterian church formed in Canada in 1951. It subsequently spread to the United States as congregations affiliated with it.

Reformed Presbyterian Church General Assembly
P.O. Box 2757
Belleview, FL 34421
www.rpcga.org

The Reformed Presbyterian Church continues the work of the former Reformed Presbyterian Church, Evangelical Synod, the majority of whose members merged into the Presbyterian Church in America in 1983.

Reformed Presbyterian Church of North America
c/o Crown & Covenant Publications
7408 Penn Ave.
Pittsburgh, PA 15208
www.reformedpresbyterian.org

The Reformed Presbyterian Church continues the emphases of the Covenanter tradition from eighteenth-century Scotland which, among other emphases, refused to vote or participate in various government structures.

For further reading:

Coalter, Milton J., et al. *The Confessional Mosaic: Presbyterians and Twentieth Century Theology.* Louisville, Ky: Westminster/John Knox Press, 1990.

Longfield, Bradley J. *The Presbyterian Controversy: Fundamentalists, Modernists and Moderates.* New York, Oxford: Oxford University Press, 1991.

McGrath, Alister E. *Life of John Calvin: A Study in the Shaping of Western Culture.* Oxford: Basil Blackwell, 1990.

North, Gary. *Crossed Fingers: How the Liberals Captured the Presbyterian Church.* Tyler, Tex.: Institute for Christian Economics, 1996.

Smith, Frank Joseph. *The History of the Presbyterian Church in America: Silver Anniversary Edition.* Lawrenceville, GA: Presbyterian Scholars Press, 1999.

Smylie, James H. *A Brief History of the Presbyterians.* Louisville, Ky: Geneva Press, 1996.

Van Hoeven, James W., ed. *Word and World: Reformed Theology in America.* Historical Series of the Reformed Church in America, vol. 16. Grand Rapids: William B. Eerdmans Publishing Co., 1986.

Weston, William. *Presbyterian Pluralism: Competition in a Protestant House.* Knoxville: University of Tennessee Press, 1997.

M. The Baptists

Through the twentieth century, the Baptist tradition has emerged as by far the most appealing form of Christianity to American Protestants, and one of its representative denominations, the Southern Baptist Convention, is second only to the Roman Catholic Church in number of members. As a tradition, Baptist themes can be traced to the sixteenth-century Anabaptists (and even earlier), but as a community the Baptists emerged on the scene in England at one end of the Puritan spectrum. With the Puritans, the Baptists accepted most of the Reformed theological perspectives brought back to England by the Marian Exiles during the reign of Queen Elizabeth I. However, while the main body of Puritans fought over the manner in which the Church of England should be purified, the Baptists forsook the effort to reform the national church, called for a separation of church and state, and developed appropriate innovations in polity and theology to embody their new approach to church life.

The Baptists began with Congregationalist independency by calling for the reorganization of Christianity on a congregational system. However, they then took the additional step of calling for the separation of the church from the state and the placing of what authority was left essentially in the hands of the local congregation. Baptists thus denied to the state any authority to suppress "false" religious beliefs. Somewhat like the Anabaptists, the Separatists, as they came to be called, then followed a similar reasoning toward a new view of society. They concluded that the general population could not be considered Christian (simply by virtue of their baptism as infants and later confirmation). The population consisted of two very different groups—those who had accepted and tried to live the Christian faith, and the great majority who did not. The church's job was to gather the true Christians into fellowship and work with them in promoting Christian discipleship. A logical consequence of such a perspective was the rejection of infant baptism, the practice being limited to those who had reached an age when they could state their personal profession of faith.

Having concluded that (adult) believer's baptism was the correct form, John Smythe formed the first "Baptist" church among English believers residing in the Netherlands (1609). A short time later a member of Smythe's church, Thomas Helwys, returned home and established the first Baptist congregation in England in 1612. English Baptists struggled to exist in a rather hostile environment, but by 1630 seven congregations in the London area were able to come together and issue an initial Confession of Faith. Then a half-century later, the Baptists were able to issue a new revised Confession (written in 1677, formally adopted in 1689) that reacted to and was based upon the Presbyterians' Westminster Confession (1648) and the Congregationalists' Savoy Declaration (1658), but emphasized the several Baptist distinctives.

As the Baptist movement developed, it moved further away from its Puritan cohorts, especially on the issue of the sacraments. Having rejected Catholic theology and episcopal authority, it moved even further away from any sacramental emphasis, ultimately discarding altogether any idea of a sacramental nature to the practices of baptism and the Lord's supper. The two practices were now seen as biblically commanded ordinances. The Lord's supper was described as a memorial meal calling to memory Jesus' last meeting with his disciples prior to his crucifixion. Baptism passed no special grace to the believer, but was public affirmation of one's identification with Christ's death, burial, and resurrection. This conclusion also accompanied the changing of the mode of baptism from either sprinkling or pouring to full immersion. Having considered baptism and the Lord's Supper as ordinances, some Baptists eventually came to regard the practice of foot-washing as an additional ordinance.

Apart from its few distinctive beliefs about polity and the ordinances, the Baptists generally accepted the basics of Reformed theology. Baptists affirmed the triune God, commitment to the gospel of Jesus Christ, belief in the authority of the Bible, and the priesthood of all believers. Because of their Reformed faith, they were greatly affected by the battles over predestination and free grace that shook the Reformed Church in the Netherlands at the beginning of the eighteenth century. Baptists were divided between those who accepted predestination and those who emphasized free grace (or free will). The former were generally called Particular Baptists, meaning they affirmed that Christ died just for the elect, over against General Baptists, who affirmed that Christ died for all.

In England, Particular and General Baptists grew up side-by-side, the latter growing more rapidly as their theology suggested the need to evangelize. They later tended to suggest that God would bring to them the elect called out from the larger world of Christendom. This later opinion created a crisis in the Particular Baptist community at the end of the eighteenth century as some Baptists wished to respond to the emerging world missionary effort. In the 1730s, the small Moravian Church had launched a global missionary effort that reached the Americas, Africa, and even India. Then in 1784, Methodist leader Thomas Coke had proposed a plan for Methodist involvement in missionary activity. The Moravians and Methodists set the stage for the emergence of William Carey, who in 1792 issued a plea for Baptists to join the missionary call. This led to the first Baptist Missionary Society, an independent endeavor, as Baptists had no organizational mechanism to develop a pan-congregational denomination-wide missionary program. Carey initially met opposition from his Particular Baptist colleagues, and it fell to Carey's colleague Andrew Fuller to articulate a modified Reformed theology that emphasized the Great Commission to evangelize the nations. While many Baptist continued in their "strict" views, the majority of Particular Baptists accepted Fuller's new direction.

Baptists in America

The first Baptists emigrated to North America from England (and also the Netherlands) in the seventeenth century. Puritan exile Roger Williams established the first Baptist church in America at Providence, Rhode Island, in 1639. Williams is doubly important for his emphasis on the problem of religious persecution and identification of the Baptist community in America with the cause of religious freedom. He articulated his beliefs in great detail in his famous *Bloody Tenet of Persecution*, published in 1643, and demonstrated the implications of his belief by inviting Jewish refugees to establish a synagogue in Newport, Rhode Island.

Through the seventeenth century, General or Free Will Baptists took the lead and became the majority party. However, a number of Particular Baptists settled in William Penn's colony and formed the first Baptist association (1707). The Philadelphia Association adopted the London Confession of Faith (1677/89) and later issued a slightly revised form of it as the Philadelphia Confession of Faith (1742). Early in the nineteenth century, a slightly revised form of the Philadelphia Confession, the New Hampshire Confession of Faith (1830), became the most popular and authoritative statement of faith among Baptist groups in America.

The Philadelphia Association became the core (and the model) from which other associations were formed, and then in 1824, in order to fund a foreign missionary endeavor, created a national organization, the General Missionary Convention of the Baptist Denomination. As it met every three years, it was generally called the Triennial Convention. Its formation had been occasioned by the conversion of several Congregationalist ministers to Baptist beliefs and the need to find some way to involve American Baptists in supporting missions. Although Baptists had already split into several distinctive communities, the formation and development of the Triennial Convention led to a series of schisms that largely reordered American Baptist life.

The Triennial Convention was organized as a gathering of representatives of Baptist congregations and associations for the purpose of inviting pan-congregational participation in a foreign missionary program. It soon attracted parallel gatherings for the purpose of promoting Christian education (Sunday schools), home missions, and the publication of Baptist materials. Over its first decades it took on the trapping of a denominational structure, though in a very limited way, given the Baptist emphasis on the autonomy of the local congregation. Though the Triennial Convention remained a relatively weak organization, there were many Baptists who opposed any pan-denominational structures and who saw any regional associations as organizations for fellowship only. They also viewed Sunday schools as a modern unbiblical innovation, and opposed the cooperative foreign mission endeavor as an unbiblical method to spread the gospel. Those opposed to missions and Sunday schools withdrew from participation in the Triennial Convention and formed the Primitive Baptist movement. The great strength of the Primitive Baptists was in the American South, where they also soon came to be known for their opposition to the introduction of instrumental music (in the form of church organs).

Two decades after its formation, the Triennial Convention became the focus of the debate over slavery within the Baptist community. A variety of questions were raised over the involvement of Baptists in slaveholding, but the fight centered on whether the convention would support a slaveholder as a home missionary. Its refusal to accept such a person occasioned a split. Most of the associations and churches in the South withdrew from the Triennial Convention and reorganized as the Southern Baptist Convention in 1845. Devastated by the Civil War, the convention took some decades to recover, but in the twentieth century it expanded into a national denomination, the largest single Protestant denomination.

The Triennial Convention continued and over the next century and a half evolved into the Northern Baptist Convention and more recently into the American Baptist Churches U.S.A. Along with the northern Presbyterian church, the Northern Baptist Convention became the most visible battleground for the modernist-fundamentalist controversy. As the more liberal element appeared to gain control of the convention, a number of fundamentalist groups withdrew through the 1920s and 1930s and founded a variety of new Baptist associations, most notably the General Association of Regular Baptist Churches, the Conservative Baptist Association of America (now more popularly known as CBAmerica), and the Minnesota Baptist Association.

The Southern Baptist Convention remained more conservative in its theology than the American Baptists and did not experience the same debates that occurred in the Northern convention. However, it did experience several controversies of its own, such as the Old Landmark controversy. Landmark Baptists emphasized Baptist distinctives from other Protestants and attempted to argue for pre-Protestant Baptist origins. Support for this position found a home in the American Baptist Association and the Baptist Missionary Association. Ultimately, a greater disturbance was generated by the charismatic ultra-fundamentalist J. Frank Norris, who in the 1930s formed the World Baptist Fellowship. In the years since Norris's death (1952), the WBF has become the parent of several large fundamentalist Baptist associations, including the Baptist Bible Fellowship International, the Independent Baptist Fellowship International, and the Liberty Baptist Fellowship (founded by televangelist Jerry Falwell).

Most recently, controversy within the Southern Baptist Convention between its most conservative and more moderate leaders led many moderates (including former President

Jimmy Carter) to withdraw and form new associations, notably the Alliance of Baptists and the Cooperative Baptist Fellowship.

African American Baptists

Africans have been part of the Baptist movement in America almost from the beginning, the first known African member having joined the church in Newport, Rhode Island, in 1652. In spite of slavery, the first African American Baptist Church was founded on Silver Bluff plantation in South Carolina in 1774. Two other Baptist churches, still in existence, were soon founded in Savannah, Georgia, and Charleston, South Carolina. The Savannah congregation became the mother of Baptist churches in Jamaica, Nova Scotia, and Sierra Leone. The first Black Baptist churches emerged in the North among free blacks in Boston (1805), New York (1808), and Philadelphia (1809).

The first Baptist associations serving African American congregations were founded in Ohio in the 1830s. In 1840, representatives from the New York and Philadelphia churches formed the American Baptist Missionary Convention, which over the next decades accepted some 45 churches across the northern states and emerged as the first national denominational body.

Following the American Civil War, African American Baptists began to organize separately as black leaders called for the creation of black-led and black-controlled Baptist structures, though a minority chose to remain affiliated with predominantly white organizations, especially the Northern Baptist Convention. Pan-congregational organization proceeded around the same issues that had led to the Triennial

Convention—missions, education, and publishing. An initial set of organizations participated in a series of mergers, leading finally to the creation of the National Baptist Convention U.S.A. in 1895.

The National Baptist Convention U.S.A. remains the largest religious body serving a predominantly African-American constituency, but it has been disturbed at several points through the twentieth century by disagreements over control of publishing, and in the 1960s over support for Martin Luther King Jr. and the Civil Rights movement. These debates have resulted in the formation of three additional National Baptist churches—the National Baptist Convention of America, the Progressive National Baptist Convention, and the National Missionary Baptist Convention of America.

Exact membership counts on the several National Baptist conventions are difficult to obtain, as they do not keep the same church-by-church lists and membership counts in the manner of most of their sister Baptist denominations. In addition, they allow both associations and churches to relate to (and hence be counted by) more than one of the national bodies. It is estimated, however, that some seven million African Americans consider themselves Baptist and more than half of these are associated with the National Baptist Convention U.S.A. It is also to be noted that approximately half a million black members adhere to the American Baptist Churches U.S.A.

General Baptists

While General or Free Will Baptists lost their majority status in the Baptist community, they have continued and built a variety of strong national organizations. The oldest and largest is the National Association of Free Will Baptists, followed by the General Association of General Baptists and the United American Free Will Baptist Church. The National Association reports some 210,000 members.

Other Baptists

The local church base for the Baptist movement has allowed a wide variety of opinions to emerge and find a following, none more interesting than the Seventh Day Baptists. Sabbatarianism emerged among Baptists in the seventeenth century and was brought to America as early as 1664 by Stephen Mumford. Though never a very large group, the Seventh Day Baptists ultimately became the source for the spread of sabbath worship among Adventists.

Through the nineteenth century, the Baptist movement spread across Europe in lands where English was not the dominant language, and somewhat simultaneously among parallel ethnic communities recently settled in the United States. Thus Baptist churches serving German, Scandinavian, and Eastern European communities emerged. Most of these have adopted English and most have changed to names indicative of their integration into the larger English-speaking community. Most Scandinavian Baptists have been absorbed into various English-speaking associations, especially the American Baptist Churches U.S.A. One former German-speaking community survives as the North American Baptist Conference. Eastern European Baptists continue in a set of small conservative Baptist groups such as the Ukrainian Evangelical Baptist Convention.

The twentieth century has seen a revival of a conservative Calvinist theology within the Baptist community and the emergence of several groups under names such as Sovereign Grace, Reformed, and Strict Baptists.

The emphasis on the local church in the Baptist tradition often makes the study and assembly of basic information on different Baptist groups difficult, even among the more dedicated and knowledgeable observers of the community. Many Baptist groups have no central headquarters, general officers, or accepted stable (if informal) source of information. A variety of groups beginning with the Primitive Baptists eschew any form of authority above the local church, publish very little, and have little interest in advertising their existence. Many of these groups, including most especially the Primitive and Regular Baptists, reside in the rural South and thus require some effort to contact. They do not make any reports on such matters as membership to any information agencies. They do not participate in any ecumenical associations.

The total Baptist community in America is in excess of thirty million and appears to be approaching forty million adherents. Its boundaries are vague and in places fade imperceptively into the Independent Fundamentalist churches, which have both Baptist and Plymouth Brethren roots. Brethren dispensational theology, along with the premillennialism it espouses, has made considerable inroads in conservative Baptist circles.

The emphasis on the local church as well as other Baptist particulars has caused a certain hesitancy among Baptists relative to participation in cooperative ecumenical efforts with other Christian bodies, even with fellow Baptists. The largest number of Baptist conventions and associations participate in the Baptist World Alliance (BWA), an international fellowship of Baptist unions and conventions around the world, and its continental affiliate, the North American Baptist Fellowship. However, even here, the majority of conservative Baptist bodies have refused fellowship with what are considered the more liberal Baptist groups. The BWA was hurt in 2004 when the Southern Baptist Convention voted to sever ties with the BWA, another symbol of the very conservative turn taken by the convention through the 1990s. Current membership in the BWA includes the following American-based groups: American Baptist Churches USA, Baptist General Association of the Baptist General Conference, Baptist General Convention of Texas, Cooperative Baptist Fellowship, Czechoslovak Baptist Convention of the USA and Canada, General Association of General Baptists, Lott Carey Baptist Foreign Mission Convention, USA, National Baptist Convention of America, National Baptist Convention, USA, Inc., National Missionary Baptist Convention of America, North American Baptist Conference, Progressive National Baptist Convention, Russian-Ukrainian Evangelical Baptist Union, USA, Seventh Day Baptist General Conference, USA and Canada, Union of Latvian Baptists in America.

Several conservative Baptist groups participate in the National Association of Evangelicals, including the Baptist General Conference, Conservative Baptist Association of America, and the General Association of General Baptists. Members of the National Council of the Churches of Christ in the U.S.A. include the Alliance of Baptists, American Baptist Churches in the USA, National Baptist Convention of America, National Baptist Convention, U.S.A., Inc., National Missionary Baptist Convention of America, and the Progressive National Baptist Convention.

Contacts:

American Baptist Churches U.S.A.
P.O. Box 851
Valley Forge, PA 19482
www.abc-usa.org

The oldest national Baptist fellowship in North America, the American Baptists date to the organization of the Triennial Convention in 1814. Through the twentieth century, it was known successively as the Northern Baptist Convention (1907), American Baptist Convention (1950), and American Baptist Churches in the U.S.A. (1972).

Baptist Bible Fellowship International
Box 191
Springfield, MO 65801
www.bbfi.org

The Baptist Bible Fellowship was formed in 1950 following the break between G. B. Vick and J. Frank Norris, the most prominent leaders in the fundamentalist World Baptist Fellowship. Under Vick's leadership, the BBFI surpassed its parent body in size.

Southern Baptist Convention
901 Commerce St.
Nashville, TN 37203
Webpage:www.sbc.net

The Southern Baptist Convention originated in the regional strife between North and South in the decades prior to the Civil War, slavery being the crucial issue. The Convention has, in the last half of the twentieth century, become the largest non-Catholic religious body in America.

African American Baptists

National Baptist Convention of America
777 S R Thornton Frwy., Suite 210
Dallas, TX 75203

or
1450 Pierre Ave.
Shreveport, LA 71103
www.nbcamerica.net

The National Baptist Convention of America resulted from a dispute over the private ownership of the National Baptist publishing concern. Those who supported R. H. Boyd's continued ownership of the denomination's publishing concern reformed apart from the National Baptist Convention of the U.S.A.

National Baptist Convention of the U.S.A., Inc.
c/o World Center Headquarters
1700 Baptist World Center Dr.
Nashville, TN 37207
www.nationalbaptist.com

This oldest national Baptist structure serving a predominantly African American constituency was formed in 1895 by the merger of several previously existing educational and publishing organizations already serving Baptists congregations.

National Baptist Evangelical Life and Soul Saving Assembly of the U.S.A.
441-61 Monroe Ave.
Detroit, MI 48226

The assembly began as an evangelical movement within the National Baptist Convention of America, but became independent in 1936.

National Missionary Baptist Convention of America
Office of the General Secretary
106 North East Ivy St.
Portland, OR 97212
www.nmbca.com

The National Missionary Baptist Convention of America resulted from a controversy within the National Baptist Convention of America, some of whose members began to call for greater accountability from the denomination's publishing house, which was independently owned and operated.

Progressive National Baptist Convention
601 50th St., NE
Washington, DC 20019
www.pnbc.org

The Progressive National Baptist Convention was formed by a group of pastors and members who wished to throw their support behind the Civil Rights Movement led by Martin Luther King, Jr. The National Baptist Convention in the U.S.A. had refused to commit itself behind King.

Free Will Baptists

General Association of General Baptists
100 Stinson Dr.
Poplar Bluff, MO 63901
www.generalbaptist.com

The General Association emerged in 1824 among the United Baptists along the Ohio River. In the 1820s the United Baptists became intolerant of those who did not believe in predestination continuing in their fellowship.

National Association of Free Will Baptists
5233 Mount View Rd.
Antioch, TN 37013-2306
www.nafwb.org

The National Association dates to 1727 and the work of Paul Palmer, a Baptist who preached an Arminian theology in North Carolina.

Sabbatarian Baptists

Seventh Day Baptist General Conference USA and Canada Ltd.
Seventh Day Baptist Center
3120 Kennedy Rd.
P.O. Box 1678
Janesville, WI 53547
www.seventhdaybaptist.org

The conference dates itself to the migration of sabbatarian Baptists from England to the American colonies in the eighteenth century. The first conference was organized in 1801.

Additional Baptist Churches

American Baptist Association
4605 N. State Line Ave.
Texarkana, TX 75501
www.abaptist.org

The ABA is one of several groups to perpetuate the idea that Baptists pre-exist Protestantism and can be traced through Christian groups that practiced adult baptism by immersion to the first century of the Christian era.

Association of Evangelicals for Italian Missions
314 Richfield Rd.
Upper Darby, PA 19082

The association, founded in 1899, primarily serves Italian-American Baptists.

Baptist General Conference
2002 S. Arlington Heights Rd.
Arlington Heights, IL 60005
www.bgcworld.org

The Baptist General Conference originated in 1852 from the effort of former Lutheran lay reader Gustaf Palmquist. Most members share a Swedish heritage.

Baptist General Convention of Texas
333 N. Washington
Dallas, TX 75246-1798
www.bgct.org

The Baptist General Convention of Texas dates to 1883, the culmination of a series of mergers of several regional Texas Baptist associations. In the 1990s, the Baptist General Convention ended its long affiliation with the Southern Baptist Convention and has become an independent body, though it has friendly relations with the Cooperative Baptists.

Baptist Missionary Association of America
c/o Baptist Publishing House
4613 Loop 245
Texarkana, AR 71845
or
Department of Church Ministries
P.O. Box 10356
Conway, AR 72034
www.bmaweb.net

The Baptist Missionary Association was formed in 1950 by former members of the American Baptist Association and continues the parent body's belief in pre-Protestant origins of the Baptists.

CBAmerica
1501 West Mineral Ave.
Littleton, CO 80120
www.cbamerica.org

CBAmerica (the Conservative Baptist Association of America) is a fellowship of evangelical Baptist churches that separated from the Northern Baptist Convention (now the American Baptist Churches in the U.S.A.) in 1946.

Continental Baptist Churches
P.O. Box 20308
Roanoke, VA 24018

Formed in 1983, the Continental Baptists hold to a Puritan covenant theology that emphasizes God's sovereign grace.

Cooperative Baptist Fellowship
P.O. Box 450329
Atlanta, GA 31145-0329
www.thefellowship.info

The fellowship is the primary group to emerge from the lengthy controversy for control of the Southern Baptist Convention in the 1980s and 1990s. It was officially constituted in 1991.

Czechoslovak Baptist Convention of the USA and Canada
c/o George Sommer, Executive Secretary
Route 4, Box 58D
Philippi, WV 26416
www.ab.edu/czslbaptconv

Formed in 1912, as the name suggests, the convention primarily serves members with a Czech or Slovak heritage.

Fundamental Baptist Fellowship International
c/o Tabernacle Baptist Church
717 N. Whitehurst Landing Rd.
Virginia Beach, VA 23464-2399
www.f-b-f.org

The Fundamentalist Baptist Fellowship was constituted by former members of the Conservative Baptist Association (now CBAmerica) who rejected cooperation with conservative Baptists who remained members of predominantly liberal Baptist associations.

General Association of Regular Baptist Churches
1300 N. Meacham Rd.
Schaumburg, IL 60173
www.garbc.com

The fundamentalist General Association was formed by former members of the Northern Baptist Convention (now the American Baptist Churches in the U.S.A.) in 1932.

Independent Baptist Fellowship International
724 North Jim Wright Frwy.
Ft. Worth, TX 76108
www.ibfi-nbbi.org

Independent Baptist Fellowship of North America
754 E. Rockhill Rd.
Sellersville, PA 18960
www.ibfna.org/IBFNA/index.htm

The fellowship was formed in 1993 by former members of the General Association of Regular Baptist Churches who felt that the association was compromising its strict position on separation from apostasy.

Liberty Baptist Fellowship
c/o Elmer L. Towns, Exec. Dir.
Candler's Mountain Rd.
Lynchburg, VA 24506

The Liberty Baptist Fellowship has grown out of the ministry of fundamentalist televangelist Jerry Falwell and the several schools for training pastors he founded.

Minnesota Baptist Association
224 Fifth Ave. NW
Hutchinson, MN 55350
www.mbaoc.org

In 1948 the Minnesota Baptist Convention, formerly a constituent part of the Northern Baptist Convention (now the American Baptist Churches in the U.S.A.) voted to become independent of the Northern Baptists and has subsequently remained a fundamentalist independent Baptist fellowship.

Nationwide Independent Baptist Fellowship
Peoples Baptist Church
850 Mill Rd.
McDonough, GA 30253
www.nationwidefellowship.com

The Nationwide Baptist Fellowship was formed in 1905 by former members of the fundamentalist Southwide Baptist Fellowship who felt that the organization had fallen into apostasy.

New Testament Association of Independent Baptist Churches
c/o Dr. Richard Paige
8856 East Fairfield St.
Mesa, AZ 85207-5124

The New Testament Association is a fundamentalist Baptist fellowship formed by former members of the Conservative Baptist Association (now CBAmerica).

North American Baptist Conference
c/o Reverend Harvey Mehlhaff, Mod.
1 S. 210 Summit Ave.
Oakbrook Terrace, IL 60181

The North American Baptist Conference primarily serves German-American Baptists.

Southwide Baptist Fellowship
c/o Faith Baptist Church
1607 Greenwood Rd.
Laurens, SC 29360

The Southwide Baptist Fellowship is a fundamentalist association of churches located primarily in the southern United States.

Sovereign Grace Baptist Association of Churches
No central headquarters. For information:
Lemoyne Baptist Church
P.O. Box 436
Lemoyne, OH 43444
www.sgba.net

Sovereign Grace churches emphasize a Calvinist Puritan theology coupled with a Baptist understanding of the autonomous local church.

World Baptist Fellowship
3001 W. Division
Arlington, TX 76012
www.wbfi.net

The World Baptist Fellowship, founded as the Premillennial Baptist Missionary Fellowship in 1932, grew out of the ministry of fundamentalist pastor J. Frank Norris (1877–1952).

For further reading:

Ammerman, Nancy T., ed. *Southern Baptists Observed: Multiple Perspectives on a Changing Denomination.* Knoxville: University of Tennessee Press, 1993.

Brackney, William H. *Baptist Life and Thought 1600–1980: A Source Book.* Valley Forge: Judson Press, 1983.

__________. *The Baptists.* New York: Greenwood Press, 1988.

__________. *Historical Dictionary of the Baptists.* Metuchen, NJ: Scarecrow Press, 1999.

Cook, Henry. *What Baptists Stand For.* London: Carey Kingsgate, 1961.

Crowley, John G. *Primitive Baptists of the Wiregrass South.* Gainesville: University of Florida Press, 1998.

Dorgan, Howard. *The Old Regular Baptists of Central Appalachia: Brothers and Sisters of Hope.* Knoxville: University of Tennessee Press, 1989.

Fitts, Leroy. *A History of Black Baptists.* Nashville: Broadman Press, 1985.

Fletcher, Jesse. *The Southern Baptist Convention: A Sesquicentennial History.* Nashville: Broadman and Holman Publishers, 1994.

George, Timothy, and David S. Dockery, eds. *Theologians of the Baptist Tradition.* Nashville: Broadman and Holman Publishers, 2001.

Goodwin, Everett C. *Baptists in the Balance: The Tension between Freedom and Responsibility.* Valley Forge: Judson Press, 1997.

Leonard, Bill. *Dictionary of Baptists in America.* Downer's Grove, Ill.: InterVarsity Press, 1994.

Macbeth, Leon. *The Baptist Heritage: Four Centuries of Baptist Witness.* Nashville: Broadman Press, 1975.

Mullins, Edgar. *Baptist Beliefs.* Valley Forge: Judson Press, 1983.

Payne, Ernest. *The Story of the Baptists.* London: Baptist Union Publishers, 1978.

Stanley, Brian. *The History of the Baptist Missionary Society: 1792–1992.* Edinburgh: T & T Clark, 1992.

Stricklin, David. *A Genealogy of Dissent: Southern Baptist Protest in the Twentieth Century.* Lexington: The University Press of Kentucky, 1999.

Torbet, Robert G. *A History of the Baptists.* Philadelphia: Judson Press, 1950, 1975.

Wardin, Albert W., ed. *Baptists Around the World.* Nashville: Broadman and Holman Publishers, 1995.

Washington, James Melvin. *Frustrated Fellowship.* Macon, Ga.: Mercer University Press, 1986.

N. The Society of Friends

The Friends movement appeared in seventeenth-century England as the most radical expression of the Puritan movement. Founder George Fox was a mystic and social activist who began to preach in 1647 following an experience of inner illumination. Fox ran into trouble soon after he began making known his critical views on the Church of England and social view on war (he was a pacifist). Soon after the establishment of the Commonwealth under Oliver Cromwell (1649), he was arrested.

Only after the demise of the Puritan Commonwealth and the restoration of the monarchy in England was Fox's movement able to make headway. In the late 1660s, the pioneering Friends organized a set of monthly (congregations), quarterly (district) and yearly (national) meetings. The Society of Friends accepted the notion that the Bible was not the end of revelation, but that each believer had access to an inner light through which he or she could contact the living Spirit. At their meetings, Friends waited quietly for the Spirit to speak. During these times, members frequently would shake with involuntary body movements, leading people to call them Quakers. More important, members would receive various messages and guidance that would, before being accepted, be examined in light of the teachings and example of Jesus.

Friends believed that they should lead simple lives and avoid the vanities of the world. They stayed away from colorful clothing, wigs, or jewelry. When most people discarded the use of the English familiar tense (thy and thou) in daily speech, they continued to employ it, which over time further set them apart. Finally, they became known for their activism in various social crusades including abolitionism and prison reform, but most notably, peace. Heightened tension over their pacifism regularly arose in times of war.

The first Quakers found a haven in the New World after one of their number, William Penn (1644–1718) turned his land grant into the colony of Pennsylvania. Penn invited his fellow believers (and many other persecuted religious minorities) to settle there. The first Quakers had arrived in the Colonies as early as 1655, but after Penn received his charter in 1681, they tended to congregate in and around Philadelphia and across the Delaware River in southern New Jersey. They promoted religious freedom in Pennsylvania and subsequently passed this ideal to the new nation following the Revolutionary War.

The Friends became a distinct minority group in the United States, even in Pennsylvania, and their efforts to rid the country of slavery limited the potential growth in the American South. Nevertheless, they established churches across the country. National organization began in 1681 with the first General Meeting of Friends held in New Jersey. That Meeting evolved into the General Yearly Meeting of Friends in Philadelphia, East Jersey, and Adjacent Provinces, now the Philadelphia Yearly Meeting, the oldest Quaker association in North America.

As the Friends established new congregations, they affiliated regionally in what were termed yearly meetings (usually including all the congregations in a state or a set of adjacent states). Yearly meetings are now affiliated with one of several national/international associations. The Friends grew out of a context of acceptance of common Christian beliefs, which they activated through their experience of the inner light. Then in the nineteenth century, the consensus through which the movement developed was strongly affected by two movements. On the one hand, Elias Hicks called for an emphasis on the Inner Light that threatened the commitment to essential Christian affirmations. On the other hand, Joseph John Gurney called for Quakers to align themselves with the Holiness movement (discussed in chapter 5 below). As both the Hicksite and Gurneyite factions separated, the mainstream of the Friends movement eventually formed what is today known as the Friends United Meeting, the largest organization of Friends internationally. Hicksite yearly meetings have come together in the Friends General Conference. The Holiness yearly meetings have formed the Evangelical Friends International.

In spite of their very real differences, Friends find a sense of unity in their shared history and their pacifism. The three main groups cooperate with the Friends World Committee for Consultation. Interestingly, the Quakers enjoyed some success in Africa in the nineteenth century, and the East Africa Yearly Meeting of Friends has become the largest Quaker association in the world.

Given the influence it has exerted in American culture, the relatively small size of the Quaker community surprises many. They number 125,000, with about 45,000 affiliated with the Friends United Meeting, a little over 30,000 in the other two larger associations, and the rest in the several unaffiliated yearly meetings. About that many more Quakers exist in various countries around the world.

Contacts:

Evangelical Friends International
5350 Broadmoor Circle, NW
Canton, OH 44709
www.evangelical-friends.org/about/contact.html

In 1990 the Evangelical Friends International superseded the former Evangelical Friends Alliance as a representative body for the more conservative Wesleyan-Holiness oriented Friends meetings.

Friends General Conference
1212 Arch St., 2B
Philadelphia, PA 19107
www.quaker.org/fgc

The Friends General Conference serves as a fellowship for the Hicksite Friends who have emphasized the world of the Inner Light in the inspiration and experience of Christians.

Friends United Meeting
101 Quaker Hill Dr.
Richmond, IN 47374
www.fum.org

The Friends United Meeting, the largest fellowship of Quakers in North America, serves the orthodox Friends tradition that survived after the Evangelical Friends and the Hicksite Friends had withdrawn to the right and left.

For further reading:

Bacon, Margaret Hope. *The Quiet Rebels : The Story of the Quakers in America.* Wallingford, Penn.: Pendle Hill Publications, 2000.

Barbour, Hugh, and J. William Frost. *The Quakers.* New York: Greenwood Press, 1988.

Comfort, William Wistar. *The Quaker Way of Life.* Philadelphia: The Blakiston Co., 1945.

Cooper, Wilmer A. *Living Faith: A Historical and Comparative Study of Quaker Beliefs.* Richmond, Ind.: Friends United Press, 2001.

Hamm, Thomas D. *The Transformation of American Quakerism : Orthodox Friends, 1800-1907.* Religion in North America. Bloomington: Indiana University Press, 1988.

Peck, George. *What Is Quakerism? A Primer.* Wallingford, Penn.: Pendle Hill Publications, 1988.

Quakers Around the World. London: Friends World Committee for Consultation, 1994.

Trueblood, D. Elton. *The People Called Quakers.* New York: Harper & Row, 1966.

Vipont, Elfrida. *The Story of Quakerism.* Richmond, Ind.: Friends United Press, 1977.

Whitmire, Catherine. *Plain Living: The Quaker Path to Simplicity.* Notre Dame, Ind.: Sorin Books, 2001.

4. Evangelical Pietism

In each generation Christian voices arise to remind the church that it cannot live on past accomplishments and leaders and that they must continually be the instruments of God's breathing the Spirit into the forms that give structure to the body of Christ. Occasionally such reform, revival, and revitalization movements take on conditions of more than local impact and reach out to affect Christianity internationally. Such a movement traces its origins to the modest efforts of eighteenth-century Lutheran pastor Johann Arndt (1555–1621), the author of *True Christianity* (1605), a volume emphasizing the author's belief that the Christian life involved right living and the union of the soul with God. Arndt's concerns were passed on to countrymen Philip Jacob Spener and August Hermann Francke. Some seventy years after its first appearance, Spener saw to a republication of Arndt's book, to which he attached a lengthy preface, the *Pia Desideria.* Here Spener presented a program for reform of the church with the goal of leading its members into an experience of personal faith and a life of piety. To this end he organized a number of informal meetings, which he termed the *Collegia Pietatis,* that met in his home for prayer, Bible study, and a discussion of the sermon preached in the local parish church the previous Sunday.

The *Pia Desideria* met significant opposition from the Lutheran clergy, but Spener finally established a fruitful ministry and founded a new university whose students were trained in assisting people to experience personal faith. Spener also discovered a capable student to carry on his work in August Francke, who came to lead the new university at Halle (1794) and guide the growing movement that had resulted from Spener's life and thought. Among the many people influenced by the new Pietist movement was Count Nikolaus von Zinzendorf, who also attended Halle during the years that Francke taught. In the 1720s, the relatively youthful Count made his estate a haven for Czech Protestant exiles and took an active role in their reorganization as the Moravian Church, also known as the Renewed United Brethren.

As the eighteenth century began, Pietism assumed a special role in the spread of Protestantism from its European base. Franz Lutkens, the chaplain to the king of Denmark, reached out to Halle for help finding ministers to work at Tranquebar, the Danish settlement in India. Two Halle graduates, Bartholemew Ziegenbalc and Heinrich Plütschau, volunteered to go as the first missionaries and began the first Protestant missionary enterprise in Asia in 1706. Then, on a visit to Copenhagen in 1730, Von Zinzendorf and his Moravian companions encountered Anthony, a slave from the Caribbean who pleaded with them to come and assist the Africans who had been brought to the Danish East Indies. In response to Anthony's pleas, the Moravians moved to complete a process of reorganization that now included a major effort to spread Christianity globally. Within a decade Moravian missionaries arrived in India, Africa, the Caribbean, and North America. Their effort launched the worldwide Protestant missionary movement that attracted Methodist and Baptist attention later in the century and would come to involve most Protestant denominations through the nineteenth century.

The redistribution of Moravians from von Zinzendorf's estate at Herrnhut led to the chance encounter of Moravian bishop Augustus Spangenberg, on his way to the Carolinas in 1734, with John Wesley, a young Anglican minister soon to take up residence in Savannah. Spangenberg pressed the issue of a personal relationship with Jesus Christ with Wesley, who struggled with Spangenberg's challenge off and on through the next few years of what proved a disastrous ministry in Georgia. Upon his return to England, Wesley spent time with another Moravian, Peter Böhler, who served as an additional catalyst for Wesley's eventual awakening. Following his "heart-warming experience" in 1738, Wesley deepened his relationship with the Moravians by visiting their center in Herrnhut.

In 1739 Wesley began his career as an evangelist with the formation of a religious society, modeled on the many informal lay groups in the Church of England that met for prayer and spiritual edification. The London society became the core from which the Methodist movement spread throughout the British Isles and to the British colonies in America. He recruited a cadre of lay preachers who soon became the instrument of spreading Methodism far and wide. Somewhat contemporaneous with Wesley's awakening was that of his brother Charles Wesley, who served the movement with his hymn-writing talents, and of George Whitefield, who had attended Oxford with the Wesleys.

George Whitefield was responsible for getting Wesley out of London and introducing him to open-air preaching, a major step in the spread of Wesley's movement. Whitefield then left for the American colonies, where he spread the Awakening throughout the length and breath of the land and introduced a variety of colonial ministers to the idea of revivalism, including Jonathan Edwards.

Methodism attracted a capable successor to Wesley in the person of Anglican minister Thomas Coke, who became charged with the fateful task of cutting American Methodists free after the Revolution but then went on to build a vision of the global spread of Wesley's movement. In the 1780s Coke helped launch Methodism's entrance into the global Protestant missionary movement, initially in the Caribbean and then in Asia.

In various ways Evangelical Pietism created tensions with older Protestant establishments, often expressed as a battle between confessionalism and piety. Confessionalism placed an emphasis on correct doctrine, usually as summarized in the great sixteenth-century Protestant confessions of faith, while the Pietists suggested that an over-emphasis on doctrine often led to a loss of the very essence of the faith of which the confessions spoke. In spite of opposition, however, Pietism spread throughout the Protestant world and became the source of new life in some of the older churches and, where resistance to the movement was strongest, brought new churches into existence.

For further reading:

Brown, Dale. *Understanding Pietism.* Grand Rapids: Eerdmans, 1978.

Sattler, Gary R. *God's Glory, Neighbor's Good: A Brief Introduction to the Life and Writings of August Hermann Francke.* Chicago: Covenant Press, 1982.

Stoeffler, F. Ernest. *The Rise of Evangelical Pietism.* Leiden: Brill, 1965.

O. German Baptist Brethren

One of the original expressions of the personal appropriation of faith urged by Philip Jacob Spener and the Pietists originated in western Germany. Here a group of members of the German Reformed Church struggled with what they felt was a spiritually dry and pastorally unresponsive church. They came to see the demand for doctrinal conformity as an obstacle to the emergence of personal faith and a barrier to a life of piety for individuals. Following the Pietist model, they began to meet for prayer, Bible study, and hymn-singing.

Alexander Mack, one of the leading Pietists, also began to challenge the local church leadership, an action that met with opposition and forced him to move from his hometown to Schwarzenau near Marburg, Hesse. Over the next year he came to feel that only in separation from the established church could a true Christianity be found. Thus, in 1708, he led a group of eight people who covenanted together to create a "church of Christian believers." Mack had come to believe that, as the Mennonites taught, baptism should be for adults who understood its significance. Further he came to believe that immersion was the proper mode, and should be done three times in the name of the triune God. The eight cast lots. Mack was baptized first, and he then rebaptized the other seven in the new way.

The small group, informally referred to as the Schwarznau Baptists, also rethought the Lord's supper, which they came to practice through a shared meal, the washing of each others feet, and the taking of bread and wine. In their separation from the government, they also came to believe in pacifism. Over the next decade, the group grew and additional congregations formed, but as it became visible to the authorities, persecution threatened to destroy them. In 1719 they began to leave Germany, some to America, others to Holland.

Through the 1720s, the groups settled in Germantown, then a German-speaking community outside of Philadelphia. Following Mack's arrival in 1729, he became their leader. They referred to themselves simply as the Brethren, and became known to their neighbors as the German Baptist Brethren or the Dunkers, a reference to their unique form of baptism. They found a broad agreement with the Mennonites and Quakers of the area and joined them in emphasizing simplicity and adopting simple dress codes, their appearance marking them as one group of the "Plain People." Like the other Plain People, they refused to bear arms in the American Revolution.

The Brethren operated informally for a generation, but as the movement spread they began to hold annual conferences. These became increasingly formal, though not until the 1780s was it felt necessary to keep written minutes. Slowly through the nineteenth century, English came to dominate the movement but it did not adopt its English name as the Church of the Brethren until 1908 (the bicentennial of the original baptisms in Germany).

The adoption of English was one adaptation to the changing culture of the modern world accepted by the Brethren. Other changes were the dropping of dress codes, the acceptance of modern education, and the development of relationships with other Christian churches. The gradual accommodation to change came to a head in the 1880s. The most conservative faction among the Brethren separated in 1881 and since then have been known as the Old German Baptist Brethren. The most liberal faction, in terms of accepting innovation in practice, separated two years later. They became known as the Brethren Church and have their headquarters at Ashland, Ohio.

The progressives among the Brethren were the first to move toward an educated (seminary-trained) ministry. Though liberal in their dropping of many of the cultural forms that had distinguished Brethren life, the progressives were very conservative in their theology and identified with the Fundamentalists in the 1920s. They split into two factions in the 1930s over whether they should adopt a statement of faith. Those supporting the particular statement in question, the "Message of the Brethren Ministry," coalesced around Grace Theological Seminary at Winona Lake, Indiana, and eventually emerged as the Fellowship of Grace Brethren Churches.

Today the Brethren remain a relatively small movement, the Church of the Brethren reporting some 140,000 members and the Brethren Church (Ashland, Ohio) and Fellowship of Grace Brethren churches reporting 13,000 and 35,000 respectively. The Church of the Brethren is a member of the National Council of Churches and the Brethren Church has affiliated with the National Association of Evangelicals.

Contacts:

Brethren Church (Ashland, Ohio)
524 College Ave
Ashland, OH 44805
www.brethrenchurch.org

The Brethren Church continues the fellowship of the progressive Brethren of the late nineteenth century who were among the first to advocate a professionally trained ministry and abandoned the necessity of "plain" dress among the German Baptist Brethren

Church of the Brethren
1451 Dundee Ave.
Elgin, IL 60120
www.cob-net.org

The Church of the Brethren is the oldest and largest of the several churches that have emerged out of the German Baptist Brethren movement.

Fellowship of Grace Brethren Churches
P.O. Box 386
Winona Lake, IN 46590
www.fgbc.org

The Fellowship of Grace Brethren was formed by members of the Church of the Brethren who were affected by the Fundamentalist movement of the 1920s. The issue of their split was the refusal of the Church of the Brethren to adopt a formal doctrinal statement apart from the Bible.

Old German Baptist Brethren
5215 Hess-Benedict Rd.
Waynesboro, PA 17268

The Old German Baptist Brethren withdrew from the Church of the Brethren in the 1880s, protesting the introduction of innovations such as Sunday schools, missions, and congregational auxiliary organizations into Brethren church life.

For further reading:

The Brethren Encyclopedia. 2 Vols. Philadelphia: The Brethren Encyclopedia, Inc., 1983.

Durnbaugh, Donald F. *The European Origins of the Brethren.* Elgin, Ill.: Brethren Press, 1958.

__________. *Fruit of the Vine: A History of the Brethren, 1708–1995.* Elgin, Ill.: Brethren Press, 1997.

Sappington, Roger E. *The Brethren in the New Nation.* Elgin, Ill.: Brethren Press, 1976.

Thompson, Charles D., Jr. *The Old German Baptist Brethren: Faith, Farming, and Change in the Virginia Blue Ridge.* Urbana: University of Illinois Press, 2006.

Willoughby, William G. *Counting the Cost.* Elgin, Ill.: Brethren Press, 1979.

P. Methodism

The Methodist movement emerged from the spiritual quest of John Wesley (1703–1791), who in the 1730s was thrown into inner turmoil by a variety of negative experiences in his first ministerial post with the newly established colony of Georgia. Upon his return to England, his spiritual struggle was assisted by his association with the Moravians, but it culminated during his attendance of an informal meeting of an Anglican religious society. As he later reported, during this gathering he felt his heart "strangely warmed" and became conscious of his personal relation with Christ. He visited Germany, where his time with the Moravians helped him consolidate his religious experience, though he would later break with them over the practice of Quietism, in which seekers waited in inactivity for an experience of God before beginning their practice of the Christian life.

Wesley formed his own religious societies, which through a series of innovations took on a distinctive tone. He adopted the practice of using unordained lay preachers, of preaching in settings away from church buildings wherever people gathered, and of asking society members to accept a disciplined Christian lifestyle. He soon organized the society members into small groups, called classes, which met weekly for edification and prayer. The multiplying societies were tied together by a set of conferences. Local conferences were held quarterly for a sacramental meal and examination of local leadership. Annual conferences were held with all the preachers, where Wesley would answer their questions and give them their preaching assignments for the next year.

Methodism grew up in the British Isles as a fellowship within the Church of England. Then in the 1760s it spread to the American colonies, the first classes being initiated by immigrants from Ireland. As the movement emerged, Wesley sent preachers to nurture the gathered believers. They discovered that a number of Africans, both free and slave, had been attracted to the movement. Their presence had a role in changing the nature of the movement from that of simply a revitalization movement within the Church of England into an evangelical movement reaching out to the unchurched.

Methodists inherited a Reformed theological tradition, but Wesley aligned himself with the variant theology developed by Dutch theologian Jacob Arminius (1560–1690) that rejected the emphasis upon predestination. Wesley championed the idea that Christ died for all and his death had resulted in God's grace spreading to all people. This prevenient grace, as Wesley termed it, allowed individuals to respond to the gospel and accept God's saving grace. The Wesleyan emphasis on the free grace of God became the basis of the focus on evangelism that led Methodism to become the largest religious grouping in America in the early nineteenth century. Wesley also proposed a doctrine of perfection as the goal of the Christian life that led to an emphasis on both holy living and social action.

Wesley faced a significant crisis following the American Revolution. As a lay movement, Methodists generally relied upon the parishes of the Church of England as a source for sacraments. However, the overwhelming majority of Anglican ministers left America during the Revolution, and Americans were in general hostile to the idea of continuing subordination to a British authority. Unable to gain episcopal orders, Wesley assumed the role of a bishop and ordained representatives to facilitate the formation of an independent American Methodist organization.

In 1784, the American leaders organized the Methodist Episcopal Church and accepted orders from Wesley through his representative, Thomas Coke. They chose Francis Asbury as their first leader and gave him the title bishop—as opposed to superintendent, the title Wesley favored. British Methodists, never calling their leaders bishops (which would have suggested competition with Anglican bishops), remained a fellowship within the Church of England until 1795 when the Wesleyan Conference was reorganized as a dissenting church.

Following its organization as the Methodist Episcopal Church, Methodism exploded upon the new nation and from a few thousand members soon became the largest church in the country. Significant in Methodism's growth was its singular willingness among American churches at the time to evangelize African Americans, who soon came to make up around 20 percent of its total membership. In its first two decades, an African preacher, Harry Hosier, became the churches' most effective preacher. Though never ordained, he was regularly sent by Bishop Asbury to shore up the weaker areas in the expanding church.

While Methodism appealed to African Americans, a growing membership in the South kept the church from welcoming them into the ordained ministry and led to a growing relegation of lay members to a second-class status. Beginning in

1813 in Wilmington, Delaware, the church experienced a series of schisms by Black members that led to the founding of three independent Methodist churches, the African Union Church (1813), the African Methodist Episcopal Church (1816), and the African Methodist Episcopal Zion Church (1820). Racial issues continued to plague the church, and adherents of the new abolitionist movement were forced out in the 1840s and formed the Wesleyan Methodist Church.

Wesley had presented the church at the time of its organization with a form of organization and a set of doctrines. The form of organization and rules for the church were printed in a small book, *The Discipline*, which was revised and reissued every four years following the meeting of the General Conference, the highest legislative body in the church. *The Discipline* also included the doctrinal statement, adopted as the 25 Articles of Religion, which Wesley had excerpted from the Church of England's 39 Articles. While organization and doctrine were important, they were simply the means of the church carrying out what it saw as its primary directive, to spread scriptural holiness over the land. To that end, Bishop Asbury took control of the church and annually for the rest of his long life traveled the length and breath of the land overseeing its progress. He also assumed the same authority as Wesley in appointing the ministers to their assigned territory.

The strong episcopal authority in the church allowed the church to grow with the country, but also occasioned a variety of protests from those who felt most abused by it—ministers who did not like the posts to which the bishop assigned them and emerging congregations that often did not have regular ministerial leadership for their Sunday services. A major protest to episcopal authority led in the 1820s to the establishment of the Methodist Protestant Church and later to movements like the Congregational Methodist Church.

At the height of its success in the 1840s, the Methodist Episcopal Church found itself unable to reach a workable consensus on slavery. The northern conferences were dominated by those opposed to slavery and the southern conferences by those who had come to feel that some accommodation was their only recourse. A new problem, however, arose in 1844 when the general conference gathered with the news that one of the church's bishops had become a slaveholder. For several reasons, the bishop refused to rid himself of the slaves, and before the conference adjourned, the general conference voted to split the church into two autonomous jurisdictions, the northern branch retaining the name Methodist Episcopal Church and the southern becoming known as the Methodist Episcopal Church, South.

Both of the two larger branches of the Methodist Church retained a large African membership until the end of the Civil War. Following the southern church's reorganization, the majority of its Black members chose to organize a new church, the Colored (now Christian) Methodist Episcopal Church, while a minority chose to reaffiliate with the Methodist Episcopal Church. The majority of these joined the African Methodist Episcopal Church or the African Methodist Episcopal Zion Church, both of which grew rapidly following the war and became national bodies.

While the main English-speaking body of Methodists had spread across the country, the Evangelical Awakening had entered the German-speaking community. Two churches resulted—the Evangelical Association growing out of the work of Jacob Albright and the United Brethren in Christ from that of Philip Otterbein and Martin Boehm. These two churches followed a parallel course in the rapidly expanding German-American community through the nineteenth century. The United Brethren faced a major crisis in 1889 when a new constitution was adopted that, among other things, allowed church members to join secret societies. A minority under the leadership of Bishop Milton Wright (father of the Wright brothers of airplane fame) left the church to continue under the previous constitution. This group continues as the Church of the United Brethren in Christ. The Evangelical Association suffered a schism in 1894. The breakaway group reunited in 1922, the Association taking the name Evangelical Church at that time. However, a minority refused to rejoin and continues as the Evangelical Congregational Church.

During the twentieth century, the larger Methodist bodies became major advocates of the ecumenical movement. Most were charter members of the Federal Council of Churches, which adapted the Social Creed of the Southern Methodists for its own social statement. Beginning in 1939 the Methodists went through a series of mergers that led to the formation of the presently existing United Methodist Church in 1968. The Methodist Episcopal Church, the Methodist Episcopal Church, South, and the Methodist Protestant Church merged in 1939. The Evangelical Church and the United Brethren merged in 1946. The churches produced by these two mergers, the Methodist Church and the Evangelical United Brethren merged in 1968. The 1939 and 1968 mergers produced new churches formed by small groups that did not wish to join in the merged body. These new churches include the Southern Methodist Church, the Fellowship of Fundamental Bible Churches, the Association of Independent Methodists, and Evangelical Church of North America (1968). The latter group has identified with the Holiness movement (discussed below in chapter 5).

The United Methodist Church, now the third largest Christian church in the United States, has become one of the building blocks of the liberal Protestant establishment, though by its very nature it includes within its membership and ordained ministry a wide spectrum of beliefs, including a large number of conservative Evangelicals. Its constituent bodies were active in the formation of the National Council of Churches, the World Council of Churches, and the World Methodist Council. It now reports more than eight million members. The United Methodist Church now maintains close fraternal ties with the three large African Methodist churches, who also share membership in the three councils. Each of these churches reports more than a million members, with the African Methodist Episcopal Church now reporting approximately 2.5 million.

A variety of additional Methodist churches formed in the nineteenth century. The largest of these—the Wesleyan Church, the Free Methodist Church, and the Church of the Nazarene—identified with the Holiness movement (and are discussed below in chapter 5). Others have remained relatively small, counting their members in the tens of thousands. The Church of the United Brethren in Christ and the Evangelical Methodist Church are both members of the National Association of Evangelicals, and the Evangelical Methodist Church of America and the Fellowship of Fundamental Bible Churches are members of the American Council of Christian Churches.

Contacts:

United Methodist Church
No central headquarters. For information:
United Methodist Communications
P.O. Box 320
Nashville, TN 37202-0320
or
810 12th Ave., South
Nashville, TN 37203
www.umc.org

The United Methodist Church was constituted in 1968 following mergers that produced the uniting churches in 1939 and 1946.

African American Methodists

African Methodist Episcopal Church
500 8th Ave., S.
Nashville, TN 37203
www.ame-church.org

The AME Church was formed by African Americans meeting in Philadelphia in 1816. They were formerly members of the Methodist Episcopal Church (now a constituent part of the United Methodist Church).

African Methodist Episcopal Zion Church
Box 23843
Charlotte, NC 28232

The AMEZ Church was founded in 1820 by former members of the Methodist Episcopal Church in New York City.

African Union First Colored Methodist Protestant Church
2611 N. Claymont St.
Wilmington, DE 19802

The AUFCMPC traces its beginning to African Methodists who left the Methodist Episcopal Church (now a constituent part of the United Methodist Church) in 1813. Originally known as the African

Independent Church, it is the first of the several independent Black Methodist denominations that formed in the nineteenth century.

Christian Methodist Episcopal Church
c/o the General Secretary
564 Frank Ave.
P.O. Box 3403
Memphis, TN 38101
www.c-m-e.org

The CME Church was founded in 1870 by former members of the Methodist Episcopal Church, South (now a constituent part of the United Methodist Church).

Free Christian Zion Church of Christ
c/o Chief Pastor Willie Benson
1315 Hutchinson
Nashville, AR 71852

The Free Christian Church was formed in 1905 by former members of the African Methodist Episcopal Zion Church.

Reformed Methodist Union Episcopal Church
c/o Right Reverend Leroy Gethers
1136 Brody Ave.
Charleston, SC 29407

The Reformed Methodist Union Episcopal Church was formed in 1885 by former members of the African Methodist Episcopal Church.

Reformed Zion Union Apostolic Church
Rt. 1
Box 64D
Dundas, VA 23938
www.rzua.com

The Reformed Zion Union Apostolic Church was formed in 1869 by former members of the African Methodist Episcopal Church.

Union American Methodist Episcopal Church
c/o Bishop George W. Poindexter
3101 Market St.
Wilmington, DE 19802

The UAMEC is one of the two churches to derive from the initial efforts of Peter Spencer of Wilmington, Delaware, early in the nineteenth century.

Additional Methodist Churches

Association of Independent Methodists
405 Marquis Dr.
Jackson, MS 39206
www.aim2020.com

The AIM was formed in 1965 by some Methodists in the American South who did not wish to participate in the merger that produced the United Methodist Church in 1968.

Congregational Methodist Church
Box 9
Florence, MS 39073
congregationalmethodist.net

The Congregational Methodist Church was organized by members of the Methodist Episcopal Church, South (now a constituent part of the United Methodist Church) who rejected that church's episcopal leadership.

Evangelical Congregational Church
c/o Evangelical Congregational Church Center
100 W. Park Ave.
Box 186
Myerstown, PA 17067
www.eccenter.com

The Evangelical Congregational Church was formed by members of the United Evangelical Church who did not wish to participate in its 1922 merger with the Evangelical Association to form the

Evangelical Church (now a constituent part of the United Methodist Church).

Evangelical Methodist Church
P.O. Box 17070
Indianapolis, IN 46217
www.emchurch.org

The Evangelical Methodist Church was founded in 1946 by former members of the Methodist Church (1939–1968) who rejected the modernist tendencies that had become part of the parent church's life.

Evangelical Methodist Church of America
c/o Jim Felds, Gen. Sup.
Box 751
Kingsport, TN 37662
www.setlinc.com/emc

Shortly after the Evangelical Methodist Church was founded, some more fundamentalist members left to found the Evangelical Methodist Church of America.

Fellowship of Fundamental Bible Churches
112 South Main St.
Glassboro, NJ 08028
jrpeet.truepath.com/ffbc

The fellowship was founded by former members of the Methodist Protestant Church who rejected the 1939 merger that produced the Methodist Church (now the United Methodist Church).

First Congregational Methodist Church of the U.S.A.
Decatur, MS 39327

In 1941 members of the Congregational Methodist Church withdrew over a variety of issues that had emerged and formed a new denomination.

Fundamental Methodist Church, Inc.
1034 N. Broadway
Springfield, MO 65802

The Fundamental Methodist Church was founded by former members of the Methodist Protestant Church who rejected the 1939 merger that produced the Methodist Church (now the United Methodist Church).

Methodist Protestant Church
722 Highway 84 West
P.O. Box 2454
Collins, MS 39428
www.pointsouth.com/mpc/index.html

The Methodist Protestant Church was founded by former members of the Methodist Protestant Church who rejected the 1939 merger that produced the Methodist Church (now the United Methodist Church).

New Congregational Methodist Church
c/o Bishop Joe E. Kelley
354 E. 9th St.
Jacksonville, FL 32206

The New Congregational Methodist Church was formed in 1881 in Waycross, Georgia, by former members of the Methodist Episcopal Church, South, who rejected its parent church's episcopal polity.

Primitive Methodist Church in the U.S.A.
c/o Kerry R. Ritts, Pres.
723 Preston Lane
Hatboro, PA 19040-2321
www.primitivemethodistchurch.org/general.html

The Primitive Methodist Church was founded in England after the introduction of American-style revivalism into British Methodism. The church then spread to America early in the nineteenth century.

Southern Methodist Church
P.O. Box 39
Orangeburg, SC 29116-0039
www.southernmethodistchurch.org

The Southern Methodist Church was founded in South Carolina by members of the Methodist Episcopal Church, South, who rejected the 1939 merger that produced the Methodist Church (now the United Methodist Church). The possible integration of African American Methodists into the church was a pervasive issue and the new church added a belief in segregation of the races to their statement of beliefs.

For further reading:

Albright, Raymond W. *A History of the Evangelical Church.* Harrisburg, Penn.: The Evangelical Press, 1956.

Davies, Rupert, and Gordon Rupp, eds. *A History of the Methodist Church in Great Britain.* 3 vols. London: Epworth Press, 1965–1983.

Green, Vivian H. H. *John Wesley.* London: Thomas Nelson, 1964.

Harmon, Nolan B. *Encyclopedia of World Methodism.* 2 vols. Nashville: United Methodist Publishing House, 1974.

Kinghorn, Kenneth Cain. *The Heritage of American Methodism.* Nashville: Abingdon Press, 1999.

Nagler, Arthur Wilford. *Pietism and Methodist.* Nashville: Publishing House of the M. E. Church, South, 1918.

Schmidt, Martin. *John Wesley, A Theological Biography.* 2 vols. New York: Abingdon, 1963–73.

Stokes, Mack B. *Major United Methodist Beliefs.* Nashville: Abingdon, 1971.

Tuell, Jack M. *The Organization of the United Methodist Church.* Nashville: Abingdon, 1977.

Wigger, John H., and Nathan O. Hatch, eds. *Methodism and the Shaping of American Culture.* Nashville: Kingswood Books, 2001.

World Methodist Council, Handbook of Information. Lake Junaluska, N.C.: World Methodist Council, 1997.

Yrigoyen, Charles, Jr., and Susan E. Warrick. *Historical Dictionary of Methodism.* Metuchen, N.J.: Scarecrow Press, 1996.

Q. Moravians

The Moravian Church traces its origins to the attempts at church reform made at the beginning of the fifteenth century by Catholic priest Jan Hus (c. 1373–1415), the popular preacher at the Bethlehem Chapel in Prague. His calls for change led to his excommunication in 1410. His attacks on the granting of indulgences as a means of raising money and his advocacy of using the Bible as a standard by which to measure theological affirmation and practices in the church were singled out for specific condemnation, as was his call for the reception of communion in both kinds (bread and wine).

In 1414 Hus was called to present his views at the church council then gathering at Constance. The council was dealing specifically with issues of reform. Granted safe passage, Hus attended. However, once in the city, he was arrested and detained for a year before being allowed to speak of his concerns. Subsequently, the safe passage was revoked and Hus was burned at the stake in 1415. A Hussite church survived in Moravia and Bohemia.

One of several groups that emerged in the years after Hus' death, the Unitas Fratrum (United Brethren) survived through the next centuries. However, early in the seventeenth century, a new attempt to impose Catholicism on the region was launched. Catholic forces won a major victory in 1620 and in 1652 Protestants were expelled. For the next two generations, members of the United Brethren lived an underground existence or fled in exile. Finally, in 1722 they found a haven on the estate of Prussian Count Nikolaus von Zinzendorf. Having created the village of Herrnhut, they began reordering their church life and reviving their spirituality. In 1727 they initially accepted a new order to rule their lives, an event from which they mark the beginning of what is now the Moravian Church. Still unresolved was whether they would become Lutherans or reestablish their own independent existence.

Hastening the resolution of their self-understanding was an encounter with an African slave named Anthony in 1730. The community responded quickly and enthusiastically to his plea for ministers to assist his fellow slaves in the Caribbean. The initial venture in foreign missions developed quickly into a global missionary program supported by those who remained behind in Herrnhut. It also led to their beginning work in the British American colonies in 1734.

The Moravians sought an ancient episcopal lineage, which they received in 1735 from Daniel Ernst Jablonski (1660–1741), a German Calvinist who had orders that traced to the Polish Moravian community. In 1745 the Moravian Church was more formally reorganized as a new episcopal body and its order subsequently recognized by the Church of England in 1749.

More than just their landlord, Count von Zinzendorf, himself deeply influenced by Pietism, took an active part in Moravian Church life and leadership. Through him, the community absorbed the lively spirituality of the Pietist movement, which it shared with John Wesley, the founder of Methodism.

The Moravian movement came to the New World in 1734, when a group under the leadership of August Gottlieb Spangenberg moved to the new colony of Georgia. They ran into initial trouble when they refused to serve in the local militia, and had to leave Georgia. They subsequently settled in Pennsylvania on land owned by evangelist George Whitefield, John Wesley's colleague, but in 1741 they purchased land for a new settlement which they called Bethlehem, Pennsylvania, and then a second plot that became the town of Nazareth. These became the centers from which they spread around the colonies and launched a mission to Native Americans.

Spangenberg then established a second headquarters for Moravians in North Carolina at Salem. Over the next century, Bethlehem, Pennsylvania, and Winston-Salem, North Carolina, emerged as the centers from which the movement spread and the center of the two provinces (Northern and Southern) of the American branch of the Moravian Church. The American work became autonomous in 1848 and now stands in close fraternal relationship with other autonomous Moravian provinces in Europe, the Caribbean, and southern Africa. There is an international gathering of Moravian leaders from around the world every seven years.

The Moravians retain the essentials of Protestant Christianity, but they have adopted a motto to govern their approach to theology: "In essentials unity; in nonessentials liberty; in all things love." They accept the Bible as the source of Christian doctrine, and saw as central to their expression of the faith what they termed "heart religion," a personal relationship with Jesus, which they saw as far more important than doctrinal purity. They continue to hold simple communal meals called love feasts, and they developed an early emphasis on music that nurtured a rich hymnody.

The Moravian Church in America now reports some 50,000 members in North America (including a Canadian district), with approximately half of its members found in the states of

Pennsylvania and North Carolina. The church is a member of the National Council of Churches and the World Council of Churches.

The Moravian Church shares a historical relationship with the Unity of the Brethren, another church that claim the original United Brethren as part of their history. Following the suppression of Protestantism in Bohemia and Moravia, many Brethren remained in their homeland and perpetuated the faith underground. In the middle of the nineteenth century, some of these Brethren made their way to Texas where they organized the Evangelical Union of Bohemian and Moravian Brethren in North America. It differs somewhat from the Moravian Church, as it did not pass through the Pietist phase of the Moravians at Herrnhut nor engage in a missionary program. They also have a Presbyterian polity rather than episcopal leadership.

Contacts:

Moravian Church in America
Northern Province
1021 Center St.
Box 1245
Bethlehem, PA 18016-1245
or
Southern Province
459 S. Church St.
Winston-Salem, NC 27108
www.moravian.org

The American Moravians are an integral part of the worldwide Moravian movement that emerged early in the eighteenth century in Germany.

Unity of the Brethren
c/o Kim Ulmer, Sec. of Synodical Committee
1417 Windcrest Dr.
Round Rock, TX 77065
www.unityofthebrethren.org

The Unity of the Brethren, never a part of the Moravian Church, shares a similar heritage among independent Protestants in Moravia and Bohemia.

For further reading:

Allen, Walter H. *Who Are the Moravians?* Bethlehem, Penn.: Walter H. Allen, 1966.

Hamilton, J. Taylor, and Kenneth G. Hamilton. *History of the Moravian Church: The Renewed Unitas Fratrum, 1722–1957.* Bethlehem, Penn., and Winston-Salem, N.C.: Interprovincial Board of Christian Education, Moravian Church in America, 1967.

Rican, Rudolf. *The History of the Unity of Brethren.* Bethlehem, Penn.: The Moravian Church in America, 1992.

Schattschneider, Allen W. *Through Five Hundred Years.* Bethlehem, Penn.: Comenius Press, 1956. Rev. ed.: 1982.

Weinlick, John Rudolf. *Count Zinzendorf.* New York: Abingdon, 1956.

_________. *The Moravian Church through the Ages.* Bethlehem, Penn.: Moravian Church in America, 1988.

5. Nineteenth-Century Free Churches

With some liberty, one can see the sixteenth century as having produced a Reformation in the church that led to Protestant establishments replacing Roman Catholic ones across much of northern and western Europe. The Puritan movement then emerged in force in England in the seventeenth century in an attempt to further the gains of the Reformation. The Evangelical Awakening of the eighteenth century saw itself, at least initially, as a revitalization movement within the established churches. The end result of each of the movements, however, was the founding of a set of new rival ecclesiastical bodies. By the beginning of the nineteenth century, any hope of replacing the older establishments had largely disappeared, and while movements to revive the church could do much good, they would reach only a percentage of churchgoers.

By the beginning of the nineteenth century, one sees a subtle change in the process of forming new churches. This change is largely influenced by the spread of ideals of freedom—the freedom of (i.e., separation of) church from the state, the freedom to inquire and question, the freedom to dissent. The fact that the established churches were not going away should not be an obstacle to the establishment of a church that more closely conformed to truth, to which the aware and/or the elect could subscribe. Given the new freedoms won in the previous centuries with the spread of notions of toleration of religious differences, the number of new churches disconnected from state control (if not from state regulation) multiplied. Outsiders generally called these churches sects, noting that they retained a close resemblance to the older churches but offered several unique sectarian differences, be they doctrinal, organizational, or devotional.

Throughout the nineteenth century, one can see the emergence of a variety of themes that dominate the thinking of the founders of the new movements. For example, many of the founders were affected by the scandal of Protestant divisiveness and sought different platforms upon which a reunited church could be built. Their quest was for a certain New Testament simplicity, affirmation of a set of essentials, or even abandoning denominational designations in favor of biblical designations—the church of God or just Christians.

On the opposite extreme of those who sought to heal the brokenness of the church were those who proposed a range of new teachings, usually derived from their personal study of the Bible. Many of these new teachings took believers far from the core of Christian orthodoxy and actually created a new religion, though utilizing Christian symbols—the Latter-day Saints and Christian Science stand as prime examples. Others retained more or less faithfully the central affirmations of the faith, but cast them in a very different context. None were more successful than the Adventist movement of William Miller and the Brethren movement of John Nelson Darby. Both movements found their origin in an individualized interpretation of the belief in the priesthood of all believers and the appeal to the authority of the Bible put forth during the Reformation.

Most theological innovations that led to the founding of new denominations, however, resulted from a new emphasis on older ideas that had been present but relatively neglected. Adventism, for example, picked up very real beliefs in the second coming of Christ and placed them at the center of the church's agenda. The urgency given the doctrine was based on the belief that the Bible revealed heretofore missed clues about the timing of endtime events. The Holiness movement took the belief in sanctification taught within the Methodist movement and placed it at the center of what initially was a revitalization effort within the Methodist Church.

Also at the opposite end of the drive to heal the divisions between the various Protestant churches was an assertion of freedom that took on many expressions. Most of the older churches had hierarchical organizations that gave real power to church leaders—bishops, synods, and presbyteries. Many revolted against what they saw as the arbitrary exercise of authority by church officials and the undemocratic actions of church councils. Thus one sees through the century the establishment of versions of older churches that maintained traditional theological affirmations but reorganized church life to redistribute power away from national leadership and place it in the hands of congregations and ministers. One sees this most vividly illustrated in the Restoration Movement, where any kind of pan-congregational organization, even for fellowship and building a sense of oneness in the movement, was questioned.

Nowhere did the freedom issue take a more central place, and for very good reasons, than in the African American churches. First, when the growth of the free black community in the northern cities and the end of the slave system in the 1860s failed to destroy the racial attitudes that had supported slavery and anti-black legislation, African American leaders took the opportunity that their freedom allowed to found churches that directly served their community's needs. Initially, African American leaders created African-led organizations reflective of older white churches, primarily Methodist and Baptist jurisdictions (as discussed in previous chapters), but by the end of the nineteenth century they took the lead developing innovative approaches to the Christian life.

The result of the development of ideals of personal freedom of choice in religion and the very real freedom to propose new innovations in church life resulted in the radical proliferation of churches. At the beginning of the nineteenth century there were some twenty different Christian churches operating in America. By the end of the century, there were more than three hundred. Most of the three hundred were variations on the original twenty churches, but some were the products of completely new movements.

While these overall patterns would work themselves out through the nineteenth century, at the beginning of the century they were not on the mind of most church leaders. They were focused on two new realities that presented themselves in the decades immediately after the founding of the new nation. Throughout the colonial era, most Europeans resided relatively close to the Atlantic Ocean or the Gulf of Mexico, only a few hearty souls venturing inland along the river systems that served as the highways of the era. Then the frontier was opened, with the United States claiming all the land west to the Mississippi River. As a result thousands of pioneers began streaming into the newly opened territory, ready to make their fortune or at least carve out a means of surviving. Church leaders saw the immediate need to plant churches in the newly populated lands, but also quickly grasped the second reality—the lack of support they had from the general population. The destruction of the semblance of religious establishments in the middle and southern colonies made most aware of the unchurched nature of the population. Far from being a Christian country, less than 15 percent (a conservative estimate) of Americans were attached to any church. Not only was there a need to evangelize the residents of the older population centers in the East, but planting any sort of church in the West would require a monumental effort.

The very different responses made to these very new realities were the major factors that led to the restructuring of American religious life. Methodists, Baptists, and Roman Catholics were best equipped to respond to a missionary situation.

Traditional Protestants were suspicious of anything that smacked of revivalism and had little experience with missionary activity. Their experience was limited to reforming already Christianized communities rather than building new ones. Relative to the frontier, they tended to wait until enough church members had migrated to the newly emerging centers of population and issued a call for a minister before they acted. Thus while their numbers grew, they fell far behind the population growth.

Meanwhile, the Methodists deployed circuit riders to the very edge of the moving frontier to establish preaching points and classes that could grow into congregations. Baptists empowered numerous lay preachers who worked farms or engaged in business during the week and preached to neighbors on the weekend. Catholic priests sought out church members among the pioneers and established missions that could evolve into parishes.

The context of the frontier nurtured the development of new forms of mass evangelism that quickly became the possession of all the older groups and led to the emergence of new ones. One thinks immediately of the camp meeting, used most effectively by Methodists and Baptists, but whose origins are intimately tied to the emergence of the Restoration movement and the Cumberland Presbyterians. Included in the techniques that became a common part of life west of the Alleghenies were the protracted meetings and other "new measures" introduced by Congregationalist evangelist Charles G. Finney, and the urban crusades and Bible conferences most associated with Dwight L. Moody during the last decades of the century.

R. Restoration Movement

Those who do not attend a congregation of the Churches of Christ or the Disciples of Christ may be unfamiliar with the reference to them under the collective heading as the Restoration Movement, a term that has become an increasingly popular designation for a group of believers who wished originally to be known simply as Christians. The term Restoration in this context indicates the founders' collective desire to return to and restore primitive Christianity in their day, one aspect of which included the unity they saw in the apostolic generation.

Among the founders of the movement were four former Presbyterians: Barton Stone, Thomas Campbell and his son Alexander Campbell, and Walter Scott. Censured for his participation in camp meetings, Stone left the Presbyterian Synod of Kentucky and formed the independent Springfield Presbytery. However, in 1809, having concluded that a congregational polity was more biblical, he dissolved the presbytery, after which the members began to refer to themselves as simply the Christian Church. Meanwhile, the Campbells, having departed from the Presbyterians, founded an independent church that in 1913 united with the Red Stone Baptist Association in Pennsylvania. While largely agreeing with the Baptists, their desire to restore New Testament Christianity led to some disagreements and in 1830, after almost two decades of affiliation, the Campbells withdrew. Crucial in their decision was the idea that even the very loose pan-congregational associations of the Baptists were not biblical. Walter Scott is credited with holding the following together as the transition away from fellowship with the Baptists was made.

The Restorationists continued many practices that they had adopted from the Baptists. They moved away from any understanding of sacraments and practiced the baptism and the Lord's supper as ordinances. They dropped infant baptism as practiced by Presbyterians, and would baptize only adults who professed faith. They also baptized only by immersion. They saw the Lord's supper as a memorial meal. Uniquely, since some of the Restoration leaders had gone through long periods when the Lord's supper was unavailable in their frontier locations, they included it as part of their weekly Sunday worship. They did not, as had some Baptists, adopt foot washing as a third ordinance.

Meanwhile in other parts of the country, fellowships of congregations that shared many of the anti-organizational ideals of Stone and the Campbells emerged in response to the likes of Methodist James O'Kelly and Baptists Abner Jones and Elias Smith. Each strain of the movement was committed to evangelism and to the formation of congregations of Christians throughout America, but especially in the lands west of the Allegheny Mountains. Some unity was given to the various strains of this larger movement by Alexander Campbell, who was well educated, traveled widely, spoke frequently, and published a popular magazine, the *Millennial Harbinger,* which he founded in 1830.

The movement was an integral part of the revivalistic culture being spread by the Methodists and Baptists. The several Christian groups were associated with the origins of the camp meeting, which had slowly evolved as a new from of evangelistic activity from a variety of sources, including the Presbyterians' popular, if occasional, weekend sacramental gatherings. The same interest in evangelism and revivalism that motivated the

Restorationist break with Presbyterianism led some Presbyterians to form the Cumberland Presbyterian Church, a church that followed Presbyterian order but was deeply involved with the mass evangelistic efforts on the frontier.

The two branches of the movement led by Barton Stone and by the Campbells came together in a loose association in 1832. Believing strongly in a congregational polity, the movement had no formal headquarters. In the years after the Civil War, the congregations in the North and South began to drift apart. That split was formalized in 1906. The use of instrumental music was the most visible outward difference between the two groups. The southern congregations (the Churches of Christ), adopting as their rallying cry, "Speak where the scriptures speak, keep silent where the scriptures are silent," forbad the use of musical instruments. The northern congregations (the Christian Church [Disciples of Christ]) began to identify with the other denominations and increasingly looked to a formally educated ministry and developed pan-congregational structures. The northern group also took an active part in the formation of the ecumenical movement, seen by some Disciples leaders as a way of actualizing the Restorationists' goals of healing the divisions in Protestantism.

The development of a spectrum of structures to serve the various needs of the Christian congregations (publishing, missionary outreach, etc.), culminating in the formation of the International Convention that unified the various organizations serving the churches, was rejected by a significant minority of the church. In 1968, the more organizationally conservative of the Disciples withdrew support from the Convention and continued to operate with the variety of decentralized structures they had previously learned to follow. The dissenting group subsequently was designated as the Christian Churches and Churches of Christ.

Thus, at present, the Restoration movement consists of three separate branches. The Churches of Christ (non-instrumental) report about 1.5 million members, with the Christian Churches and Churches of Christ reporting about a million, and the Disciples of Christ about 800,000. Within the very loosely organized Churches of Christ several sub-groups have been identified by (1) their adoption of one or more distinctive beliefs or practices, (2) their orientation toward a periodical that champions their unique stance, and (3) a Bible school that teaches their different perspective. In this respect, some Churches of Christ have come to teach a premillennial eschatology as opposed to the postmillennialism that dominates the movement. Some see Sunday schools as an unbiblical innovation, while others have become open to the charismatic renewal.

The newest division within the Churches of Christ emerged as a revitalization group and proved most successful in building some large congregations. At the same time it created an intense controversy as it tried to introduce a number of new innovations into the movement. Most controversial was the practice of discipling in which older members are assigned to younger members as part of an intense program designed to make every church member an active Christian. Eventually taking the name International Churches of Christ, the new group departed significantly from the mainstream of the Churches of Christ polity by adopting elements of a centralized structure in order to carry out a plan for world evangelism. As the new century began, the ICOC launched a significant process of decentralization and transformation that continues as this volume goes to press. There is no way to predict where this process will take the group. As part of the process, conversations with representatives of the Christian Churches and Churches of Christ have been held to begin a process of healing past divisions.

The larger mainline branch of the Churches of Christ has persisted in its unwillingness to form centralized structures, but has nevertheless been able to sustain a group consciousness through the fellowship of churches and nurture support for a number of institutions such as Lipscomb University in Nashville, Tennessee, Harding University in Searcy, Arkansas, and Pepperdine University in suburban Los Angeles. Two prominent periodicals, *Firm Foundation* and the *Gospel Advocate,* serve the Churches of Christ.

The Christian Churches and Churches of Christ extend the ministries of their local congregations through a variety of independent missionary and parachurch organizations, including a set of Bible schools, colleges, and universities. Some gathering for the whole fellowship is provided by the annual meetings of the North American Christian Convention. Two periodicals are closely identified with the churches, the *Christian Standard* and *Lookout.*

The Christian Church (Disciples of Christ), while retaining its loose congregational polity, has developed a centralized structure for handling the church's missionary, publishing, and educational programs (not unlike many Baptist groups). It has also taken its place among mainline liberal Protestant groups. It is a member of the National Council of Churches and the World Council of Churches. In 1995, the Disciples' Division of Overseas Ministries merged its work with the

United Board of World Ministries of the United Church of Christ to create a common Global Ministries Board.

The Evangelical Christian Church is a church in the Barton-Stone tradition serving primarily in the African American community.

Among the most interesting offshoots of the Restoration movement are the Christadelphians, a movement formed in the 1840s by Dr. John Thomas, a Virginia physician and contemporary of Alexander Campbell. The movement grew out of Thomas' doubts about the doctrine of the Trinity and opinions on some fine points concerning eschatology, including a belief that those who reject Christ would be annihilated rather than sent to an eternal hell. After his break with Campbell, Thomas' group still considered themselves just Christians, but they had to assume a distinctive name during the Civil War to gain recognition for their pacifist beliefs. They began to call themselves the Brethren of Christ or Christadelphians.

While assuming a low profile, the Christadelphians spread internationally through the English-speaking world. They maintained the loose congregation-centered organization and were tied together by several periodicals. An intense controversy on the destiny of individuals in the final judgment divided the Christadelphians in the 1890s and, in spite of several efforts, the division has not been healed.

The controversy concerned the destiny of those who had died without hearing the gospel. Robert Roberts, the editor of a popular Christadelphian periodical, *The Christadelphian,* favored admitting such persons to the kingdom. He was opposed by a prominent leader, J. J. Andrew. Those who accepted Roberts' position are now known as the Amended

Christadelphians and Andrew's following as the Unammended Christadelphians.

The Christadelphians have neither national nor international headquarters, but may be contacted through the several periodicals and publishing houses that serve the two branches of the movement. These publishing concerns have produced a wealth of literature and the movement has spread into more than a hundred countries.

Contacts:

Christadelphians-Amended
No central address. For information:
Christadelphian Book Supply
14651 Auburndale
Livonia, MI 48154

The Amended Christadelphians developed from a doctrinal controversy within the larger Christadelphian movement over several points of eschatology.

Christadelphians-Unamended
No central address. For information:
Edward W. Farrar
4 Mountain Park Ave.
Hamilton, ON, Canada L9A 1A2
www.christadelphian-advocate.org

The Christadelphians developed as a movement within the Restoration tradition from which it broke in 1844 over several doctrinal disagreements.

Christian Churches and Churches of Christ
No central address. For information:
North American Christian Convention
110 Boggs Lane, Ste. 330
Cincinnati, OH 45246
www.naccthecconnectingplace.org

Differentiated as a separate fellowship of congregations, the Christian Churches and Churches of Christ rejected the move toward a more centralized organization of the Christian Church (Disciples of Christ).

Christian Church (Disciples of Christ)
222 S. Downey Ave.
Box 1986
Indianapolis, IN 46206
www.disciples.org

The Christian Church (Disciples of Christ) is the most centralized of the loosely organized groupings coming out of the Restoration Movement of the nineteenth century.

Churches of Christ (Non-Instrumental)
No central headquarters. For information:
Firm Foundation
P.O. Box 17200
Pensacola, FL 32522
or
Gospel Advocate
Box 150
Nashville, TN 37202
www.church-of-christ.org

The Churches of Christ differentiated themselves from the Christian Church (Disciples of Christ) early in the twentieth century as its members rejected a number of innovations the Disciples had introduced such as the use of instrumental music in worship.

Evangelical Christian Church
P.O. Box 742
Granbury, TX 76048
ecc.dayspringmi.com

The Evangelical Christian Church is a theologically conservative fellowship in the Restoration tradition with a centralized organization.

International Churches of Christ
No central headquarters:
Webpage (unofficial): www.icocinfo.org
www.disciplestoday.com/MainSummary.aspx

The International Churches of Christ developed as a distinctive revitalization movement within the Churches of Christ in the 1980s, characterized by its strong program for the nurture and discipling of members.

For further reading:

Allen, Leonard. *The Transforming of a Tradition: Churches of Christ in the New Millennium.* ed. by Lynn Anderson. New Leaf Books, 2001.

Casey, Michael W., and Douglas A. Foster, eds. *Stone-Campbell Movement: An International Religious Tradition.* Knoxville: University of Tennessee Press, 2002.

Foster, Douglas A. et al, eds. *The Encyclopedia of the Stone-Campbell Movement.* Grand Rapids: Eerdmans, 2004.

Garret, Leroy. *The Stone-Campbell Movement: The Story of the American Restoration Movement.* Joplin, Mo.: College Press, 1994.

Harrell, David Edwin. *The Social Sources of Division in the Disciples of Christ.* Athens, GA: Publishing Systems, Inc., 1973.

McAllister, Lester G., and William Tucker. *Journey in Faith: A History of the Christian Church (Disciples of Christ).* St. Louis: Bethany Press, 1975.

Murch, James DeForest. *Christians Only.* Cincinnati: Standard Publishing, 1962.

Webb, Henry E. *In Search of Christian Unity, A History of the Restoration Movement.* Cincinnati: Standard Publishing Co., 1990.

Williams, D. Newell, ed. *A Case Study of Mainstream Protestantism: The Disciples' Relation to American Culture, 1880–1989.* Grand Rapids: Eerdmans, 1991.

S. Adventism

During the 1820s, a Baptist layman residing in rural New York named William Miller devoted his free time to the study of the Bible. As a result, he came to believe that he had discerned the overall system for understanding the chronology of the Bible's prophecies concerning future events, especially the imminent Second Coming, or Advent, of Jesus Christ that would bring to a culmination human history and society. From his study, he concluded that Christ would return in 1843.

He initially published his views in a series of articles in a newspaper, the *Vermont Telegraph*, which were turned into a pamphlet the next year. In 1833, the Baptists gave Miller a license to preach, and for the next decade he spent most of his time traveling. In 1836, he published a more detailed volume to inform people of his beliefs: *Evidences from Scripture and History of the Second Coming of Christ about the Year 1843: Exhibited in a Course of Lectures.*

Miller's system is anchored in a set of easily dated events in biblical history, and a key interpretive principle that in the Bible a prophetic day is equal to a year (see Ezek.4:6). The key passages in unlocking the prophetic scheme were Daniel 8:14, "unto 2,300 days, then shall the sanctuary be cleansed, or justified," and Daniel 9:24, "Seventy weeks are determined upon thy people . . . to make an end of sins." God's effort to make an end of sins at the end of the 70 weeks (490 days or 490 years) was set at A.D. 33, then the commonly accepted date of Jesus' crucifixion. Four hundred and ninety years earlier brought him to 457 B.C. This date, when Ezra began his effort to restore the law, was also the beginning of the 2,300 days. Two thousand three hundred years from 457 B.C. brought him to 1843, the date of the beginning of the cleansing of the sanctuary, which he interpreted to be the date of Christ's return.

By the time the predicted date approached, a large movement had emerged. Increasingly, church leaders who had entertained Miller's views in the 1830s had become hostile to his ideas, and church members who adhered to them began to withdraw from their former congregations. Christ did not return as expected in 1843, nor in 1844 as some suggested (possibly a miscalculation had occurred in the move from B.C. to A.D.), and believers experienced what was termed the Great Disappointment. Miller lost faith in his own speculations and withdrew support from further attention to his ideas.

Most people, however, who had already committed to the predictions and burned their bridges with previous church life, continued to believe the basic scheme of prophetic history and sought ways to salvage it. One group began to offer alterations of the chronology and suggest that Miller's calculations had been slightly off. The result was the project of a new set of dates for Christ's return. The other possibility, posed most successfully by Ellen G. White, suggested that Christ had indeed returned as predicted, but the event had been misunderstood. In 1843, he had returned to cleanse the heavenly sanctuary (Hebrews 9), an event imperceptible to us. Upon completion of that task, he would return to earth fully visible. Her new interpretation provided the basis for the founding of the Seventh-day Adventist Church. Taking something from both approaches to the chronology of the Second Coming, a generation later, Charles Taze Russell proposed a new timetable for return that centered upon the dates 1879 and 1914. His ideas led to the formation of a community of Bible students that saw themselves announcing the dawn of the millennium.

Following Russell's death, that Millennial Dawn community evolved into the Jehovah's Witnesses.

Through the nineteenth century, the Adventist movement split into several major divisions, and then in the twentieth century each of these major divisions splintered into a number of groups. The overwhelming majority of these (more than a hundred) remained relatively small, but three emerged to become large prominent international organizations: the Seventh-day Adventists, the Jehovah's Witnesses, and the Worldwide Church of God.

The Adventist movement was launched by a Baptist and took its leadership from the other churches prominent in the United States in the 1830s—Methodists, Congregationalists, Presbyterians, etc. As such, the movement inherited a Protestant theological consensus, differing only in its expectation of Christ's Second Coming in 1843. However, in the aftermath of the Great Disappointment, the movement became open to a variety of theological innovations—sabbatarianism being an early issue introduced into the movement. Later in the century, various leaders also began to express doubts about the Trinity, and a spectrum of opinion emerged. The Seventh-day Adventists affirmed, for example, that "There is One God: Father, Son, and Holy Spirit, a unity of three co-eternal Persons," a clear affirmation of the Trinity. However, other groups, such as the Advent Christian Church, affirmed the existence of God the Father, Jesus Christ the Lord, and the Holy Spirit, in such a way that a variety of theologies, both trinitarian and non-trinitarian were possible. Still others, such as the Church of God General Conference (Abrahamic Faith) specifically denied the Trinity along with the divinity and personal pre-existence of Jesus Christ. Charles Taze Russell inherited these latter teachings and went on to identify himself with the ancient Arian tradition.

Meanwhile, acceptance of the seventh-day Sabbath led to additional speculation on other elements of Jewish laws and practices. Among the most interesting were proponents of the continuing relevance of the annual cycle of Jewish festivals for contemporary Christians. Renewed interest in the Old Testament also led to a focus on the issue of God's name and how best to render that into English. That issue became an important element of the change of the Millennial Dawn Bible students into the Jehovah's Witnesses. It also spawned a new movement that argued that the references to God and Jesus should be replaced with Hebrew equivalents—Yahweh and Yahshua.

After the Great Disappointment

Following the non-appearance of Christ in 1844, Adventists reorganized while waiting for further light on their predicament. Over the next decades several options were proposed. One opinion that gained some popularity suggested that Miller's calculation had been off by a decade and hence 1854 was the actual date for Christ's return. Following the lack of any fulfillment of the 1854 date, several new groups emerged, including the Advent Christian Church, the Life and Advent Union, the Evangelical Adventists, and the Church of God (Abrahamic Faith). Influenced somewhat by the Christadelphian movement, they tended to reorient their attention away from the Second Coming to a consideration of life after death. Jonathan Cumming, founder of the Advent Christian Church, questioned the immortality of the soul, suggesting that immortality was conditional, a gift of faith in Christ. These groups remained small, some surviving only a generation, but collectively they provided the context from which the Jehovah's Witnesses arose.

Contacts:

Advent Christian Church
P.O. Box 23152
Charlotte, NC 28227
www.adventchristian.org

The Advent Christian Church emerged in the years immediately after the Adventists' Great Disappointment in 1844. It is distinguished by it rejection of the idea of inherent immortality, believing instead in an immortality conferred upon believers by Christ.

Church of God General Conference (Abrahamic Faith)
c/o Atlanta Bible College
Box 100,000
Morrow, GA 30260
www.abc-coggc.org

This Church of God was organized in the 1850s among Adventists who accepted the idea that "Church of God" was the only proper name for Christian believers.

Jehovah's Witnesses and the Bible Student Movement

In the years immediately after the Civil War, a young man in the Pittsburgh area associated with the surviving Adventist movement and in 1870 left his Congregationalist church to found a Bible study group and pursue his own private study of the Scriptures. Among the Adventists with whom he associated were some who had suggested 1879 as a new date for the Second Coming. Charles Taze Russell eventually developed an overall understanding of the Bible and of church history, but his understanding of the Second Coming determined what he proposed as God's Plan for the Ages. In 1879 he began publishing a periodical, *Zion's Watch Tower and Herald of Christ's Presence.*

Russell suggested that the Greek word *parousia,* generally translated "coming," actually could better be translated as "presence." Thus he reasoned that Christ had in fact returned in 1879, but had done so invisibly. His presence signaled the dawning of the Millennium, which would begin as this last generation of the old order passed away, in about 35 years, thus around 1914. When World War I began in 1914, many Witnesses believed that Russell's dates had been correct. Russell died in 1916, before the war ended.

Russell had built a loosely organized movement around his periodical and the small corporation that had been organized to handle the movement's business affairs, especially the publication of Russell's books. J. F. Rutherford succeeded Russell as head of the corporation. Once Rutherford assumed control of the movement, several groups pulled out and organized separately. Their number increased as Rutherford introduced further changes in belief and practice and began to build a more tightly organized movement around what were termed "kingdom halls." He changed the name of the movement to Jehovah's Witnesses in 1931.

Rutherford continued Russell's non-trinitarian theology, which pictured Jesus as God's human son whose sacrificial death primarily balanced Adam's introduction of sin into the world. He also set the Witnesses in a position strongly opposed to the powerful structures of society, especially the government and the larger churches. His opposition to government authority led Witnesses to become pacifists, and hence to reject any service in the armed forces (in whatever country they lived). They also came to see the saluting of the flag as an act of idolatry. As World War II approached, Witnesses were often seen as unpatriotic. In Germany, many were placed in concentration camps. In America, it led to a number of court cases that have played a significant role in defining the boundaries of religious freedom. Witnesses, in essence, won the right to proselytize through door-to-door evangelism, to refrain from saluting the flag, to be treated justly under conscientious objector laws, and generally to propagate unorthodox religious ideas.

The founding of the Jehovah's Witness and its transformation into a highly organized group that consumed most of the leisure time of its members led to another round of separations by members and the establishment of more Bible study groups that continued Russell's teachings and loose organization. Several of the groups became national organizations, notably the Dawn Bible Students and the Pastoral Bible Institute, but none experienced the success of the Witnesses. The low-key approach of the continuing Bible student groups has kept them virtually invisible on the religious landscape.

Meanwhile, the Witnesses built on the international spread of the Bible student movement during Russell's lifetime, and developed a highly aggressive evangelism program. That evangelism has continued to the present and has made them one of the largest religious groups in Europe (at the very time when many mainline Christian churches are losing members) and has led to their establishing worshipping communities in more than 200 countries. In the United States, their door-to-door evangelism has made them an object of on-going criticism.

Orthodox Christians have pursued a campaign of warning people of the Witnesses' departures from orthodox beliefs.

As the new century begins, the Witnesses have reported approximately six million members worldwide, of which approximately one million reside in the United States. Their constituency is more than double their membership and is measured by attendance at the annual Memorial of Christ's death (Lord's supper). More than fifteen million have attended in recent years. International headquarters is located in Brooklyn, New York.

Contacts:

Jehovah's Witnesses
25 Columbia Heights
Brooklyn, NY 11201
www.watchtower.org

Jehovah's Witnesses are the primary organization to come out of the ministry of Charles Taze Russell (1852–1916), who in the late-nineteenth century organized Bible students around his distinctive presentation of Christian teachings and belief in the imminent end of the present order of society. Following his death, his work was continued by the Watchtower Society he founded, and has grown into a large international fellowship.

Bible Student Groups

Christian Millennial Fellowship
P.O. Box 31
Port Murray, NJ 07865-0031
www.cmfellowship.org

The Christian Millennial Fellowship emerged as the teachings of Charles Taze Russell spread among Italian Americans.

Dawn Bible Students Association
199 Railroad Ave.
East Rutherford, NJ 07073
www.dawnbible.com

The Dawn Bible Students Association is likely the strongest of the several groups that rejected the changes offered by the Watchtower Society as it evolved into the Jehovah's Witnesses after the death of founder Charles Taze Russell.

Epiphany Bible Students Association
Box 97
Mount Dora, FL 32757

The Epiphany Bible Students Association formed out of a dispute in the Layman's Home Missionary Movement between its leadership and John J. Hoefle (1895–1984), a prominent leader. Hoefle withdrew and founded the Epiphany Bible Students Association in 1956.

Laodicean Home Missionary Movement
Rte. 38, 9021 Temple Rd.
W. Fort Myers, FL 33912

The Laodicean Home Missionary Movement was formed by former members of the Layman's Home Missionary Movement who rejected the leadership of Raymond Jolly, the successor of founder Paul S. L. Johnson.

Layman's Home Missionary Movement
Chester Springs, PA 19425

The Layman's Home Missionary Movement, one of several groups to reject changes in the movement founded by Charles Taze Russell that led to the formation of Jehovah's Witnesses, was founded by Paul S. L. Johnson a few years after Russell's death in 1916.

Pastoral Bible Institute
1425 Lackman Ln.
Pacific Palisades, CA 90272
www.heraldmag.org

The Pastoral Bible Institute was formed in 1918 by leaders of the Watchtower Society who rejected the leadership chosen to direct its work following the death of founder Charles Taze Russell in 1916.

Seventh-day Adventists

Shortly after the Great Disappointment, when Christ did not appear in 1844, a prophetess arose among the Adventists in the person of Ellen G. White. She picked up a proposal originally made by Hiram Edson concerning the 1844 date and offered it to the larger Adventist community. She suggested that Christ had indeed begun his work of return in 1844, but had begun by moving into the heavenly sanctuary mentioned in Hebrews 8 and was now engaged in its cleansing. Once that work was completed, at a near but indeterminate time, he would appear on earth, fully visible. Edson's idea solved a variety of essential problems for the Adventists by both confirming William Miller's calculations and removing the predicted return from the realm of verifiable beliefs.

Ellen G. White also offered to the followers what competing movements did not, a person with divine prophetic abilities. She was a visionary who claimed direct access to supernatural realities. Also, through her spoken prophecies, she pointed the church in various directions and offered it new doctrines, though these doctrines were not to contradict Scriptures. Among the first changes she proposed was the adoption of sabbatarianism. This idea was confirmed in a vision in which she saw a tablet of the Ten Commandments with the fourth commandment ("Remember the Sabbath day and keep it holy") highlighted.

Enough Adventists responded to White that she and her husband launched a periodical, the *Review and Herald,* in 1850. They began calling their activity the Seventh-day Adventist Church, under which name it was officially founded in 1863. Headquarters was established in Battle Creek, Michigan.

The church became associated with the larger health reform movement then active across America. White considered health reform in light of some of the health regulations contained in the ancient Hebrew laws. In 1866 she led in the founding of the Battle Creek Sanitarium (originally known as the Western Health Reform Institute). The institute later became identified with the career of its medical superintendent, Dr. John Harvey Kellogg. Though a pioneer in many forms of therapy, he has become best known as the inventor of flaked cereal. Two large cereal companies, Kellogg's and Post's, were formed by former sanitarium employees. In the twentieth century, the Seventh-day Adventist Church sponsored a network of hospitals, several of which, such as the one at Loma Linda, California, became well-known for their pioneering medical research.

Enlivened by a belief in the soon return of Christ, Adventists have energetically supported a global missionary endeavor, which has led to the planting of churches in more than 200 countries around the world. As the new century begins, the church reports some 900,000 members in the United States and more than eleven million worldwide.

The Seventh-day Adventists are by far the largest group to grow out of the original work of William Miller. A variety of dissenting groups have broken from them, the most important being those generated by arguments over the church's abandonment of its early pacifist stance. Most Adventist splinters have remained relatively small.

Davidians

In the 1930s, an Adventist layman with some new views on eschatology, Victor T. Houteff, broke with the church in California, and in 1935 moved with a small cadre of followers to Waco, Texas. They took the name Davidian, as their ultimate goal was the reestablishment of the Davidic kingdom. Shortly after Houteff's death, his widow Lois declared that the 1,260 days (42 months) mentioned in Revelation 11:2 would end on April 22, 1959, and God would intervene in Palestine. She called the Davidians to Waco to await God's action and the subsequent movement to the Holy Land. When that event failed to occur, the movement splintered, and now exists as several distinct groups in different parts of the United States.

The Davidians and the Seventh-day Adventists were both surprised and embarrassed when one of the small Davidian groups became the subject of government interest in 1993. A raid on their center, called Mt. Carmel, near Waco, resulted in the death of eight people, including four officers of the Bureau of Alcohol, Tobacco, and Firearms. Fifty-one days later, a number of the Davidians died when the FBI attempted to end the siege. Neither the Seventh-day Adventists nor the other Davidian groups that still exist had any relationship with the Waco Davidians at the time.

Contacts:

Seventh-day Adventist Church
12501 Old Columbia Pike
Silver Spring, MD 20904
www.adventist.org

The Seventh-day Adventist Church was founded in 1865 and continued the primary emphases of the Millerite Adventist movement, with the additional beliefs in the prophetic leadership of Ellen G. White and sabbatarianism.

Additional Seventh-day Adventist Groups

Creation Seventh Day Adventist Churches
1162 Old Highway 45 South
Guys, TN 38339

International Missionary Society/ Seventh-day Adventist Reform Movement
P.O. Box 261093
Tampa, FL 33685-1093
www.imssdarm.org

The International Missionary Society emerged out of the reform movement that appeared during World War I as the Seventh-day Adventists backed away from traditional standards regarding pacifism and conscientious objection.

Seventh-day Adventist Church, Reform Movement
Box 7239
Roanoke, VA 24019
www.sdarmgc.org

The SDA Reform Movement originated during World War I among pacifists who decried the SDA's rejection of its historical pacifism. In 1951, the movements split into two branches, with the majority of American believers adhering to the SDA Reform Movement while the majority of Europeans gave their allegiance to the International Missionary Society.

Unification Association of Christian Sabbath Keepers
255 W. 131st St.
New York, NY 10027

The Unification Association primarily serves African American sabbatarian Adventist believers.

Davidians

Davidian Seventh-day Adventist Association
Bashan Hill
Exeter, MO 65647

In 1961, M. J. Bingham, one of the leaders of the movement founded by Victor J. Houteff, reorganized some of the splintered followers as the Davidian SDA Association. The association is now built around an intentional community in rural Missouri.

General Association of Branch Davidian Seventh-day Adventists
c/o Doug Mitchell
P.O. Box 1004
Kingsland, TX 78639
www.the-branch.org

The General Association is one of several groups of followers of Victor T. Houteff who rejected the leadership of his successor, Florence Houteff, and reorganized separately.

General Association of Davidian Seventh-day Adventists
Mt. Carmel Center
P.O. Box 450
Salem, SC 29676
www.davidian.org

The Davidian movement founded by Victor T, Houteff (1885–1955) split during the leadership of his successor and widow, Florence Houteff, especially after her failed prophecy of 1959. In 1961, a group of members reorganized around Houteff's original teachings and writings as the General Association.

Sabbatarian Churches of God

As teachings about the Sabbath spread through the Adventist community, some accepted these along with the associated renewed emphasis on the Jewish Law's continuing role in the Christian's life, but did not accept the prophetic ministry of Ellen G. White. They also came to view the idea that the proper name for the church was Church of God. Over time, the group splintered on some relatively minor issues, but became the home for speculations on a variety of topics, including the need to observe the Jewish festival holidays and British Israelism, the idea that the Anglo-Saxon people are the direct descendants of the ancient Hebrew tribes.

The sabbatarian Churches of God remained very small bodies through the 1930s, but in the years before World War II one of their ministers, Herbert W. Armstrong, began a radio ministry in Eugene, Oregon, that over several decades gained a relatively large following. Armstrong accepted the millennial imperative that remained alive in the Adventist community and came to believe that it was the primary mission of the church to publish and freely disseminate the gospel message of the kingdom. He also saw his mission in terms of restoring biblical truth that had been lost through the centuries by an apostate church. He accepted a non-Trinitarian theology, British Israelism, the need to practice the Hebrew festivals, and Saturday as the primary day for weekly worship.

His radio show, originally called the Radio Church of God and given to religious comment on the news of the day, continued to grow. Many listened to the radio and then the television show; a lesser number supported the show's ministry; a lesser number still became members of the church. Full membership in what became the Worldwide Church of God included the acceptance of a strict code of personal behavior, attendance at the main annual festival, and a commitment of personal income to support the work through tithing. At its peak, the church was circulating hundreds of books and pamphlets (all given away to any who requested them), millions of copies of each issue of their magazine, *The Plain Truth*, and a Bible correspondence course. Armstrong's son, Garner Ted Armstrong, the main speaker on the radio and television show, had become one of the most recognizable faces in the United States, and the church was growing internationally, especially in the countries of the former British Commonwealth.

The Worldwide Church of God began to face problems in the 1970s. It was briefly moved into receivership when authorities took the side of former members that funds were being misused. Garner Ted Armstrong was dismissed from the church for sexual improprieties. Some intellectual leaders questioned a few of the biblical interpretations Armstrong had proposed. Then, following Herbert W. Armstrong's death in 1986, leadership fell to Joseph W. Tkach, Sr. as the new Apostle. Tkach lived only nine additional years, but during that time he began to call for a review of the church's teachings. Within only a few years of assuming office he began to withdraw some of the church's literature, a signal that teachings were in process of change.

Through the 1990s, one-by-one, the church abandoned all of Armstrong's unique teachings, including the non-Trinitarian theology, and adopted a centrist evangelical Christian theology. Under the leadership of Joseph Tkach, Jr., who succeeded his father in 1995, the church completed its abandonment of the teachings of its founder and was accepted as a member of the National Association of Evangelicals.

The changes that occurred in the Worldwide Church of God were not accepted by all, and it is estimated that as much as one half of the membership left. Those who did leave have associated primarily with three groups, the United Church of God, the Global Church of God, and the Philadelphia Church of God, the latter most closely attempting to reestablish the pre-1986 church and its teachings. However, the break-up of the Worldwide Church led to the establishment of dozens of splinter groups, most consisting of only one or two congregations. The larger groups continue the practice of printing and distributing their literature without charge, and look to their membership to largely support the publishing effort. Prior to Herbert Armstrong's death, there had been several splinters of the Worldwide Church formed, the most important being the two churches founded by Garner Ted Armstrong, the Church of God International and the Intercontinental Church of God.

Contacts:

Associates for Scriptural Knowledge
P.O. Box 25000
Portland, OR 97298-0990
askelm.com

Association for Christian Development
c/o Association for Church Development
P.O. Box 4748
Federal Way, WA 98063
godward.org/

Formerly known as Associated Churches, Inc., the association was founded by former members of the Worldwide Church of God who withdrew in the midst of a doctrinal dispute in the mid 1970s.

Christian Biblical Church of God
P.O. Box 1442
Hollister, CA 95024-1442
www.cbcg.org

The Christian Biblical Church of God was founded in 1982 by Fred Coulter, formerly a minister in the Worldwide Church of God.

Christian Churches of God
P.O. Box 1537
Blue Springs, MO 64013-1537
www.logon.org

Formed by former Worldwide Church of God members based in Australia, the Christian Churches of God have spread internationally.

Church of God, The Eternal
P.O. Box 775
Eugene, OR 97440-0775
www.cogeternal.org

The Church of God, The Eternal, was founded in 1975 by Raymond C. Cole, formerly a minister with the Worldwide Church of God.

Church of God Evangelistic Association
908 Sycamore St.
Waxahachie, TX 75165
www.newswatchmagazine.org

The Church of God Evangelistic Association was organized in 1980 by former members of the Worldwide Church of God.

Church of God, In Truth
Box 2109
Corona, CA 91718-2109
www.postponements.com

The Church of God in Truth was founded in 1991 by James Russell and others formerly associated with the Worldwide Church of God.

Church of God International
Box 2525
Tyler, TX 75710
www.cgi.org

The Church of God International was founded by Garner Ted Armstrong, the son of the founder of the Worldwide Church of God, after being removed from his leadership positions within the WCG. He later left the CGI to found the Intercontinental Church of God.

Church of God (Jesus Christ the Head)
c/o Pastor M. L. Bartholomew
Box 02026
Cleveland, OH 44102

The Church of God (Jesus Christ the Head) is a loosely organized fellowship of sabbatarian believers formed in 1972 by former members of the Sabbatarian Church of God.

Church of God (O'Brien)
P.O. Box 81224
Cleveland, OH 44181

The Church of God (O'Brien) was founded in 1970 by Carl O'Brien, formerly a minister with the Worldwide Church of God.

Church of God (Seventh Day, Salem, West Virginia)
79 Water St.
Salem, WV 26426

This branch of the Sabbatarian Church of God continues a branch headquartered in Salem, West Virginia, which rejected a 1949 merger with the General Conference of the Church of God (Seventh Day).

Church of the Great God
10409 Barberville Rd.
Fort Mill, SC 29715-9131
www.cgg.org

The Church of the Great God was founded in 1992 by former members of the Worldwide Church of God concerned about its drift away from the doctrines taught by founder Herbert W. Armstrong.

General Conference of the Church of God (Seventh Day)
General Conference Offices
Box 33677
Denver, CO 80233
home.cog7.org

The General Conference is the largest and oldest of the sabbatarian Churches of God to form in the years after the Adventist Great Disappointment of 1844. While associating together as early as 1863, the churches have through the years created a more formal organization under various names.

General Council of the Church of God
1827 W. 3rd St.
Meridian, ID 83642-1653

The General Council was formed in 1950 by former members of the General Conference of the Church of God (Seventh Day).

Independent Churches of God
c/o Church of God in Miami
P.O. Box 831566
Miami, FL 33283-1566
or
House of God in Daytona Beach
138 Madison Ave.
Daytona Beach, FL 32114
www.godschurch.org

The Independent Churches of God was founded by former members of the Worldwide Church of God.

Intercontinental Church of God
P.O. Box 1117
Tyler, TX 75710
www.intercontinentalcog.org

The Intercontinental Church of God was founded by televangelist Garner Ted Armstrong (1930–2003) in 1997 after his disagreement with the leadership of the Church of God International.

Living Church of God
P.O. Box 3810
Charlotte, NC 28227-8010
www.livingcog.org

The Living Church of God was founded by Roderick C. Meredith, one of the leaders of the Worldwide Church of God during the lifetime of founder Herbert W. Armstrong. Meredith rejected most of the changes instituted in the years following Armstrong's death.

Philadelphia Church of God
P.O. Box 3700
Edmond, OK 73083
www.keyofdavid.com

The Philadelphia Church of God, headed by Gerald Flurry, most closely adheres to the perspective the Worldwide Church of God held prior to its transformation in the 1990s.

Seventh-Day Church of God
Box 804
Caldwell, ID 83606-0804

The Seventh-Day Church of God was founded in 1954 by ministers and members formerly associated with the Church of God (Seventh Day, Salem, West Virginia).

Twentieth Century Church of God
Box 25
Ninevah, PA 15344

The Twentieth Century Church of God was founded in 1990 by C. Kenneth Rockwell and David E. Barth, Jr., both formerly associated with the Worldwide Church of God.

United Church of God
P.O. Box 541027
Cincinnati, OH 45254-1027
www.ucg.org

The United Church of God, formed in 1995, is the largest of the several groups to emerge as a result of the changes instituted by the Worldwide Church of God following the death of its founder Herbert W. Armstrong.

World Insight International
Box 35
Pasadena, CA 91102

World Insight International was formed in 1977 by Kenneth Story, formerly a prominent minister with the Worldwide Church of God.

Worldwide Church of God
300 W. Green St.
Pasadena, CA 91129
Webpage; www.wcg.org

The Worldwide Church of God emerged in the late-nineteenth century as the most successful sabbatarian Adventist group apart from the Seventh-day Adventist Church. Then, through the 1990s, the WCG rejected most of the ideas with which it had been identified and adopted a more traditional orthodox Protestant Evangelical theological perspective. Because of its drastic changes, it became the "parent" of a number of groups which adhered, more or less, to the beliefs expressed by the church at the time of the death of its founder Herbert W. Armstrong (1892–1986).

Sacred Name Movement

In the early decades of the twentieth century, within the sabbatarian Church of God tradition, speculation on a range of issues arising out of the attention on the Hebrew scriptures led some to concentrate on the issue of God's name. Once raised as an issue, certain biblical passages (such as 2 Sam. 7:26, which called for the magnifying of God's name) appeared to support the effort to know God's name and use it. The main body of the groups called together by Charles Taze Russell gave some impetus to the effort with the adoption of the name Jehovah's Witnesses in 1931. Members of what would become the Sacred Name Movement went with the spelling (in English) of the Hebrew transliterations Yahweh and Yeshua (Jesus), with several groups adopting slight variations.

A movement around the Sacred Name issue emerged in the late 1930s, one prominent early leader being C. O. Dodd, editor of *The Faith* magazine. Several early assemblies (congregations) were formed and efforts to produce Bible translations that dropped the words God, Lord, and Jesus, in favor of the Hebrew transliterations were published.

The Sacred Name movement is possibly the smallest segment of the larger Adventist movement. The only group of any size is the Assemblies of Yahweh that grew out of the broadcast ministry of Jacob O. Meyer, which has some 75 congregations.

Contacts:

Assemblies of Yahweh
Bethel, PA 19507
www.AssembliesofYahweh.com

The largest of the several Sacred Name groups, the Assemblies of Yahweh grew out of the radio ministry of Jacob O. Meyer launched in 1966.

Assembly of Yahvah
Box 89
Winfield, AL 35594

The Assembly of Yahvah is distinguished by the spelling of the name of the Creator (Yahvah rather than Yahweh) and of his Son, Yahshua. It is a sabbatarian group.

Assembly of Yahweh (Eaton Rapids, Michigan)
P.O. Box 102
Holt, MI 48842
www.assemblyofyahweh.com

This fellowship is centered on the oldest surviving Sacred Name congregation in Eaton Rapids, Michigan, which continues to publish *The Faith*, the magazine founded by Sacred Name pioneer Elder C. O. Dodd in 1937.

Assembly of YHWHHOSHUA
c/o Pastor Laycher Gonzales
1998 58th Ln.
Boone, CO 81025

This small Sacred Name group is distinguished by its spelling of the Creator's name as YHWH and his Son as YHWHHOSHUA.

Church of God (Jerusalem)
International Hq: Box 10184
Jerusalem 91101, Israel

The Church of God headquartered in Jerusalem is an American-based group whose founder, A. N. Dugger, formerly with the

Church of God (Salem, West Virginia), moved to Jerusalem where he believed the church would eventually be headquartered.

House of Yahweh (Abilene, Texas)
Box 242
Abilene, TX 79604
www.yahweh.com

The House of Yahweh headquartered in Abilene, Texas, was founded and is headed by Yisrayl Hawkins, the brother of Jacob Hawkins (d. 1991), founder of the House of Yahweh in Odessa, Texas. He allied himself with his brother's work, and then in the early 1990s became independent of the center in Odessa.

Worldwide Assembly of YHWH
8503 Cooksteel Dr.
Houston, Texas 77072-4810
www.yah-way.org

The Worldwide Assembly was founded in the early 1990s by former members of the Worldwide Church of God.

Yahweh's Assembly in Messiah
Rte. 1, Box 364
Rocheport, MO 65279
www.yaim.org

Yahweh's Assembly in Messiah was founded by former members of the Assemblies of Yahweh.

Yahweh's New Covenant Assembly
P.O. Box 50
Kingdom City, MO 65262
www.ynca.com

Yahweh's New Covenant Assembly was founded in 1988.

For further reading:

Bull, Malcolm, and Keith Lockart. *Seeking a Sanctuary: Seventh-day Adventism and the American Dream.* San Francisco, CA: Harper and Row, 1989.

Kyle, Richard. *The Last Days Are Here Again.* Grand Rapids: Baker Books, 1998.

Land, Gary, ed. *Adventism in America: A History.* Berrien Springs, MI: Andrews University Press, 1998.

Landes, Richard, ed. *Encyclopedia of Millennialism and Millennial Movements.* New York: Routledge, 2000.

Morgan, Douglas, and Martin Marty. *Adventism and the American Republic: The Public Involvement of a Major Apocalyptic Movement.* Knoxville: University of Tennessee Press, 2001.

Nichol, Francis D. *The Midnight Cry.* Washington, D.C.: Review and Herald Publishing Association, 1944.

Nickels, Richard C. *A History of the Seventh Day Church of God.* Vol. I. Sheridan, WY: The Author, 1977.

Penton, M. James. *Apocalypse Delayed.* Toronto: University of Toronto Press, 1985.

Tkach, Joseph, Jr. *Transformed by Truth.* Sisters, Ore.: Multnomah Books, 1997.

T. Brethren (Christian Brethren; Plymouth Brethren)

In the nineteenth century, a group emerged in the British Isles who wished to separate from the state church (Anglican) and to return to what it saw as the simple life of the biblical church, including the rejection of the various denominational labels being used by the dissenting churches (Baptist, Congregational, Presbyterian, Unitarian, etc.). Trying to resist being seen as just another dissenting group, they rejected the adoption of any formal designation, but they came to call themselves and to be referred to by others as the Brethren. Since an early prominent congregation was located at Plymouth, England, outsiders commonly called the group the Plymouth Brethren.

Most prominent in the founding and development of the Brethren was John Nelson Darby, an Anglican priest who withdrew from his clergy role to advocate the founding of assemblies of faithful believers who adhered to a simple New Testament pattern of church life and broke bread together as a sign of their unity. As multiple assemblies emerged and as people began to move between assemblies, a congregational polity was adopted, with fellowship and mutual recognition of assemblies based upon doctrinal unity and willingness to accept each other's members at the table of the Lord.

Without the formal adoption of a statement of belief, the beliefs of the Brethren grew out of their study of the Bible and the new and unique understanding of biblical history proposed by Darby called dispensationalism. Darby saw the Bible as the history of God's dealing with humanity through various successive periods of history (the dispensations). In each period God's expectation of believers is different. Thus in the first period, life in the Garden of Eden, the basic demand was not to eat of the Tree of the Knowledge of Good and Evil. In the early twentieth century, Darby's scheme was reworked by C. I. Scofield and became the basis of the notes to the famous *Scofield Reference Bible.* Schofield's revision of Darby is the primary starting point of contemporary discussions of dispensationalism.

In the last half of the nineteenth century, the Brethren movement grew significantly. Several Brethren leaders, such as George Müller, became well-known. The China Inland Mission, the first of the successful faith missions, drew heavily on the Brethren's support. The movement also did two things not anticipated by the founders. First, it splintered into several factions, the most important being the split between inclusive and exclusive Brethren. The inclusive position, originally advocated by Benjamin W. Newton, suggested an open relationship with evangelical believers outside the Brethren movement itself. Darby opposed this approach. Today, the open or inclusive Brethren, generally known as the Christian Brethren, have become the largest segment of the movement. Following the break between Newton and Darby, the exclusive Brethren divided into more than a dozen groups based on disagreements over doctrinal and administrative matters. These factions became known by the names of the leaders whose particular view on the issue at hand was followed, and they generally found some outward unity around one or more publishing houses the group supported.

A second unexpected occurrence was the spread of Darby's dispensational theology outside of the movement. The most notable person to accept dispensationalism without aligning with the Brethren was the famous nineteenth-century evangelist Dwight L. Moody. Through the many organizations he founded, he introduced dispensational teachings to many American evangelicals and was an early supporter of C. I. Scofield.

One of the concerns that made dispensationalism so attractive was a primary concern for prophecy and speculation on the expected return of Jesus, a belief common to many branches of Christianity. The new wave of interest on Jesus' Second Coming launched by William Miller found a new expression in a series of prophecy conferences conducted by mainline Baptist, Presbyterian, and Congregationalist ministers and scholars beginning late in the nineteenth century. Dispensationalism aligned very easily with an expectant premillennialism, a belief that Jesus will return soon and establish a millennial reign of a thousand years on earth. Many of the leaders of the fundamentalist movement of the 1920s and 1930s were premillennial dispensationalists and they popularized Brethren ideas far beyond the Brethren movement.

The Brethren, though forming an important segment of modern Evangelicalism and being everywhere present in the Evangelical world, remain almost invisible on the religious landscape. Congregations meet in unassuming buildings with names like "gospel assembly" that do not identify their group alignments. Like other ultra-congregational groups, there is no formal headquarters, and educational and missional endeavors are carried out through independent schools and missionary agencies that normally do not identify themselves as Brethren organizations. A spectrum of Brethren leaders have become prominent in Evangelical circles (one thinks immediately of F. F. Bruce, Luis Palau, and Harry Ironside) without the majority of people who read their books or listen to their sermons being aware of their membership.

As the new century begins, the Brethren have become a global movement, the result of their support of a vigorous missionary program through the twentieth century. A primary open or Christian Brethren missionary agency based in the United States is Missions in Many Lands, headquartered in Spring Lake, New Jersey. Walterick Publishers periodically publishes a directory of all the Christian Brethren assemblies under the title, *Address Book of Some Assemblies of Christians.* There are several exclusive Brethren groups operating in the United States, of which the largest appears to be the Reunited Brethren, formed by a series of mergers of several of the larger exclusive Brethren groups. Brethren groups do not have a central headquarters, but they may be contacted through their publishing and literature distributing agencies.

Worldwide, there are approximately one and a half million people associated with Brethren assemblies, of which some 1,100 congregations and about 100,000 members reside in the United States. Emmaus Bible College in Dubuque, Iowa, is the major Brethren educational institution.

Contacts:

Christian Brethren
For Information:
Walterick Publishing Ministries/The Christian Bookstore
6549 State Ave.
Kansas City, KS 66102-3000
www.walterick.org

Exclusive Brethren groups

Ames Brethren
Christian Literature, Inc.
P.O. Box 1052
Anoka, MN 55303-0599

Reunited Brethren
c/o Believers Bookshelf
P.O. Box 261
Sunbury, PA 17801-0261
www.bbusa.org

Tunbridge Wells Brethren
c/o Bible Truth Publishers
59 W. Industrial Rd.
Addison, IL 60101-4582
www.biblecounsel.homestead.com

For further reading:

Coad, Roy. *A History of the Brethren Movement.* Exeter: The Paternoster Press, 1968.

Darby, John Nelson. *The Collected Writings.* 35 vols. Oak Park, Ill.: Bible Truth Publishers, 1971.

Kraus, C. Norman. *Dispensationalism in America: Its Rise and Development.* Richmond: John Knox Press, 1958.

Neatby, William Blair. *A History of the Plymouth Brethren.* London: Hodder and Stoughton, 1901.

Noel, Napoleon. *The History of the Brethren.* 2 vols. Denver: W. F. Knapp, 1934.

Pickering, Hy. *Chief Men Among the Brethren.* London: Pickering & Inglis, 1918.

Scofield, C. I. *Rightly Dividing the Word of Truth.* Westwood, N.J.: Fleming H. Revell, 1896.

Turner, W. G. *John Nelson Darby.* London: C. A. Hammond, 1944.

Wilson, Bryan R. *The Brethren: A Current Sociological Appraisal.* Oxford: All Souls College, 1981.

U. Holiness Movement

The Holiness Movement developed in the nineteenth century as a revival of interest in the teachings of John Wesley (1703–1791), the founder of Methodism. Wesley had pictured the life of the Christian as one of growing in grace and culminating in the attainment of a level of perfection, which he termed sanctification. Methodists understood their striving in the words of Paul to the Philippians 2: 12-13, "... work out your own salvation with fear and trembling. For it is God who works within you both to will and to do of his good pleasure." They might view the Christian life as one of human effort, but the gains, including the attainment of the sanctified state, were seen as results of God's gracious action, not the result of human striving.

Methodism emerged in England as a revitalization movement among people generally assumed to be Christians who had lost their immediate experience of God's grace and become lax in piety. In America, the situation shifted markedly as Methodists saw an unchurched and largely religiously indifferent public. The emphasis was placed upon introducing people to Christianity, and the preaching of sanctification, while never disappearing, certainly was deemphasized.

In the 1840s, two new thrusts on the preaching of sanctification appeared. One emerged within the Methodist movement around Timothy Merritt, who edited a periodical, the *Guide to Christian Perfection* (later changed to the *Guide to Holiness*). The second thrust came from Congregationalist evangelist Charles G. Finney, who had been deeply affected by his reading of Wesley's *Plain Account of Christian Perfection.* Finney's revivalistic activities raised the issue of sanctification for Protestantism in general and Methodists in particular. His participation in the anti-slavery movement helped tie the issue of perfection to the great social crusades of the century, the drive for women's rights being as prominent a Holiness concern as any.

By the 1850s a Holiness movement had emerged in strength, only to be temporarily dampened by the Civil War. It was quickly revived, and few leaders had the impact of Phoebe Palmer, who with her husband, Walter, purchased Merritt's periodical and toured the country speaking on Holiness to large audiences. The camp meeting received a new shot in the arm as a center for the dissemination of Holiness teachings. Palmer championed another important idea. She joined with a new generation of writers, including Salvation Army co-founder Catherine Booth, in calling for a role for women in the pulpit.

Palmer also led in a new emphasis in Holiness circles, the search for sanctification as a new experience of the Holy Spirit immediately after the experience of salvation. Wesley, and for a century most Methodists, had conceived of the Christian life as one aimed at sanctification over a period of years and decades and the experience of sanctification to be the actual attainment of a few toward the end of their life. Palmer and the new generation of Holiness preachers began to see holiness as a work that God would do in the believer at any time in answer to prayer. Thus sanctification was a gift available to the majority, she believed, and most church members should be able to live the great part of their Christian life as sanctified individuals. Sanctification thus replaced the striving for sanctification as the norm for church members.

This new emphasis on sanctification gained favor throughout the several Methodist churches in the decades immediately after the American Civil War, signaled by the election of several known supporters, Randolph S. Foster and Jesse T. Peck, to the bishopric of the Methodist Episcopal Church. However, by the 1880s, vocal critics began to appear. Bishops and district superintendents worried about excesses and questionable teachings coming from the camp meetings over which they had no control. They also faced problems in churches divided between those who professed sanctification and the feeling of superiority they assumed over others.

The tension between Holiness advocates and detractors through the next generation led (or forced) many Holiness advocates to leave the Methodists and create new independent Holiness congregations. In the late nineteenth and early twentieth centuries these congregations began to coalesce into the major Holiness denominations such as the Church of the Nazarene, the Pilgrim Holiness Church (now a constituent part of the Wesleyan Church), and the Church of God (Anderson, Indiana). In the meantime, several of the old Methodist denominational bodies, especially the Wesleyan Methodist Church (now a constituent part of the Wesleyan Church) and the Free Methodist Church of North America, identified with the Holiness movement and the social crusades it supported. As these churches emerged, the several larger Methodists churches (later to merge into the United Methodist Church) backed away from any form of Holiness teachings. Through the efforts of Joseph Gurney, Holiness teachings also entered the Quaker movement and now forms one of the larger segments of the Society of Friends. In like measure Holiness teachings affected the Mennonite community and survives in such groups as the Missionary Church and the Brethren in Christ.

Holiness teachings tended to identify the experience of sanctification with the baptism of the Holy Spirit and the welcoming of women into the pulpit as part of the endtime message that "your sons and daughters shall prophesy" (Acts 2:17). The emphasis on the baptism of the Holy Spirit prompted some Holiness people who looked for more to change their emphasis on the baptism of the Spirit from sanctification to speaking in tongues. Thus the Holiness movement gave birth to the Pentecostal movement (discussed in the next chapter) in the early twentieth century.

In the years after World War I, the larger Holiness churches launched expansive missionary programs, and, though relatively late in the mission fields, through the twentieth century they became global churches. Holiness churches also made efforts to cooperate with one another, originally through the National Campmeeting Association for the Promotion of Holiness, which has gone through several transformations and has emerged as the contemporary Christian Holiness Partnership.

Within the larger Protestant community, the Holiness movement has survived as a relatively small elite. The largest Holiness church is the Salvation Army, known far better for its social endeavors and its unique modeling of the Christian life on military service. The other larger Holiness churches hover around 100,000 members each in the United States, though their worldwide membership is significantly larger. Several of the groups have in recent years become affiliated with the National Association of Evangelicals. Today the movement is home to several dozen relatively small but active denominations in which, due to the high standards of membership, many local churches will have a far larger active constituency than membership. Among these many small Holiness denominations are some of the African American Sanctified churches, which grade into and are often indistinguishable from the Holiness Pentecostal churches.

Through the twentieth century, Holiness churches became identified with a strict code of personal behavior which was expected of members. Much of that code involved a detachment from what were seen as immoral and frivolous forms of popular entertainment (from alcohol and tobacco to movies and television). In the decades after World War II, a reaction set in to what was seen as the lukewarmness of Holiness churches and their abandonment of many traditional behavioral standards. As a result most of the larger Holiness churches experienced schisms among their more conservative constituency. Former Nazarene minister Glenn Griffith led the new effort to separate and led in the establishment of a set of new Holiness denominations.

In England, Holiness teachings were spread through what was termed the Keswick movement. Here, the baptism of the Holy Spirit and sanctification were identified with a certain indwelling of the Holy Spirit and empowerment of Christians. Keswick has tended to occupy the place in British church life that both the Holiness and Pentecostal movements have in America, and accounts for the fact that neither movement had the response in England that they had in some other European countries. In the United States, Keswick teachings are most identified with Albert Benjamin Simpson (1843–1919) and the Christian and Missionary Alliance.

Contacts:

Christian and Missionary Alliance
P.O. Box 35000
Colorado Springs, CO 80935-3500
www.cmalliance.org

The Christian and Missionary Alliance was the major organizational result of the evangelical ministry of Albert Benjamin Simpson (1843–1919).

Church of God (Anderson, Indiana)
c/o the Executive Secretary
Box 2420
Anderson, IN 46018
www.chog.org

The Church of God (Anderson) emerged from the ministry of Daniel S. Warner (1842–1895), who had formerly been associated with a non-Holiness Church of God movement initiated by John Winebrenner (1797–1860).

Church of the Nazarene
6401 The Paseo
Kansas City, MO 64131
www.nazarene.org

The Church of the Nazarene was founded by former Methodist minister Phineas P. Bresee (1838–1915).

Free Methodist Church of North America
World Ministries Center
770 N. High School Rd.
Indianapolis, IN 46214
www.freemethodistchurch.org

The Free Methodist Church emerged as a reform movement in the Methodist Episcopal Church (now a constituent part of the United Methodist Church) in the 1850s, noted for its advocacy of abolitionism and opposition to the common practice of selling pews for Sunday worship.

Salvation Army
615 Slaters Ln.
Alexandria, VA 22313
www.salvationarmyusa.org/usn/www_usn.nsf
or
International Hq: 101 Queen Victoria St.
London EC4P 4EP, England
www.salvationarmy.org.uk/

The Salvation Army began in 1865 as an inner city mission in London and eventually spread globally. It is best known for the adoption of a military organizational model.

Wesleyan Church
13300 Olio Rd.
Fishers, IN 46037

or
Box 50434
Indianapolis, IN 46250-0434
www.wesleyan.org

The Wesleyan Church was founded in 1968 by the merger of two older Holiness churches, the Wesleyan Methodist Church and the Pilgrim Holiness Church.

Additional Holiness Churches

Allegheny Wesleyan Methodist Connection (Original Allegheny Conference)
P.O. Box 357
Salem, OH 44460
or
2161 Woodsdale Rd.
Salem, OH 44460
www.awmchurch.org

The Allegheny Wesleyan Methodist Connection was formed by members of the Wesleyan Methodist Church who rejected the church's merger with the Pilgrim Holiness Church in 1968.

American Rescue Workers
25 Ross St.
Williamsport, PA 17701
www.arwus.com

The American Rescue Workers was founded in 1882 by Thomas E. Moore, formerly the head of the Salvation Army in the United States.

Associated Churches of Christ (Holiness)
1302 E. Adams Blvd.
Los Angeles, CA 90011

The Associated Churches date to 1915 and the work of Bishop William Washington, who for a time was associated with the Church of Christ (Holiness).

Bible Holiness Church
c/o Gerald Broadway, Gen. Superintendent.
600 College Ave.
Independence, KS 67301

The Bible Holiness Church was founded in Kansas in 1890 as the Fire Baptized Holiness Church (Wesleyan), assuming its present name in 1995.

Bible Holiness Movement
Box 223
Postal Station A
Vancouver, BC, Canada V6C 2M3
www.bible-holiness-movement.com

The Bible Holiness Movement is rooted in the Salvation Army, with which its founder, W. J. E. Wakefield, had been associated in the early twentieth century. Most of its work is in Canada.

Bible Methodist Connection of Churches
Rev. Walter Hedstrom, Pres.
Box 523
Pell City, AL 35125
www.biblemethodist.org

The Bible Methodists, who protested the decline of Holiness in the former Wesleyan Methodist Church (now part of the Wesleyan Church), formed in Ohio in 1966. In 1966 the Bible Methodists united with the Wesleyan Connection of Churches to form the Bible Methodist Connection of Churches.

Bible Missionary Church
P.O. Box 6070
Rock Island, IL 61204-6070

The Bible Missionary Church is the primary result of a conservative revitalization movement within the Church of the Nazarene in the 1950s by Rev. Glenn Griffith.

Brethren in Christ Church
431 Grantham Rd.
P.O. Box A
Grantham, PA 17027
www.bic-church.org

The Brethren in Christ, one branch of the Mennonite movement, was deeply affected by Wesleyan holiness teachings in the nineteenth century, and by the end of the century the church had become a Holiness church.

Christ's Holy Sanctified Church of America
5201 Willie St.
Ft. Worth, TX 76105

Christ's Holy Sanctified Church of America is a predominantly African American body operating primarily in Louisiana and Texas.

Christ's Sanctified Holy Church (South Carolina)
Box 1376
CSHC Campgrounds and Home for the Aged
Perry, GA 31068
cshc.org/about.htm

Christ's Sanctified Holiness Church is a predominantly white Holiness church operating in the American South.

Church of Christ (Holiness)
P.O. Box 3135
Jackson, MS 39207-3135
www.cochusa.com

The Church of Christ (Holiness) is one of the oldest Holiness bodies operating in the African American community, originally founded as the Church of God in Christ in 1894.

Church of God (Guthrie, Oklahoma)
c/o Faith Publishing House
7415 W. Monsur Ave.
Guthrie, OK 73044
www.theshop.net/faithpub/fpcog.html

The Church of God headquartered in Guthrie, Oklahoma, was founded in 1910 by former members of the Church of God (Anderson, Indiana).

Church of God (Holiness)
7415 Metcalf
Overland Park, KS 66204
www.cogh.net/generalinfo.php (unofficial)

The Church of God (Holiness) was founded in the 1880s as an independent Holiness denomination.

Church of God (Sanctified Church)
1037 Jefferson St.
Nashville, TN 37208
www.cogsanctified.org

The Church of God (Sanctified Church) was formed by Elder Charles W. Grey of Nashville, Tennessee, formerly associated with the Church of God in Christ (now the Church of Christ [Holiness]).

Churches of Christ in Christian Union
P.O. Box 30
1426 Lancaster Pike
Circleville, OH 43113
www.cccuhq.org

The Churches of Christ in Christian Union was formed by former members of the Christian Union in 1909, after the Christian Union moved to suppress Holiness teachings in its fellowship.

Churches of God (Holiness)
170 Ashby St., NW
Atlanta, GA 30314

The Churches of God (Holiness) date to 1914 and the work of African American Holiness minister King H. Burress (d. 1963) in Atlanta, Georgia.

Emmanuel Association
2713 W. Cucharas
Colorado Springs, CO 80904

The Emmanuel Association was formed in 1937 by Ralph G. Finch, formerly with the Pilgrim Holiness Church (now a constituent part of the Wesleyan Church).

Evangelical Church of North America
7733 West River Rd.
Minneapolis, MN 55444

The Evangelical Church of North America was formed in 1968 by members of the Evangelical United Brethren who did not wish to join in the merger that produced the United Methodist Church. The following year, the Holiness Methodist Church, a Midwestern group dating to 1909, merged into the Evangelical Church.

God's Missionary Church
Penn View Bible Institute
125 Penn View Dr.
Penns Creek, PA 17862
www.pvbi.edu

Gospel Spreading Church
2030 Georgia Ave., NW
Washington, DC 20003

This conservative Holiness body was formed in 1935 by former members of the Pilgrim Holiness Church, now a constituent part of the Wesleyan Church.

Grace and Hope Mission
4 S. Gay St.
Baltimore, MD 21202

This small group was founded in 1914 in Baltimore by Mamie E. Caskie and Jennie E. Goranflo, both formerly associated with the Mennonite Brethren in Christ (now a constituent part of the Missionary Church).

International Fellowship of Bible Churches
3511 N. Geraldine Ave.
Oklahoma City, OK 73112
www.ifbc.org

The International Fellowship of Bible Churches was founded in 1988 by the merger of several conservative Holiness churches, including Church of the Bible Covenant.

Kentucky Mountain Holiness Association
c/o Dr. J. Eldon Neihof, Sr.
Box 2
Vancleve, KY 41385

The association was started by Lea G. McConnell, formerly a deaconess in the Methodist Episcopal Church.

Lumber River Annual Conference of the Holiness Methodist Church
c/o Bishop C. N. Lowry
Rowland, NC 28383

The conference was organized in 1900 by former members of the Methodist Episcopal Church, South.

Metropolitan Church Association
323 Broad St.
Lake Geneva, WI 53147

The Metropolitan Church Association was formed in 1900 by former members of the Free Methodist Church.

Missionary Church, Inc.
3811 Vanguard Dr.
Fort Wayne, IN 46899-9127
www.mcusa.org

The Missionary Church was formed in 1969 by the merger of two older Holiness churches, both with Mennonite roots, the Missionary Church Association and the United Missionary Church.

Missionary Methodist Church of America
c/o Poarch Chapel Missionary Methodist Church
3580 Playmore Beach Rd.
Lenoir, NC 28645
mmc-oa.org

The Missionary Methodist Church was formed in 1913 by former members of the Wesleyan Methodist Church (now a constituent part of the Wesleyan Church).

National Association of Holiness Churches
351 S. Park Dr.
Griffith, IN 46319

The National Association is a conservative Holiness church founded in 1967 by H. Robb French (1891–1985), a former minister in the Wesleyan Methodist Church (now a constituent part of the Wesleyan Church).

New Testament Church of God
Box 611
Mountain Home, AR 72653

The New Testament Church of God was founded in 1942 by C. W. and Martha Pendleton, both former members of the Church of God (Anderson, Indiana).

Oriental Missionary Society Holiness Church of North America
3660 S. Gramercy Pl.
Los Angeles, CA 90018
www.omsholiness.org

This Japanese-American Holiness church began with the Los Angeles Holiness church formed in 1925 by six seminarians.

Original Church of God (Sanctified Church)
1803 County Hospital Rd.
Nashville, TN 37218
originalchurchofgod.net

The Original Church of God (Sanctified Church) began in 1927 when the leadership of the Church of God (Santified Church) moved to incorporate. Church founder Charles W. Gray rejected the idea and with his supporters continued to operate as an unincorporated association as the Original Church of God (Sanctified Church).

Pilgrim Holiness Church of New York
32 Cadillac Ave.
Albany, NY 12205
phcofny.homestead.com/files/index.htm

The Pilgrim Holiness Church of New York was formed by former members who rejected the 1968 merger of the Pilgrim Holiness Church into the Wesleyan Church.

Pilgrim Holiness Church of the Midwest
Union Bible College
434 S. Union St.
Westfield, IN 46074

The Pilgrim Holiness Church of the Midwest was formed by former members who rejected the 1968 merger of the Pilgrim Holiness Church with the Wesleyan Methodist Church to form the Wesleyan Church.

Pillar of Fire
10 Chapel Dr.
Zarephath, NJ 08890
www.pillar.org/index.shtml

The Pillar of Fire was formed by Alma White (1862–1946), the first woman in modern times to assume the office of bishop.

Redeemed Church of God
P.O. Box 710874
Houston, TX 77271-0874

or
4307 Hwy. 90A
Stafford, TX 77477
main.rccg.org

The Redeemed Church of God is an African American Holiness church that was founded in Nigeria by Pa Akindayomi (1909–1981).

Triumph the Church and Kingdom of God in Christ
Chief Apostle Zepheniah Swindle
7843 Siskin Ave.
Jacksonville, FL 32209
www.triumphchurch-jax2.org

Triumph the Church and Kingdom of God in Christ is a predominantly African American church founded in 1902 by Elder S. D. Smith.

Voice of the Nazarene Association of Churches
6 Conklin Rd.
Washington, PA 15301
www.voiceofthenazarene.org

The Voice of the Nazarene is an extremely conservative Holiness church founded in the 1950s by Walter L. King (b. 1923).

Volunteers of America
110 S. Union St.
Alexandria, VA 22314-3324
www.voa.org

Volunteers of America was founded in 1896 by Ballington (1857–1940) and Maud Booth (1865–1948), the son and daughter-in-law of William Booth, the founder of the Salvation Army. It is modeled on the Salvation Army, but somewhat more democratic in its structure.

Wesleyan Holiness Association of Churches
c/o Reverend J. Stevan Manley, Gen. Superintendent
108 Carter Ave.
Dayton, OH 45405

The Wesleyan Holiness Association was formed in 1959 by Glenn Griffith after he left the Bible Missionary Church which he had founded in the mid-1950s.

Wesleyan Tabernacle Association
c/o Candy Run Wesleyan Tabernacle
1054 Lucasville-Minford Rd.
Lucasville, OH 45648

For further reading:

Bassett, Paul M., and William M. Greathouse. *Exploring Christian Holiness.* Vol. 2. The Historical Development. Kansas City, Mo.: Beacon Hill Press of Kansas City, 1985.

Dieter, Melvin Easterday. *The Holiness Revival of the Nineteenth Century.* 2d edition. Metuchen, N.J.: Scarecrow Press, 1996.

Finney, Charles G. *Sanctification.* Fort Washington, PA: Christian Literature Crusade, n.d.

Jones, Charles Edwin. *A Guide to the Study of the Holiness Movement.* Metuchen, N.J.: Scarecrow Press, 1974.

Kostlevy, William C. *Historical Dictionary of the Holiness Movement.* Metuchen, N.J.: Scarecrow Press, 2001.

Lindstrom, Harold. *Wesley and Sanctification.* New York: Abingdon Press, 1946.

Manskar, Steven W. *A Perfect Love: Understanding John Wesley's A Plain Account of Christian Perfection.* Nashville: Discipleship Resources, 2003.

Peters, John Leland. *Christian Perfection and American Methodism.* New York: Abingdon, 1956.

Wesley, John. *A Plain Account of Christian Perfection.* Kansas City, Mo.: Beacon Hill Press, 1966.

White, Charles. *The Beauty of Holiness: Phoebe Palmer as Theologian, Revivalist, Feminist, and Humanitarian.* Grand Rapids: Zondervan, 1986.

V. Additional European and American Evangelical Churches

Through the nineteenth and twentieth centuries, several new free-church groups, primarily of European origin and not clearly identified with one of the larger denominational traditions, arrived in America. Some of the groups adopted a form of communal living. The Hutterites were the most successful communal group not affiated with the Roman Catholic Church in the modern era. Others were new Protestant groups whose origin was peculiar to the situation in the country from which they came. The Churches of God General Conference was the original group proposing that the name of the church should be simply the "Church of God."

Contacts:

Amana Church Association
Box 103
Middle Amana, IA 52307
showcase.netins.net/web/amanachurch

The Amana Colonies in Iowa were established in the mid 1850s by a group of German free-church pietists who were attempting to establish a biblical church complete with communal sharing structures. The communal system was abandoned in 1932.

Apostolic Christian Church of America
c/o Bill Schlatter
14834 Campbell Rd.
Defiance, OH 43512
www.apostolicchristian.org

The Apostolic Christian Church has its roots in a free-church movement in Switzerland begun by Samuel H. Froelich (1803–1857).

Bruderhof Communities
c/o Woodcrest
2032 Rt. 213
Rifton, NY 12471

The Bruderhof is a Christian communal fellowship begun early in the twentieth century. It was strongly influenced by the Hutterites.

Churches of God, General Conference
700 East Melrose Ave.
Findlay, OH 45840
www.cggc.org

The Church of God movement was begun by John Winebrenner (1797–1860) who, in the midst of a growing number of Protestant sects, called for church unity and the dropping of any name for the church except the "Church of God."

Evangelical Covenant Church
5101 North Francisco Ave.
Chicago, IL 60625
www.covchurch.org/cov

The Evangelical Covenant Church began as a Swedish free-church pietist movement, whose members moved to the United States in the last half of the nineteenth century.

Evangelical Free Church of America
901 East 78th St.
Minneapolis, MN 55420-1300
www.efca.org

The Evangelical Free Church was formed in 1950 by the merger of the Swedish Evangelical Free Church and the Norwegian-Danish Evangelical Free Church Association, two Scandinavian evangelical revivalist groups.

Hutterites
No central organization or headquarters
www.hutterites.org

The Hutterites, with roots in the radical reformation of the sixteenth century, have become the largest, longest-lived, and most successful communal group in modern history. The group is divided into four major branches, or leuts, that have emerged since the major Hutterite migration to America in the 1870s.

Hutterite Brethren (Dariusleut)
Elder Martin Walter
Spring Point Colony, AB

The Dariusleut, the most loosely organized of the Hutterite communities, is named for Darius Walter, who founded the first of its colonies.

Hutterite Brethren (Lehrerleut)
Elder John Wipf
Rose Town Colony, SK

The Lehrerleut is named for its original leader, Jacob Wopf, an accomplished teacher or lehrer. It is considered the most liberal of the Hutterite communities.

Hutterite Brethren (Schmiedeleut)
Elder Jacob Kleinsasser,
Crystal Spring, MB

The Schmiedeleut is named for visionary "Schmied Michael" Waldner and is considered the most conservative of the several Hutterite communities.

Hutterite Brethren (Schmiedeleut-Committee of Elders)
No address available

The Committee of Elders emerged in 1992 when a group rejected the Schmiedeleut leadership at the time.

Molokans
c/o United Molokan Christian Association
16222 Soriano Dr.
Hacienda Heights, CA 91745-4840
www.molokane.org

The Molokans are part of a Russian free-church movement founded by Simeon Uklein (b. 1733). Their name, which means milk drinkers, refers to their refusal to give up drinking milk during Lent, a practice in the Russian Orthodox Church.

6. Contemporary Evangelical Movements

Most American church historians see the great debates that occurred between Fundamentalists and Modernists in the 1920s and 1930s as having long-term consequences of dividing American Protestantism into two large communities. One community acquired labels such as Modernist, liberal, and ecumenical. The other was known as Fundamentalist, conservative, and evangelical. The issues that produced these two large communities in the first half of the twentieth century were, as a whole, very different from those that had previously divided Protestantism into its large denominational families—Baptists, Lutherans, Methodists, Presbyterians, etc. Some mistakenly saw these new issues as overriding the older issues, thus making denominations obsolete and leading to their gradual disappearance. In hindsight, the newer issues were added to those dividing denominations without displacing them.

The new arguments developed around a collection of issues that had arisen in the nineteenth century and demanded a response from the churches. Some issues originated within the churches, while other came from developments in the fast-paced secular culture. Prominent issues from within the church community included the movement of denominationalism onto the global mission fields and the emergence of new critical tools with which to analyze the Bible.

The scandal of competition between the different Protestant churches on the mission field provided possibly the strongest motivation for the formation of an ecumenical movement to overcome the divisions. While many became enthusiastic for the possibilities of creating a united Protestant church, a variety of issues stood in the way. For example, many people held very real sectarian perspectives and believed their own perspective most closely approached biblical truth. Correlatively, they had concluded that to put aside truth was a sin. Others feared that the emergence of a large Protestant church that served the majority of Christians in any location would on the practical level result in the creation of a new tyrannical ecclesiastical leadership.

Meanwhile, university and seminary professors had begun looking at the Bible as not only a sacred text but an important ancient historical document that could be studied like other ancient documents. Their new approach, however, led to a reappraisal of the Bible itself. The primary insight offered by the new biblical scholars was that the process of the writing and development of the biblical text was much more complex than previously believed. The most controversial elements of the findings concerned the first five books of the Hebrew Scriptures (the Old Testament). Scholars asserted that, rather than being five books written by Moses, Genesis and the other books were assembled in steps over several centuries by the merging of a set of four main documents (generally labeled the

J, E, P, and D documents). Some scholars also were calling into question the biblical stories of so-called miraculous events which seemed to question what science said was possible—the sun standing still, an axe head floating on water, etc.

At the same time, a set of issues impinged upon the church from outside. The biological sciences, for example, were suggesting that life had evolved over a long period of time as one species gave birth to another and that at the end of that process humans had arisen in a process of evolution from lower mammalian forms. Many saw those teachings as contradicting the idea of God creating the world, animal life, and humanity. Simultaneously, the new discipline of geology was suggesting that the earth had been formed over hundreds of thousands of years by a slow process of continental development. Together, these disciplines suggested a much different picture of the origin of life and humanity than that portrayed by a literal reading of the first chapters of the Book of Genesis.

Meanwhile, psychology and sociology were emerging as separate disciplines. Both were suggesting that previously hidden social and psychological processes were active in society and that manipulation of them could bring about notable improvement in human life. In their more extreme forms, the social sciences tended to reinterpret the concept of sin as psychological disorder and the consequence of destructive social structures. One offered redemption through psychological counseling and the other the production of an ideal society by restructuring it on a more equitable basis.

The acceptance/rejection of the array of new ideas occurred along a spectrum, with those who fully accepted or fully rejected them at either extreme. Some accepted them joyfully, as providing a way forward for the churches, and others reluctantly, as unwelcome truths that demanded an adjustment in thinking. Some people rejected some of the new approaches and accepted others, with some reluctance. Some saw the whole trend of contemporary culture as disastrous, possibly the sign of society's final plunge into sin before the endtime.

As prominent champions of the new ideas arose, they found themselves under attack. Some were pastors in congregational churches, so their job was not threatened as long as the congregations supported them. Seminary professors were more vulnerable, and many were forced out by more conservative forces in their denominations. A few faced heresy trials, with mixed results.

In the 1920s, those who supported the new ideas seemed to be gaining ground in some of the larger denominations, and this occasioned battles for control of denominational agencies—especially the seminaries and foreign mission boards. Debates between modernists and fundamentalists became a regular part of the national meetings of the Northern Baptists and Presbyterians. The end result was that the majority of the leadership of both the Baptists and the Presbyterians shifted and modernists gained control. The Methodist shift toward modernism was accomplished more slowly and with much less heated debate, their most conservative segment having already left to identify with the Holiness movement. The shift, which became quite visible to all in the 1930s, led to a number of the more conservative voices in the different churches leaving and establishing new denominations.

Among those who separated from the older denominations, three issues immediately came to the fore. First, how should they relate to their conservative colleagues who did not leave the denomination but chose to remain as continuing conservative voices? Many of the most important conservative leaders in the older churches were at the height of their career and would have lost everything, including their pensions, if they had left. Some who did leave, however, demanded complete separation from what they saw as the apostate denominations, including former colleagues who did not leave. Others who left were quite willing to continue to work with conservative colleagues within the older churches.

Second, many of those who left the denominations had abandoned the traditional Calvinist theology of their denomination in favor of dispensationalist teachings that had been introduced in the nineteenth century by the Brethren (see chapter 5) and spread by evangelist Dwight L. Moody and his associates. The dispensationlist issue disturbed, for example, the Presbyterian leadership and led to a break of relations between J. Gresham Machen (who rejected dispensation premillennialism) and Carl McIntire (who accepted it).

By the 1940s, a third issue came to the fore: how conservatives would approach contemporary culture, especially the new sciences of sociology and psychology, and the new consensus in the natural sciences, most important, geology and biology. Some tended to reject any hope of reconciling the essential Protestant affirmations with contemporary culture and tended to withdraw into a bastion of theological purity. After the shock of the break with the older denominations, the larger group decided that it was possible to engage contemporary culture in a fruitful dialogue/debate and that a positive program of evangelism should be their keynote.

By the end of World War II, thc theologically conservative Protestants who had left the larger denominations found themselves further divided into two communities—the separatist fundamentalists and the neo-evangelicals. The former coalesced around Carl McIntire and many joined the American Council of Christian Churches. The latter found their center in the National Association of Evangelicals and found institutional support through Fuller Theological Seminary in Pasadena, California, and the magazine, *Christianity Today.*

Most of those who separated from the older denominations formed theologically conservative groups that mirrored their former denominations, for example the General Association of Regular Baptists, the Bible Presbyterian Church, the Orthodox Presbyterian Church, and the Evangelical Methodist Church. However, some felt that a separation from these denominational traditions was also required, and in the case of the more hierarchal churches a move toward a more democratic congregationally based organization was called for. Among most fundamentalists, a dispensational theology replaced traditional Reformation theologies.

W. Independent Fundamentalist and Evangelical Churches

Beginning in the 1920s, a set of new fundamentalist and evangelical denominations were founded. Many, though by no means all, adopted dispensationalism either formally or informally. Most related to and drew pastors from the many Bible colleges that had emerged out of the work of Dwight Moody's colleagues and successors such as Moody Bible Institute, Bob Jones University, Dallas Theological Seminary, and the Bible Institute of Los Angeles (BIOLA). The new group of ministers who received their training either from independent Bible colleges or in a more informal manner created a need for organized associations that could charter congregations and ordain ministers who wished to operate independent ministries.

During the last half of the twentieth century, the conservative churches founded in the 1920s and 1930s rebuilt and strengthened their educational and missionary structures, recruited a new intelligensia, and proved innovative in their use of radio and television. Given a certain amount of academic freedom, scholars found ways to engage the ever-changing world of sciences and a means of appropriating their findings.

Evangelical leaders began to envision a community that included (1) the larger conservative denominations such as the Southern Baptist Convention, (2) the smaller newer denominations that had separated from the older liberal churches beginning in the 1920s, and (3) members and pastors still within the older churches but holding to an evangelical theology. If they could unite those three groups, a new Evangelical movement could arise and take its place beside the Roman Catholic community and mainstream Protestantism. That Evangelical movement grew considerably by welcoming the Pentecostal movement (discussed later in this chapter).

Increasingly important within that Evangelical movement are those churches that emerged as direct products of the fundamentalist movement of the 1920s and 1930s and severed any direct ties to either the Reformation or Puritan traditions. Some saw themselves as nondenominational and some as interdenominational, others as being based strictly upon a contemporary appropriation of biblical teachings (hence Bible churches).

As noted above, the majority of the new independent fundamentalist, evangelical, or Bible churches adopted dispensationalism as their tool for interpreting the Scriptures. This dispensationalist theology nurtured two movements within the larger community. First, some people adopted a variation on dispensationalist theology originally developed by Anglican scholar Ethelbert William Bullinger. This form of dispensationalism is now advocated within what is termed the Grace Gospel Movement. Second, dispensationalism has always nurtured an interest in eschatology, the doctrine of the last things—hence prophecy and the events surrounding the Second Coming of Christ. For many, the founding of the State of Israel was such an event and some came to believe that 1948 was an important date in prophetic history. Such speculations also affected the many organizations engaged in Jewish evangelism, and directly supported the emergence of a new movement called Messianic Judaism.

Both the Grace Gospel Movement and Messianic Judaism are discussed later in this text. Immediately below, however, is the directory of the twentieth-century independent fundamentalist and evangelical denominations.

Contacts:

Alliance for Renewal Churches
365 Straub Rd., E.
Mansfield, OH 44903
www.arcchurch.org

The alliance is a fellowship of conservative evangelical congregations that emerged in the 1990s.

American Coalition of Unregistered Churches
P.O. Box 1224
Indianapolis, IN 46206

The American Coalition of Unregistered Churches is a fellowship of fundamentalist congregations that have come together to assert their independence from government interference in their ministries. Under the First Amendment, the coalition deals with issues as varied as tax regulations and the inspection of church-owned property by fire inspectors.

American Mission for Opening Churches
P.O. Box 130
6419 East Lake Rd.
Olcott, NY 14126-0130
www.amoc-nbc.com

The American Mission began as a home mission in the 1940s to revive fundamentalist Christian congregations that had closed their doors, especially in rural areas.

Antioch Network
8801 W. Union Hills Dr.
Bldg. D-200
Peoria, AZ 85382-8195
www.antiochnetwork.org

Founded in 1987, the Antioch Network is an evangelical, mission-oriented fellowship of local churches organized to plant new churches and nurture existing congregations as vital centers of discipleship.

Armenian Evangelical Union of North America
c/o Minister to the Union, Rev. Joseph D. Matossian
609 East Colorado St.
Glendale, CA 91205-1709
www.aeuna.org

The union is a fellowship of congregations primarily serving evangelical Christians of an Armenian heritage.

Associated Gospel Churches
1919 Beach St.
Pittsburgh, PA 15221

The Associated Gospel Churches was founded in 1939 by former members of the Methodist Protestant Church who had adopted a fundamentalist dispensational theological perspective and did not wish to enter the merger that produced the Methodist Church (now a constituent part of the United Methodist Church).

Association of Gospel Rescue Missions
1045 Swift St.
Kansas City, MO 64116-4127
www.iugm.org

The association, formerly the International Union of Gospel Missions, serves the many inner city mission congregations that serve the poor and homeless.

Berachah Church
2815 Sage Rd.
Houston, TX 77056
www.berachah.org

The Berachah Church is the base of a fellowship of Christians tied together by their attention to the Bible-teaching ministry of Robert B. Thieme, Jr., as delivered through the R. B. Thieme, Jr., Bible Ministries.

Berean Fundamental Churches
P.O. Box 1264
Kearney, NE 68848
www.bereanchurchfellowship.org

The Berean Fundamental Churches constitute a fellowship of fundamentalist congregations formed in 1936.

Christian Evangelistic Assemblies
P.O. Box 591876
Houston, TX 77259-1876
www.ceanatl.org

Christian Evangelistic Assemblies began in 1933, when O. C. Harms founded the Colonial Tabernacle Church of Long Beach, California. That church soon became the center of a fellowship of like-minded ministers, congregations, and ministries.

The Church Which Is Christ's Body
No central headquarters:
For information:
Robert A. Grove
P.O. Box 7253
Fredericksburg, VA 22404
or
wc/o Bible Truth.org
www.bibletruths.org/

This fundamentalist association of congregations refuses any labeling that might imply it is just another sectarian fellowship. The church grew out of the teachings of former-Methodist Maurice M. Johnson.

Covenant Ministries International
C.M.I. Bible Research Center
P.O. Box 446
Leslie, AR 72645
www.cmintl.org/

Covenant Ministries is a fellowship of independent evangelical congregations and ministries.

Deaf Ministries Worldwide Fellowship
P.O. Box 985
Sulphur, OK 73086
www.brightok.net/~dmw/

As its name implies, Deaf Ministries Worldwide is a fellowship of Christians founded in the 1990s and connected by the mutual challenges caused by deafness.

Destiny Ministries
c/o Gene Edwards
P.O. Box 3450
Jacksonville, FL 32206
www.geneedwards.com

Destiny Ministries ties together believers who have responded to the independent ministry of evangelist-teacher Gene Edwards.

Ecumenical Fellowship of Ministers International
c/o Aletheia Fellowship & Ministry Center
2502 Faith Dr.
Anderson, IN 46013

The Ecumenical Fellowship, formed in 1996, is a fellowship of independent ministers, churches, and laypeople brought together by Bishops Joe Huff, Harold Brinkley, and Gordon Barrett.

Evangelical Church Alliance
P.O. Box 9
205 W. Broadway St.
Bradley, IL 60915
www.ecainternational.org/

The Evangelical Church Alliance is a fellowship of independent churches and ministers that grew out of the World's Faith Missionary Association founded in 1887.

Evangelistic Messengers Association
100 Charity Lane
Huntingdon, TN 38344
www.shekinah.com/emai/

The association is a fellowship of independent churches and ministers founded in 1933 by Mr. and Mrs. Walter Willis, and Revs. Sales Malcomb Smith, Robert Adkins, and O. L. Ford.

Evangelistic Missionary Fellowship
5403 W. 1st Ave.
Lakewood, CO 80226

The Evangelistic Missionary Fellowship is an association of churches that grew out of the radio ministry of S. H. Patterson, the Radio Prayer League.

Fellowship of Fundamental Bible Churches
112 South Main St.
Glassboro, NJ 08028
jrpeet.truepath.com/ffbc/

The fellowship is an association of independent congregations that adhere to a fundamentalist faith.

Great Commission Association of Churches
P.O. Box 29154
Columbus, OH 43229
www.gcachurches.org/

The Great Commission Association is a fellowship of churches that grew out of a campus ministry that subsequently matured into a substantial association.

Greater Grace World Outreach
6025 Moravia Park Dr.
Baltimore, MD 21206
www.ggwo.org/

Greater Grace World Outreach, founded by fundamentalist Baptist minister Carl H. Stevens, began in 1964 as The Bible Speaks.

Independent Churches Affiliated
c/o Dr. Robert E. Mayer
810 E. Canal
Lebanon, PA 17042

Independent Churches Affiliated is a fellowship of independent fundamentalist congregations founded in 1953.

Independent Fundamental Churches of America
Box 810
Grandville, MI 49468
www.ifca.org

The Independent Fundamental Churches of America is a fellowship of fundamentalist churches founded in 1922 by Dr. R. Lee Kirkland.

The (Local) Church
c/o Living Stream Ministry
P.O. Box 2121
Anaheim, CA 92814-0121
www.lsm.org/

The Local Church (also known as the Little Flock or Assembly Hall Churches) continues the international ministry of Chinese ministers Watchman Nee and Witness Lee.

National Conservative Christian Church
5260 Paylor Lane
Sarasota, FL 34240
www.ncchurch.org/

The church is a national fellowship of independent ministers and ministries.

Ohio Bible Fellowship
c/o The Bible Institute of Ohio
3865 N. High St.
Columbus, OH 43214-3797
www.obf.net/

The Ohio Bible Fellowship was formed in 1968 by former members of the independent Fundamental Churches of America.

Worldwide Missionary Evangelism
1285 Millsap Rd.
Fayetteville, AR 72701
www.wmeinc.org/

Worldwide Missionary Evangelism is a fellowship of independent ministers with a commitment to global evangelism.

Grace Gospel Churches

The Grace Gospel Movement developed in the early twentieth century as an extension of the dispensational theology popularized by the Brethren Movement and the followers of evangelist Dwight L. Moody. Dispensationalists divide Bible history into seven periods, each marked by a distinct way that God related to humanity and his creation. Dispensationalists generally see a break between dispensations created by Jesus' death and resurrection. The Grace Gospel movement changed that break to a time after Pentecost when the apostle Paul began his ministry to the Gentiles. This initiated the Dispensation of Grace. Leading up to this dispensation were the period of Jesus' ministry (indicated by the water baptism of John), the time of the early church (with the two baptisms of John and of the Holy Spirit), and the present dispensation of grace (with one baptism, of the Holy Spirit). This movement has also been called ultra-dispensationalism.

Contacts:

Berean Bible Fellowship (Chicago)
P.O. Box 6
Collinsville, IL 62234

The Berean Bible Fellowship is a fellowship of churches founded in 1968 by Win Johnson and Cornelius R. Stam (1909–2003), the head of the important Grace Gospel teaching ministry, the Berean Bible Society.

Concordant Publishing Concern
15570 W. Knochaven Dr.
Canyon Country, CA 91351
concordant.org/

The Concordant Publishing Concern was founded in 1909 as a ministry of Adolph Ernst Knoch (1874–1965).

Grace Gospel Fellowship
1011 Aldon SW
Box 9432
Wyoming, MI 49509
www.ggfusa.org/

The Grace Gospel Fellowship was formed in 1944 by J. C. O'Hair (1876–1968), Charles Baker, and other pastors as a ministerial fellowship, subsequently growing into a congregational association.

Timely Messenger Fellowship
c/o Pastor Charles Wages
Grace Bible Church
1450 Oak Hill Rd.
Ft. Worth, TX 76112
www.gracebiblechurch-fw.com

The Timely Messenger Fellowship grew out of the ministry of grace gospel pastor Ike T. Sidebotton (1897–1970) of Fort Worth, Texas.

Truth for Today Bible Fellowship
c/o Joseph L. Watkins
Box 6358
Lafayette, IN 47903
www.tftmin.org/

Truth for Today emerged from the ministry of Bible teachers Ethelbert W. Bullinger, Charles Welch, and Stuart Allen and was founded in the United States by Oscar M. Baker (1898–1987).

The Way International
Box 328
New Knoxville, OH 45871
theway.com

The Way International was started by Victor Paul Wierwille (1916–1985) as a radio ministry in 1942.

Messianic Judaism

Following the establishment of the State of Israel (1948) and especially after the Six-Day War (1967), some Christians, especially dispensationalists, began to speculate about the meaning of the reinstitution of the nation of Israel relative to biblical prophecy. Some, like popular prophecy writer Hal Lindsey, even speculated that forty years after Israel's founding we would see visible signs of the endtime events.

Through most of the nineteenth and twentieth centuries, Jews who converted to Christianity were encouraged to integrate themselves into the existing denominations, and they were discouraged from forming exclusively Jewish ethnic congregations. In the latter half of the twentieth century, the Jews for Jesus emerged, articulating a form of Christianity that could affirm Protestant theological emphases on grace within a general context of Jewish culture. Based on that idea, some began to found Jewish Christian synagogues and call their clergy rabbis. Thus was born the idea of Messianic Judaism. Once the idea of Messianic Judaism was articulated, it attracted a number of Jewish Christians as well as non-Jews who felt a strong connection with Jewish believers. Over the years a number of associations of synagogues have been born, several of which adopted a Pentecostal theology.

Contacts:

House of David/Messianic Israel Ministries
P.O. Box 3263
Lebanon, TN 37088
www.mim.net/front.html

Messianic Israel Ministries was founded in 1999 to unite Jewish believers and non-Jewish believers in the Messiah as the new Israel.

International Alliance of Messianic Congregations and Synagogues
P.O. Box 20006
Sarasota, FL 34276-3006
www.iamcs.org

The International Alliance formed in 1986 as a fellowship of congregations that had been formed over the previous decade through the efforts of the leadership of the previously existing Messianic Jewish Alliance of America.

International Federation of Messianic Jews
P.O. Box 271708
Tampa, FL 33688-1708
www.ifmj.org

The International Federation began in 1978 with the founding of Beth Israel, a pioneering messianic congregation in Tampa, Florida, and the associated school for training messianic rabbis. The Federation is a "Torah Faithful" organization that believes that Yeshua (Jesus) did not abolish the Jewish law.

Messianic Bureau International
c/o The Messianic Center
701B Industrial Park Dr.
Newport News, VA 23608
www.messianicbureau.org

Begun in 1984 as a messianic Jewish information service, MBI has grown into a fellowship of charismatic rabbis and congregations.

Messianic Jewish Movement International
P.O. Box 1212
Chandler, AZ 85244-1212
www.mjmi.org

The Messianic Jewish Movement International was founded in the 1990s by Nathan L. Jacobus.

Union of Messianic Jewish Congregations
529 Jefferson St. NE
Albuquerque, NM 87108
www.umjc.net

The union grew out of the original messianic movement that emerged among Jewish Christians in the 1960s.

Union of Nazarene Yisraelite Congregations
c/o Bnai Avraham
P.O. Box 556
Ottumwa, IA 52501
www.uonyc.org

The union was founded at the beginning of the twenty-first century by Rabbi Moshe Koniuchowsky, formerly associated with the Messianic Israel Alliance. It was originally known as the Union of Two House Messianic Congregations.

For further reading:

Ellingsen, Mark. *The Evangelical Movement: Growth, Impact, Controversy, Dialog.* Minneapolis: Augsburg Publishing House, 1988.

Falwell, Jerry. *The Fundamentalist Phenomenon.* Garden City, N.Y.: Doubleday, 1981.

Harris-Shapiro, Carol. *Messianic Judaism: A Rabbi's Journey through Religious Change in America.* Boston: Beacon Press, 1999.

Kraus, C. Norman. *Dispensationalism in America: Its Rise and Development.* Richmond: John Knox Press, 1958.

Sandeen, Ernest R. *The Roots of Fundamentalism.* Chicago: University of Chicago Press, 1970.

Shibley, Mark A. *Resurgent Evangelicalism in the United States: Mapping Cultural Change Since 1970.* Columbia: University of South Carolina Press, 1996.

Sweet, Leonard I. *The Evangelical Tradition in America.* Macon, Ga.: Mercer University Press, 1984.

Tidwell, Derek J. *Who Are the Evangelicals?: Tracing the Roots of the Modern Movement.* Grand Rapids: Zondervan Publishing House, 1994.

Weber, Timothy P. *Living in the Shadow of the Second Coming.* New York: Oxford University Press, 1979.

Wells, David F., and John D. Woodbridge. *The Evangelicals: What They Believe, Who They Are, Where Are They Changing.* Nashville: Abingdon, 1975.

X. Pentecostalism/Charismatic Movement

From its beginning as a revitalization movement in the Holiness churches in the American Southwest, it would have been hard to project the impact that Pentecostalism would have on American religion. The fledgling movement seemed but another variation of Holiness teachings which had placed an emphasis on the work of the Holy Spirit in the Christian's life and suggested, following the lead of Methodist founder John Wesley (1703–1791), that it was possible for believers to be made perfect in love by an act of God. This act of sanctifying the believer was often described by Holiness teachers as the baptism of the Holy Spirit. However, it was also the case that day-to-day life in Holiness churches too often centered merely on maintaining a strict set of moral and behavioral codes. The Holiness movement was continually tempted to fall into a legalistic approach to the faith.

Different Holiness leaders initiated a variety of explorations concerning the goals of the Christian life. One such effort began at an independent Bible school in Topeka, Kansas, in December of 1900. The school's leader, former Methodist minister Charles F. Parham (1873–1929), assigned a research project to the students. They were to search the New Testament for reported incidents of the baptism of the Holy Spirit. At the end of the month, they reported that the baptism was always accompanied by the phenomenon of speaking in an unknown tongue. On New Year's Eve of 1900, he led the students in a prayer for the baptism and the accompanying experience. In the early morning of January 1, 1901, one of the students, Agnes Ozman, became the first to speak in tongues. She was soon followed by Parham and the other students.

Parham began to preach about the baptism of the Holy Spirit and share accounts of speaking in tongues through Kansas and the surrounding states, eventually ending up in Houston, Texas, where he opened another Bible school. Though operating in a highly segregated atmosphere, he accepted an African American Methodist preacher, William J. Seymour, as a student. Before he actually received the baptism, Seymour in 1906 took the teachings to Los Angeles, where he had taken a job as the pastor of a small church. His preaching about speaking in tongues caused him to be locked out of the church and with a few supporters he founded an independent mission on Azusa Street. From this mission, the Pentecostal movement spread across North America and within a decade around the world.

The original Pentecostal teachings built directly upon Holiness teachings. Holiness believers claimed to have experienced sanctification as a second work of God's grace in their life (a life that had begun with faith in Christ, their initial experience as a Christian). Thus the baptism of the Holy Spirit and the accompanying experience of speaking in tongues were taught as a third experience with God. For Holiness Pentecostals, the experience of Holiness was considered a prerequisite for experiencing the baptism of the Holy Spirit, and for Holiness people, the baptism was a logical development of what they already had accepted. This understanding of Pentecostalism would be accepted and is still taught by such groups as the Church of God (Cleveland, Tennessee), the Church of God in Christ (the largest single Pentecostal group), and the International Pentecostal Holiness Church.

As Pentecostal teachings spread beyond Holiness circles, some found the Holiness approach to Pentecostalism a cumbersome and unnecessary barrier. They did not accept the assumptions of Holiness teachings and declared that the baptism of the Holy Spirit should be and actually was available to every believer quite apart from any experience of sanctification. This perspective was built upon a more traditional Puritan Calvinist theology rather than a Wesleyan Holiness theology. Termed the "Finished Work" approach, this teaching split the Pentecostal movement almost at its beginning. Among the churches that followed the Finished Work approach to Pentecostalism are the Assemblies of God and the International Church of the Foursquare Gospel.

The Pentecostal movement unleashed believers to return to their study of Scripture with fresh eyes and motivated people who had experienced this event, seemingly described so vividly in the Book of Acts, to search the New Testament on a variety of additional issues. In each case, the goal was to reorder the church in a more biblical pattern. That effort in several years saw the emergence of new reflections on water baptism. Reports on water baptism in the Book of Acts seem to differ from the common practice of baptizing people with a formula developed from the Great Commission (Matt. 28:19). The call to baptize converts in the name of "Jesus Only" led to a reexamination of the common understanding of the Christian doctrine of the Trinity. The new "Jesus Only" believers placed a renewed emphasis on the Oneness of God. God's name is Jesus and he manifests as Father, Son, and Holy Spirit. Such groups as the United Pentecostal Church International and the Pentecostal Assemblies of the World are among the prominent Oneness or Apostolic churches.

The Pentecostal movement found a new beginning in the small African American mission on Azusa St. in Los Angeles. As the number of people who spoke in tongues grew, their collective experience was seen as a new Pentecost and an event heralding the last days (Acts 2:17). The initial outbreak of speaking in tongues also occurred near the time of the great earthquake that destroyed San Francisco. Within a few weeks, thousands of tracts were spread along the West Coast tying the two events together and emphasizing their eschatological implications.

As the movement grew, the outlines of a distinctive Pentecostal perspective emerged. The movement offered people a new experience of the Holy Spirit in their lives. That a new life in the Spirit had begun was signaled by speaking in tongues. Subsequently, different believers began to manifest the gifts of the Spirit mentioned by Paul in 1 Corinthians 12 in their lives. Pentecostal meetings came to be distinguished by people speaking in tongues, others rising to translate what had been said, physical healing of those who were the object of prayer, and spoken prophecies concerning the future. Each generation saw the emergence of individuals who specialized in healing ministries that would operate trans-denominationally.

As the revival at Azusa grew, those who experienced the baptism of the Holy Spirit were motivated to spread the word across North America and then, very quickly, around the world. The new movement found notable response in Scandinavia,

Africa, and Latin America, where numerous independent Pentecostal churches emerged. The Danish, Finnish, Norwegian, and Swedish Pentecostals came to form the largest segment of Christians apart from the state churches. In Africa, the Apostolic and Zionist churches led in the spread of Pentecostalism from South Africa north to the Sahara. Mexican believers at Azusa took the movement to Mexico and Central America. In the last half of the twentieth century it became the major movement contesting Roman Catholicism across South America.

From the initial burst of energy that led to the founding of a number of independent Pentecostal congregations, the movement has passed through several broad stages. In the early decades of the twentieth century, a variety of Pentecostal denominations were founded, which included among their number several Holiness churches that as a group accepted Pentecostal teachings about the baptism of the Holy Spirit. These new denominations represented all three major perspectives to emerge in the early years in Los Angeles—the Holiness Pentecostals, the Finished Work Pentecostals, and the Oneness or Apostolic Pentecostals. Early on, there was an attempt to keep the interracial fellowship that had manifested at the Azusa mission, but gradually most of the denominational bodies came to serve either a Black or white membership exclusively. The one exception has been the Pentecostal Assemblies of the World, a predominantly Black organization that has a measurable white minority within it.

The Pentecostal movement grew up in a quite hostile environment. They were dismissed by the older churches as an over emotional group—the Holy Rollers—who exemplified the worst side of religious experience. In spite of the attempts to marginalize them, the movement grew steadily. In the years immediately after World War II, it experienced a new revival called the Latter Rain movement. This movement attempted to reinstitute what it saw as a biblical organization headed by apostles, prophets, evangelists, pastors, and teachers in a five-fold ministry as mentioned in Ephesians 4:11. The movement challenged Pentecostal church structures and called for a reorganization around independent congregations tied together by charismatic individuals who had manifested trans-congregational leadership as apostles.

Several decades later a new wave of Pentecostal teachings began to spread among the older Protestant churches and the Roman Catholic Church. Known as the charismatic movement (from the Greek word for gifts, *charisma*), the charismatic movement developed national fellowships of new believers in the baptism of the Holy Spirit in the 1970s. While many charismatic believers have remained in the older churches, others, after receiving cool or even hostile receptions, left their former churches and formed new churches that perpetuate Pentecostal distinctives. Some of these churches take the form of mega-congregations in a single location, and others are new denominations.

In the last half of the twentieth century, Pentecostals have attempted to develop ecumenical relations both among the different Pentecostal organizations and with the older churches. That effort was significantly stimulated by the work of the late South African Pentecostal leader David T. duPlessis. A Pentecostal World Conference first convened in 1947 and has met periodically since. Hesitant to see the conference as doing anything more than providing fellowship, the movement's international leadership was slow to form the

Pentecostal World Fellowship to offer some ongoing cooperation and consultation between the different global Pentecostal bodies.

The Pentecostal World Conference spawned the Pentecostal Fellowship of North America (1948), which included most of the larger white Pentecostal bodies. That organization disbanded in 1994 and was superseded by an interracial body, the Pentecostal Charismatic Churches of North America. Meanwhile, several Pentecostal groups joined the National Association of Evangelicals that had been founded during World War II. Four Pentecostal churches affiliated from its beginning and others soon joined. Today, the following groups are members:

Assemblies of God
Association of Life-Giving Churches
Association of Vineyard Churches-USA
Bi-lingual Churches of America
Christian Church of North America
Church of God (Cleveland, Tennessee)
Church of God Mountain Assembly
Congregational Holiness Church
Elim Fellowship
Evangelical Assembly of Presbyterian Churches
Evangelical Presbyterian Church
Evangelistic Missionary Fellowship
International Church of the Foursquare Gospel
International Pentecostal Church of Christ
International Pentecostal Holiness Church
Northern Pacific Latin American Assemblies of God
Open Bible Churches
Pentecostal Church of God
Pentecostal Free Will Baptist Church Inc.
Southern Pacific Latin American Churches

Third Day Worship Centers
World Harvest Church

These churches represent the entire spectrum of Pentecostal denominations with the exception of the non-trinitarian Oneness churches.

Through the twentieth century, more than a hundred "denominations" have been founded within the Pentecostal community. Because of the manner in which some Pentecostal leaders were treated in the older denominational bodies, they tended to favor congregational polities when they engaged in the work of creating new Pentecostal denominations. Many Pentecostal denominations like to think of themselves as a loose fellowship or association, relegating the designation "denomination" to more centrally organized churches. In a few cases, such associations may welcome congregations that have dual membership in two or more associations, though relatively few congregations can maintain dual affiliations over time. Several Pentecostal associations exist primarily to license independent Pentecostal ministers and charter otherwise independent Pentecostal congregations.

In the list of Pentecostal churches below, we first list the several Pentecostal bodies that have become large international churches. It is to be noted that three Pentecostal churches now have more than a million members in the United States, with a fourth just falling short of that mark. Following that initial spotlighting is a list of the many Pentecostal and charismatic churches operating in America.

Within the main body of traditional Pentecostal and charismatic churches, African American churches have played an important role. In fact, the largest Pentecostal body in America is an African American church, the Church of God in Christ. To highlight their important role, and provide easy access to them, a separate list of African American Pentecostal churches is included below.

The Pentecostal Assemblies of the World, a Oneness Pentecostal church, also reports over a million members, while the United Pentecostal Church International reports a half million members in the United States and over three million worldwide. These two churches, because of their different theology, constitute a distinct community within the larger Pentecostal world, and they have been listed separately in the section on Apostolic Pentecostal Churches.

It is also to be noted that several additional Pentecostal associations are found among the Jewish Christian groups listed above under "Messianic Judaism."

Assemblies of God, General Council of the
c/o Thomas E. Trask, Gen. Superintendent.
1445 Boonville Ave.
Springfield, MO 65802
www.ag.org

The largest of the predominantly white Pentecostal churches, the Assemblies of God has since its founding in 1914 expanded into an international fellowship with members in almost 200 countries.

Church of God in Christ
c/o Bishop Chandler David Owens
272 S. Main St.
P.O. Box 320
Memphis, TN 38103
www.cogic.org

The Church of God in Christ was founded by Holiness minister Charles H. Mason following his experience with a Pentecostal awakening at Azusa Street in 1907.

Church of God (Cleveland, Tennessee)
Keith St. at 25th St., NW
Cleveland, TN 37311
www.chofgod.org

The Church of God began as a Holiness church in 1886. In 1908 it received news of the Pentecostal outpouring in Los Angeles and accepted it.

Contacts:

Abbott Loop Fellowship of Churches
c/o Reverend Richard Benjamin
2626 Abbott Rd.
Anchorage, AK 99507
www.abbottloopcommunitychurch.org

What became the Abbott Loop Fellowship of Churches began with the founding of Abbott Loop Community Church in 1959 by Dick Benjamin, earlier associated with Bethel Temple in Seattle. In the 1970s, the church adopted the five-fold ministry pattern of Ephesians 4:11 and began to found branch congregations.

Abundant Life Church Evangelistic Association
556 Greenwood Ave.
P.O. Box 285
Mannford, OK 74044

AEGA International (Assn. of Evangelical Gospel Assemblies)
2151 Hwy. 139
Monroe, LA 71203
www.aega.org

AEGA International was founded in 1976 in Monroe, Louisiana, by Harry A. Harbuck.

Agape Ministries *See:* **International Convention of Faith Ministries**

Ambassadors Ministerial Fellowship
P.O. Box 393
Roanoke, AL 36274
usamf.org

Ambassadors Ministerial Fellowship is a cooperative association of Pentecostal ministers and churches founded by Lyndon B. Hutcherson, who also founded Amazing Grace Ministries.

American Evangelistic Association
3507 Carriage Gate Dr.
Melbourne, FL 32904
www.aeaintl.org

American Evangelistic Association, best known for its overseas missionary activity, is also an association of independent ministers and churches, many but not all Pentecostal. It was formed by John E. Douglas (1925–2002) and others in 1954.

Anchor Bay Evangelistic Association
P.O. Box 406
Maryville, IL 62062
www.abea.cc

The association was founded by Roy John (1880–1945) and Blanche Turner, who assumed leadership of a congregation originally formed by evangelist Mrs. M. B. Woodworth-Etter (1844–1924). In 1940, the Turners left the International Church of the Foursquare Gospel and began the association as an independent body.

Anointed Word Ministries and Fellowships International
P.O. Box 3006
Springfield, OH 45501

Anointed Word Ministries was founded in 1984 by Pentecostal evangelist Drew Pruzaniec.

Antioch International Ministries
207-E Cowden Rd.
New Wilmington, PA 16142
www.aiministries.org

Antioch International Ministries is a fellowship of charismatic churches. It was founded in the mid-1990s by former United Methodist minister Jim Erb.

Antioch Network of Churches and Ministers
8801 W. Union Hills Dr., Bldg. D-200
Peoria, AZ 85382-8195
www.antiochnetwork.org

Antioch Network was begun in 1987 by George Miley as a network of ministers and churches with a strong emphasis on the local church.

Apostolic Christian Churches, International
c/o Pastor Wayne Miller
P.O. Box 2160
Myrtle Beach, SC 29578-2160
www.cathedralministries.org

Apostolic Christian Churches, International began in the 1980s as the Gloryland Fellowship of Churches. Leading in its founding was Dr. R. Wayne Miller, the pastor of the Grand Strand Cathedral in Myrtle Beach, South Carolina.

Apostolic Church
Hq: 142 N. 17th St.
Philadelphia, PA 19103
or
International Hq: P.O. Box 389
24-27 St. Helens Rd.
Swansea, SA2 1ZH
United Kingdom
www.apostolic-church.org

The Apostolic Church was founded in 1916 in England by former members of the Apostolic Faith Church, Britain's original Pentecostal church. Congregations were established in Canada in the 1920s and subsequently spread to the United States.

Apostolic Faith (Kansas)
1009 Lincoln Ave.
Baxter Springs, KS 66713

The first of the Pentecostal churches, the Apostolic Faith grew out of Charles F. Parham's rediscovery of the Pentecostal experience in 1901.

Apostolic Faith Mission of Portland, Oregon, Inc.
6615 SE 52nd Ave.
Portland, OR 97206-7660
www.apostolicfaith.org

The Apostolic Faith Mission was founded by Florence L. Crawford, who had been active in the original Apostolic Faith Mission in Los Angeles. She began work in Portland, Oregon, in 1908.

Apostolic Ministers Conference of Philadelphia
c/o Bishop Robert Doub, President
1516 W. Master St.
Philadelphia, PA 19121-4321

Apostolic Missions International
c/o Emanuele Cannistraci
Gate Way City Church
5883 Eden Park Place
San Jose, CA 95138
www.gatewaycitychurch.org

Apostolic Missions International is an international fellowship of Pentecostal churches and ministers brought together by the charismatic ministry of Apostle Emanuele Cannistraci.

Ascension Fellowships International
1050 Boylan Rd., Unit # 15
Bozeman, MT 59715
www.afichurches.net

Ascension Fellowships International is an Apostolic organization that unites local churches in a ministry model based on the five-fold ministry of Ephesians 4:11.

Assemblies of God International Fellowship (Independent/Not Affiliated)
P.O. Box 22410
San Diego, CA 92192-2410
www.agifellowship.org

In 1986 the Assemblies of God International Fellowship superseded the Independent Assemblies of God, which had emerged as the Pentecostal movement spread among Scandinavian Americans early in the twentieth century.

Assembly of Free Spirit Baptist Churches
3627 Mt. Elliott
Detroit, MI 48527

Association of Charismatic Reformed Churches
c/o Jacksonville Christian Fellowship
2213 North Loop Rd.
Jacksonville, AK 72076

The association began in 2001 as a network for congregations from conservative Reformed tradition that were experiencing the charismatic renewal.

Association of Covenant Charismatic Churches
13320 Lake Magdalene Blvd.
Tampa, FL 33618

The association networks Presbyterian churches that have experienced the charismatic renewal.

Association of Evangelical Congregations and Ministries
c/o Reverend Bob Swanger
1050 Polaris Pkwy.
Columbus, OH 43240

Association of Faith Churches and Ministries
P.O. Box 2330
Branson, MO 65615-2330
www.jkmafcm.org

The association was founded in 1978 by Jim Kaseman, a graduate of Rhema Bible Training Center in Tulsa, Oklahoma.

Association of International Gospel Assemblies
411 S. 3Rd. St.
De Soto, MO 63020-2016
www.aigahq.com

The association was founded by Dr. Granville M. Rayl (1917–1997) to bring together ministers of like mind to fulfill the Great Commission.

Association of Life-Giving Churches
11025 Voyager Parkway
Colorado Springs, CO 80921
www.lifegivingchurch.com

The ALC is a network of churches that grew out of the charismatic ministry of Ted Haggard.

Bethel Apostolic Churches Pentecostal Movement Association
c/o Bishop Dr. D. McCollough
5433 W. Jackson Blvd.
Chicago, IL 60644

Bethel Fellowship International
P.O. Box 7174
Sumner, WA 98390
www.bethelfellowshipinternational.com

The fellowship, based in the Northwest, was founded to bring together a group of independent ministers and churches that emerged out of the Latter Rain Revival of the late-1940s.

Bethel Temple
2033 Second Ave.
Seattle, WA 98121

Bethel Temple was founded in 1914 and subsequently became the center of a loose association of congregations in the northwest United States, Holland, and Indonesia.

Bethesda Community Churches
c/o Bishop Raleigh Lee, Jr.
11597 Islandale Dr.
Cincinnati, OH 45240

Bibleway Association
c/o Reverend Leslie Buckner
P.O. Box 370
Doniphan, MO 63935
www.biblewayassociation.com

The Bibleway Association was founded in 1958 by Rev. Leslie Buckner.

Body of Christ Movement
c/o Immanuel's Church
16819 New Hampshire Ave.
Silver Spring, MD 20905
www.immanuels.org

The Body of Christ Movement is a charismatic fellowship founded and headed by Charles E. and Dorothy E. Schmitt.

Branham Tabernacle and Related Assemblies
William Branham Evangelistic Association
Branham Tabernacle
Box 325
Jeffersonville, IN 47130
or
Voice of God Recordings
P.O. Box 950
Jeffersonville, IN 47131
www.branham.org

or
Believers International
P.O. Box 78270
Tucson, AZ 85703-8220
www.biblebelievers.org/belint.htm

William Branham (1909–1965) was a prominent healing evangelist in the mid-twentieth century whose followers came to see him as the Prophet Elijah whose appearance was promised in Malachi 4:5.

Called to All Nations
P.O. Box 680993
San Antonio, TX 78268-0993
www.ctan.us/index.htm

Called to All Nations was founded in the 1990s by Ray Popham, its Apostolic Overseer, and includes in its complex of related organizations and ministries an international network of like-minded ministers and churches.

Calvary Chapel Churches
c/o Calvary Chapel Outreach Fellowships
3232 W. MacArthur Blvd.
Santa Ana, CA 92704
www.calvarychapel.com

Calvary Chapel Church, an international fellowship of congregations, grew out of the initial work of Pastor Charles "Chuck" Smith (b. 1927), a former minister in the International Church of the Foursquare Gospel.

Calvary Grace Christian Churches
c/o Dr. Michael K. Lake
P.O. Box 559
Dixon, MO 65459

Calvary Ministries Inc., International
P.O. Box 11228
Fort Wayne, IN 46856-8069
www.cmifellowship.com

Calvary Ministries began in 1971 with the work of Dr. Paul E. Paino (d. 2005), formerly associated with the Assemblies of God, at Calvary Temple in Fort Wayne, Indiana.

Carolina Evangelistic Association
Garr Memorial Church
7700 Wallace Rd.
Charlotte, NC 28121

The Carolina Evangelistic Association was founded by Dr. Alfred G. Garr (1874–1944), who began his Pentecostal career as a missionary in Asia.

Cathedral of the Holy Spirit
c/o Cathedral at Chapel Hill
4650 Flat Shoals Parkway
Decatur, GA 30034-5000
or
P.O. Box 371289
Decatur, GA 30037-1289

The Cathedral of the Holy Spirit is the center of the networking ministry of Archbishop Earl Paulk.

Catholic Charismatic Church
c/o Most Reverend W. Edwin DeVoy
256 Higby Rd.
New Hartford, NY 13413

The Catholic Charismatic Church was founded in the 1990s by Most Rev. Paul A. Boucher, and combines the Catholic tradition with the contemporary charismatic renewal.

Charismatic Episcopal Church
c/o Most Rev. Randolph Adler, Patriarch
107 West Marquita
San Clemente, CA 92672
www.iccec.org

Founded in 1992, the Charismatic Episcopal Church is a liturgical church that fully participates in the contemporary charismatic renewal.

Charismatic Orthodox Church
110 Masters Dr.
St Augustine, FL 32086

The Charismatic Orthodox Church was founded in 1998 under the leadership of Bishop Symeon John (Mark D. Kersey), a former Jehovah's Witness who made a pilgrimage to Eastern Orthodoxy and the charismatic renewal.

Christ Gospel Churches International
c/o Reverend Delbert Brooks
P.O. Box 786
Jeffersonville, IN 47131-0786
www.christgospel.org

Christ Gospel Churches was founded by Rev. Bernice R. Hicks in the 1950s.

Christian Church of North America, General Council
Rt. 18 & Rutledge Rd.
Box 141-A, R.D. #1
Transfer, PA 16154
www.ccna.org

Formally created in 1927, the Christian Church of North America traces its beginning to the early response in the Italian American community to the Pentecostal message.

Christian Faith Ministers' Fellowship International
c/o Brenda Timberlake
P.O. Box 100
Creedmoor, NC 27522
www.timberlakeministries.com

Christian Faith Ministers' Fellowship International was founded by Bishop Mark Timberlake (d. 2002) and his wife, Brenda Timberlake, as a national fellowship of ministers and ministries.

Christian Fellowship International
310 Country Wood Dr.
San Antonio, TX 78216
www.cficonnection.com

Christian Fellowship International began in 1982 and subsequently grew into a fellowship of churches in Mexico, New Mexico, and Texas under the leadership of founder Ron Corzine.

Christian International Network of Prophetic Ministries
P.O. Box 9000
Santa Rosa Beach, FL 32459
bishophamon.org

A primary manifestation of the Latter-Rain Movement that spread through Pentecostalism in the late 1940s, the network was founded in 1988 by Bill Hamon (b. 1934) and a number of ministers he had trained through his Christian International School of Theology.

Church Foundational Network
4900 Forest Creek Dr.
Pace, FL 32571
www.churchfoundationalnetwork.com

The Church Foundational Network was founded in 1995 by Ken Sumrall as a fellowship of independent Pentecostal ministers who wish oversight from the network's apostolic teams.

Church of God by Faith, Inc.
1315 Lane Ave., SO. #6
Jacksonville, FL 32205
www.cogbf.org

The Church of God by Faith was founded in 1914 by Elder John Bright. It is currently led by its General Overseer, Bishop James E. McKnight.

Church of God for All Nations
Bishop Samuel Doffe
1401 Wildwood Ave.
P.O. Box 5569
Cleveland, TN 37320-5569
www.thechurchofgodnations.org

The Church of God for All Nations was founded in 1981 by Bishop Samuel Doffee, formerly with the Church of God (Jerusalem Acres).

Church of God, USA
c/o Bishop Danny R. Patrick
P.O. Box 525
Scottsville, Kentucky
www.ourchurch.com/view/?pageID=1748

The Church of God, USA was founded by Homer A. Tomlinson (1892–1968) after he withdrew from the Church of God of Prophecy when he was not named to succeed his father as general overseer.

Church of God (Jerusalem Acres)
Box 1207
1826 Dalton Pike (Jerusalem Acres)
Cleveland, TN 37364-1207

The Church of God (Jerusalem Acres) was founded by Grady R. Kent (1909–1964), formerly a minister in the Church of God of Prophecy.

Church of God/Mountain Assembly
c/o Rev. Fred R. Cornelius, Gen. Overseer
110 S. Florence Ave.
Jellico, TN 37762
www.cgmahdq.org

This Church of God began as a Baptist Holiness church, which in 1907 accepted the ideas and experience concerning the baptism of the Holy Spirit being preached at the Azusa Revival in Los Angeles.

Church of God of Prophecy
Bible Place
P.O. Box 2910
Cleveland, TN 37320
www.cogop.org

The Church of God of Prophecy was founded in 1922 after A. J. Tomlinson (1865–1943) was removed from office as the general overseer of the Church of God (Cleveland, Tennessee).

Church of God of the Union Assembly
2211 South Dixie Highway
P.O. Box 1323
Dalton, GA 30722-1323
www.thechurchofgodua.org

The Church of God of the Union Assembly was formed in 1920 by former members of the Church of God/Mountain Assembly.

Church of the Lord (Aladura)
Provincial Head-office, Province of U.S.A.
1697 Monro Ave.
Bronx, NY 10457

The Church of the Lord was founded in 1930 by Josiah Ositelu (d. 1966), a Nigerian and former Anglican. He raised up the Aladura (or praying people) across West Africa, and in recent decades the church has spread internationally.

Church on the Rock International
1615 W. Belt Line Rd.
Carrollton, TX 75006-6633
www.northchurch.org

Church on the Rock International is a network of ministers-pastors, evangelists, and missionaries founded by Dr. Lawrence Kennedy.

Churches of Christ (Pentecostal)
No central headquarters.
For information:
Conference on Spiritual Renewal
RENOVARÉ
8 Inverness Dr. East, Suite 102
Englewood, CO 80112-5609
www.renovare.org

In the 1980s, some congregations associated with the Churches of Christ accepted the charismatic renewal, a move that has separated them from the main body of the Churches of Christ.

Congregational Bible Churches International
P.O. Box 165
Hutchinson, KS 67501

The Congregational Bible Churches was created in 1977 by the merger of the Way Open Door Church and the Independent Holiness Church, whose ministry began in the 1920s.

Congregational Holiness Church
3888 Fayetteville Hwy.
Griffin, GA 30223
chchurch.com

The Congregational Holiness Church was formed in 1920 by former members of the Pentecostal Holiness Church under the leadership of Rev. Watson Sorrow.

Covenant Church of Pittsburgh
c/o Bishop Joseph Garlington
RECONCILIATION! Ministries International
1111 Wood St.
Pittsburgh, PA 15221
www.ccop.org/home

The Covenant Church of Pittsburgh is the home base for the international ministry of Bishop Joseph and Pastor Barbara Garlington.

Destiny Fellowship of Churches International
1781 Ellington St.
Decatur, GA 30032

Destiny Fellowship of Churches International was founded by Bishop D. Jerome Watson, its International Presiding Prelate.

Door of Faith Church and Bible School
1161 Young St.
Honolulu, HI 96814

The Door of Faith Church was founded in 1940 by Mildred Brostek (1911–2005), formerly a minister with the Pentecostal Holiness Church.

DOVE Christian Fellowship International
c/o Larry Kreider
11 Toll Gate Rd.
Lititz, PA 17543
www.dcfi.org

DOVE Christian Fellowship International, launched in 1971, has pioneered the cell church movement as a means of organizing church life.

Eagle's Nest Ministries
c/o Gary Greenwald
P.O. Box 15000
Santa Ana, CA 92735
www.eaglesnestministries.org/home.htm

Healing evangelist Gary Greenwald launched Eagle's Nest Ministries as both a local church and a network of people affected by his ministry and working within the five-fold ministry of Ephesians 4:11.

Ecclesia Word Ministries International
1638 Bronxdale Ave.
Bronx, NY 10462
www.ecclesiaword.org

Dr. John Tetsola, who moved to America from his native Nigeria, founded Ecclesia Word Ministries International and the associated Reformers Ministries International, a network of ministers and their ministries.

Elim Fellowship
1703 Dalton Rd.
P.O. Box 57A
Lima, NY 14485-0857
www.elimfellowship.org

Elim Fellowship developed from the Elim Bible Institute opened at Endwell, New York, in 1924 by Ivan Q. (1888–1970) and Minnie Spencer.

Emmanuel Holiness Church
Box 818
Bladenboro, NC 28320

The Emmanuel Holiness Church was formed in 1953 by former members of the Pentecostal Fire-baptized Holiness Church.

Evangel Fellowship of Ministers and Churches International
c/o Houston Miles, President
200 Evangel Rd.
Spartanburg, SC 29301-1139
www.evangelfellowshipintl.org

A group of ministers under the leadership of Bishop Houston Miles founded the Evangel Fellowship in 1983 as a network of ministers, missionaries, and churches.

Evangelical Assembly of Presbyterian Churches
EAPC General Assembly Office
65 Broadway Ave., Suite 1805
New York, NY 10006
www.ea-pc.org

The Evangelical Assembly was formally organized in 1999 to give structure to a set of Presbyterian churches that had been called into existence through the decade by a group of Spirit-filled ministers.

Evangelical House of God
c/o Bishop Juanita Troy
106 Pearson St.
Spring Lake, NC 28390

Evangelistic Missionary Fellowship
5403 W. 1st Ave.
Lakewood, CO 80226

The Evangelistic Missionary Fellowship is a national organization of pastors, churches, Christian workers, and missionaries, and a member of the National Association of Evangelicals.

Evangelization Society
c/o Reverend David Vogel
Road #1, Box 391
Gibsonia, PA 15044

Every Nation Ministries
P.O. Box 1787
Brentwood, TN 37024
www.everynation.org/en/home.html

Every Nation is a worldwide family of churches and ministries engaged in church planting, campus ministry, and world missions. It was founded in Manila, the Philippines, and now has affiliated congregations in some 50 countries.

Faith Assembly
2214 E. Winona Ave.
Warsaw, IN 46580
frontpage.kconline.com/faithassembly/index.htm

Faith Assembly was founded by Hobart Freeman (1920–1984) in 1963 in Indiana and subsequently founded associated congregations through middle America.

Faith Christian Fellowship International
2448 E. 81st St., Ste. 5400
Tulsa, OK 74137
or
P.O. Box 35443
Tulsa, OK 74153
www.fcf.org

Faith Christian Fellowship International is a fellowship of charismatic ministers and churches founded in 1977 by Doyle "Buddy" Harrison (1939–1998).

Faith Fellowship Ministries
Faith Fellowship Ministries World Outreach Center
2707 Main St.
Sayreville, NJ 08872
www.ffmwoc.org

Faith Fellowship Ministries was founded in 1980 by David T. Demola, who also leads Covenant Ministries International, an international association for pastors and ministers.

Faith Ministries Christian Church
Hq: c/o David Duell
Box 609
Littleton, CO 80160-0609

Federation of Ministers and Churches
P.O. Box 40042
Grand Junction, CO 81504
www.fmci.org/

The federation is an association of charismatic congregations and pastors founded in 1988.

Fellowship of Charismatic Churches and Ministers International
c/o Pastor William T. Ligon
P.O. Box 1218
Brunswick, GA 31521-1218

Fellowship of Christian Assemblies
520 N. 34th Ave. E.
Duluth, MN 55804
www.foca.org

The Fellowship of Christian Assemblies originated in 1922 by the affiliation of several Scandinavian-American Pentecostal assemblies.

Fellowship of Churches and Ministers International
P.O. Box 2165
Reidsville, CA 20456
www.fellowshipcmi.org

The loosely organized Fellowship of Churches and Ministers International was formed in the late 1980s.

Fellowship of Covenant Ministries
c/o Grace Henderson Ministries
P.O. Box 2051
Germantown, MD 20874

The fellowship is a network of ministers sponsored by Grace Henderson Ministries.

Fellowship of Vineyard Harvester Churches
1890 Rome Hwy.
Cedartown, GA 30125
www.fvhc.net

The fellowship is an association of ministers and churches centered on the Cedar Lake Christian Center in Cedartown, Georgia, founded in 1986 by Bishop David Huskins.

First Church of Jesus Christ
c/o Bishop H. E. Honea
1100 E. Lincoln St.
Tullahoma, TN 37388

Fountain of Life Outreach Ministries
P.O. Box 1016
Chicopee, MA 01021
www.folomi.org

Fountain of Life Outreach Ministries is an international fellowship of charismatic ministers and churches.

Free Temple Revival Center Ministries
937 U.S. Hwy. 13-17 S.
Windsor, NC 27983

Freedom Chapel Church of Christ
c/o Bishop William D. Madison
13101 Rhame Dr.
Fort Washington, MD 20744

Full Counsel Christian Fellowship of Churches
P.O. Box 2160
North Little Rock, AR 72115-0160

Full Faith Church of Love
6824 Lackman Rd.
Shawnee Mission, KS 66217-9595
www.fullfaith.com

Full Gospel Assemblies International
c/o Dr. Charles E. Strauser, Pres.
P.O. Box 1230
Coatesville, PA 19320

Full Gospel Assemblies International is a fellowship of charismatic churches and ministers founded in 1972 by Gerald E. Strauser.

Full Gospel Christian Association
c/o Reverend John Brady
P.O. Box 24284
Little Rock, AR 72221

Full Gospel Church in Christ
P.O. Box 6899
Stockton, CA 95206-6899

Full Gospel Evangelistic Association
1400 East Skelly Dr.
Tulsa, OK 74105-4742

The Full Gospel Evangelistic Association was formed in 1952 by former members of the Apostolic Faith Church based in Kansas.

Full Gospel Fellowship of Churches and Ministers International
1000 North Belt Line Rd., Suite 201
Irving, TX 75061-4000
www.fgfcmi.org

The Full Gospel Fellowship, formed in 1962, grew out of the ministry of healing evangelist Gordon Lindsay (1906–1973) and his wife Freda Lindsay (b. 1916). They also founded Christ for the Nations in Dallas, Texas.

Full Gospel Minister's Association
P.O. Box 1324
Paducah, KY 42002-1324

Full Gospel Ministerial Association
6905 Eighth Ave.
Brooklyn, NY 11220

Full Gospel Restoration Ministers and Churches
P.O. Box 840
Corning, CA 96021
fullgospelminister.com

Full Gospel Truth, Inc.
304 3rd St.
P.O. Box 886
East Jordan, MI 49727
members.aol.com/jeraldc

Fullness in Christ Ministries
c/o Reverend Ras Robinson
P.O. Box 136117
Fort Worth, TX 76136
www.fullnessonline.org/

Gate Fellowship of Churches
1638 13th Ave.
Columbus, GA 31901

General Conference of the Evangelical Baptist Church, Inc.
Kavetter Bldg.
3400 E. Ash St.
Goldsboro, NC 27530

Global Network of Christian Ministries
P.O. Box 154747
Irving, TX 75015
www.global-ministries.com

The Global Network is a fellowship of independent Pentecostal ministries founded in the 1980s.

Gospel Assemblies (Sowders/Goodwin)
c/o Gospel Assembly Church
7135 Meredith Dr.
Des Moines, IA 50322

The Gospel Assemblies developed out of the pioneering work of William Sowders (1879–1952). In 1963, Lloyd Goodwin, an associate of Sowders', became pastor of the Gospel Assembly Church in Iowa and from that base founded a number of associated churches.

Gospel Christian Ministries
c/o Reverend L. H. Hardwick
15354 Old Hickory Blvd.
Nashville, TN 37211

Gospel Crusade Ministerial Fellowship
c/o Gerald G. Derstine
1200 Glory Way Blvd.
Bradenton, FL 34212
www.gcmf.org

Gospel Crusade Ministerial Fellowship is an association of ministers, ministries, and churches founded by charismatic evangelist Gerald G. Derstine (b. 1928).

Gospel Ministers and Churches International/Gospel Alliance Church
3593 W. Northern Ave., Ste. 8
Phoenix, AZ 85051
www.gmci.org

Gospel Ministers and Churches International is a charismatic ministerial association closely related to the Gospel Alliance Church, a congregational association. Both organizations are headed by Gordon H. Douglas.

Gospel Outreach (c/o Dave Sczepanski)
Verbo Ministries
P.O. Box 190
Kenner, LA 70063-0190
www.verbo.org

Grace Bible Ministries
c/o Grace Bible Church
Reverend Sam Webb
1052 Ilima Dr.
Honolulu, HI 96817
netministries.org/see/churches.exe/ch01255

Grace Christian Fellowship
c/o Reverend John L. Bayles
P.O. Box 920
Germantown, MD 20875

Grace Fellowship
Bob Yandian Ministries
P.O. Box 55236
Tulsa, OK 74155
www.gracetulsa.com

Great Commission Association of Churches
P.O. Box 7101
Winter Park, FL 32793-7101
www.greatcommission.org

Greater Bible Way Temple
c/o Bishop Huie L. Rogers
261 Rochester Ave.
Brooklyn, NY 11213
www.biblewaychurch.org

Greater Grace World Outreach
6025 Moravia Park Dr.
Baltimore, MD 21206.
www.ggwo.org

Greater Works Church of Jesus Christ
c/o Bishop Charles Warren
110 William St.
Sikeston, MO 63801

Hall Deliverance Foundation
Box 9910
Phoenix, AZ 85068

The Hall Deliverance Foundation was founded by healing evangelist Franklin Hall (1907–1993), who taught the concept of "body-felt" salvation, by which he meant that salvation was for the body as well as the soul.

Harvest Evangelism
Apostolic Transformation Network
6472 Camden Ave., Ste. 110
San Jose, CA 95120
www.harvestevan.org

Harvest Time Revivals
c/o Reverend David Livingston
P.O. Box 10
Stanley, NC 28164

Hillcrest Church
12123 Hillcrest Rd.
Dallas, TX 75230
www.hillcrestchurch.org

Holiness Assemblies of God
9414 East 46th St.
Tulsa, OK 74125

Holy Church of God
707 Little Neck Rd.
Savannah, GA 31419
www.holychurchofgod.org

The Holy Church of God is a Holiness Pentecostal church with congregations primarily in the South.

Hope Chapel Kihei
300 E. Welakahao Rd.
Kihei, HI 96753

Impact Ministries
4410 University Dr., Suite 109
Huntsville, AL 35816
www.impactministries.com

Independent Assemblies Fellowship
c/o Reverend Jim Robinson
P.O. Box 1546
Ada, OK 74821
www.independentassemblies.org

Independent Ministries International
c/o Reverend Don Young
P.O. Box 150
Paducah, KY 42002

Indonesian Full Gospel Fellowship
12345 8th Ave. NE
Seattle, WA 98125
www.ifgf.org

Interdenominational Ministries International
P.O. Box 2107
Vista, CA 92085-0107

Interdenominational Ministries International began in 1980 as a set of home prayer groups led by Rev. Rocco and Mary Bruno.

International Apostolic Evangelistic and Missionary Fellowship
1322 E. Memorial Blvd.
Lakeland, FL 33801

International Christian Church and Ministerial Association
P.O. Box 1295
Plymouth, FL 32768-1295
www.internationalseminary.com

International Church of the Foursquare Gospel
Angelus Temple
1100 Glendale Blvd.
Los Angeles, CA 90026
www.foursquare.org

The Foursquare Church was founded by pioneering female evangelist Aimee Semple McPherson (1890–1944).

International Conference of Word Ministries
7547 Olive Blvd.
University City, MO 63130

International Convention of Faith Ministries
5500 Woodland Park Blvd.
Arlington, TX 76013
www.icfm.org

The International Convention was founded in 1979 by Doyle "Buddy" Harrison and a number of charismatic ministers, many of whom have subsequently grown their own fellowships of ministers and churches.

International Evangelical Church (IEC)
Evangel Cathedral
13901 Central Ave.
Upper Marlboro, MD 20772

The International Evangelical Church began in Italy as an evangelical movement headed by John McTernan, and was brought to the United States when Evangel Cathedral, founded by John Levin Meares (b. 1924) in suburban Washington, D.C., affiliated with it.

International Evangelism Crusades
c/o Dr. Frank E. Stranges, Pres.
14617 Victory Blvd.
Van Nuys, CA 91411

The International Evangelism Crusades was founded in 1959 by Pentecostal minister Dr. Frank E. Stranges. Stranges is better known for his study of flying saucers (UFOs) and his founding of the National Investigations Committee on UFOs.

The International Fellowship of Ministries
5710 22nd Ave.
Seattle, WA 98107
www.ifm7.org

The fellowship was founded by people drawn around healing evangelist John G. Lake (1870–1935) and as a means of continuing his ministry in the years since his death.

International Ministerial Association
5201 W. Homosassa Trail
Lecanto, FL 34461
www.interma.net

International Ministerial Fellowship
P.O. Box 32366
Minneapolis, MN 55432-0366
www.i-m-f.org

The fellowship is an association of independent charismatic ministers and churches founded in 1958.

International Ministers Forum
c/o Pastor Doris J. Swartz
P.O. Box 1717
Dayton, OH 45401-1717

The forum was founded in 1950 by Rev. Louise Copeland as a fellowship of independent Pentecostal ministers and churches.

International Pentecostal Church of Christ
c/o Clyde M. Hughes, Gen. Overseer
Box 439
2245 St. Rte. 42
London, OH 43140-0439
www.ipcc.cc

The International Pentecostal Church of Christ was formed when the International Pentecostal Assemblies and the Pentecostal Church of Christ merged in 1976. It traces its heritage to the founding of a periodical, *The Bridegroom's Messenger,* in 1907.

International Pentecostal Holiness Church
P.O. Box 12609
Oklahoma City, OK 73157-2609
www.iphc.org

The IPHC derived from the fire-baptized movement initiated by Holiness minister B. H. Irwin (b. 1854) in the 1890s. After the events at Azusa, the church accepted the Holiness Pentecostal perspective.

International Union of Gospel Missions
1045 Swift St.
Kansas City, MO 64116-4127
www.iugm.org

Jesus Is Lord Ministries
c/o Pastor Michael H. Yeager
Rt. #30
Cashtown, PA 17310

Ken Stewart Ministries
c/o Pastor Ronald Deeble
P.O. Box 2493
Broken Arrow, OK 74013
www.kenstewart.com

Kingdom and World Mission of Our Lord Jesus Christ
4179 Edenhurst Ave
Los Angeles, CA 90039

The mission was founded in 1984 by Elie Khoury, who migrated to the United States from Egypt.

Kingdom Expansion International Ministries
P.O. Box 2051
Germantown, MD 20874

Kingdom Ministries International
c/o George Kouri
126 NW 10th St.
Oklahoma City, OK 73103
www.kmintl.org

Kingdom Ministries Network International
P.O. Box 8842
Coral Springs, FL 33075
www.kmni.org

Kingdom Ministries Network was founded in 2001 in South Africa under the leadership of Apostle John Boney to provide apostolic oversight to ministries, ministers, and organizations who are in covenant with the Network.

Kingsway Fellowship International
3707 SW 9th St.
Des Moines, IA 50315-3047
www.kingsway.edu

The Kingsway Fellowship was created in 1966 by Dr. D. L. Browning to serve otherwise independent Pentecostal ministers and churches.

Lakewood Church
c/o John Osteen
P.O. Box 23297
Houston, TX 77028
www.lakewood.cc/site/PageServer

Lakewood Church, founded in 1959, became the center for the global ministry of John (d. 1999) and Dotie Osteen, and is continued today by their son Joel Osteen.

Lamb of God Church
612 Isenburg St.
Honolulu, HI 96817

The Lamb of God Church is a Pentecostal church founded in 1942 by Rev. Rose H. Kwan, serving the Hawaiian Islands.

LeSea Ministries Network
c/o David Sumrall
P.O. Box 12
South Bend, IN 46624

Liberty Fellowship of Churches and Ministers
5229 Kelly Elliott Rd.
Arlington, TX 76017
www.libertyfellowship.org

Liberty Fellowship was founded in 1977 by Ken Sumrall, a former Southern Baptist minister, and a number of colleagues who wished to fellowship together and work with the five-fold ministry structure of Ephesians 4:11.

Life Links International Fellowship of Churches and Ministers
International Hq: 2202 8th Ave. N
Regina, SK S4R 7T9
Canada
lifelinks.org

Life Links is a continent-wide fellowship of independent Pentecostal and charismatic churches. It was founded in 1978 in Alberta.

Life Ministerial Fellowship International
P.O. Box 1220
Sand Springs, OK 74063-1220

Lighthouse Gospel Fellowship
P.O. Box 2058
Tulsa, OK 74101-0349

The Lighthouse Gospel Fellowship was founded in 1958 by Drs. H. A. and Thelma Chaney of Tulsa, Oklahoma.

Living Bread Ministries
c/o Sandra L. Ambroso
3304 E. Yorba Linda Blvd.
Fullerton, CA 92631

Living Faith Leaders' Fellowship
c/o Karl Barden
1035 S. Grand
Pullman, WA 99163

Living Word Fellowship
P.O. Box 3429
Iowa City, IA 52244-3429
Or
Living Word Publications
Box 858
North Hollywood, CA 91063
www.thelivingword.org

The fellowship (originally the Church of the Living Word) emerged in the 1950s around John Robert Stevens (1919–1983), formerly a minister with the Assemblies of God.

Logos Christian Fellowship
107 2nd St.
Leesburg, FL 34748
www.logoschristian.org

Logos Christian Fellowship was founded in 1989 by Christopher Brian Ward, formerly affiliated with Calvary Chapel, who pioneered a deliverance ministry (exorcisms) and a web ministry based at Leesburg, Florida.

Metro Fellowship of Kansas City
12411 Wornall Rd.
Kansas City, MO 64145
www.metro-kc.org

Midwest Ministers' Fellowship
23300 Pink Hill Rd.
Blue Springs, MO 64015
www.mmfellowship.org

Ministers Fellowship International
9200 NE Fremont St.
Portland, OR 97220
www.mfi-online.org

The fellowship was founded in 1987 to bring together a group of independent ministers and churches that emerged out of the Latter Rain Revival of the late-1940s.

Ministers for Christ Assembly of Churches
6630 W. Cactus, Ste. B107
Glendale, AZ 85304
www.ordination.org

Miracle Life Fellowship International
11052 N. 24th Ave.
Phoenix, AZ 85029
www.donstewartassociation.com

Miracle Life Fellowship International was founded by evangelist A. A. Allen (1911–1970), who started his career with the Assemblies of God. Allen was succeeded by evangelist Don Stewart.

Miracle Revival Fellowship
c/o Trans World Evangelism, Inc
913 Canyon St.
Plainview, TX 79072
miraclerevival.net/MRF.html

Miracle Revival Fellowship was founded by evangelist Neal Frisby (d. 2005).

Miracles Ministry Fellowship
P.O. Box 21
Griffin, GA 30223
miraclestoday.org

Miracles Ministry Fellowship grew out of the ministry of independent Pentecostal evangelist Don Walker.

Missionary Church International
c/o Bishop Bob Coulter
P.O. Box 1761
Columbia, SC 29202-1761
www.themissionarychurchinternational.org

Music Square Church
Tony Alamo Christian Ministries Worldwide
P.O. Box 398
Alma, AR 72921
www.alamoministries.com

Music Square (also known as the Tony Alamo Christian Church) began as a Jesus People street ministry under the leadership of Tony and Susan (d. 1982) Alamo.

N.A.T.I.O.N. Strategy
c/o Ed Delph
7145 W. Mariposa Grande Lane
Peoria, AZ 85383
www.nationstrategy.com

Network International
c/o Mr. Darrel Eaton
126 S. Jackson St.
San Angelo, TX 76901

Network of Equipping Ministries
c/o Dale L. Stoll
50755 C. R. 23
Bristol, IN 46507

New Covenant Churches of Maryland
804 Windsor Rd.
Arnold, MD 21012

The New Covenant Churches of Maryland were called together by Robert Wright, director of the New Life Christian Center in Arnold, Maryland. Wright also has founded a national federation of church schools.

New Covenant Ministries International
c/o Southland Church International
1920 South Brea, Canyon Cutoff Rd.
Walnut, CA 91789
www.ncmi.net

New Covenant Ministries International is a network of otherwise autonomous charismatic churches that agree to cooperate with the apostolic leadership based in South Africa.

New Frontiers International
c/o Reverend John Lanferman
930 Walron Rd.
Crestwood, MO 63126
or
International Hq:
17 Claredon Villas
Hove, East Sussex BN3 3RE, UK
www.n-f-i.org

New Frontiers International is a network of churches, based in the United Kingdom, that accept the leadership pattern of the five-fold ministry of Ephesians 4:11.

New Testament Holiness Church
P.O. Box 24409
Dallas, TX 75224

The New Testament Holiness Church grew out of the efforts of Pentecostal healing evangelist David Terrell.

New Wine Ministerial Fellowship
109 East Main St.
Morganfield, KY 42437

Open Bible Standard Churches, Inc.
2020 Bell Ave.
Des Moines, IA 50315-1096
www.openbible.org

The Open Bible Standard Churches was formed in 1935 by the merger of two older Pentecostal bodies, the Open Bible Evangelistic Association and Bible Standard, Inc.,

(Original) Church of God, Inc.
c/o Reverend W. D. Sawyer, Gen. Overseer
Box 3086
Chattanooga, TN 37404

The (Original) Church of God was founded in 1917 by former members of the Church of God (Cleveland, Tennessee).

Overcoming Faith Fellowship International
3310 W. Magnolia Blvd.
Burbank, CA 91505-2907
abcd.co.za/offi

PDI Ministries
7881-B Beechcraft Ave.
Gaithersburg, MD 20879

PDI Ministries (also known as People of Destiny International) was founded by Larry Tomczak and C. J. Mahaney, who were influenced by the charismatic revival and began a small teaching ministry in Washington, D.C., in the late 1970s.

Pentecostal Church of God
c/o Dr. James D. Gee, Gen. Superintendent
4901 Pennsylvania
Box 850
Joplin, MO 64802
www.pcg.org

The Pentecostal Church of God was formed in 1919 by a group of ministers who had become Pentecostals meeting in Chicago.

Pentecostal Conference of North American Keralites
P.O. Box 294940
Lewisville, TX 75029
www.pcnak.org

Pentecostal Free Will Baptist Church, Inc.
Box 1568
Dunn, NC 28334
www.pfwb.org

The Pentecostal Free Will Baptist Church originated in the spread of Pentecostalism among Free Will Baptists in the decade after the Azusa revival. Four conferences were formed in the Carolinas, and in 1943 these conferences formally affiliated. A 1959 reorganization produced the current church.

Pentecostal Ministerial Association of America
P.O. Box 311
Dayton, OH 45401
www.thepma.org

Pentecostal 7th-Day Assemblies
c/o Chairman Elder Garver C. Gray
4700 NE 119th St.
Vancouver, WA 98686

Praise Chapel Christian Fellowship Churches and Ministries International
Larry Neville, Senior Minister
Praise Chapel
P.O. Box 787
Rancho Cucamonga, CA 91730
www.praisechapel.com

Praise Chapel was initiated in Maywood, California, in 1976 by Michael Neville (d. 1996).

Revival Centres International
c/o Pastor Rocky Schimelfining
12345 SW Main St.
Portland, OR 97223
www.rci.org.au

Revival Fellowship Group
c/o Pastor George Rohrig
Living Faith Church
5600 Carbon Canyon Rd.
Brea, CA 92621

Rhema Churches
c/o Kenneth Hagin Ministries
P.O. Box 50126
Tulsa, OK 74150-0126
www.rhema.org

Rhema is the center of a fellowship of ministers trained at Rhema Bible School and the churches they have founded and/or serve. Rhema was founded by televangelist Kenneth Hagin, Sr. (1917–2003).

The Rock Church and Ministerial Fellowship
c/o Bishop John Gimenez
640 Kempsville Rd.
Virginia Beach, VA 23464
www.rockchurch.org/rmf.htm

The Rock Church and Ministerial Fellowship was founded by John Gimenez, who in 1965 was saved from his addiction to drugs.

R. W. Schambach Ministries
22525 Hwy. 155 S.
Flint, TX 75762
or
P.O. Box 9009
Tyler, TX 75711
www.schambach.org

St. Peter's World Outreach Center
1249 E. Sprague St.
Winston-Salem, NC 27107

Set Free Ministries, International
c/o Kingdom Lifestyles Institute
P.O. Box 591
Katy, TX 77493
www.apostle.org

SHEM Ministries International
Dr. Glenn T. and Terrie L. Smith
25016 Maple Valley Highway
Maple Valley, WA 98038
www.shem.net

Shem Ministries (Servant House Evangelistic Ministries) was founded in 1996 by Glenn Smith and grew as a fellowship of ministers and churches/ministries as a means of fellowship and encouragement.

Shiloh Apostolic Churches USA
c/o Shiloh Apostolic Church (New York)
1607 Nostrand Ave.
Brooklyn, NY 11226

Shiloh Christian Fellowship
c/o David Kitely
3295 School St.
Oakland, CA 94602
www.shilohcf.org

Souls Outreach and Ministerial Association
900 Weeks Rd.
Cleveland, TN 37312

Sovereign Grace Ministries
7505 Muncaster Mill Rd.
Gaithersburg, MD 20877
www.sovereigngraceministries.org

Strategic Christian Services
c/o Dennis T. Peacocke
2425 Mendocino Ave.
Santa Rosa, CA 95403
www.gostrategic.org

Tulsa Christian Fellowship
2121 E. 3rd St.
Tulsa, OK 74104
www.tulsachristianfellowship.com

The Tulsa Christian Fellowship was started in 1969 by Bill Sanders, a former Southern Baptist minister. Beginning as a congregation ministering to Hippies, it has grown into a network of house-churches scattered throughout Tulsa, with two of the leaders serving in apostolic and prophetic roles in other churches.

United Christian Church and Ministerial Association
Box 700
Cleveland, TN 37364-0700
www.unitedchristianchurch.com

The United Christian Church was established by independent Pentecostal minister H. Richard Hall (1920–2002) Cleveland, Tennessee, in1956.

United Full Gospel Churches International
c/o Bishop Michael K. Lake
P.O. Box 588
Marshfield, MO 65706-0588
www.biblical-life.com/ufgc/index.htm

UFGC was founded in 1965 as a fellowship of independent Pentecostal ministers and ministries. In 1999, the Biblical Life Fellowship merged into the United Full Gospel Church.

United Full Gospel Ministries Association
2345 Lafayette Ave.
St. Louis, MO 63104-2519

United Fundamentalist Church
3236 Larga Ave.
Los Angeles, CA 90039-2247

The United Fundamentalist Church was organized in 1939 by Leroy M. Kopp, who passed the leadership to his son, E. Paul Kopp.

United Gospel Fellowship Covenant Ministries
c/o J. Venturnio Porter Ministries
P.O. Box 2709
Fayetteville, NC 28302-0709
www.jvporter.org

United Network of Christian Ministers and Churches
c/o Don Pfotenhauer
804 131st Ave.
Blaine, MN 55434

The United Network was formed in 1985 by Rev. Don Pfotenhauser, a former Lutheran Church-Missouri Synod minister who became a charismatic.

Universal Faith Ministries of Jesus Christ
c/o Bishop Albert L. Henderson
P.O. Box 1344
Douglasville, GA 30133-1344

Universal World Church
123 N. Lake St.
Los Angeles, CA 90026
groups.msn.com/TheUniversalWorldChurch

The Universal World Church was founded by Dr. O. Lee Jaggers, previously serving with the Assemblies of God, in 1952 in Los Angeles.

Victory Churches International
c/o California Victory Church
P.O. Box 20034
Fountain Valley, CA 92708

or
International Hq: c/o Victory Village
P.O. Box 65077
North Hill
Calgary, AB Canada T2N 4T6
www.victoryint.org

Victory Churches International is a Pentecostal fellowship that began at Victory Christian Church in Lethbridge, Alberta, in 1979 with the ministry of George and Hazel Hill.

Victory Fellowship of Ministries
7700 S. Lewis Ave.
Tulsa, OK 74136-7700
www.victory.com

VFM is organized around the Victory Christian Center in Tulsa, Oklahoma, and is home to a network of like churches around the country, many pastored by graduates of Victory Bible Institute.

Victory New Testament Fellowship International
P.O. Box 850146
Mesquite, TX 75185-0146
www.fellowshipintl.org

Victory New Testament Fellowship International dates its beginning to the call to the ministry of H. Donald Skelton in 1934. However, it was formally organized in 1953, at which time Skelton began to ordain ministers and found additional congregations.

Vineyard USA
P.O. Box 2089
Stafford, TX 77497
www.vineyardusa.org

Vineyard USA is the American branch of the movement started by John Wimber (1934–1997), a former minister with the Calvary Chapel Church, which grew into an international charismatic fellowship.

World Bible Way Fellowship
P.O. Box 70
DeSoto, TX 75115-0070
www.brainerd.net/~wjc/IRCC/wbwf.html

World Bible Way Fellowship was founded in 1943 as a Pentecostal fellowship of ministers and churches.

World Council of Independent Christian Churches
Bowling Green Station
P.O. Box 76
New York, NY 10274-0076
www.wcicc.org

The World Council of Independent Christian Churches was formed in 1988 in Malawi, Central Africa, the first elder being Dr. Edward Thomas Chikumba of Wa La La Mission in Namandzi, Malawi. The council soon expanded to include members from countries across Africa, Europe, and North America.

World Evangelism Fellowship
c/o Reverend Jimmy Swaggart
Box 262550
Baton Rouge, LA 70826-2550
www.jsm.org

World Evangelism Fellowship continues the ministry of televangelist Jimmy Swaggart (b. 1935), who left the Assemblies of God in 1988 and began to work independently.

World Harvest Church Ministerial Fellowship
c/o Rod Parsley
P.O. Box 32903
Columbus, OH 43232-0903
www.whcmf.net/Index.aspx

World Ministries Fellowship
c/o Reverend Robert Terrell
P.O. Box 1868
Texarkana, AR 71854

World Ministry Fellowship
801 E. Plano Pkwy., #150
Plano, TX 75074-6797
www.worldministry.com

World-Wide Association of Full Gospel Churches
Dr. Lance Keeling–Bishop
1110 Penn St.
Borger, TX 79007
www.ourchurch.com/view/?pageID=68802

Worldwide Missionary Evangelism
1285 Millsap Rd.
Fayetteville, AR 72701
www.wmeinc.org

Worldwide Missionary Evangelism, founded in 1956 by Norris Plotts (1906–1997) for missionary work in Africa, began to work in the United States and charter churches in the 1970s, at which time Plotts separated from the Assemblies of God.

African American Pentecostal Churches

Though Pentecostalism began in a small Bible school led by Charles Parham (a white man), its real growth was launched from the revival that began in the small African American Azusa Street Mission in Los Angeles in 1906. Pentecostalism was thus really born as an interracial movement, but very early divided along racial lines. It initially spread through several black Holiness denominations and then found a life of its own and became an established part of the African American community, rivaling Baptists and Methodists in strength. The largest African American Pentecostal church, the Church of God in Christ, is also the largest Pentecostal church in America, with approximately twice the membership of the predominantly white Assemblies of God.

The Azusa Street Mission was officially known as the Apostolic Faith Mission of Los Angeles. It passed its name to several predominantly white groups, several African American churches, and to a whole movement: the Jesus Only or Oneness movement that dissented from the orthodox doctrine of the Trinity.

Contacts:

African Universal Church
2236 SW 48th Ave.
Hollywood, FL 33023

The African Universal Church grew out of the ministry of Mother Laura Adorkor Koffey (d. 1928), who preached in the South in the 1920s and founded the church in 1927.

Apostolic Faith Church of God
5211 "A" St., SE
Washington, DC 20019
or
841 Griggs Rd.
Jefferson, OH 44047

Apostolic Faith Church of God and True Holiness
c/o Bishop O. Key
825 Gregg Rd.
Jefferson, OH 44047

Apostolic Faith Church of God Giving Grace
c/o Bishop Geanie Perry
Rt. 3, Box 111A
Warrenton, NC 17589

Apostolic Faith Church of God, Live On
c/o Bishop Richard Cross
2300 Trenton St.
Hopewell, VA 23868.

The Apostolic Faith Church of God, Live On was founded in 1952 by groups formerly associated with the Apostolic Faith Church of God and True Holiness.

Apostolic Faith Churches of God
700 Charles St.
Franklin, VA 23851

The Apostolic Faith Churches developed out of evangelical efforts of Pentecostal pioneers William J. Seymour and Charles H. Mason, who visited Washington, D.C., in 1909. Congregations resulting from that effort took more formal steps to organize in 1934.

Apostolic Faith Churches of a Living God
3416 Carver St.
Columbia, SC 29203

Azusa Interdenominational Fellowship of Christian Churches
c/o Reverend Carlton Pearson
8621 S. Memorial Dr.
Tulsa, OK 74133-4312

The Azusa Interdenominational Fellowship was founded by Tulsa minister Carlton D. Pearson (b. 1953) in 1990. The fellowship serves as both an ecumenical association and a denominational home for the different churches and ministries associated with it.

Bible Church of Christ
100 West 2nd St.
Mt. Vernon, NY 10550
www.thebiblechurchofchrist.com

The Bible Church of Christ was founded in 1959 by Bishop Roy Bryant, Sr. (b. 1923), who became known in the African American community as an exorcist.

Celestial Church of Christ
No central headquarters:
For information contact:
Christ Ambassador Parish
2805 Linden St.
Oakland, CA 94607
or
International Hq:
Mission House Ketu
P.O. Box 1237
Ikeja, Lagos, Nigeria
www.celestialchurch.com

Central Holiness Church of Deliverance
c/o Bishop J. T. Barnet
1069 Washington St., S.W.
Atlanta, GA 30315

Christ Apostolic Church of America
(Christ Apostolic Church WOSEM)
108-02 & 04 Sutphin Boulevard
Jamaica, New York 11435
or
International headquarters:
World Soul Winning Evangelistic Ministry
c/o Prophet T. O. Obadare
P.O. Box 151
Akure, Ondo State, Nigeria

Christ Apostolic Church is the American affiliate of the World Soul Winning Evangelistic Ministry founded in Nigeria by Apostle Joseph A. Babalola. It currently is led by Prophet T. O. Obadare, who brought the church to the United States in 1981.

Christ Holy Sanctified Church of America
5204 Willie St.
Fort Worth, TX 76105

Church of Christ Holiness unto the Lord
1650 Smart St.
P.O. Box 1642
Savannah, GA 31401

Church of God and True Holiness
7710 Euclid Ave.
Cleveland, OH 44103
www.trueholinesstemple.com

Church of God in Christ, Congregational
1905 Bond Ave.
East St. Louis, IL 62201

The Church of God in Christ, Congregational, was founded in 1932 by former members of the Church of God in Christ who rejected its episcopal polity.

Church of God in Christ, International
c/o Presiding Bishop Rt. Reverend Carl E. Williams
170 Adelphi St.
Brooklyn, NY 11025

The Church of God in Christ, International, was founded in 1969 by former members of the Church of God in Christ who rejected the reorganization of the church that occurred that year.

Church of God, the House of Prayer
c/o Reverend Charles Mackenin
Markleysburg, PA 15459

Church of God (Which He Purchased with His Own Blood)
1628 NE 50th
Oklahoma City, OK 73111

Church of the Holy Trinity
1618 11th St., NW
Washington, DC 20001

Church of the Kingdom of God
P.O. Box 577
Eustis, FL 32727

Church of the Living God
P.O. Box 55090
Indianapolis, IN 46205
www.cotlgnet.org

Church of the Living God (Christian Workers for Fellowship)
c/o Bishop W. E. Crumes
434 Forest Ave.
Cincinnati, OH 45229

The Church of the Living God was founded in 1889 by William Christian (1856–1928), formerly a Baptist.

Church of the Living God, Pillar and Ground of Truth
c/o M. H. Lewis, General Overseer
4520 Ashland City Highway
Nashville, TN 37208
www.clgpgt.org

The Church of the Living God, Pillar and Ground of Truth is one of several branches of the movement founded in 1903 by evangelist Mary Lena Lewis Tate (1871–1930). This branch resulted from a three-way split in the original church when the three people chosen to the office of general overseer separated. This branch was originally led by F. E. Lewis.

Church of the Living God, The Pillar and Ground of Truth Which He Purchased with His Own Blood
P.O. Box 55090
Indianapolis, IN 46205
www.cotlgnet.org

The Church of the Living God is one branch of the church originally founded by Mary L. L. Tate early in the twentieth century. This branch was founded in the 1930s by general overseer B. L. McLeod (d. 1936) and is currently led by Bishop Faye Moore.

Church of Universal Triumph/ the Dominion of God
c/o Reverend James Shaffer
8317 LaSalle Blvd.
Detroit, MI 48206

Deliverance Evangelistic Centers
505 Central Ave.
Newark, NJ 07017
or
621 Clinton Ave.
Newark, NJ 07108

The Deliverance Evangelistic Centers was founded in the 1950s by Arturo Skinner (d. 1975).

Deliverance Evangelistic Church
2001 West Lehigh Ave.
Philadelphia, PA 19132
www.decministry.org

The Deliverance Evangelistic Church began in the early 1960s as an independent prayer meeting in Philadelphia led by Rev. Benjamin Smith, Sr. (d. 2002).

Faith Tabernacle Council of Churches, International
7015 NE 23rd Ave.
Portland, OR 97211

The Faith Tabernacle Council was founded in 1962 by Bishop Louis B. Osborne, Sr., of Portland, Oregon.

Fellowship of Inter-City Word of Faith Ministries
c/o Crenshaw Christian Center
7901 S. Vermont Ave.
Los Angeles, CA 90044
www.faithdome.org

The fellowship developed out of the ministry of televangelist Fred Price (b. 1932), a former associate of Kenneth Hagin, Sr., of Rhema, and pastor of the Crenshaw Christian Center in Los Angeles.

Fire-Baptized Holiness Church of God of the Americas
c/o Bishop W. E. Fuller, Jr.
901 Bishop W. E. Fuller Hwy.
Greenville, SC 29601-4103
www.fbhchurch.org

The Fire-Baptized Holiness Church of God of the Americas was founded in 1908 by Bishop W. E. Fuller, who complained of racism in the original white-led Fire-Baptized Holiness Church (now defunct). The church soon accepted the new Pentecostal perspective that was introduced into the American South about the time of its founding.

Free Gospel Church of the Apostles Doctrine
c/o Apostle Dr. Ralph E. Green
Free Gospel Deliverance Temple
Coral Hills, MD 20734
www.freegospel.org

Freedom Worldwide Covenant Ministries
c/o Apostle Gilbert Coleman, Jr.
Freedom Christian Bible Fellowship
P.O. Box 4587
Philadelphia, PA 19131
www.freedomworldwide.org

The Freedom Worldwide Covenant Ministries was founded by Apostle Gilbert Coleman, Jr.

Full Gospel Baptist Church Fellowship
4185 Snapfinger Woods Dr.
Decatur, GA 30035

The Full Gospel Baptist Church Fellowship emerged in 1995 as a result of the Pentecostal experience spreading into many Baptist congregations. Leading in the founding of the fellowship was Paul S. Morton, pastor of the Greater St. Stephen Full Gospel Baptist Church in New Orleans. In the wake of Hurricane Katrina, the fellowship has moved its headquarters to Georgia, while committing itself to the rebuilding of New Orleans.

Full Gospel Holy Temple
39727 LBJ Freeway
Dallas, TX 75237
www.fght.org

The Full Gospel Holy Temple was founded as a Holiness Pentecostal church in 1961 by Apostle Lobias Murray.

Full Gospel Pentecostal Association
1032 N. Sumner
Portland, OR 97217
or
Tabernacle Evangelism Community Church
1300 N. La Brea Ave.
Inglewood, CA 90302

The Full Gospel Pentecostal Association is a fellowship of independent Pentecostal churches, founded in 1970 by Adolph A. Wells, Edna Travis, and S. D. Leffall.

General Assembly Church of the Living God Pillar and Ground of the Truth
c/o Bishop C. C. Berry, Jr.
1112 S. Ewing Ave.
Dallas, TX 75216
www.cotlg.org

The General Assembly, under the leadership of Bishop C. C. Berry (b. 1930), has most of its congregations in the state of Texas.

Holy Temple of God, Inc.
c/o Walter Camps, Sr., Presiding Bishop
1220 NE 23rd Ave.
Gainesville, FL 32609
www.htog.org/htog

House of God Which Is the Church of the Living God, the Pillar and Ground of Truth, Inc.
Bishop Raymond W. White
6107 Cobbs Creek Pkwy.
P.O. Box 5319
Philadelphia, PA 19142
www.houseofgodclg.org

The House of God was founded in 1919 by Philadelphia members who left the Church of the Living God, the Pillar and Ground of Truth led by Mary Lena Lewis Tate.

House of God Which Is the Church of the Living God, the Pillar and Ground of Truth without Controversy (Keith Dominion)
2717 Heiman St.
Nashville, TN 37208
or
P.O. Box 22675
Nashville, TN 37202-2675
www.hogc.org

One of three branches of the Church of the Living God originally founded by Mary L. L. Tate early in the twentieth century, the Keith Dominion was founded in the 1930s by Mary F. L. Keith (d. 1962). It is currently led by Bishop Rebecca W. Fletcher.

House of Prayer, Church of God
Rt. 9, Box 131
Charleston, WV 25311

House of the Lord Pentecostal Church
415 Atlantic Ave.
Brooklyn, NY 11217

Mount Calvary Holy Church of America
c/o Greater Mt. Calvary Holy Church
610 Rhode Island Ave., NE
Washington, DC 20002
www.gmchc.org

Mount Calvary United Church of God
223-25 First St.
Elizabeth, NJ 07201

Mount Sinai Holy Church
c/o Bishop Joseph Bell
1601 N. Broad St.
Philadelphia, PA 19148
www.mtsinaichurch.org

The Mount Sinai Holy Church grew out of the lengthy ministry of pioneering female minister Ida Robinson (1891–1946). She founded the church in 1924.

Original United Holy Church International
Bishop H. W. Field
Box 263
Durham, NC 27702

The Original United Holy Church International emerged in 1977 from a controversy within the United Holy Church of America.

Pilgrim Assemblies International
c/o Bishop Roy E. Brown
135 Schaefer St.
Brooklyn, NY 11207
www.roybrownministries.org

Pilgrim Assemblies International was founded by Roy E. Brown (b. 1943) in Brooklyn, New York.

Prayer Band Fellowship Union
Gospel Temple Community Holiness Church
P.O. Box 9109
Bridgeport, CT 06601

Redeemed Christian Church of God
P.O. Box 710874
Houston, TX 77271-0874
www.rccg.org

or
International Hq: Nigeria

Salvation and Deliverance Church, Worldwide
c/o Apostle William Brown
37 West 116th St.
New York, NY 10026
churches.net/churches/sdcchurch/index1.html

The Salvation and Deliverance Church was founded in 1975 by William Brown, formerly a minister with the African Methodist Episcopal Church.

Seventh Day Pentecostal Church of the Living God
1443 S. Euclid
Washington, DC 20009
www.7dpc.com

Triumph the Church and the Kingdom of God in Christ (International)
c/o Chief Bishop Right Reverend A. J. Scott
213 Farrington Ave., SE
Atlanta, GA 30315

Triumph the Church in Righteousness
P.O. Box 1572
Fort Lauderdale, FL 33302

True Grace Memorial House of Prayer
205 V St., NW
Washington, DC 20001

The True Grace Memorial House of Prayer was founded in the early 1960s by former ministers and leaders of the United House of Prayer for All People.

True Vine Pentecostal Holiness Church
929 Bethel Ln.
Martinsville, VA 24112

The True Vine Pentecostal Holiness Church was founded in the 1940s by William Monroe Johnson and Robert L. Hairston.

United Church of the Living God, the Pillar and Ground of Truth
601 Kentucky Ave.
Fulton, KY 42041

The United Church of the Living God, the Pillar and Ground of Truth was founded in 1946 by Bishop Clifton Okley, who left the Church of the Living God, the Pillar and Ground of Truth Which He Purchased with His Own Blood. Most congregations are on the West Coast.

United Covenant Churches of Christ
9730 South Western, Suite 712
Evergreen Park, IL 60805
www.upccweb.com

United Crusade Fellowship Conference
14250 SE 13th Pl.
Bellevue, WA 98007-5521

The United Crusade Fellowship Conference was founded by Bishop Richard E. Taylor and operates primarily in the Northwest.

United Holy Church
c/o Bishop Ralph Houston
173 Brian Circle
Antioch, TN 37013

United Holy Church of America
825 Fairoak Ave.
Chillum, MD 20783

The United Holy Church formed as a Holiness church in 1886 and later accepted Pentecostalism. It originated in a revival held at Method, North Carolina, by Rev. Isaac Cheshier.

United House of Prayer for All People
c/o Bishop S. C. Madison
601 M St. NW
Washington, DC 20001
www.uhop.org

The United House of Prayer is the original organization established by Bishop C. M. "Sweet Daddy" Grace (1882?–1960), who emerged as a popular and controversial African American church leader in the 1930s.

United Pentecostal Churches of Christ
c/o Bishop Jesse Ellis
10515 Chester Ave.
Cleveland, OH 44106

United Pentecostal Council of the Assemblies of God
P.O. Box 308
Cambridge MA 02139
www.upcag.net

The United Pentecostal Council traces its beginning to the formation of a small African American Holiness congregation in Cambridge, Massachusetts, in 1909. The council was founded to facilitate overseas missions.

Unity & Faith Full Gospel Association
c/o Bishop Donald A. Mcknight Sr.
Auburn, WA 98092
www.ourchurch.com/view/?pageID=138805

Word of Faith International Christian Centers
c/o Bishop Keith A. Butler
20000 W. Nine Mile Rd.
Southfield, MI 48075

World Link of Churches and Ministries
World Outreach Ministries
Apostle Lloyd Benson
P.O. Box 477
Baton Rouge, LA 70821
www.wlcm.org

Oneness/Apostolic Pentecostal Church

The first Pentecostals understood that they were fulfilling events described in Acts 2. This led many of the movement's young leaders to go back and reread the Bible (and especially the Book of Acts) with their new understanding of the baptism of the Holy Spirit. Some began to question the mode of baptism, which, they said, should be administered in the name of Jesus only. This idea then led to speculation on the nature of Jesus as God, and some concluded that Jesus was the Only God. This idea pushed to its logical conclusion dissented from orthodox teachings on the Trinity, and led to the movement's adoption of what is generally termed a form of modalism that denies the essential nature of the Trinity. The most famous Oneness spokesperson at the present is Texas preacher T. D. Jakes.

The two largest Apostolic churches by far are the Pentecostal Assemblies of the World, an interracial but predominantly African American association, and the United Pentecostal Church International, which is predominantly white. The former is larger inside the United States, but the UPCI has the larger international membership.

Pentecostal Assemblies of the World
c/o Dr. Horace E. Smith, Presiding Bishop
3339 Meadows Dr.
Indianapolis, IN 46205
www.pawinc.org

The Pentecostal Assemblies was the first of the Pentecostal fellowships to grow out of the Azusa Revival. It was formed in Los Angeles in 1907 and was incorporated in 1919.

United Pentecostal Church International
8855 Dunn Rd.
Hazelwood, MO 63042
www.upci.org

The United Pentecostal Church was founded in 1945 by a merger of the Pentecostal Church, Inc., and the Pentecostal Assemblies of Jesus Christ, two groups that had roots in the Pentecostal Assemblies of the World.

Contacts:

Apostolic Assemblies of Christ, International
c/o Bishop G. M. Boone
8425 Fenkell Ave.
Detroit, MI 48238
www.apostolicassembliesofchrist.com

The Apostolic Assemblies was founded in 1970 by Bishop G. N. Boone and other former members of the Pentecostal Churches of Apostolic Faith.

Apostolic Assemblies of the Faith in Christ Jesus
10807 Laurel St.
Rancho Cucamonga, CA 91730
www.acnavafoundation.com/pages/2/index.htm

Apostolic Church of Christ
2044 Martin Luther King Jr. Dr.
Winston-Salem, NC 27107

The Apostolic Church of Christ was formed in 1969 by Bishop Johnnie Draft and Elder Wallace Snow, formerly with the Church of God (Apostolic).

Apostolic Church of Christ in God
1217 E. 15th St.
Winston-Salem, NC 27105

The Apostolic Church of Christ in God was formed by five elders formerly in the Church of God (Apostolic).

Apostolic Church of Jesus
1130 Merritt St.
Altamonte Springs, FL 32701
www.acoj.com/Home.htm

The Apostolic Church of Jesus was founded in 1942 by an African American minister, Bishop Harry Johnson, and subsequently developed congregations across the state of Florida.

Apostolic Church of the Lord Jesus Christ
c/o Bishop Carl E. Angle
P.O. Box 106
Niles, OH 44446

Apostolic Churches of Jesus Christ International
c/o Reverend E. G. Valverde
P.O. Box 10271
Salinas, CA 93912

Apostolic Faith (Hawaii)
1043 Middle St.
Honolulu, HI 96819

The Apostolic Faith church was started by Charles Lochbaum, who arrived in Honolulu in 1923.

Apostolic Faith Churches of God in Christ
330 King St.
Hertford, NC 27944

Apostolic Faith Mission Church of God
c/o Ward's Temple
8906 Muscogee Rd.
Cantonment, FL 32532
or
Bishop Houston Ward
P.O. Box 551
Cantonment, FL 32522

The Apostolic Faith Mission Church of God is a predominantly African American church founded by Frank W. Williams, one of the first ministers affected by the 1906 revival at Azusa. However, he broke with the Apostolic Faith Mission in 1915 and proceeded to lead an Apostolic "Jesus Only" church.

Apostolic Ministries of America, Inc.
c/o Elder Charles Ford Walker, General Overseer
Post Office Drawer 39
Titusville, FL 32781-0039
www.apostolic-ministries.net

Apostolic Overcoming Holy Church of God, Inc.
c/o Bishop Jasper C. Roby
1120 N. 24th St.
Birmingham, AL 35234

The Apostolic Overcoming Holy Church of God was organized in 1920 by William Thomas Philips (1893–1973), who had been ordained by Frank W. Williams of the Apostolic Faith Mission Church of God.

Assemblies of the Lord Jesus Christ, Inc.
875 N. White Station Rd.
Memphis, TN 38122
www.aljc.org

The Assemblies of the Lord Jesus Christ was formed in 1952 by the merger of the Assemblies of the Church of Jesus Christ, the Jesus Only Apostolic Church of God, and the Church of the Lord Jesus Christ.

Associated Brotherhood of Christians
c/o Rev. Richard Burgett
P.O. Box 3256
Hot Springs, AR 71914
www.abofc.org

The brotherhood is a fellowship of Apostolic churches founded in 1933 by S. E. Partridge and H. A. Riley.

Beth-el Churches of Christ
c/o Bishop Bernard N. Bragg
New Life Restoration Temple
38-40 Centre St.
Dorchester Center, MA 02124
www.beth-elchurchesofchrist.org

Bethel Ministerial Association
7055 Manker St.
Indianapolis, IN 46227
www.daveweb1.com/bma

The association was formed in 1934 by evangelist Albert Franklin Varnell.

Bible Way Church of Our Lord Jesus Christ World Wide, Inc.
261 Rochester Ave.
Brooklyn, NY 11213
www.biblewaychurch.org

The Bible Way Church was formed in 1957 by some former ministers and members of the Church of Our Lord Jesus Christ of the Apostolic Faith, most notably Smallwood E. Williams (1907–1991).

Biblical Apostolic Organization
c/o Biblical Apostolic University
P.O. Box 755
Greenbrier, TN 37073
www.geocities.com/ba_org/mission.html
www.geocities.com/merlinthd/BAO_.html

The Biblical Apostolic Organization was formed in 1983 by a group of Apostolic ministers led by Marvin M. Arnold (b. 1921).

Christian Fellowship Church Ministries International
c/o General Pastor Peter F. Paine
P.O. Box 318
Waukegan, IL 60079-0318

Church of God (Apostolic)
3683 Old Lexington Rd.
Winston-Salem, NC 27107-5262

The Church of God (Apostolic) was founded as a Holiness church, the Christian Faith Band, in 1877, and took its present name in 1915 after accepting Pentecostalism.

Church of Jesus Christ (Kingsport)
2300 Bloomingdale Rd.
Kingsport, TN 37664
www.tcojc.us

The Church of Jesus Christ was formed in 1927 by former members of the Church of God (Cleveland, Tennessee).

Church of Our Lord Jesus Christ of the Apostolic Faith, Inc.
2081 Adam Clayton Powell Jr. Blvd.
New York, NY 10027

The Church of Our Lord Jesus Christ was founded in 1919 by Robert Clarence Lawson (1883–1961), formerly with the Pentecostal Assemblies of the World.

Church of the Living God, the Pillar and Ground of the Truth
400 21st St.
McComb, MS 39648
www.cotlg.net

Not to be confused with the churches derived from the ministry of Mary L. L. Tate, this church is a sabbatarian Pentecostal church that accepted the Sacred Name ideal of using YHVH and Yahshua as the names for God and Jesus respectively.

Church of the Lord Jesus Christ of the Apostolic Faith
22nd & Bainbridge Sts.
Philadelphia, PA 19146

The Church of the Lord Jesus Christ of the Apostolic Faith was founded in 1933 by Bishop Sherrod C. Johnson (1897–1961), formerly with the Church of Our Lord Jesus Christ of the Apostolic Faith.

Churches of Christ in the Apostles Doctrine
c/o Bishop M. J. Hernandez
9501 SW 1675th Terr.
Miami, FL 33157

The church was founded in the 1980s by Bishop M. J. Hernandez and has its strength in the Hispanic community of southern Florida.

Emmanuel Tabernacle Baptist Church Apostolic Faith
329 N. Garfield Ave.
Columbus, OH 43203

The Emmanuel Tabernacle was founded in 1916 by Bishop Martin Rawleigh Gregory (1885–1960). It is distinguished by it stance on female equality and welcoming of women into both the ordained ministry and episcopacy.

Eternal Light Church of the Apostolic Faith
149 E. Third St.
Mount Vernon, NY 10550
www.eternallight.org

The Eternal Light Church was founded in 1980 by Apostle Anderson Morehead, Sr. (d. 1997), Mother Betty Sue Morehead, and Pastor Robert Moe, Sr. (d. 2001).

First Assembly Holiness Church of God in Christ
P.O. Box 503
Trenton, FL 32693

Free Church of God in Christ in Jesus' Name
1904 East Weir Ave.
Phoenix, AZ 85401

Greater Emmanuel International Fellowship of Churches and Ministries
c/o Office of the Presiding Bishop
P.O. Box 091086
Columbus, OH 43209
www.geif.org

Highway Christian Church of Christ
432 W St., NW
Washington, DC 20001

The Highway Christian Church was founded in 1927 by James Thomas Morris (1892–1959), formerly with the Pentecostal Assemblies of the World.

Holy Bethel Pentecostal Church Apostolic Faith
c/o Bishop Henry Borrah
2726 Nottingham Rd.
Bethlehem, PA 18017

Holy Temple Church of the Lord Jesus Christ of the Apostolic Faith
c/o Bishop Belton Green
2075 Clinton Ave.
Bronx, NY 10457
www.theholytemplechurch.org

The Holy Temple Church is under the leadership of Pastor, Apostle, and General Overseer Belton Green.

House of God, Holy Church of the Living God, the Pillar and Ground of Truth, the House of Prayer for All People
548 Georgetown St.
Lexington, KY 50608
www.houseofgod.org

The House of God was founded in 1914 by Bishop R. A. Johnson (d. 1940), a former Methodist. It is a sabbatarian "Jesus Only" church. Following the death of Bishop F. C. Scott in 2005, Bishop James Embry became the new Chief Apostle.

International Apostolic Fellowship
P.O. Box 4085
Kingsport, TN 37665
www.apostolicfellowship.com/home2.htm

International Ministerial Association
9455 Lackland Rd.
St. Louis, MO 64114

The International Ministerial Association was formed by a group of ministers under the leadership of W. E. Kidson, who had withdrawn from the United Pentecostal Church.

Light of the World Apostolic Churches
c/o Bishop G. H. Brewton
All Nations Apostolic Church of Christ
15801 Central Park
Markham, IL 60426

Mount Hebron Apostolic Temple of Our Lord Jesus of the Apostolic Faith
Mount Hebron Apostolic Temple
27 Vineyard Ave.
Yonkers, NY 10703

The Mount Hebron Apostolic Temple was founded in 1963 by George H. Wiley III, formerly with the Apostolic Church of Christ in God.

New Gospel Churches of Christ
c/o Dr. Obriwe Hamilton, Bishop
P.O. Box 1360
East Orange, NJ 07019
netministries.org/see/churches/ch05670

New Life Apostolic Fellowship
P.O. Box 311
St Albans, VT 05478

Original Glorious Church of God in Christ Apostolic Faith
995 Foster Ave.
Elvira, OH 44035

The Original Glorious Church of God in Christ Apostolic Faith was formed in 1952 by a group of members under W. O. Howard who left the Glorious Church of God.

Pentecostal Assemblies of the Apostolic Faith
c/o Bishop W. T. Smith
P.O. Box 352
#5 Henson Cir.
Carrollton, GA 30117

Pentecostal Assemblies of Jesus Christ
220 Country Club Rd.
Forsyth, GA 31029
www.pajc.org

Pentecostal Assembly Churches of Jesus Christ
c/o Bishop Alfred W. Johnson
109 Lloyd
Wilmington, DE 19804-2821

Pentecostal Church of God
9244 Delmar
Detroit, MI 48211

The Pentecostal Church of God is a predominantly African American church founded by Apostle Willie James Peterson (1921–1969) in the 1950s.

Pentecostal Churches of the Apostolic Faith
c/o Bishop Rayford Bell
14 S. Ashland
Chicago, IL 60607

In 1957, Bishop Samuel N. Hancock (d. 1963) left the Pentecostal Assemblies of the World, as he had come to believe that Jesus was only the Son of God, not divine. He formed the Pentecostal Churches of the Apostolic Faith, but following his death the church returned to the Apostolic position of its parent body.

Primitive Church of Jesus Christ
c/o Bethel Church of Jesus Christ
Highway 19 North
Inglis, FL 34449

The Primitive Church of Jesus Christ resulted from a dispute within the Church of Jesus Christ (Kingsport).

Progressive Church of Our Lord Jesus Christ
c/o Bishop Edward Smith
2222 Barhamville Rd.
Columbia, SC 29204-1203
www.progressivechurch.org

The Progressive Church of Our Lord Jesus Christ was founded by Bishop Joseph D. Williams (d. 1966), formerly a minister with the Church of Our Lord Jesus Christ of the Apostolic Faith.

Pure Holiness Church of God
Saint Timothy's Pure Holiness Church
408 McDonough Blvd. SE
Atlanta, GA 30315

The Pure Holiness Church of God was founded in 1927 by John Isaac Woodly and others in the Church of God in Christ who had accepted the Apostolic "Jesus Only" doctrinal perspective.

Shiloh Apostolic Temple
1516 W. Master
Philadelphia, PA 19121

The Shiloh Apostolic Temple was founded in 1953 by Robert O. Doub, Jr., formerly with the Apostolic Church of Christ in God.

The True Apostolic Church Of Jesus Christ
16 Helena St.
Rochester, NY 14605
www.trueapostolicchurchofjesuschrist.org

True Bibleway Church of the Lord Jesus Christ of the Apostolic Faith
c/o Bishop F. M. Dawson
520 Hickory St.
Clarksdale, MS 38614

True Jesus Church, International Assembly of the
314 S. Brookhurst St., #104
Anaheim, CA 92801
www.tjc.org

The True Jesus Church was founded in China in 1917 and spread internationally during the 1920s. It initially reached the United States (Hawaii) in 1930. In the wake of the Communist takeover of China, headquarters of the church shifted to Taiwan and then the United States (1985). This sabbatarian church serves primarily Chinese Americans.

True Vine Pentecostal Churches of Jesus (Apostolic Faith)
c/o Bishop Robert L. Hairston
929 Bethel Ln.
Martinsville, VA 24112

Robert L. Hairston founded the True Vine Pentecostal Church in 1961 after accepting the Apostolic Pentecostal perspective.

United Apostolic Church International
c/o Reverend Dr. William Kidd
208 Embassy Dr.
Lexington, KY 40511
members.tripod.com/~Rev_Kidd/index.html

The United Apostolic Church International was founded at the end of the 1990s by a group of Pentecostal ministers who set a goal of moving beyond denominational remnants they claimed that still remained in older Pentecostal churches.

United Apostolic Church of Jesus Christ
c/o Bishop Kenneth Brown
Apostolic Pentecostal Church
1202 East 5th St.
Greenfield, IN 46140-1518
uac-jc.org/home.php

United Church of Jesus Christ Apostolic
Bishop James B. Thornton
934 Gorsuch Avenue
Baltimore, Maryland 21218
www.unitedapostolic.org

The United Church was founded in 1963 by Bishop James B. Thornton, formerly with the Church of Our Lord Jesus Christ of the Apostolic Faith.

United Church of Jesus Christ Apostolic
c/o Bishop Monroe Saunders
5150 Baltimore National Pike
Baltimore, MD 21219-1216
www.unitedchurchofjesuschrist.org

The United Church was founded by Bishop Monroe Saunders in 1965 after his departure from the Church of God in Christ (Apostolic).

United Churches of Jesus Apostolic
1500 N. Dunleith Ave.
Winston Salem, North Carolina 27102
www.ucjaonline.com/home.aspx

United Way of the Cross Churches of Christ of the Apostolic Faith
c/o Bishop Joseph H. Adams
Rt. 2, Box 532
Axton, VA 24054

Universal Church of Christ
19-23 Park St.
P.O. Box 146
Orange, NJ 07050

Way of the Cross Church of Christ
c/o Bishop Alphonzo D. Brooks
1177 Largo Rd.
Upper Marlboro, MD 20774

The Way of the Cross Church was founded in 1927 by Henry C. Brooks, an independent African American minister in Washington, D.C.

Spanish-Speaking Pentecostal Churches

Attending the Azusa Street Mission almost from the beginning were several Spanish-speakers, mostly of Mexican heritage. They launched the movement back into their native land, and from there it spread throughout Latin America (with additional starting points added by others). Its spread into Mexico also meant that many of the new believers could be found along the Mexico-United States border. Besides its development in Mexico, Pentecostalism swept across Puerto Rica after World War I and was then brought by immigrants into the New York Metropolitan Area.

Contacts:

Assembly of Christian Churches
Bethel Christian Temple
7 West 110th St.
New York, NY 10026

The Assembly of Christian Churches was founded in 1939 in New York City by Bishop Carlos Sepúlveda, formerly associated with the Concilio Olazabal de Iglesias Latino Americano.

Centro Amistad Cristiana
c/o Samuel & Edith Lozano
P.O. Box 5326
Santa Ana, CA 92704

Concilio Olazabal de Iglesias Latino Americano
1925 E. First St.
Los Angeles, CA 90033

The Concilio Olazabal was founded in 1923 by Rev. Francisco Olazabal, a minister with the Assemblies of God.

Damascus Christian Church
c/o Reverend Enrique Melendez
170 Mt. Eden Parkway
Bronx, NY 10473

The Damascus Christian Church was founded in 1939 in New York City by Francisco and Leoncai Rosado.

Defenders of the Faith
P.O. Box 2816
Bayamon, PR 00621-0816

Defenders of the Faith, an organization headed by Baptist preacher Gerald Winrod, began to sponsor an evangelistic/missionary effort in Puerto Rico in 1931. That effort, led by Juan Francisco Rodriguez-Rivera, produced a number of congregations on the island and the exporting of the movement to New York before the end of the decade. The doctrine is Baptist with some Pentecostal influence.

Filipino Assemblies of the First Born
229 Glenwood
Delano, CA 93215

Iglesia de Dios Pentecostal, Movimento Internacional
P.O. Box 360455
San Juan, PR 00936-0455

Iglesia Evangelica Congregacional, Inc., of Puerto Rico
Hq: Box 396
Humacao, PR 00792

The Iglesia Evangelica Congregacional grew out of the spread of Pentecostalism in Puerto Rico in the 1930s. Congregations were founded in the United States in the 1970s.

Igreja Universal do Reino de Deus
(Universal Church of the Kingdom of God)
307 S. Broadway
Los Angeles, CA 90013
or
International headquarters:
Av: Suburbana 4242
Del Castilho/Rio de Janeiro, Brasil
www.igrejauniversal.org.br

The Universal Church of the Kingdom of God began in 1977 with the decision of Edir Macedo, an independent Pentecostal layman, to become an evangelist. Beginning in Rio de Janeiro, he built a church that spread through the Portuguese-speaking world and most recently has been established across Europe, North America, and South Africa.

Latin-American Council of the Pentecostal Church of God of New York
115 E. 125th St.
New York, NY 10035

The Latin-American Council of the Pentecostal Church of New York was formed in 1957 in New York City. It primarily serves Puerto Rican Americans.

Light of the World Church/Iglsia la Luz del Mundo
4765 E. 1st St.
Los Angeles, CA 90022

The Light of the World Church is an expansive Mexican Pentecostal church founded in 1926 by Eusibio Joaquin Gonzalez, who was named Aaron at the time of his baptism. International headquarters is in Guadalajara.

Missionary Church of the Disciples of Jesus Christ
15906 East San Bernardino Rd.
Covina, CA 91722
www.disciplesofjesuschrist.org

The Missionary Church was founded in 1970 by Rolando G. Washington, formerly associated with the Soldiers of the Cross of Christ, Evangelical International Church.

Mita's Congregation
Calle Duarte 203
Hata Rey, PR 60919
www.congregacionmita.org/siguiente_e.htm

Mita's Congregation was founded in Puerto Rico in 1940 by Juanita García Peraza, who assumed the name Mita, meaning "Spirit of Life." She was joined in this endeavor by eleven men.

Philippine Apostolic Christian Fellowship
P.O. Box 313
Burnsville, MS 38833

Soldiers of the Cross of Christ, Evangelical International Church
641 West Flagler St.
Miami, Florida 33130
www.soldadosdelacruzdecristo.org.mx

The Soldiers of the Cross of Christ was founded in the early 1920s in Havana, Cuba, by Ernest William Sellers (1953).

Worldwide Pentecostal Church of Christ
c/o Bishop John E. Ayudtud
4172 Victory Blvd.
Staten Island, NY 10314
or
International Hq: 104 Malaya St.
Caloocan City, Metro Manila, Philippines

Founded in the Philippines in 1984, the Worldwide Church was brought to the United States the next year by its founder John E. Ayudtud.

A Distinct Pentecostal Community, the Signs Movement

As a prank, some kids let a rattlesnake loose in a Pentecostal revival meeting led by Church of God preacher George Went Hensley in 1914. As the story goes, rather than allow the prank to disturb the service, he simply picked the snake up and continued preaching. From that event, Church of God (Cleveland, Tennessee) believers began to explore the truth of Mark 16:17–18, that certain signs would follow those who professed faith in Christ, namely that they would be able to handle poisonous serpents without being harmed. When the leadership decided to discontinue snake-handling in their services, the practice continued in independent Pentecostal congregations now found scattered along the Appalachian Mountains. Most congregations operate under the name Church of God with Signs Following. There is no central headquarters.

For further reading:

Anderson, Allan. *An Introduction to Pentecostalism.* Cambridge: Cambridge University Press, 2004.

Blumhofer, Edith. *The Assemblies of God: A Popular History.* Springfield, Mo.: Radiant Books, 1985.

Blumhofer, Edith L., Russell P. Spittler, and Grant A. Wacker, eds. *Pentecostal Currents in America.* Urbana: University of Illinois Press, 1999.

Burgess, Stanley M., and Gary McGee, eds. *Dictionary of Pentecostal and Charismatic Movements.* Grand Rapids: Regency Reference Library, 1988.

Burgess, Stanley M., and Eduard M. van der Maas, eds. *The New International Dictionary of Pentecostal and Charismatic Movements.* Grand Rapids: Zondervan, 2002.

Covington, Dennis. *Salvation on Sand Mountain: Snake Handling and Redemption in Southern Appalachia.* New York: Penguin, 1996.

Cox, Harvey. *Fire from Heaven: The Rise of Pentecostal Spirituality and the Reshaping of Religion in the Twenty-first Century.* Reading, Mass.: Addison-Wesley, 1995.

Dempster, M. W., B. D. Klaus, and D. Petersen, eds. *The Globalization of Pentecostalism: A Religion Made to Travel.* Oxford: Regnum, 1999.

Faupel, D. William. *The Everlasting Gospel: the Significance of Eschatology in the Development of Pentecostal Thought.* Sheffield: Sheffield Academic Press, 1996.

Foster, Fred J. *Their Story: Twentieth Century Pentecostals.* Hazelwood, N.J.: World Aflame Press, 1981.

Goff, James. *Fields White Unto Harvest: Charles Fox Parham and the Missionary Origins of Pentecostalism.* Fayetteville: University of Arkansas Press, 1988.

Hollenweger, Walter J. *Pentecostals: The Charismatic Movement in the Church.* Minneapolis: Augsburg, 1972.

Hunter, Harold D. *Spirit Baptism: A Pentecostal Alternative.* Washington, D.C.: University Press of America, 1983.

Jones, Charles Edwin. *The Charismatic Movement: A Guide to the Study of Neo-Pentecostalism with Emphasis on Anglo-American Sources.* Philadelphia: Scarecrow Press, 1995.

MacRobert, Iain. *The Black Roots and White Racism of Early Pentecostalism in the USA.* Basingstoke, UK: Macmillan, 1988.

Riss, Richard Michael. *The Latter Rain Movement of 1948 and the Mid-Twentieth Century Evangelical Awakening.* Vancouver, BC: Regent College, 1979.

Robeck, Cecil M., Jr. *The Azusa St. Mission and Revival: The Birth of Global Pentecostalism.* Nashville: Thomas Nelson, Inc., 2006.

Samarin, William. *Tongues of Men and Angels.* New York: Macmillan Company, 1972.

Synan, Vinson. *The Century of the Holy Spirit: 100 Years of Pentecostal and Charismatic Renewal, 1901–2001.* Nashville: Thomas Nelson, 2001.

Wacker, Grant. *Heaven Below: Early Pentecostals and American Culture.* Cambridge: Harvard University Press, 2001.

Wagner, C. Peter, ed. *The New Apostolic Churches.* Ventura, Calif.: Regal, 1998.

7. Parachurch Organizations

Parachurches are organizations that do the work typically carried on by traditional denominational boards and agencies, but do so corporately independent of such denominations. As organizationally independent, the parachurches possess a degree of flexibility for innovation than is often lacking to agencies that work as an arm of a larger denominational hierarchy. They provide a space for some dissent from majority decisions that set the direction and priorities for the denominational organization as a whole. Most important, parachurch organizations often provide the means for exercising ministry in ways that the denominations, most of which are rather small and lacking in the resources of the few larger church structures, could never do.

Many smaller denominations, especially those that have adopted a congregational form of church government, are unable or unwilling to gather the funding to build schools, create missionary boards, or even publish church school materials. They rely upon independent colleges and seminaries, interdenominational missionary agencies, and privately-owned publishing houses to supply the needs and expectations of the members of congregations.

The existence of parachurch organizations is often traced to the formation of the Baptist Missionary Society in England at the end of the eighteenth century.[114] A sizeable group of individual Baptists wished to respond positively to William Carey's call for a world missionary enterprise. Supporters faced stiff opposition from those who raised significant theological questions about engaging in such an enterprise, along with an additional obstacle created by those Baptists who felt that the development of such pan-denominational programs contradicted the group's congregational polity. Thus those who wished to support Carey organized separately.

A few years later, the London Missionary Society was organized to carry out the same goal as the Baptist Society, but from a slightly different perspective. Its founders sought to bring together Christians who were interested in missions from several British denominations that had yet to become involved in missions. As the different churches developed their own mission boards, their members withdrew support from the London Society, eventually leaving it as the missionary agency of the Congregationalists.

American Protestants formed many new parachurch organizations in the early nineteenth century as Christians from various denominations banded together to pursue a common goal (such as Bible publication) or present a united front on social reform (anti-slavery, temperance, Sabbath observance). This era led to the formation of some of the oldest and most respected of parachurch organizations, like the American Bible Society and the American Tract Society. Through the rest of the century the issues tackled by parachurch groups broadened to include education, peace, women's rights, and the reform of prisons, health, immigration, and public morals. Parachurch groups operated from two very different worldviews. Some looked toward the building of a more Christian (just and loving) society, and others, seeing secular society as somewhat of a lost cause, developed efforts that would nurture and spread the church.

In the twentieth century, the number of parachurch groups grew exponentially. Leading this growth were the many independent "faith" missionary groups. These often rose to pioneer missionary work in the remote parts of the world. These groups could target specific areas such as the interior of China or Africa, or specialize in a specific task (medicine, education). Paralleling the development of foreign missions was the attention given to home missions that targeted various minority groups or needful regions (Appalachia, the West) within the United States.

The proliferation of parachurches in the twentieth century was nurtured by the proliferation of denominations (from less than twenty when the nation was founded to more than a thousand as the 21st century began). Many of the newer denominations, formed out of older hierarchical churches, have adopted congregational polities with weak central authorities. Such groups either have been unable to or have been ideologically opposed to the development of structures to meet the needs of their congregations. Thus they have self-consciously depended on parachurch organizations to supply Sunday school literature, a structure to reach the mission field, a place to educate ministers, or a means to respond to the social environment. Those groups which specialized in meeting the needs of local churches, while operating in an interdenominational context (serving congregations with different denominational affiliations), generally served congregations from a relatively narrow spectrum of the Christian community (that is, otherwise closely related denominations).

Since the early decades of the nineteenth century, Christians have organized to show support for various moral values and have entered the political arena on behalf of some legislation to support or oppose their beliefs. In the late nineteenth century, the Woman's Christian Temperance Union, the largest women's rights group in the country at the time, wedded the temperance issue to a number of women's issues as distinct as voting, the hiring of female police officers, and dress reform. Recent decades have seen a proliferation of social reform groups that have wedded the issue of family values to a broad spectrum of issues—from opposing abortion and challenging the content of television programming to protection of missionaries from foreign governments.

A second factor leading to the proliferation of parachurch organizations, now numbering in the tens of thousands, has been a relatively new trend to institutionalize personal ministries. The personal ministries allow ministers, for example, to develop programs about which they have a particular passion, apart from the involvement of the church they serve or the denomination in which they hold credentials. Such personal ministries also allow lay people, who are somewhat disenfranchised in some denominations, to develop new ministries in what they feel are neglected areas. Over the last century, such ministries became a significant opportunity for women to explore new avenues for ministry.

Among the new parachurch organizations that emerged in the twentieth century were the many religious broadcast organizations. These were formed in the 1920s, were given new life as the government has regulated and deregulated the airwaves, and then rapidly expanded with the development of cable television. Different broadcasting organizations own and operate radio and television stations, produce programming, operate networks, and/or attempt to coordinate the efforts of stations, networks, and programs.

Finally, we note the existence of a variety of organizations that attempt to reverse the process of denominational fragmentation that has been a major theme of the American Christian community since the founding of the country. More than forty national/international organizations, usually called councils or associations, attempt to provide some level of fellowship between different denominations. Some, like the National Council of Churches and the National Association of Evangelicals, operate across a broad range of Christian groups, but the majority tend to operate solely within one denominational family tradition, such as the Baptist Fellowship of North America or the World Methodist Council. These organizations are discussed in their own section of the directory of churches (see chapter 8 below).

Given the special focus of this issue of the *Guide to Denominations*, in the first section below we have highlighted those agencies engaged in Bible translation and distribution.

A. Bible Translation and Publishing

In the nineteenth century, Protestant Christianity visibly changed by its programs to translate the Bible into all the then known languages. In the twenty-first century it is again changing the world by its support of a massive global program to reduce all of the world's remaining languages to writing, teach that written system to the people who speak the language, and produce a Bible for the people to read as a first book. This process had been documented as one of the most effective tools for the conversion of large groups of people. The following organizations are among the those based in the United States that are taking the lead in translating, publishing, and/or distributing of Bibles around the world.

American Bible Society
1865 Broadway
New York, NY 10023
www.americanbible.org

Audio Scripture Ministries
760 Waverly Rd.
Holland, MI 49423
www.audioscriptureministries.org

Bible League
P.O. Box 28000
Chicago, IL 60628
www.bibleleague.org

Bibles For The World
P.O. Box 49759
Colorado Springs, CO 80949-9759
www.biblesfortheworld.org

Braille Bibles International
P.O. Box 378
Liberty, MO 64069-0378
www.braillebibles.org

Christian Literature International
P.O. Box 777
Canby, OR 97013
www.newlifebible.org

Evangel Bible Translators
P.O. Box 669
Rockwall, TX 75087-0669
evangelbible.org

The Gideons International
50 Century Blvd.
P.O. Box 140800
Nashville, TN 37214-0800
www.gideons.org

International Bible Society
1820 Jet Stream Dr.
Colorado Springs, CO 80921
www.ibs.org

Pioneer Bible Translators
7500 W. Camp Wisdom Rd.
Dallas, TX 75236
www.pioneerbible.org

Pocket Testament League
P.O. Box 800
Lititz, PA 17543-7026
www.pocketpower.org

World Bible Translation Center
P.O. Box 820648
Fort Worth, TX 76182
www.wbtc.com

Wycliffe Bible Translators
P.O. Box 628200
Orlando, FL 32862-8200
or
11221 John Wycliffe Blvd.
Orlando, FL 32832
www.wycliffe.org

B. World Ministries

Most organizations with a globally focused ministry are missionary organizations that have focused on certain areas of the world, and most, simply by their own doctrinal commitments, draw the majority of their support from a particular segment of the Christian community. Thus we have groups such as OMS International working in Southern Asia or Arab World Ministries working in predominantly Arab countries. Some such as Baptist Mid-Missions or Lutheran Literature Society for the Chinese are easily recognizable for their working out of a particular theological tradition, while others such as Advancing Renewal Ministries (Lutheran) or African Mission Evangelism (Restoration movement) are less obvious, at least from their names.

For a more complete list of American-based missionary sending agencies, see the latest edition of the *Mission Handbook*, periodically updated and published by the Evangelism and Missions Information Service (EMIS), the publishing division of the Billy Graham Center (formerly issued by the Missions Advanced Research and Communications Center [MARC] affiliated with World Vision). This list concentrates on some specialized missionary agencies that work at supplying other agencies with needed resources (research data, materials, supplies) that allow them to focus more completely on their evangelistic task, and organizations that have carved out a special niche in the missionary world, such as medical missions.

Over the last century Christians discovered and brought attention to a broad spectrum of people and their needs and found an ever-increasing number of creative ways to tie together the Great Commission and Christian compassion for suffering humanity, ways hardly imaginable a century ago. Today, ministries exist for almost any need that God puts upon one's heart to meet. If one wants to feed the hungry, comfort the afflicted, visit the prisoner, heal the sick, or reach the outcast—there are other people waiting to hear from you. The list below, focused on medical and health-related ministries, is but a few of hundreds of organizations, some of which are already doing what you are ready to do.

American Leprosy Missions
1 ALM Way
Greenville, SC 29601
www.leprosy.org

Baptist Missions to Forgotten Peoples
P.O. Box 37043
Jacksonville, FL 32236-7043
www.bmfp.org

Blessings International
5881 S. Garnett
Tulsa, OK 74146
www.blessing.org

Caleb Project
10 West Dry Creek Circle
Littleton, CO 80120
www.calebproject.org

Children's Medical Ministries
P.O. Box 3382
Crofton, MD 21114
www.childmed.org

Christian Dental Society
P.O. Box 296
Sumner, IA 50674
www.christiandental.org

Christian Mission for the Deaf
P.O. Box 28005
Detroit, MI 48228-0005
www.cmdeaf.org

Deaf Ministries International
c/o Peter Pfeil
50 Knollwood Dr.
Hilton Head, SC 29926-2500
www.deafmin.org

Emmanuel International
3878 Concord Rd.
York, SC 29745
www.e-i.org

Engineering Ministries International
130 East Kiowa, Suite 200
Colorado Springs, CO 80903
www.emiusa.org

Farms International
P.O. Box 270
Knife River, MN 55609-0270
www.farmsinternational.com

Global Mapping International
15435 Gleneagle Dr., Suite 100
Colorado Springs, CO 80921
www.gmi.org

Heifer Project International
P.O. Box 8058
Little Rock, AR 72203
www.heifer.org

IFMA (Interdenominational Foreign Mission Association)
P.O. Box 398
Wheaton, IL 60189-0398
www.ifmamissions.org

Interdev Partnerships Associates(IPA)
IPA USA
P.O. Box 1331
Edmonds, WA 98020
www.interdev.org

International Medical Assistance
P.O. Box 429
New Windsor, MD 21776
www.interchurch.org

Joshua Project
A ministry of the U.S. Center for World Mission
P.O. Box 64080
Colorado Springs, CO 80962

MAP (Medical Assistance Programs International)
2200 Glynco Parkway
Brunswick, GA 31525-6800
www.map.org

Medical Ambassadors International
P.O. Box 576645
Modesto, CA 95357-6645
www.medicalambassadors.org

Mission America Coalition
P.O. Box 13930
Palm Desert, CA 92255
www.missionamerica.org

Mission India
P.O. Box 141312
Grand Rapids, MI 49514-1312
www.missionindia.org

Mission Safety International
328 E. Elk Ave., Ste.1
Elizabethton, TN 37643
www.msisafety.org

Samaritan's Purse
P.O. Box 3000
Boone, NC 28607
www.samaritan.org

U.S. Center for World Mission
1605 E. Elizabeth St.
Pasadena, CA 91104-2721
www.uscwm.org

World Emergency Relief
P.O. Box 131570
Carlsbad, CA 92013
www.wer-us.org

World Relief
7 East Baltimore St.
Baltimore, MD 21202
www.worldrelief.org

World Vision International
800 West Chestnut Ave.
Monrovia, CA 91016-3198
www.wvi.org/wvi

Youth with a Mission
P.O. Box 350
Kealakekua, HI 96750
or
P.O. Box 7206
Ventura, CA 93006
www.ywam.org

C. Education

In a separate section of this *Guide to Denominations*, one can find a list of schools offering a theological education. It is to be noted, however, that the Christian education enterprise is carried on at all levels and assisted by a variety of professional and coordinating groups, such as those listed below, which work continually to improve and maintain high standards in the field.

American Theological Library Association
300 South Wacker Dr., Suite 2100
Chicago, IL 60606-6702
www.atla.com/atlahome.html

Association of Christian Librarians
P.O. Box 4
Cedarville, OH 45314
www.acl.org

The Association of Theological Schools in the United States and Canada
10 Summit Park Dr.
Pittsburgh, PA 15275-1103
www.ats.edu

Council for Christian Colleges and Universities
321 Eighth Street, NE
Washington, DC 20002
www.cccu.org

Faith Tech Ministries
900 Long Blvd. #463
Lansing, MI 48911
www.faithtech.org

D. Evangelism

Possibly the largest number of parachurch organizations in America today are devoted to evangelism, as many pastors have formed evangelistic associations to give structure to their activities beyond the walls of their congregation. At the same time, a variety of ministers not serving in particular congregations have devoted their lives to evangelistic activity, often targeting a particular segment of the population (tied together by a shared ethnic background, age, occupation, or geographical location). Several organizations such as Campus Crusade have grown into large international organizations.

Association of Gospel Rescue Missions
1045 Swift St.
Kansas City, MO 64116-4127
www.iugm.org

Bible Believers Fellowship, Inc.
P.O. Box 0065
Baldwin, NY 11510-0065
www.prisonministry.org

Billy Graham Evangelistic Association
1 Billy Graham Parkway
Charlotte, NC 28201
www.billygraham.org

Campus Crusade for Christ
100 Lake Hart Dr.
Orlando, FL 32832
www.ccci.org

Christian Military Fellowship
P.O. Box 1207
Englewood, CO 81050-1207
cmf.com

Fellowship of Christian Athletes
8701 Leeds Rd.
Kansas City, MO 64129
www.fca.org

Youth for Christ
7670 S. Vaughn St.
Englewood, CO 80112
or
P.O. Box 4478
Englewood, CO 80155
www.yfc.net

E. Christian Nurture

A variety of organizations provide opportunities for fellowship among Christian who also share a second characteristic such as a stage in one's educational career or a common occupation. Such groups allow people who exist in a specialized realm to meet as students or professionals sharing not only secular commonalities but their Christian faith.

Awana Clubs International
1 East Bode Rd.
Streamwood, IL 60107-6658
www.awana.org

Christian Medical & Dental Associations
P.O. Box 7500
Bristol, TN 37621
www.cmdahome.org

Healthcare Chaplains Ministry Association
377 E. Chapman Ave., Ste. 260
Placentia, CA 92870-5094
www.hcmachaplains.org

InterVarsity Christian Fellowship/USA
6400 Schroeder Rd.
P.O. Box 7895
Madison, WI 53707-7895
www.intervarsity.org

Life Action Ministries
P.O. Box 31
Buchanan, MI 49107-0031
or
2727 Niles-Buchanan Rd.
Buchanan, MI 49107
www.lifeaction.org/lam

Navigators
P.O. Box 6000
Colorado Springs, CO 80934
or
3820 N. 30th St.
Colorado Springs, CO 80904
www.navigators.org/us

Pure Life Ministries
14 School St.
Dry Ridge, KY 41035
www.purelifeministries.org

Teen Challenge
P.O. Box 1015
Springfield, MO 65801
www.teenchallengeusa.com

F. Gender Issues

Among the issues Christians have expressed opinions about in the last generation, few have as diverse a range of comments as the changing social roles of women that followed on the heels of the feminist movement, which in turn led to a post-feminist redefinition of manhood. This has been paralleled by the more narrowly focused movement to open ordination to the ministry to females, a movement that has led to a growing number of denominations that have ordained female clergy and female bishops.

The very success of the movement supporting female clergy and the rise of lay women to prominent roles in denominations nationally has led to the demise of many of the women's organization of the 1970s and the emergence of a set of new organizations that are focused on contemporary issues.

African-American Women's Clergy Association
214 P Street NW
Washington, DC 20001

Association of Full Gospel Women Clergy
P.O. Box 1504
Annandale, VA 22003-9504
netministries.org/see/charmin/CM00038

Christians for Biblical Equality
122 West Franklin Ave., Suite 218
Minneapolis, MN 55404-2451
www.cbeinternational.org

Church Women United
475 Riverside Drive, Ste. 1626
New York, NY 10115
www.churchwomen.org

Council on Biblical Manhood and Womanhood
2825 Lexington Rd., Box 926
Louisville, KY 40280
www.cbmw.org

Evangelical and Ecumenical Women's Caucus
P.O. Box 67
Davis, IL 61019-0067
www.eewc.com

International Association of Women Ministers
c/o Carol Brown, Treasurer
579 Main Street
Stroudsburg, PA 18360
www.hnet.net/~seater/iawm1.html

Promise Keepers
P.O. Box 11798
Denver, CO 80211-0798
www.promisekeepers.org

Women's Ministry Network
1730 E. Republic Rd., Suite A-220
Springfield, MO 65804
www.womensministry.net

G. Religious Broadcasting

Christianity had been radically altered by the emergence of new media in the twentieth century, and a variety of evangelistic ministries have arisen to exploit the new opportunities. The list below includes networks that specialize in Christian programming and bring together the many participants in religious broadcasting to coordinate their work and increase their effectiveness.

The Christian Broadcasting Network
977 Centerville Turnpike
Virginia Beach, VA 23463
www.cbn.com

Christian Internet Radio and Television Network
9775 SW 87 Avenue
Miami, FL 33176-2900
www.citv.com

Eternal Word Television Network
5817 Old Leeds Rd.
Irondale, AL 35210
www.ewtn.com

Faith & Values Media
74 Trinity Place, Suite 1550
New York, NY 10006
www.faithandvaluesmedia.org

or
FaithStreams
c/o The FaithStreams Team
3470 Blazer Parkway, Suite 150
Lexington, KY 40509
www.faithstreams.com

Far East Broadcasting
P.O. Box 1
La Mirada, CA 90637-0001
www.febc.org

National Association of Broadcasters
1771 N Street, NW
Washington, DC 20036
www.nab.org

Sky Angel
P.O. Box 7609
Naples, FL 34101
www.skyangel.com

Trinity Broadcasting Network
P.O. Box A
Santa Ana, CA 92711
www.tbn.org

World Association for Christian Communications
c/o Adán Medrano, President
JM Communications
1402 Banks St.
Houston, TX 77006
www.wacc.org.uk/wacc

H. Public Forum

Continuing the early nineteenth century organizations that search to build what some called the "Benevolent Empire" to spread Christian values in the larger society, are a set of organizations that deal with a range of social issues—poverty, prisons, racism, war—by mobilizing Christians to fight social evils and calling for a more just society.

Bread for the World
Bread for the World Institute
50 F Street, NW, Suite 500
Washington, DC 20001
www.bread.org

Call to Renewal
3333 14th Street NW, Ste. 200
Washington, DC 20010
www.calltorenewal.com
Poverty issues

Center on Conscience & War
1830 Connecticut Avenue NW
Washington, DC 20009
www.centeronconscience.org

Chalcedon Foundation
P.O. Box 158
Vallecito, CA 95251
www.chalcedon.edu

Christian Children's Fund
2821 Emerywood Parkway
Richmond, VA 23294
www.christianchildrensfund.org

Churches for Middle East Peace
110 Maryland Ave., NE #311
Washington, DC 20002
www.cmep.org

Compassion International
12290 Voyager Parkway
Colorado Springs, CO 80921
www.compassion.com

Evangelicals for Social Action
10 E. Lancaster Avenue
Wynnewood, PA 19096-3495

Food for the Hungry
1224 E. Washington St.
Phoenix, AZ 85034-1102
www.fh.org

Habitat for Humanity International
121 Habitat St.
Americus, GA 31709-3498
www.habitat.org

Protestants for the Common Good
77 W. Washington St.
Suite 1124
Chicago, IL 60602
www.thecommongood.org

Religious Freedom Coalition
P.O. Box 77511
Washington, DC 20013
rfcnet.org

Prison Fellowship

Justice Fellowship
44180 Riverside Parkway
Lansdowne, VA 20176
www.pfm.org

Prison Mission Association
P.O. Box 2300
Port Orchard, WA 98366
www.pmabcf.org

Southern Christian Leadership Conference
P.O. Box 89128
Atlanta, GA 30312

or
591-A Edgewood Ave.
Atlanta, GA 30312
www.sclcnational.org

I. Human Rights

A variety of organizations have arisen to promote human freedoms, including the freedoms guaranteed to religion in the United States constitution.

Alliance Defense Fund
15333 North Pima Rd., Suite 165
Scottsdale, AZ 85260
www.alliancedefensefund.org

American Center for Law and Justice
P.O. Box 90555
Washington, DC 20090-0555
www.aclj.org

Christian Freedom International
P.O. Box 535
Front Royal, VA 22630
www.christianfreedom.org

International Christian Concern
2020 Pennsylvania Ave., NW, #941
Washington, DC 20006-1846
www.persecution.org

International Justice Mission
P.O. Box 58147
Washington, DC 20037-8147
www.ijm.org

J. Science and Religion

Few developments in the secular society have so affected the shape of the religious community as the emergence of science and the challenges it posed for theology, Christian education, and even personal piety. A spectrum of organizations has arisen to answer challenges to traditional Christian affirmations, to make use of new scientific and technological advances, and to articulate contemporary Christian stances relative to science. Much of the dialogue on these issues is carried forward in the many Christian colleges, universities, and seminaries.

Access Research Network
P.O. Box 38069
Colorado Springs, CO 80937-8069
www.arn.org

Affiliation of Christian Geologists
c/o Keith B. Miller
Dept of Geology, Kansas State University
Manhattan, KS, 66506-3201
www.wheaton.edu/ACG

American Scientific Affiliation
Executive Director, Dr. Donald Munro
P.O. Box 668
Ipswich, MA 01938-0668
cesc.montreat.edu/ceo/ASA

Answers in Genesis
P.O. Box 510
Hebron, KY 41048
www.answersingenesis.org

Center for Theology and the Natural Sciences
2400 Ridge Rd.
Berkeley, CA 94709-1212
www.ctns.org

Creation Moments
P.O. Box 839
Foley, MN 56329

or
19365 65th St. NE
Foley, MN 56329
creationmoments.org

Creation Research Society
P.O. Box 8263
St. Joseph, MO 64508-8263
www.creationresearch.org

Discovery Institute
1402 Third Ave., Suite 400
Seattle, WA 98101
www.discovery.org

Institute for Creation Research
10946 Woodside Ave.
Santee, CA 92071
www.icr.org

Reasons To Believe
P.O. Box 5978
Pasadena, CA 91117
www.reasons.org

Science & Theology News
c/o Eastern Nazarene College
162 Old Colony Ave.
Quincy, MA 02170
www.stnews.org/guide.php

K. Traditional Values

A variety of Christians have concluded traditional Christian values, especially those that undergird family life, have been undermined by large-scale social trends in the decades since World War II. Several organizations have arisen to counter such trends and promote healthy families. By the very nature of the family, the majority of family-oriented parachurch organizations operate on the local level, many devoted to working directly with families in trouble or promoting family enrichment activities.

American Family Association
P.O. Drawer 2440
Tupelo, MS 38803
www.afa.net

Christian Coalition of America
P.O. Box 37030
Washington, DC 20013-7030
www.cc.org

Christian Family Movement
FM USA National Office
P.O. Box 925
Evansville, IN 47706-0925
www.cfm.org/

Christian World Adoption
111 Ashley Ave.
Charleston, SC 29401
or
777 South Allen Rd.
Flat Rock, NC 28731
www.cwa.org

Concerned Women for America
1015 Fifteenth St. NW, Suite 1100
Washington, DC 20005
www.cwfa.org/main.asp

Family Life Communications
P.O. Box 35300
Tucson AZ 85740
www.flc.org

Family Research Council
801 G Street, NW
Washington, DC 20001
www.frc.org

Focus on the Family
Colorado Springs, CO 80995
www.family.org

Threads of Love
c/o Sissy Davis
37184 Oak Shadows
Denham Springs, LA 70706
www.threadsoflove.org

Traditional Values Coalition
139 "C" Street, SE
Washington, DC 20003
or
100 S. Anaheim Boulevard, Suite 350
Anaheim, CA 92805
www.traditionalvalues.org

8. Christian Cooperative Organizations

During the nineteenth century, two things happened to the global Protestant community. First, the missionary movement begun in the previous century turned Protestantism into a worldwide phenomenon. What had been largely confined to northern and western Europe and North America was suddenly challenging the Roman Catholic and Eastern Orthodox churches on their own turf and establishing itself in most countries of the world. Second, the four basic Reformation traditions had, in the course of this spreading, multiplied into hundreds of different denominations—some large and multinational in scope and others quite small and confined to one region of a single country, with most fitting somewhere in the middle.

By the closing decades of the century, farsighted church leaders saw the two trends and the problems each was creating. First of all, the multiplication of denominations was itself a scandal that further divided the one body of Christ. Second, the missionary movement was taking the divisions and the arguments that undergirded them into all corners of the world. Leaders from all branches of the church began to ponder ways to stop unnecessary competition and the exporting of differences that seemed of little relevance in the global context. Others concentrated on ending the divisions, many of which seemed to be accidents of history and unfortunate misunderstandings. The result of these forces was an international movement looking toward healing the divisions within the Protestant community. That movement has come to be known as the ecumenical movement.

During the twentieth century, the trends of the nineteenth century led to further key developments. First, the expanding missionary enterprise was challenged by the destruction of colonialism. Many came to see the nineteenth-century missionary effort as extremely flawed in that churches had more-or-less formally allied themselves with colonial powers and used their political ties to impose Christianity on conquered peoples. Increasingly, missionary leaders began to see how such alliances had delayed the development and empowering of indigenous leadership and how the spreading of the gospel had been confused with the spreading of Western civilization. In its worst forms, the missionary enterprise had supported and perpetuated European ideas of racial superiority.

The ideological changes that moved to correct the major flaw in the missionary enterprise were given added impetus by the changes wrought by and following World War II. The end of colonialism and the establishment of numerous new governments brought radical changes to the church. In most cases, this meant the end of many international denominations whose foreign wings were now cut loose to form national churches. These organizational changes radically multiplied the number of "denominations" and changed the substance and rhetoric of the missionary enterprise. No longer would Western churches spread the gospel to a heathen world; rather, Western churches would form partnerships with Christian nationals in local evangelization efforts, and former mission churches would be recognized as equals in the work of spreading the gospel.

At the same time that the end of colonialism radically changed the missionary enterprise, developments in Protestantism's home base radically changed the ecumenical movement. In the 1920s and 1930s, American Protestantism was shaken by the Modernist-Fundamentalist controversy. Out of that controversy, three communities developed: mainline Protestant liberalism (representing most of the larger older churches), the new Evangelicalism (which inherited the bulk of what had been Fundamentalists), and separatist Fundamentalism (which disagreed with the Evangelicals on any cooperation with members of the mainline churches).

Each of the three groups that had emerged by the end of the 1930s operated pan-denominationally, and each sought to create structures that aided communication and cooperation across denominational lines. Many of the mainline churches were already members of what was then the Federal Council of

Churches. The Separatist Fundamentalists then formed the American Council of Christian Churches, while the Evangelicals formed the National Association of Evangelicals. Shortly after World War II, the Federal Council of Churches went through a massive reorganization and emerged as the National Council of the Churches of Christ in the U.S.A.

In the aftermath of the second global war, the international ecumenical movement moved quickly to complete the organization of the World Council of Churches, the single largest body representing Protestant churches worldwide. The Council has also included Eastern Orthodox bodies from its beginning.

The organization of the World Council of Churches prompted more conservative church leaders to organize internationally. Separatist fundamentalists organized the International Council of Christian Churches, and Evangelicals revived the largely moribund Evangelical Alliance as the World Evangelical Fellowship. All three world organizations are represented locally by national and regional organizations.

Even before the pan-Protestant ecumenical organizations appeared, cooperative organizations related to single traditions emerged. The Methodists were among the first. They held a World Ecumenical Methodist Conference in 1881, the herald of the present World Methodist Council. Reformed and Presbyterian leaders were even earlier, holding their first gathering in 1875 to form what is now the World Alliance of Reformed Churches. Baptists followed soon afterward. At the height of the hope that many held for the development of something resembling a united Protestant church, the greatest number of mergers actually occurred between churches that shared a family tradition. Cross-family mergers did occur, but they typically happened in countries where Protestant Christianity was a distinct minority (India, Sri Lanka, Korea).

Cooperation always raises the question of grounds and limits of such cooperation. The larger churches have generally called for a minimal level of agreement among members of coopering organizations. The World Council of Churches, for instance, has defined itself as a coming together of churches that "confess the Lord Jesus Christ as God and Saviour according to the scriptures and therefore seek to fulfil together their common calling to the glory of the one God, Father, Son and Holy Spirit." More conservative groups have generally demanded a higher degree of doctrinal conformity for member groups.

Organizations have also differed on areas of possible cooperation. Lutherans have been most insistent on maintaining the integrity of the sacraments. Reformed and Presbyterians have been most insistent about doctrinal conformity. Some organizations have been quite willing to involve themselves in major social questions, but others have been content simply to promote fellowship and cooperation. Most denominations of any size are members of one or more cooperative organizations, the Southern Baptist Convention being a notable exception.

Different churches, in choosing to associate with various cooperative bodies, will often emphasize the areas of agreement and the possible realms for cooperative actions, while others will emphasize those aspects of other churches with which they wish to avoid being associated.

A bold new ecumenical effort to overcome some of the longstanding differences between the churches of the National Council of Churches and those of the National Association of

Evangelicals emerged at the beginning of the twenty-first century. Christian Churches Together in the USA is a new effort to invite churches from across several dividing lines, most crucially the conservative-liberal theological split of the 1920s, to find a common ground for conversation. To date, over a hundred denominations, including such diverse groups as the Church of God (Anderson, Indiana), the Coptic Orthodox Church, the Evangelical Lutheran Church in America, and the National Baptist Convention of America have given their initial approval to the effort.

Among the more interesting of the ecumenical endeavors of the past generation was the Consultation on Church Union (COCU), which brought together representatives of a cross-section of Protestant churches which looked to a merger across some significant family traditions—Episcopalian, Methodist, Presbyterian. After a number of attempts floundered, it became obvious that the barriers to merger were not going to be overcome, and COCU reinvented itself as Churches Uniting in Christ (CUIC). The participating churches have made an agreement that falls far short of union, but does focus on items of a broadly held consensus—mutual respect, a shared worship life, a recognized need to combat continuing racism in the Christian community, and a broad agreement on the essentials of proclaiming Christ as Savior. It is the hope that in participating together in areas already agreed upon, a closer relationship can be developed otherwise. Current participants in the conversation of CUIC are the African Methodist Episcopal Church, the African Methodist Episcopal Zion Church, the Christian Church (Disciples of Christ), the Christian Methodist Episcopal Church, the Episcopal Church, the International Council of Community Churches, the Presbyterian Church

(USA), the United Church of Christ, the United Methodist Church, the Evangelical Lutheran Church in America, and the Moravian Church Northern Province.

Multi-traditional Organizations

American Council of Christian Churches
P.O. Box 5455
Bethlehem, PA 18015
www.amcouncilcc.org

Bible Sabbath Association
3316 Alberta Dr.
Gillette, WY 82718
www.biblesabbath.org

Christian Churches Together in the USA
c/o Wes Granberg-Michaelson, Steering Committee Chair
4500 60th St., SE
Grand Rapids, MI 49512
www.christianchurchestogether.org

Churches Uniting in Christ
c/o Rev. Thomas E. Dipko, Director
700 Prospect Ave.
Cleveland, OH 44115-1100
www.cuicinfo.org

International Council of Christian Churches
North American Regional Council, ICCC
P.O. Box 2453
Collins, MS 39428-2453
www.iccc.org.sg

Love in the Name of Christ
430 Oak Grove St., Ste. 400
Minneapolis, MN 55403
www.loveinc.org

National Association of Evangelicals
Office of the President
11025 Voyager Parkway
Colorado Springs, CO 80921
www.nae.net
or
Office of Governmental Affairs
P.O. Box 23269
Washington, DC 20026

National Black Evangelical Association
P.O. Box 4311
Chicago, IL 60680-4311

National Council of Churches of Christ in the USA
475 Riverside Dr., Rm. 880
New York, NY 10015-0050
www.ncccusa.org

World Council of Biblical Churches
625 E. 4th St.
P.O. Box 5455
Bethlehem, PA 18015

World Council of Churches
United States Office: 475 Riverside Dr., Rm. 915
New York, NY 10015-0050
or
International Hq: 150, route de Ferney
P.O. Box 2100
1211 Geneva 2, Switzerland
www.wcc-coe.org

World Evangelical Fellowship
644 Strander Blvd, #154
Seattle, WA 98188

or
MIP Box 3740
Markham, ON L3R 5J1
Canada
www.worldevangelicalalliance.com

Organizations Serving Churches of a Single Tradition

Alliance Churches

Alliance World Fellowship
Driemaster 18
3904 RK Veenendaal
The Netherlands
www.allianceworldfellowship.org

Anglicans

Anglican Church, Inc.
c/o Right Reverend Frank H. Benning
Box 52702
Atlanta, GA 30355
www.angelfire.com/ga/anglicanepiscopal

Anglican Consultative Council
c/o Anglican Communion Secretariat
Partnership House
157 Waterloo Rd.
London, UK SE1 8UT
www.anglicancommunion.org

Communion of Evangelical Episcopal Churches
c/o Right Reverend Michael D. Owen
6825 West Wilshire Blvd.
Oklahoma City, OK 74137
www.theceec.org

International Anglican Fellowship
5712 Pommel Ct.
West Des Moines, IA 50266-6355
www.zeuter.com/accc/accc/iaf.htm

Lambeth Conference of Bishops of the Anglican Communion
c/o Archbishop of Canterbury
Lambeth Palace
London, UK SE1 7JU

Traditional Anglican Communion
c/o Reverend Gregory Wilcox
4510 Finley Ave.
Los Angeles, CA 90027
www.zeuter.com/~accc/tac.htm

Baptists

Baptist World Alliance
405 North Washington St.
Falls Church, VA 22046
bwanet.org

North American Baptist Fellowship
P.O. Box 6412
Falls Church, VA 22040

Seventh Day Baptist World Federation
Seventh Day Baptist Center
3120 Kennedy Rd.
P.O. Box 1678
Janesville, WI 53547
www.seventhdaybaptist.org

Churches of Christ

World Convention of Churches of Christ
1101 19th Ave. S.
Nashville, TN 37212-2196

Eastern Orthodoxy

Ecumenical Patriarchate
Ecumenical Centre
150, route de Ferney
P.O. Box 2100
1211 Geneva 2, Switzerland
www.patriarchate.org

Standing Conference of Canonical Orthodox Bishops in the Americas
8-10 E. 79th St.
New York, NY 10021
www.oca.org/OrthodoxChurches/SCOBA.html

Free Evangelicals

International Federation of Free Evangelical Churches
c/o Paul A. Cedar, President
901 E. 78th St.
Minneapolis, MN 55420-1300
or
International Hq:
Tégnergatan 8
S-113 81 Stockholm, Sweden

Friends

Friends World Committee for Consultation--Section of the Americas
c/o Margaret Fraser, Executive Secretary
1506 Race St.
Philadelphia, PA 19102
www.fwccworld.org

Holiness

Christian Holiness Partnership
c/o Martin Hotle
263 Buffalo Rd.
Clinton, TN 37716

Independent Catholic/Orthodox

Council of Old Roman Catholic Bishops
704 Old Harrods Creek Rd.
Louisville, KY 40223
www.orccna.org/info/indbishops.htm

Ecumenical Communion of Catholic and Apostolic Churches
c/o Most Rev. Dan Gincig
14100 E. Jewell Ave.
Aurora, CO 80012
www.aocc.org/ECCAC.htm

Federated Orthodox Catholic Churches International (FOCUS)
c/o the Most Reverend Seraphim MacLennan
407 Donovan Rd.
Brushton, NY 12916
www.jesusfocus.org/focus2.htm

Holy Eastern Orthodox Catholic and Apostolic Church in North America (THEOCACNA)
c/o His Beatitude Victor, Metropolitan Archbishop of North America
P.O. Box 477
Sudan, TX 79371
www.geocities.com/theocacnainc

Independent Catholic Churches International
1033 Indiana St.
Vallejo, CA 94590
www.independentcatholics.org/staff.html

Synod of Autonomous Canonical Orthodox Churches in North America
Box 72102
Akron, OH 44372

World Bishops' Council
238 Lexington Ave.
Brooklyn, NY 11216
www.worldbishopscouncil.org

Lutheran

International Lutheran Council
1333 S. Kirkwood Rd.
St. Louis, MO 63122-7295
www.ilc-online.org

Lutheran World Federation
Hq: c/o Office of Ecumenical Affairs
Evangelical Lutheran Church in America
8765 W. Higgins Rd.
Chicago, IL 60631
or
International Hq: 150, route de Ferney
P.O. Box 2100
1211 Geneva 2, Switzerland
www.lutheranworld.org

Mennonites

Mennonite World Conference
2529 Willow Ave.
Clovis, CA 93612
www.mwc-cmm.org
or
International Hq: 7 Ave. de la Gorét-Nopire
F- 67000 Strasbourg, France

Methodists

World Methodist Council
P.O. Box 518
Lake Junaluska, NC 28745
www.worldmethodistcouncil.org

Old Catholic

International Old Catholic Bishops Conference
International Hq: Kon. Wilhelminalaan 3
NL-3818 HN Amersfoort, Netherlands

Pentecostals/Charismatics

Apostolic World Christian Fellowship
11 West Iowa St.
Evansville, IN 47711
www.awcf.org

International Revival Network
2041 Harvey Ave.
Kelowna, BC V1Y 6G7
Canada
www.revivalnow.com

Pentecostal/Charismatic Churches of North America
c/o General Council of the Assemblies of God
1445 N. Boonville Ave.
Springfield, MO 65802
www.iphc.org/iccna/unfinished.html

Pentecostal World Fellowship
P.O. Box 12609
Oklahoma City, OK 73157
www.pentecostalworldfellowship.org

Reformed/Presbyterian/Congregational

International Association of Reformed and Presbyterian Churches
756 Haddon Ave.
Collinswood, NJ 08108

International Conference of Reformed Churches
c/o The Rev. C. Van Spronsen
8586 Harbour Heights Rd.
Vernon, BC V1H 1J8 Canada.
www.icrconline.com

International Congregational Fellowship
c/o Rev. Dr. Janet Wootton, Moderator
36 Olivier Ct.
Union St., Bedford
MK40 2UU, UK
www.intercong.org

North American Presbyterian and Reformed Council
No central headquarters
www.naparc.org

Reformed Ecumenical Council
2117 Eastern Ave., SE, Ste. 201
Grand Rapids, MI 49507-3234
www.recweb,org

World Alliance of Reformed Churches
Ecumenical Centre
150, route de Ferney
P.O. Box 2100
CH-1211 Geneva 2, Switzerland
www.warc.ch

World Reformed Fellowship
c/o Dr. Samuel Logan, Executive Secretary
Westminster Theological Seminary
2960 W. Church Rd.
Glenside, PA 19038
www.wrfnet.org

IV

Educational Institutions For Ministerial Training

Over the years, Christian churches have formed schools—seminaries, biblical institutes, Bible colleges—for training ordained ministers, and most of these schools are attached to one of the larger denominations and primarily exist to serve the needs of the denomination(s) that support them. The number of training schools relative to the size of the denomination is a factor of the value placed on specialized study of the theological disciplines (Bible, theology, church history, church administration, ethics, etc.). Most seminaries are post-graduate schools and require students to have a four-year bachelor's degree from a college or university for admission.

The largest number of seminaries are attached to the larger denominational bodies, though some schooling for prospective ministers soon becomes a priority for smaller groups which move either to found a school or designate an independent school as an acceptable institution for the group. The larger denominations also have founded many college and universities which future seminarians may attend, though they are primarily designed to produce an educated and theologically literate laity.

The list below has two parts. The first lists those schools primarily serving the larger denominations. Information about these schools is readily available now, as each has an internet site containing basic information and the answers to the most frequently asked questions about the school.

The second part of the list, arranged alphabetically by the name of the institution, lists those schools serving smaller denominations and those independent schools that serve an interdenominational student body, though most such schools tend to clearly identify with a particular denominational family tradition. For each school, the address and sponsoring groups (general orientation) is given.

BAPTISTS

Southern Baptist Convention

The largest Protestant body in America has six seminaries that are officially sponsored and recognized by the Convention:

Golden Gate Baptist Theological Seminary, Mill Valley, California
Midwestern Baptist Theological Seminary, Kansas City, Missouri
New Orleans Baptist Theological Seminary, New Orleans, Louisiana
Southeastern Baptist Theological Seminary, Wake Forest, North Carolina
Southern Baptist Theological Seminary, Louisville, Kentucky
Southwestern Baptist Theological Seminary, Fort Worth, Texas

Disagreements within the Convention through the 1990s led to the formation of a new association of former Southern Baptists, the Cooperative Baptist Fellowship. At the local and state level, many Baptists are somewhat divided in loyalties, with some local congregations financially supporting both the SBC and the CBF. The Fellowship has established what it terms a network of ministry partnerships with thirteen seminaries in the United States and supports these schools financially. In addition, two schools of theology partner with Cooperative Baptist Fellowship state organizations.

Baptist House of Studies, Divinity School, Duke University, Durham, North Carolina
Baptist Seminary of Kentucky, Lexington, Kentucky
Baptist Studies Program, Brite Divinity School, Texas Christian University, Fort Worth, Texas
Baptist Studies Program, Candler School of Theology, Emory University, Atlanta, Georgia
Baptist Studies Program at the Lutheran Theological Southern Seminary, Columbia, South Carolina (CBF of South Carolina)
Baptist Studies Program at Phillips Theological Seminary in Tulsa, Oklahoma (CBF of Oklahoma)
Baptist Theological Seminary at Richmond, Richmond, Virginia
Baptist University of the Americas, San Antonio, Texas
Central Baptist Theological Seminary, Kansas City, Kansas
Divinity School, Campbell University, Buies Creek, North Carolina
Divinity School, Wake Forest University, Winston-Salem, North Carolina
George W. Truett Theological Seminary, Baylor University, Waco, Texas

Logsdon School of Theology, Hardin-Simmons University, Abilene, Texas
M. Christopher White School of Divinity, Gardner-Webb University, Boiling Springs, North Carolina
McAfee School of Theology, Mercer University, Atlanta, Georgia

American Baptist Churches in the U.S.A.

The oldest Baptist group in the United States supports ten seminaries:

American Baptist Seminary of the West, Berkeley, California
Andover Newton Theological Seminary, Newton Centre, Massachusetts
Central Baptist Theological Seminary, Kansas City, Kansas
Colgate Rochester/Bexley Hall/Crozer, Rochester, New York
Evangelical Seminary of Puerto Rico, Hato Rey, Puerto Rico
Morehouse School of Religion, Atlanta, Georgia
Northern Baptist Theological Seminary, Lombard, Illinois
Palmer Theological Seminary, Philadelphia, Pennsylvania
The School of Theology, Richmond, Virginia
Samuel DeWitt Proctor School of Theology, at Virginia Union University, Richmond, Virginia

African American Baptists

The several larger Baptist bodies serving a predominantly African American membership—the National Baptist Convention, U.S.A., Inc.; the National Baptist Convention of America, Inc.; the National Missionary Baptist Convention of America; and the Progressive National Baptist Convention, Inc.—support the Central Baptist Theological Seminary, Indianapolis, Indiana, and the Morehouse School of Religion, Atlanta, Georgia. The latter is the primary Baptist institution that participates in the Interdenominational Theological Center, a cooperative effort of seven African American seminaries.

In addition, the National Baptist Convention, U.S.A., Inc. sponsors Selma University, in Selma, Alabama, the American Baptist Theological Seminary, in Nashville, Tennessee, and Shaw University Divinity School, Shaw University, Raleigh, North Carolina.

Congregationalists

United Church of Christ

The United Church of Christ, the primary body carrying the Congregationalist tradition in the United States, sponsors and/or officially approves of the following seminaries for ministerial training:

Andover Newton Theological Seminary, Newton Center, Massachusetts
Bangor Theological Seminary, Bangor, Maine
Chicago Theological Seminary, Chicago, Illinois
Eden Theological Seminary, St. Louis, Missouri
Hartford Seminary, Hartford, Connecticut
Harvard University School of Divinity, Cambridge, Massachusetts
Howard University School of Divinity, Washington, D.C.
Interdenominational Theological Center, Atlanta, Georgia
Lancaster Theological Seminary, Lancaster, Pennsylvania
Pacific School of Religion, Berkeley, California
Seminario Evangelico de Puerto Rico, Hato Rey, Puerto Rico
Union Theological Seminary, New York, New York
United Theological Seminary of the Twin Cities, New Brighton, Minnesota
Vanderbilt University Divinity School, Nashville, Tennessee

Yale Divinity School, New Haven, Connecticut

Eastern Orthodox

Armenian Apostolic Church

St. Nersess Armenian Seminary, New Rochelle, New York

Ecumenical Patriarchate

Patriarch Athenagoras Orthodox Institute, at the Graduate Theological Union, Berkeley, California.

Greek Orthodox Archdiocese of America

Holy Cross School of Theology, and Hellenic College, Brookline, Massachusetts.

Orthodox Church in America

St. Herman's Orthodox Theological Seminary, Kodiak, Alaska

St. Tikhon's Orthodox Theological Seminary, South Canaan, Pennsylvania

St. Vladimir's Orthodox Theological Seminary, Crestwood, New York

Ukrainian Orthodox Church

St. Sophia Ukrainian Orthodox Seminary, South Bound Brook, New Jersey

Episcopalians

Episcopal Church

Berkeley Divinity School at Yale, New Haven, Connecticut
Bexley Hall, Colgate-Rochester, Rochester, New York
Church Divinity School of the Pacific, Berkeley, California
Episcopal Divinity School, Cambridge, Massachusetts
Episcopal Theological Seminary of the Southwest, Austin, Texas
General Theological Seminary, New York City, New York
Nashotah House, Nashotah, Wisconsin
School of Theology of the University of the South, Sewanee, Tennessee
Seabury-Western Theological Seminary, Evanston, Illinois
Trinity Episcopal School for Ministry, Ambridge, Pennsylvania
Virginia Theological Seminary, Alexandria, Virginia.

Lutherans

Evangelical Lutheran Church in America

Luther Seminary, St. Paul, Minnesota
Lutheran School of Theology at Chicago, Chicago, Illinois
Lutheran Seminary Program in the Southwest, Austin, Texas
Lutheran Theological Center, Atlanta, Georgia
Lutheran Theological Seminary, Gettysburg, Pennsylvania
Lutheran Theological Seminary at Philadelphia, Philadelphia, Pennsylvania
Lutheran Theological Southern Seminary, Columbia, South Carolina
Pacific Lutheran Theological Seminary, Berkeley, California
Trinity Lutheran Seminary, Columbus, Ohio

Wartburg Theological Seminary, Dubuque, Iowa

Lutheran Church–Missouri Synod

Concordia Seminary, St. Louis, Missouri
Concordia Theological Seminary, Ft. Wayne, Indiana

METHODISTS

United Methodist Church

The United Methodist Church directly sponsors and supports the following seminaries:

Boston School of Theology, Boston, Massachusetts
Candler School of Theology, Atlanta, Georgia
Drew University, the Theological School, Madison, New Jersey
Duke University, the Divinity School, Durham, North Carolina
Gammon Theological Seminary, Atlanta, Georgia (Gammon is the primary Methodist school that participates in the Interdenominational Theological Center)
Garrett Evangelical Theological Seminary, Evanston, Illinois
Iliff School of Theology, Denver, Colorado
The Methodist Theological School of Ohio, Delaware, Ohio
Perkins School of Theology, Dallas, Texas
Saint Paul School of Theology, Kansas City, Missouri
School of Theology at Claremont, Claremont, California
United Theological Seminary, Dayton, Ohio
Wesley Theological Seminary, Washington, D.C.

In addition to the schools directly sponsored by the United Methodist Church, a number of others schools, primarily schools sponsored by denominations with which it has strong ecumenical ties, have been approved for students by the church's University Senate. Many of these schools offer special courses for United Methodist students that meet requirements in Methodist history and polity.

Andover Newton Theological School
Asbury Theological Seminary
Ashland Theological Seminary
Associated Mennonite Biblical Seminary
Austin Presbyterian Theological Seminary
Bangor Theological Seminary
Bexley Hall (Colgate Rochester/Crozer)
Brite Divinity School
Chicago Theological Seminary
Christian Theological Seminary
Colgate Rochester Divinity School
Eastern Baptist Theological Seminary
Eastern Mennonite Seminary
Eden Theological Seminary
Episcopal Theological Seminary of the Southwest
Erskine Theological Seminary
Evangelical School of Theology
Evangelical Seminary of Puerto Rico
Fuller Theological Seminary
Gordon-Conwell Theological Seminary
Harvard University Divinity School
Hood Theological Seminary
Howard University Divinity School
Lancaster Theological Seminary
Louisville Presbyterian Theological Seminary
Luther Theological Seminary
Lutheran Theological Seminary at Philadelphia

Lutheran Theological Southern Seminary
McCormick Theological Seminary
Memphis Theological Seminary
Moravian Theological School
New Brunswick Theological Seminary
New York Theological Seminary
North American Baptist Seminary
Pacific School of Religion
Palmer Theological Seminary
Phillips Theological Seminary
Pittsburgh Theological Seminary
Princeton Theological Seminary
School of Theology and Ministry (Seattle University)
The School of Theology (University of the South)
The University of Chicago Divinity School
Union Theological Seminary
Union Theological Seminary in Virginia
United Theological Seminary of the Twin Cities
University of Dubuque Theological Seminary
Vanderbilt University Divinity School
Virginia Union University School of Theology
Yale University Divinity School

African American Methodists

The oldest of the ministerial training schools sponsored by African American Methodists are the African Methodist Episcopal Church's Payne Theological Seminary, Wilberforce, Ohio, and the African Methodist Episcopal Zion Church's Hood Theological Seminary, Salisbury, North Carolina.

Turner Theological Seminary in Atlanta, Georgia, also sponsored by the African Methodist Episcopal Church, is now apart of the Interdenominational Theological Seminary, as is the Phillips School of Theology, sponsored by the Christian Methodist Episcopal (CME) Church.

Pentecostals

The Church of God in Christ, the largest Pentecostal church in the United States, pioneered seminary training among Pentecostals. Most recently, Charles H. Mason Theological Seminary has moved to Atlanta, Georgia, to be part of the Interdenominational Theological Center.

The Assemblies of God has steadily upgraded its schools, three of which now offer a seminary education or its equivalent:

Assemblies of God Theological Seminary, Springfield, Missouri
School of Graduate Studies, Southwestern University, Waxahachie, Texas
Vanguard University, Costa Mesa, California

Additional theological centers among the larger Pentecostal churches are sponsored by the Church of God (Cleveland, Tennessee).

Church of God Theological Seminary, Cleveland, Tennessee

Pentecostal Assemblies of the World, Inc.

Aenon Bible School, Indianapolis, Indiana

United Pentecostal Church International

Urshan Graduate School of Theology, Hazelwood, Missouri

Presbyterians

Presbyterian Church (U.S.A.)

Austin Presbyterian Theological Seminary, Austin, Texas
Columbia Theological Seminary, Decatur, Georgia
Johnson C. Smith Theological Seminary, Atlanta, Georgia
Louisville Presbyterian Theological Seminary, Louisville, Kentucky
McCormick Theological Seminary, Chicago, Illinois
Pittsburgh Theological Seminary, Pittsburgh, Pennsylvania
Princeton Theological Seminary, Princeton, New Jersey
San Francisco Theological Seminary, San Anselmo, California
Union Theological Seminary and Presbyterian School of Christian Education, Richmond, Virginia.
University of Dubuque Theological Seminary, Dubuque, Iowa

Restoration Tradition

Christian Church (Disciples of Christ)

Brite Divinity School, Fort Worth, Texas
Christian Theological Seminary, Indianapolis, Indiana
Lexington Theological Seminary, Lexington, Kentucky
Phillips Theological Seminary, Tulsa, Oklahoma

Christian Churches and Churches of Christ

Cincinnati Christian University, Cincinnati, Ohio
Emmanuel School of Religion, Johnson City, Tennessee
Hope International University, Fullerton, Califonia
Lincoln Christian Seminary, Lincoln, Illinois

Churches of Christ

David Lipscomb University, Nashville, Tennessee
Graduate School of Theology, Abilene Christian University, Abilene, Texas
Harding Graduate School of Religion, Harding University, Memphis, Tennessee
Turner School of Theology, Southern Christian University, Montgomery, Alabama

Roman Catholic Church

Most Roman Catholic dioceses support one or more schools (junior and senior seminaries) for the training of priests. Where a school is not available, one in a neighboring diocese is used. In addition, the larger Catholic orders have also founded schools which provide education for those in the order who strive to enter the ordained ministry. For a complete list of institutions of higher learning supported by the Roman Catholic Church see the latest edition of either *The Official Roman Catholic Directory* (New York: P. J. Kenedy & Sons) or *Catholic Almanac* (Huntington, IN: Our Sunday Visitor). Each is regularly revised and updated.

Overwhelmingly, Catholic seminaries are training grounds for clergy in the Latin Western Rite. There are, however, several schools serving Eastern Rite Catholics including:

Our Lady of Lebanon Maronite Seminary, Washington, D.C.
St. Basil's Melkite Catholic Seminary, Methuen, Massachusetts
Saints Cyril and Methodius Byzantine Catholic Seminary, Pittsburgh, Pennsylvania

Additional Schools

This list has been limited to schools that have a campus and offer an array of courses appropriate for those studying for the ordained ministry.

No attempt has been made to compile a directory of schools that primarily offer distance education, though no disparagement is meant of education received from such schools.

Alliance Theological Seminary
350 N. Highland Ave.
Nyack, NY 10960-1416
Christian and Missionary Alliance

American Lutheran Theological Seminary
6600 N. Clinton St.
Fort Wayne, IN 46825
American Association of Lutheran Churches

Anderson University
School of Theology
1100 E. 5th St.
Anderson, IN 46012-3495
Church of God (Anderson, Indiana)

Andersonville Theological Seminary
54 South Butler St., Ste. A
P.O. Box 545
Camilla, GA 31730

Arlington Baptist College
3001 West Division
Arlington, TX 76012
World Baptist Fellowship

Asbury Theological Seminary
204 North Lexington Ave.
Wilmore, KY 40390
Independent, Holiness

Ashland Theological Seminary
910 Center St.
Ashland, OH 44805
Brethren Church

Assemblies of God Theological Seminary
1435 North Glenstone Ave.
Springfield, MO 65802
Assemblies of God

Associated Mennonite Biblical Seminary
3003 Benham Ave.
Elkhart, IN 46517
Mennonite Church USA

Association of Free Lutheran Theological Seminary
3110 E. Medicine Lake Blvd.
Plymouth, MN 55441
Association of Free Lutheran Congregations

Baptist Bible Graduate School of Theology
628 East Kearney St.
Springfield, MO 65803
Baptist Bible Fellowship International

Baptist Bible Seminary
538 Venard Rd.
Clarks Summit, PA 18411
Independent, Baptist (General Association of Regular Baptist Churches)

Baptist Missionary Association Theological Seminary
1530 East Pine St.
Jacksonville, TX 75766-5407
Baptist Missionary Association of America

Baptist Theological Seminary at Richmond
3400 Brook Rd.
Richmond, VA 23227
Alliance of Baptists

Beeson Divinity School
Samford University
800 Lakeshore Dr.
Birmingham, AL 35229
Baptist, Interdenominational

Belleview Christian College and Bible Seminary
3455 West 83rd Ave.
Westminster, CO 80031
Pillar of Fire

Bethany Lutheran Theological Seminary
6 Browns Ct.
Mankato, MN 56001
Evangelical Lutheran Synod

Bethany College of Missions
6820 Auto Club Rd., Suite C
Bloomington, MN 55438
Bethany Missionary Church

Bethany Theological Seminary
615 National Rd. West
Richmond, IN 47374-4019
Church of the Brethren

Bethel Seminary of the East
3900 Bethel Dr.
St. Paul, MN 55112-6999
Baptist General Conference

Bethesda Christian University
730 N. Euclid
Anaheim, CA 92801
Independent, Pentecostal

Biblical Seminary
200 N. Main St.
Hatfield, PA 19440
Independent, Evangelical

Birmingham Theological Seminary
Suite A203
2200 Briarwood Way
Birmingham, AL 35243-2923
Independent, Reformed

Bob Jones University Seminary & Graduate School of Religion
1700 Wade Hampton Blvd.
Greenville, SC 29614
Independent, Fundamentalist

Calvary Baptist Theological Seminary
1380 S. Valley Forge Rd.
Lansdale, PA 19446
Baptist, Separatist

Calvary Bible College
15800 Calvary Rd.
Kansas City, MO 64147
Baptist, Independent

Calvary Chapel School of Ministry
3800 South Fairview Rd.
Santa Ana, CA 92704
Calvary Chapel Church

Calvin Theological Seminary
3233 Burton SE
Grand Rapids, MI 49546
Christian Reformed Church in North America

Capital Bible Seminary
6511 Princess Garden Pkwy.
Lanham, MD 20706
Evangelical, Interdenominational

Carolina Evangelical Divinity School
1208 Eastchester Dr., Suite 130
High Point, NC 27265
Religious Society of Friends

Center for Traditionalist Orthodox Studies
c/o St. Gregory Palamas Monastery
Etna, CA 96027
American Exarchate of the True (Old Calendar) Orthodox Church of Greece

Central Baptist Theological Seminary of Minneapolis
900 Forestview Lane North
Plymouth, MN 55441
Baptist, Fundamentalist

Central Baptist Theological Seminary of Virginia Beach
2221 Centerville Turnpike
Virginia Beach, VA 23464
Baptist, Independent

Chafer Theological Seminary
1800 E. La Veta Ave.
Orange, CA 92866
Independent, Fundamentalist

Chapman School of Religious Studies
c/o Oakland City University
138 N. Lucretia St.
Oakland City, IN 47660
General Association of General Baptists

Christ For the Nations Institute
P.O. Box 769000
Dallas, TX 75376-9000
Pentecostal, Independent

Christ the Savior Seminary
225 Chandler Ave.
Johnstown, PA 15906
American Carpatho-Russian Greek Catholic Church

Christian International Ministry Training College
P.O. Box 9000
Myrtle Beach, SC 32459
Christian International Network of Prophetic Ministry

Christian Witness Theological Seminary
1040 Oak Grove Rd.
Concord, CA 94518
Evangelical, Inter/Multidenominational

Cincinnati Bible Seminary
2700 Glenway Ave.
Cincinnati, OH 45204
Evangelical, Independent

College for Officer Training
1032 Metropolitan Pkwy.
Atlanta, GA 30310
Salvation Army

Columbia Biblical Seminary and School of Missions
c/o Columbia International University
P.O. Box 3122
Columbia, SC 29230
Evangelical, Independent

Covenant Theological Seminary
12330 Conway Rd.
St. Louis, MO 63141
Presbyterian Church in America

Cranmer Theological House
211 Byrne Houston
Houston, TX 77009
Reformed Episcopal Church

Cummins Memorial Theological Seminary
705 S Main St.
Summerville, SC 29483
Reformed Episcopal Church

Dallas Theological Seminary
3909 Swiss Ave.
Dallas, TX 75204
Independent, Fundamentalist

Denver Seminary
6399 South Santa Fe Dr.
Littleton, CO 80120
Conservative Baptist (CBAmerica)

Earlham School of Religion
228 College Ave.
Richmond, IN 47374
Friends United Meeting

Eastern Mennonite Seminary
1200 Park Rd.
Harrisonburg, VA 22801
Mennonite Church USA

Ecumenical Theological Seminary
2930 Woodward Ave.
Detroit, MI 48201
Interdenominational, Liberal Protestant

Erskine Theological Seminary
Bowie Divinity Hall
210 West Main St.
P.O. Box 668
Due West, SC 29639
Associate Reformed Presbyterian Church

Evangelical School of Theology
121 South College St.
Myerstown, PA 17067
Evangelical Congregational Church

Faith Evangelical Seminary
3504 N. Pearl St.
Tacoma, WA 98407
Conservative Lutheran Association

Faith Theological Seminary
1900 NW 4th St.
Ankeny, IA 50021
Baptist, Fundamentalist

Faith Theological Seminary
529-531 Walker Ave.
Baltimore, MD 21212-2624
Independent, Presbyterian, Fundamentalist

Florida Center for Theological Studies
111 NE 1st St., 7th Floor
Miami, FL 33132
Interdenominational

Fuller Theological Seminary
135 North Oakland Ave.
Pasadena, CA 91182
Interdenominational, Evangelical

Geneva Reformed Seminary
1207 Haywood Rd.
Greenville, SC 29615
Free Presbyterian Church of North America

George Fox Evangelical Seminary
c/o George Fox University
414 N. Meridian St.
Newberg, OR 97132
Evangelical Friends International

God's Bible School and College
1810 Young St.
Cincinnati, OH 45202-6838
Independent, Wesleyan

Gordon-Conwell Theological Seminary
130 Essex St.
South Hamilton, MA 01982
Independent, Evangelical

Gordon-Conwell Theological Seminary
14542 Choate Circle
Charlotte, NC 28273
Independent, Evangelical

Grace Theological Seminary
200 Seminary Dr.
Winona Lake, IN 46590
Fellowship of Grace Brethren Chruches

Graduate Theological Union
2400 Ridge Rd.
Berkeley, CA 94709
Independent, Liberal Protestant

Grand Rapids Theological Seminary
1001 East Beltline Ave. NE
Grand Rapids, MI 49525
Baptist, Fundamentalist

Greenville Presbyterian Theological Seminary
P.O. Box 690
418 East Main St.
Taylors, SC 29687
Independent, Presbyterian

Haggard School of Theology
c/o Azusa Pacific University
P.O. Box 7000
Azusa, CA 91702-7000
Independent, Evangelical

Heritage Bible College
P.O. Box 1628
Dunn, NC 28335
Pentecostal Free Will Baptist Church

Hobe Sound Bible College
P.O. Box 1065
Hobe Sound, FL 33475
National Association of Holiness Churches

Holy Trinity Orthodox Seminary
P.O. Box 36
Jordanville, NY 13361
Russian Orthodox Church Outside of Russia

Houston Graduate School of Theology
2501 Central Parkway, Suite A19
Houston, TX 77092
Evangelical Friends International

Huntington University Graduate School in Christian Ministries
2303 College Ave.
Huntington, IN 46750
Church of the United Brethren in Christ

Inter-American Adventist Theological Seminary
P.O. Box 830518
Miami, FL 33283
Seventh-day Adventist Church

Inter-Lutheran Theological Seminary
P.O. Box 449
Hancock, MI 49930
Apostolic Lutheran Church of America

International Theological Seminary
3225 Tyler Ave.
El Monte, CA 91731
Independent, Presbyterian

Kansas City College and Bible School
7401 Metcalf
Overland Park, KS 66204
Church of God (Holiness)

Knox Theological Seminary
5554 North Federal Highway
Fort Lauderdale, FL 33308
Presbyterian, Independent

La Sierra University School of Religion
4500 Riverwalk Parkway
Riverside, CA 92515-8247
Seventh-day Adventist Church

Liberty Theological Seminary
Campus North 2500
Lynchburg, VA 24502-2239
Liberty Baptist Fellowship

Life Pacific College
1100 Covina Blvd.
San Dimas, CA 91773
International Church of the Foursquare Gospel

Logos Evangelical Seminary
9358 Telstar Ave.
El Monte, CA 91731
Evangelical Formosan Church

Luther Rice Seminary
c/o Luther Rice University
3038 Evans Mill Rd.
Lithonia, GA 30038
Baptist, Independent

Lutheran Brethren Seminary
Fergus Falls, MN 56537
Church of the Lutheran Brethren of America

The Master's Seminary
13248 Roscoe Blvd.
Sun Valley, CA 91352-3798
Independent, Fundamentalist

Memphis Theological Seminary
168 East Parkway South
Memphis, TN 38104
Cumberland Presbyterian Church

Mennonite Brethren Biblical Seminary
4824 E. Butler Ave.
Fresno, CA 93727
Mennonite Brethren Church of North America

Messianic Jewish Theological Institute
P.O. Box 1521
Ann Arbor, MI 48106
Messianic Jewish

Michigan Theological Seminary
41550 East Ann Arbor Trail
Plymouth, MI 48170
Independent, Evangelical

Mid-American Baptist Theological Seminary
2216 Germantown Rd. S
Germantown, TN 38138
Baptist, Independent

Mid-America Reformed Seminary
229 Seminary Dr.
Dyer, IN 46311
Independent, Reformed

Missionary Baptist Seminary
5224 Stagecoach Rd.
Little Rock, AR 72204
American Baptist Association

Moody Bible Institute
820 N LaSalle Blvd.
Chicago, IL 60610
Independent, Evangelical

Moravian Theological School
60 West Locust St.
Bethlehem, PA 18018
Moravian Church

Multnomah Biblical Seminary
8435 NE Glisan St.
Portland, OR 97220
Independent, Evangelical

Nazarene Theological Seminary
1700 E. Meyer Blvd.
Kansas City, MO 64131
Church of the Nazarene

Netzer David International Yeshiva
3190 Gulf-To-Bay Blvd.
Clearwater, FL 33759
Menorah Ministries

New Brunswick Theological Seminary
17 Seminary Place
New Brunswick, NJ 08901-1107
Reformed Church in America

New York Theological Seminary
475 Riverside Dr., Ste. 500
New York, NY 10115
Independent, Evangelical

North American Baptist Seminary
1525 S. Grange Ave.
Sioux Falls, SD 57105
North American Baptist Conference

North Park Theological Seminary
3225 W. Foster Ave.
Chicago, IL 60625-4895
Evangelical Covenant Church

Northeastern Seminary
2265 Westside Dr.
Rochester, NY 14624-1997
Free Methodist Church of North America

Northern Seminary
660 East Butterfield Rd.
Lombard, IL 60148
Baptist, Independent

Northwest Baptist Seminary
4301 N. Stevens St.
Tacoma, WA 98407
Baptist, Independent (General Association of Regular Baptist Churches)

Oral Roberts University School of Theology and Missions
7777 South Lewis Ave.
Tulsa, OK 74171
Independent, charismatic

Pensacola Theological Seminary
P.O. Box 18000
Pensacola, FL 32523-9160
Independent, Baptist, Fundamentalist

Phoenix Seminary
4222 East Thomas Rd., Ste. 400
Phoenix, AZ 85018
Independent, Interdenominational

Providence Theological Institute
P.O. Box 704
Belton, TX 76513-1535
Sovereign Grace Baptist

Puritan Reformed Theological Seminary
2965 Leonard St., NE
Grand Rapids, MI 49525
Heritage Netherlands Reformed Congregations
Free Reformed Church of North America

Reformed Presbyterian Seminary
1901 W. 166th St.
Gardena, CA 90247
Korean American Presbyterian Church

Reformed Presbyterian Theological Seminary
7418 Penn Ave.
Pittsburgh, PA 15208-2594
Reformed Presbyterian Church of North America

Reformed Theological Seminary
5422 Clinton Blvd.
Jackson, MS 39209-3099
Reformed, Interdenominational (with additional campuses at Orlando, FL, Boca Raton, FL, Atlanta, GA, Washington, DC, and Charlotte, NC)

Regent University School of Divinity
1000 Regent University Dr.
Virginia Beach, VA 23464
Independent, Evangelical

RHEMA Bible Training Center
1025 W. Kenosha St.
Broken Arrow, OK 74012
Rhema, charismatic

Saint Andrew's Theological College and Seminary
464 County Home Rd.
Lexington, NC 27292
Anglican Orthodox Church

Saint Joseph of Arimathea Anglican Theological College
P.O. Box 40020
Berkeley, CA 94704
Anglican Province of Christ the King

St. Mary's Theological College
4510 Finley Ave.
Los Angeles, CA 90027
Anglican Church in America

St. Paul's Bible Institute
37 West 116th St.
New York, NY 10026
Salvation and Deliverance Church

St. Petersburg Theological Seminary
10830 Navajo Dr.
St. Petersburg, FL 33708-3116
Evangelical, Independent

St. Thomas Aquinas Seminary
206 Tackora Trail
Ridgefield, CT 06877
Society of Pius X

Salt Lake Theological Seminary
699 East South Temple, Ste. 324
P.O. Box 2096
Salt Lake City, UT 84110-2096
Independent, Interdenominational

Salvation Army College for Officer Training
700 W. Brompton Ave.
Chicago, IL 60657
Salvation Army

Salvation Army Collegc for Officer Training at Crestmont
30840 Hawthorne Blvd.
Rancho Palos Verdes, CA 90275
Salvation Army

Savonarola Theological Seminary
1031 Cedar Ave.
Scranton, PA 18505
Polish National Catholic Church

School for Officer Training
201 Lafayette Ave.
Suffern, NY 10901
Salvation Army

School of Theology and Ministry
Seattle University
901 12th Ave.
P.O. Box 222000
Seattle, WA 98122-1090
Independent, Liberal Protestant

Seventh-day Adventist Theological Seminary
Andrews University
Berrien Springs, MI 49104-1500
Seventh-day Adventist Church

Southern Territorial Salvation Army College for Officer Training
1032 Metropolitan Parkway
Atlanta, GA 30310
Salvation Army

Southwest Bible College & Seminary
115 West Nezpique St.
Jennings, LA 70546
Independent, Fundamentalist

Southwestern Christian University Graduate School
P.O. Box 340
7210 NW 39th Expressway
Bethany, OK 73008
International Pentecostal Holiness Church

Talbot School of Theology
Biola University
13800 Biola Ave.
La Mirada, CA 90639-0001
Independent, Evangelical

Temple Baptist Seminary
1815 Union Ave.
Chattanooga, TN 37404
Baptist, Independent (Southwide Baptist Fellowship)

Theological School of the Protestant Reformed Churches
4949 Ivanrest Ave. SW
Grandville, MI 49418
Protestant Reformed Churches in America

Trinity Evangelical Divinity School
c/o Trinity International University
2065 Half Day Rd.
Deerfield, IL 60015
Evangelical Free Church of America

Tyndale Theological Seminary and Biblical Institute
6800 Brentwood Stair, Ste. 105
Fort Worth, TX 76112-3325
Independent, Fundamentalist

University of Chicago Divinity School
1025 E. 58th St.
Chicago, IL 60637
Independent, Liberal Protestant

Vanderbilt University Divinity School
411 21st Ave. South
Nashville, TN 37240-1121
Non-denominational, Liberal Protestant

Victory Bible Institute
1400 E. Skelly Dr.
Tulsa, OK 74105
Victory Fellowship of Ministries

Wesley Biblical Seminary
787 E. Northside Dr.
Jackson, MS 39206
Independent, Wesleyan

Western Seminary
5511 SE Hawthorne Blvd.
Portland, OR 97215
Conservative Baptist (CBAmerica)

Western Theological Seminary
101 East Thirteenth St.
Holland, MI 49423-3622
Reformed Church in America

Westminster Seminary California
1725 Bear Valley Parkway
Escondido, CA 92027
Orthodox Presbyterian Church

Westminster Theological Seminary
2960 W. Church Rd.
Glenside, PA 19038
Orthodox Presbyterian Church

Wheaton College Graduate School
501 College Ave.
Wheaton, IL 60187
Independent, Evangelical

Whitefield Theological Semianry
P.O. Box 6321
Lakeland, FL 33807
Reformed Presbyterian Church General Assembly

Winebrenner Theological Seminary
950 N. Main St.
Findley, OH 45840
Churches of God, General Conference

Wisconsin Lutheran Seminary
11831 N. Seminary Dr. 65W
Mequon, WI 53092
Wisconsin Evangelical Lutheran Synod

World Evangelism Bible College and Seminary
8919 World Ministry Ave.
Baton Rouge, LA 70810
Independent, Pentecostal

Endnotes

[1] Gonzalo Baez-Camargo, *Archaeological Commentary on the Bible* (Garden City, NY: Doubleday, 1984), xv.

[2] Earnest G. Wright, *Biblical Archaeology,* Rev. ed. (Philadelphia, Penn: Westminster Press, 1962), 18.

[3] Baez-Camargo, xvi.

[4] Nelson Glueck, *Rivers in the Desert; History of the Negev* (Philadelphia, Penn: Jewish Publications Society of America, 1969), 31.

[5] Millar Burrows, *What Mean These Stones?* (New Haven, CT: American Schools of Oriental Research, 1941), 6.

[6] J. A. Thompson, *The Bible and Archaeology* (Grand Rapids: Eerdmans, 1962), 4-5.

[7] Earnest G. Wright and David N. Freedman, eds., *The Biblical Archaeological Reader,* vol. 1 (Garden City, NY: Doubleday, 1961-64), 53.

[8] H. J. Franken and C. A. Franken-Battershill, *A Primer of Old Testament Archaeology* (Leiden:Brill, 1963), 110-14.

[9] Wright, 126-30.

[10] William F. Albright, *The Archaeology of Palestine and the Bible* (Cambridge, Mass: American Schools of Oriental Research, 1974), 170.

[11] Wright, 207.

[12] John 1:46.

[13] Jack Finegan, *The Archaeology of the New Testament* (Princeton, NJ: Princeton University Press, 1969), 27-33.

[14] B. Mazar, et.al., *Jerusalem Revealed* (Jerusalem: Israel Exploration Society, 1975), 24 and 88.

[15] *The Biblical Archaeologist,* vol. 37, 1974, 69.

[16] Sidney Collett, *All About the Bible* (Old Tappan, NJ: Revell, n.d.), 314-15.

[17] John W. Montgomery, *History and Christianity* (Downers Grove, Ill: InterVarsity Press, 1971), 29.

[18] Bernard Ramm, *Protestant Christian Evidences* (Chicago, Ill: Moody Press, 1957), 232.

[19] Bruce M. Metzger, *The Text of the New Testament* (New York and Oxford: Oxford University Press, 1968), 67.

[20] J. Harold Greenlee, *Introduction to the New Testament Textual Criticism* (Grand Rapids: Eerdmans Publishing, 1964), 54.

[21] Norman L. Geisler and William E. Nix, *A General Introduction to the Bible* (Chicago: Moody Press, 1968), 353-54.

[22] Charles Pellegrino, *Return to Sodom and Gomorrah* (New York: Random House, 1994), 323.

[23] Fredrick Fyvie Bruce, *New Testament Documents: Are They Reliable?* (Downers Grove, Ill: InterVarsity Press, 1972), 14f.

[24] Metzger, *The Text of the New Testament*, 67.

[25] Ibid, 34.

[26] Norman L. Geisler, *Christian Apologetics* (Grand Rapids: Baker Book House, 1976).

[27] F. F. Bruce, *The Books and the Parchments*, Rev. ed. (Westwood: Fleming H. Revell Co., 1969), 178.

[28] C. Sanders, *Introduction to Research in English Literary History* (New York: MacMillan, 1952), 143f.

[29] Bruce M. Metzger, *The New Testament its Background, Growth, and Content* (Nashville: Abingdon Press, 1965), 173.

[30] Greenlee, 16.

[31] Matthew 28:5-6.

[32] D. W. Bebbington *Evangelicalism in Modern Britain. A history from the 1730s to the 1980s* (London: Routledge, 1989). See also the doctrinal statement of the Evangelical Theological Society, which reads: "The Bible alone, and the Bible in its entirety, is the Word of God written and is therefore inerrant in the autographs. God is a Trinity, Father, Son, and Holy Spirit, each an uncreated person, one in essence, equal in power and glory."www.etsjets.org/

[33] See Gordon Fee's helpful text, *Listening to the Spirit in the Text* (Grand Rapids: Eerdmans, 2000).

[34] C. Kroeger and M. Evans, ed. *The IVP Women's Bible Commentary,* by (Downers Grove, Ill: InterVarsity Press, 2002), 644.

[35] See Linda Belleville, *Women Leaders and the Church: Three crucial questions* (Grand Rapids: Baker Books, 2000).

[36] See Genesis 2:16-17.

[37] For a more thorough exegetical work on the passages used to limit's women's equality in the church, see *Discovering Biblical Equality: Complementarity without hierarchy* (Downers Grove, Ill: InterVarsity Press, 2004).

[38] Kwok Pui Lan, "Discovering the Bible in the Non-Biblical World," *Semeia* 47(1989):35

[39] Landrum Bolling, Narrator of the Film *Conversations with Howard Thurman, Part One* (San Francisco: The Howard Thurman Educational Trust, 1978).

[40] Tape from Seminar of Religious Leaders and Practitioners with Thurman, San Francisco, 1977.

[41] Bolling.

[42] Cain Hope Felder, *Troubling Biblical Waters: Race, Class, and Family* (Maryknoll, N.Y.: Orbis Books, 1989), xi.

[43] Ibid, xiv and xiii.

[44] "Introduction" by Elisabeth Schüssler Firoenza, 1.

[45] Minneapolis: Fortress Press, 1991.

[46] Maryknoll, NY: Orbis Books, 1993.

[47] Atlanta: Scholars Press, 1989.

[48] Minneapolis: Fortress Press, 1995.

[49] Ibid, 121-43.

[50] New York: Continuum, 1995.

[51] "Reading Her Way through the Struggle: African American Women and the Bible" in *Stony the Road We Trod: African American Biblical Interpretation*, 57-77, ed: Cain Hope Felder. (Minneapolis: Fortress, 1991), 64. Weems cites sources for this perspective of the role the reader plays in construing meaning within texts as being I. A. Richards, Wolfgang Iser, Stanley Fish, Susan R. Suleiman, and Inge Crosman, 64n.

[52] Ibid, 64 . See also, William H. Myers, "The Hermeneutical Dilemma of the African American Biblical Student" in *Stony the Road We Trod*, ed: Cain Hope Felder. (Minneapolis: Fortress Press, 1991), 40-56.

[53] Reems, 64.

[54] Ibid, 64-65n.

[55] Delores Williams prefers the paradigmatic expression "survival and quality of life" rather than "liberation" in reference to God's desire for all humanity seen throughout scripture. See *Sisters in the Wilderness*, 20-22. Also Willliams's

use of the term "ministerial vision" rather than "surrogacy" and "atonement" in reference to the meaning of Jesus' death and resurrection are quite insightful and helpful as opposed to being destructive in our spiritual understanding of God's desire for human healing and wholeness. See 167-70. See also JoAnne Marie Terrell, *Power in the Blood: The Cross in the African American Experience* (Maryknoll, NY: Orbis Books, 1998), 105-08; and Kelly Brown Douglas, *The Black Christ* (Maryknoll, NY: Orbis Books, 1994), 110.

[56] "He has told you, O mortal, what is good; and what does the LORD require of you but to do justice, and to love kindness, and to walk humbly with your God?" (NRSV).

[57] Consider the Magnificat, Luke 1:46-55 (NRSV); and what is considered Jesus' first sermon: Luke 4:18-19, as well as the Sermon on the Mount, Matthew 5-7 (NRSV).

[58] Michael Wyschogrod, "Judaism and Evangelical Christianity," in *Christianity Through Non-Christian Eyes,* ed: Paul J. Griffiths (Maryknoll, New York: Orbis, 1990), 56.

[59] Tikva Frymer-Kensky, "The Image: Religious Anthropology in Judaism and Christianity," icjs.com (The Institute for Christian and Jewish Studies website), www.icjs.org/what/njsp/theimage.html. This article is a chapter from the book *Christianity in Jewish Terms,* edited by Tikva Frymer-Kensky, et. al.

[60] Leon Kleniki and Eugene J. Fisher, "Basic Jewish and Christian Beliefs in Dialogue: Covenant," in *Understanding the Jewish Experience,* ed: Leon Kleniki and Eugene J. Fisher (Winona, Min: Saint Mary's Press, 1983).

[61] Christians and Jews have proposed many theories concerning the identity of the Suffering Servant. See C. R. North, *The Suffering Servant in Deutero-Isaiah,* 2nd Ed. (New York: Oxford Press, 1956).

[62] The Jewish understanding of Messiah is complex, and not all Jews agree on the identity and nature of the Messiah. A good starting place to learn about Jewish understandings of Messiah is the Judaism 101 website, www.jewfaq.org/moshiach.htm.

[63] Wyschogrod, 55.

[64] Yechiel Eckstein, *What Christians Should Know about Jews and Judaism* (Waco, Tx: Word, 1984), Chapters 9, 10, 11.

[65] Ibid, 268.

[66] Ibid, 259.

[67] Ibid, 256-57.

[68] Ibid, 258.

[69] Ibid, 266.

[70] Isodore Epstein, *Judaism* (New York: Penguin Books, 1959), 107. See also the exposition of early Christianity in Leo Trepp, *Judaism: Development and Life,* Third Edition (Belmont, Calif: Wadsworth Publishing, 1982), Chapter 3, "The Impact of Christianity."

[71] Eckstein, 267.

[72] Eckstein, 267; Trepp, 43.

[73] Samuel Sandmel, *A Jewish Understanding of the New Testament* (Cincinnati: Hebrew Union College, 1957), 128. Quoted in Trepp, 43.

[74] For a sympathetic Christian response to Jewish concerns about the New Testament, see James C. Browning, "Telling the Gospel Story Without Defaming Jews," EthicsDaily.com, www.ethicsdaily.com/article_detail.cfm?AID=4011. For an evangelical Christian response, see Michael Brown's series on "Answering Jewish Objections to Jesus" published by Baker. See also *Review and Expositor* (Vol. 84, No. 2, Spring 1987), which includes articles on "The New Testament and Judaism."

[75] Seyyed Hossein Nassar, "The Islamic View of Christianity," in *Christianity Through Non-Christian Eyes,* ed: Paul J. Griffiths (Maryknoll, New York: Orbis, 1990.), 127.

[76] "Dhimmi," *Encyclopedia of the Orient,* i-cias.com/e.o/dhimmi.htm.

[77] Citations from the Qur'an are taken from the translation by A. Yasuf Ali.

[78] Zeba Siddiqi, "The Revealed Books,' in *The Islamic Tradition* (Allen, Tx: Argus Communications, 1978).

[79] See Geoffrey Parrinder, *Jesus in the Qur'an* (New York: Barnes & Noble, Inc., 1965).

[80] For an excellent exposition on Jesus in the Qur'an, see Jamal Badawi, "Jesus in the Qur'an," in Mir Zohai Husain, *Islam and the Muslim World* (Dubuque, IA:McGraw-Hill, 2006). See also the summary from the Islam 101 website www.islam-101.org/, which is a Christian response to the Qur'an's view of Jesus. Also see Badawi's apologetic against the orthodox Christian doctrine of Christ in isoc-unsw.org.au/main/index.php?option=com_content&task=view&id=21&Itemid=1.

[81] Badawi, 293.

[82] Sa'dullah Khan, "Crucifying Jesus?" BeliefNet.com, www.beliefnet.com/story/60/story_6002_1.html.

[83] Quoted in Ahmad Shafaat, "Islamic View of the Coming/Return of Jesus," www.islamicperspectives.com/ReturnOfJesus.htm.

[84] See the exposition on this passage on the website "A Brief Illustrated Guide to Islam", www.islam-guide.com/frm-ch1-3.htm.

[85] Jamal Badawi, "Muhammad in the Bible," on the Islamic City website, www.islamicity.com/Mosque/Muhammad_Bible.HTM.

[86] R. Blackhirst, "Barnabus and the Gospels: Was There an Early Gospel of Barnabus?", on the website for the Institute of Higher Critical Studies, www.depts.drew.edu/jhc/Blackhirst_Barnabas.html. For the text and a Muslim apologetic using the Gospel of Barnabus, see www.barnabas.net/. For a Christian response, see answering-islam.org.uk/Green/barnabas.htm.

[87] A thoroughgoing Christian response to the Muslim apologetics sketched in this essay is found in Ray Register's *Dialogue and Interfaith Witness With Muslims* (Kingsport, TN:Moody Books, 1979), Chapter IV, "Questions and Statements Encountered in Dialogue with Muslims," 24-56.

[88] Robert E. Van Voorst, *Anthology of Asian Scriptures* (Belmont, CA: Wadsworth, 2001).

[89] Vivekanda, "Christ, the Messenger" in *Christianity Through Non-Christian Eyes*, 209-11.

[90] Quoted in Samachar.com, sify.com/samacharreligion/enlightenedsouls/fullstory.php?id=13536143.

[91] Vivekanda, "Christ, the Messenger," 212.

[92] See James C. Browning, "The Story of Incarnation" EthicsDaily.com, www.ethicsdaily.com/article_detail.cfm?AID=1959.

[93] Ibid, 214.

[94] Vivekananda, "Was Christ a Yogi?" Sacred Texts Website, www.sacred-texts.com/hin/hby/hby11.htm.

[95] See this portrait at www.vedanta.com/showbook.cfm?booknum=10000139.

[96] Stephen Prothero, "Hindus for Jesus," Beliefnet.com, www.beliefnet.com/story/97/story_9719_1.html. The article is adapted from his book, *American Jesus: How the Son of God Became a National Icon* (New York: Farrar, Straus and Giroux, 2003).

[97] Mohandas K. Gandhi, "Extracts from The Story of My Experiments with Truth," in *Christianity Through Non-Christian Eyes*, 219-20.

[98] Quoted in Ananda T. Hingorani, "The Message of Jesus Christ," The Official Mahatma Gandhi Archive, www.mahatma.org.in/books/showbook.jsp?id=8&link=bg&book=bg0039&lang=en&cat=books.

[99] Quoted in Harris Wofford, "Imitation of Christ," Beliefnet.com, www.beliefnet.com/story/78/story_7803_1.html.

[100] Quoted in Hingorani.

[101] A classic evangelical apologetic for the uniqueness of Jesus in light of religious pluralism is Stephen Neill, *The Supremacy of Jesus* (Downers Grove, Ill: InterVarsity Press, 1984).

[102] See especially *Encyclopedia of American Religion* by J. Gordon Melton now in its 7th edition (Dunbass: Thompson Gale, 2002). See also the magisterial 3rd edition of the *New Historical Atlas of Religion in America* by Edwin Gaustad and Philip Barlow (New York: Oxford University Press, 2001). Online see www.thearda.com, which has the bulk of significant survey data on American religion in user-friendly form.

[103] Most of the statistics in this report can be found in one of four places: (1) Barrett, Kurian, and Johnson, *World Christian Encyclopedia*, 2nd edition (New York: Oxford UNIVersity Press, 2001); (2) Barrett and Johnson, *World Christian Trends,* AD *30–*AD *2200* (William Carey Library, 2001); (3) Barrett, Johnson, and Crossing, "Status of Global Mission, 2005, in Context of 20th and 21st Centuries", *International Bulletin of Missionary Research,* Vol. 29, No. 1, January 2005, page 29; (4) World Christian Database, online subscription service found at www.worldchristiandatabase.org.

[104] I was inspired by the plotting of the mean center of American population from colonial times to the present (using census data from 1790 to 2000). See www.census.gov/geo/www/cenpop/meanctr.pdf for more information.

[105] For a more detailed analysis of the centre of gravity of Christianity throughout its entire history see Johnson and Chung, "Tracking Global Christianity's Statistical Centre of Gravity, AD 33–AD 2100" in *International Review of Mission,* Vol. 93, No. 369, April 2004, 166-81.

[106] North is defined here in a geopolitical sense by five current United Nations regions (fifty-three countries): Eastern Europe (including Russia), Northern Europe, Southern Europe, Western Europe, and Northern America.

[107] South is defined as sixteen current United Nations regions (185 countries): Eastern Africa, Middle Africa, Northern Africa, Southern Africa, Western Africa, Eastern Asia, South-central Asia, South-eastern Asia, Western Asia, Caribbean, Central America, South America, Australia/New Zealand, Melanesia, Micronesia and Polynesia.

[108] See *The Eclipse of Christianity in Asia* by L.E. Browne (Cambridge, N.Y.: Cambridge UNIVersity Press, 1933). Three main reasons for the decline were (1) the rise of Islam, (2) the slaughter of Asian Christians under Tamerlane, and (3) the impact of the Black Death in Asia.

109 The source is U.S. Department of Homeland Security, *Yearbook of Immigration Statistics, 2004,* Washington, D.C.: U.S. Government Printing Office, 2005. The methodology is direct. The religious composition of the country of origin of immigrants was utilized to estimate the religious makeup of people from that country (assuming that immigrants matched the demographic makeup of the country they came from). These were then added together for all countries to produce the data in Graph 4.

110 Hence, Peter Berger's infamous statement in the *New York Times* in 1968 (April 25, p. 3) that by AD 2000 "religious believers are likely to be found only in small sects, huddled together to resist a worldwide secular culture." See Rodney Stark, "Secularization R.I.P.", *Sociology of Religion,* 1999, 60:249-73.

111 See *World Christian Encyclopedia,* 2nd volume, Part 8, "Ethnosphere", 13-241. This analysis did not reproduce data on all religions, but only Christianity. All religious data appeared first in the World Christian Database, launched in October 2003. The data appears there for each people in the USA.

112 For example, see Sylvia Boorstein's *That's Funny, You Don't Look Buddhist: On Being a Faithful Jew and a Passionate Buddhist* (HarperSanFrancisco, 1998).

113 There are exceptions. In recent years, for example, some old Southern Baptist congregations have found their membership split over allegiance to the Southern Baptist Convention and the Cooperative Baptist Fellowship. Rather than split the congregation, the local church splits its money between the two associations. It is also the case that on occasion, small congregations of different but friendly denominations will merge and consciously retain a double denominational affiliation. However, there is always a tendency in such cases, over time, for one of those affiliations to be lost.

114 Of course, The Baptist Missionary Society had been preceded by a spectrum of parachurch organizations such as the Society for the propagation of the Gospel in Foreign Parts, but it was historically significant in prompting the formation of additional parachurch missionary organizations.

Index